THE
JOYS OF
COMPOUNDING

THE
JOYS OF
COMPOUNDING

*The Passionate Pursuit
of Lifelong Learning*

REVISED AND UPDATED

GAUTAM BAID

Columbia University Press
New York

Columbia University Press
Publishers Since 1893
New York   Chichester, West Sussex
cup.columbia.edu

Library of Congress Cataloging-in-Publication Data
Names: Baid, Gautam, author.
Title: The joys of compounding : the passionate pursuit of lifelong
    learning / Gautam Baid.
Description: Revised and updated. | New York : Columbia University Press,
    [2020] | Includes bibliographical references and index.
Identifiers: LCCN 2019051276 (print) | LCCN 2019051277 (ebook) |
    ISBN 9780231197328 (hardback) | ISBN 9780231552110 (ebook)
Subjects: LCSH: Investments. | Value investing. | Success in business.
Classification: LCC HG4521 .B3448 2020 (print) | LCC HG4521 (ebook) |
    DDC 332.6—dc23
LC record available at https://lccn.loc.gov/2019051276
LC ebook record available at https://lccn.loc.gov/2019051277

In loving memory of my grandfather, Deepchand Nahata (1926–2007) ∾

The best thing a human being can do is to help another human being know more.

—Charlie Munger

The true value investor, who deserves my utmost respect, is somebody who devotes their life to their passion for reading. Nobody can spend their life studying for 50 years—which is what we do—if they don't enjoy it.

—Francisco García Paramés

It's startling how much life wisdom can be gleaned from the maxims and approaches of value investors.

—Rolf Dobelli

The wisdom of the wise, and the experience of ages, may be preserved by quotations.

—Isaac Disraeli

CONTENTS

FOREWORD

A little more than twenty years ago, I discovered Warren Buffett, Charlie Munger, Ben Graham and the art of Intelligent Investing. Even before attending my first Berkshire Hathaway meeting, I had become a converted disciple—such that, when I first arrived at Berkshire, I felt like I had found "my tribe." At the time, we were one or two thousand people in Omaha. But the tribe was growing. Today, tens of thousands attend the Berkshire meeting, and many more watch online.

And just as the size of the tribe has not been static, neither has its world view or self-understanding. Back in those early days, I saw value investing as merely a way to invest well, get rich, and live The Good Life. But as the years went on, I came to realize that there was far more to it than this. I began to see it as a system for living the best possible life. Thus, the Value Investor's view of life encompasses far more than concepts like Mr. Market, and Margin of Safety. It extends to questions like, "What is Worldly Wisdom and How does one Acquire it?," "How does one build a Latticework of Mental Models," "What role can and should Stoicism play in life and investing?," and "What can the Mahabarata, the Gita and other great works of Eastern Wisdom teach us about investing and life?"

Gautam Baid's book is another step in the Value Investing tribe's unfolding knowledge about the world we inhabit. In it, you will learn his lessons from the greats—as updated by more recent students. So in addition to Buffett, Munger, and Graham, you will read about what Baid has learned from people like Mohnish Pabrai, Tom Russo, Mike Mauboussin, Peter Bevelin,

Saurabh Madaan, Marcelo Lima, Paul Lountzis, and others. You will also benefit from Baid's broad reading across many disciplines as he distils his understanding of works by a broad range of authors, including Herbert Simon, Shane Parrish, Nassim Taleb, Rolf Dobelli, Richard Zeckhauser, and others.

And, just as all true value investors are travelers on a path, this book itself has come a long way since it crossed my desk not so long ago. This Columbia Business School Publishing edition benefits from improved organization around topics and a clearer focus on Gautam's voice and insights. It offers fresh opportunity to learn and relearn those key lessons that will make us better investors and better human beings.

Guy Spier
Zurich, Switzerland

THE
JOYS OF
COMPOUNDING

CHAPTER 1

INTRODUCTION: THE BEST INVESTMENT YOU CAN MAKE IS AN INVESTMENT IN YOURSELF

I constantly see people rise in life who are not the smartest, sometimes not even the most diligent, but they are learning machines. They go to bed every night a little wiser than they were when they got up and boy does that help, particularly when you have a long run ahead of you.

—Charlie Munger

I n his 2007 University of Southern California School of Law commencement speech, Charlie Munger said that lifelong learning is paramount to long-term success. Without it, we won't succeed, because we won't get far based on what we already know.

If you take Berkshire Hathaway, which is certainly one of the best-regarded corporations in the world and may have the best long-term investment record in the entire history of civilization, the skill that got Berkshire through one decade would not have sufficed to get it through the next decade with the achievements made. Without Warren Buffett being a learning machine, a continuous learning machine, the record would have been absolutely impossible.[1]

Most people go through life not really getting any smarter. But you can acquire wisdom if you truly want to obtain it. In fact, a simple formula, if followed, is almost certain to make you smarter over time. It's simple but not easy.

It involves a lot of hard work, patience, discipline, and focus.

Read. A lot.

This is how Warren Buffett, one of the most successful people in the business world, describes his typical day: "I just sit in my office and read all day."[2]

Sitting. Reading. Thinking.

Buffett credits many of his successful decisions to his incredible reading habit. He estimates that he spends as much as 80 percent of his day reading and thinking.

In a 2014 letter to Berkshire shareholders, Munger outlined his expectations of the chair of the firm: "His first priority would be reservation of much time for quiet reading and thinking, particularly that which might advance his determined learning, no matter how old he became."[3]

Once, when asked about the key to his success, Buffett held up stacks of paper and said, "Read 500 pages like this every day. That's how knowledge works. It builds up, like compound interest. All of you can do it, but I guarantee not many of you will do it."[4]

All of us can work to improve our knowledge, but most of us won't put in the effort.

> More important than the will to win is the will to prepare.
>   —Charlie Munger

Self-improvement is the ultimate form of investing in oneself. It requires devoting time, money, attention, and hard effort now for a payoff later, sometimes in the far distant future. A lot of people are unwilling to make this trade-off because they crave instant gratification and desire instant results.

These short-term costs, when applied the right way along an axis of time, offer an exponential payoff when applied over a long life (figure 1.1).

"Compound interest," Albert Einstein reputedly said, "is the most powerful force in the universe."

So what happens when you apply such an incredible power to knowledge building?

You become a learning machine.

One person who took Buffett's advice, Todd Combs, now works for the legendary investor. After hearing Buffett talk, Combs started keeping track of what he read and how many pages he was reading.

> Eventually finding and reading productive material became second nature, a habit. As he began his investing career, he would read even more, hitting 600, 750, even 1,000 pages a day. Combs discovered that Buffett's formula worked, giving him more knowledge that helped him with what became his primary job—seeking the truth about potential investments.[5]

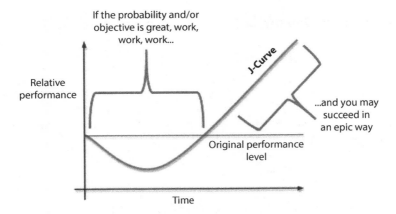

FIGURE 1.1 This is compounding in action. This illustrates what I experienced in 2018, after many years of determined efforts amid repeated setbacks. Resilience is a superpower.

Source: "5 Things I Learned from Elon Musk on Life, Business, and Investing," *Safal Niveshak* (blog), September 16, 2015, https://www.safalniveshak.com/elon-musk-on-life-business-investing/.

Reading five hundred pages a day might not be feasible for you. If, however, you can find ways to read (or to listen to an audiobook) during your day, at night, or on the weekends, you are likely to see multiple benefits.

Research published in the *Journal of American Academy of Neurology* has shown that people who engage in mentally stimulating activities like reading experience slower memory decline than those who do not. Reading is also linked with higher emotional intelligence, reduced stress, a wider vocabulary, and improved comprehension.

If you think of your mind as a library, three things should concern you:

1. The accuracy and relevance of the information you store.
2. Your ability to find or retrieve that information on demand.
3. Your ability to put that information to use when you need it—that is, your ability to apply it.

Having a repository of knowledge in your mind is pointless if you can't find and apply its contents.

Here, I am reminded of what Sherlock Holmes said in *The Reigate Puzzle*: "It is of the highest importance in the art of detection to be able to recognize, out of a number of facts, which are incidental and which vital. Otherwise your energy and attention must be dissipated instead of being concentrated."[6]

So be very careful of what you take in.

The Passionate Pursuit of Lifelong Learning

The game of life is the game of everlasting learning.

—Charlie Munger

Formal education will make you a living; self-education will make you a fortune.

—Jim Rohn

Rich people have small TVs and big libraries. Poor people have small libraries and big TVs.

—Zig Ziglar

Even after achieving such enormous success, Buffett continues to read for five to six hours every day. He often credits this good habit for much of his success in life. Reading allows him to learn the lessons of others.

What many people see as a three-hundred-page book is often the accumulation of thousands of hours and decades of work. Where else can you get the entire life's work of someone in the space of a few hours?

The most talented people in any given field are self-educated. Contrary to some belief, it doesn't mean grinding away without teachers. Rather, it's about drawing from your raw material and building out of it from a large number of sources. Books. Experiences. People. Everything in life can be a teacher when you possess the right mind-set. The benefits of recognizing just a few extra learning opportunities compound over time and unlock promising possibilities in the future.

The best way to learn something is to try to do it, but the next best way to learn is from someone who has already done it. This is the importance of reading and vicarious learning.

Understanding and learning from successful people provides insights about approaching life with the right attitude, developing a sound work ethic, and improving the quality of our decisions on a continuous basis.

In Michael Eisner and Aaron Cohen's book *Working Together: Why Great Partnerships Succeed*, Buffett talked about his and Munger's fierce dedication to lifelong learning:

I don't think any other twosome in business was better at continuous learning than we were. . . . And if we hadn't been continuous learners, the record wouldn't have been as good. And we were so extreme about it that we both spent the better part of our days reading, so we could learn more, which is not a common pattern in business. . . . We don't read other people's opinions. We want to get the facts, and then think.[7]

In the following excerpt from an October 2013 interview in *Fortune*, Buffett and Munger discuss how they were able to leap ahead of their peers and competitors:

Munger: We've learned how to outsmart people who are clearly smarter [than we are].
Buffett: Temperament is more important than IQ.
Munger: The other big secret is that we're good at lifelong learning. Warren is better in his seventies and eighties, in many ways, than he was when he was younger. If you keep learning all the time, you have a wonderful advantage.[8]

Is there a better investment than self-improvement? Here is what Buffett has had to say on the topic:

"The best investment you can make is an investment in yourself."
"The more you learn, the more you'll earn."
"Learn from your mistakes, and the mistakes of others."[9]

Self-improvement is the best way to spend some of your time every day. And finding the time to read is easier than you think. One way to make this happen is to carve out an hour of each day just for yourself. If you need inspiration, consider how Munger would sell himself the best hour of each day.

In an interview for his authorized biography, *The Snowball*, Buffett shared this story about Munger:

Charlie, as a very young lawyer, was probably getting $20 an hour. He thought to himself, "Who's my most valuable client?" And he decided it was himself. So he decided to sell himself an hour each day. He did it early in the morning, working on these construction projects and real estate deals. Everybody should do this, be the client, and then work for other people, too, and sell yourself an hour a day.[10]

It is essential to understand the opportunity cost of this one hour. On one hand, you can indulge in getting dopamine-laced rushes from emails and social media feeds while multitasking. On the other hand, you can dedicate the time to deep work and self-improvement. An hour's time spent acquiring in-depth knowledge about an important principle pays off in the long run. This current investment is minuscule compared with the significant net present value that results over a lifetime. It is akin to buying a dollar for less than one cent. This is why good books are the most undervalued asset class: the right ideas can be worth millions, if not billions, of dollars over time.

Time is a resource that becomes increasingly scarce for everyone with each passing second. Learn to value your time highly. Buffett avoids long daily commutes to work for this very reason. No matter how much money you have, you can't buy more time. We each have only twenty-four hours available to us every day. Time is the currency of life that appreciates in value the more it's spent. Minimize your commute time to work and outsource all of the noncore time-consuming menial tasks to free up valuable time for self-development. The extra money spent on these small luxuries will pinch initially, but over time, you will realize that it was well worth it. In the long term, the daily investment in learning something new and improving yourself goes a long way. So, the best investment of time is to invest in personal development. I hope the time you are investing in reading this book today yields positive results for the rest of your life. After having successfully achieved financial freedom through my passionate pursuit of lifelong learning, I can happily say that I am a better investor because I am a lifelong learner, and I am a better lifelong learner because I am an investor.

It seems fitting to end this chapter with the golden words of wisdom from two of the greatest learners and thinkers to have ever lived.

An investment in knowledge pays the best interest.
—Benjamin Franklin

Develop into a lifelong self-learner through voracious reading; cultivate curiosity and strive to become a little wiser every day.
—Charlie Munger

SECTION I

ACHIEVING WORLDLY WISDOM

CHAPTER 2

BECOMING A LEARNING MACHINE

Those who keep learning, will keep rising in life.

—Charlie Munger

The body is limited in ways that the mind is not. In fact, by the time most people are forty years old, their bodies begin to deteriorate. But the amount of growth and development that the mind can sustain has no limit.

Reading keeps our mind alive and growing. That's why we should inculcate a healthy reading habit. Reading is also meditative and calming.

Books are truly life changing, particularly once you've developed the habit of reading every day while watching your every thought. The neuronal connections that compound through the effort will make you an entirely new person after a few years.

Warren Buffett and Charlie Munger estimate that they spend 80 percent of their day reading or thinking about what they have read.

Therein lies the secret to becoming smarter.

The way to achieve success in life is to learn constantly. And the best way to learn is to read, and to do so effectively.

When someone asked Jim Rogers what was the best advice he ever got, he said it was the advice he received from an old man in an airplane: read everything.

All successful investors have a common habit. They just love to read all the time.

As Munger says, "In my whole life, I have known no wise people (over a broad subject matter area) who didn't read all the time—none, zero. You'd be amazed at how much Warren reads—at how much I read. My children laugh at me. They think I'm a book with a couple of legs sticking out."[1]

Vicarious Learning

The reading of all good books is like a conversation with the finest minds of past centuries.

—René Descartes

There is no better teacher than history in determining the future. . . . There are answers worth billions of dollars in a $30 history book.

—Bill Gross

Throughout the course of humanity, we have been recording knowledge in books. That means there's not a lot that's new; it's just recycled historical knowledge. Odds are that no matter what you're working on, somewhere, someone who is smarter than you has probably thought about your problem and put it into a book. Munger says:

I am a biography nut myself. And I think when you're trying to teach the great concepts that work, it helps to tie them into the lives and personalities of the people who developed them. I think you learn economics better if you make Adam Smith your friend. That sounds funny, making friends among the eminent dead, but if you go through life making friends with the eminent dead who had the right ideas, I think it will work better in life and work better in education. It's way better than just being given the basic concepts.[2]

Making friends with the eminent dead and the great thinkers of the past is a highly rewarding exercise. Morgan Housel writes:

Everything's been done before. The scenes change but the behaviors and outcomes don't. Historian Niall Ferguson's plug for his profession is that "The dead outnumber the living 14 to 1, and we ignore the accumulated experience of such a huge majority of mankind at our peril." The biggest lesson from the 100 billion people who are no longer alive is that they tried everything we're trying. The details were different, but they tried to outwit entrenched competition. They swung from optimism to pessimism at the worst times. They battled unsuccessfully against reversion to the mean. They learned that popular things seem safe because so many people are involved, but they're most dangerous because they're most competitive. Same stuff that guides today, and will guide tomorrow. History is abused when specific events are used as a guide to the future. It's way more useful as a benchmark for how people react to risk and incentives, which is pretty stable over time.[3]

The more you read, the more you build your mental repertoire. Incrementally, the knowledge you add to your stockpile will grow over time as it combines with everything new you put in there. This is compounding in action, and it works with knowledge in much the same way as it does with interest. Eventually, when faced with new, challenging, or ambiguous situations, you will be able to draw on this dynamic inner repository, or what Munger refers to as a "latticework of mental models."[4] (Mental models are an explanation of how things work, what variables matter in a given situation, and how they interact with one another. Mental models are how we make sense of the world.) You will then respond as someone whose instincts and judgment have been honed by the experiences of others, rather than just your own. You will start to see that nothing is truly new, that incredible challenges can and have been overcome, and that there are fundamental truths about how the world works.

So, learn from others. Figure out where you are going and find out who has been there before. Knowledge comes from experience, but it doesn't have to be your experience.

Creating Time to Read, Learn, and Think

Warren and I do more reading and thinking and less doing than most people in business. We do that because we like that kind of a life. But we've turned that quirk into a positive outcome for ourselves. We both insist on a lot of time being available almost every day to just sit and think. That is very uncommon in American business. We read and think.

—Charlie Munger

The rich invest in time, the poor invest in money.

—Warren Buffett

The rich have money. The wealthy have control over their time. And time is the scarcest resource, because of its nonrenewability. Time is a universally depleting resource, reduced at the same rate for the wealthy as for the poor.

This gives us one way of defining a successful investor, as a person for whom time has become a more binding constraint than money. The ultimate status symbol is time. Time is the new money.

My friends and colleagues often ask me how I manage to find so much time for reading while having a full-time job and managing my household chores.

For starters, I hardly watch television. I don't even have a cable television connection. I get all my desired content on Netflix, YouTube, and Amazon Prime. I watch only those select few movies, documentaries, and shows that truly pique my interest. I ensure that I don't spend a lot of time commuting to my workplace. I live in an area where I can walk to the grocery store, finish my purchases, and return home in less than twenty minutes. I have fully automated the monthly payments online for my phone, electricity, Internet, utilities, and meal plan bills.

All these choices are deliberate.

If you assume that the average person spends two hours a day watching television, an hour for commuting, and another two hours a week shopping, that adds up to twenty-three hours a week.

Twenty-three hours. That is 1,380 minutes. That is a lot of time. If you read a page in two minutes, that's almost seven hundred pages a week. Do seven hundred pages a week sound like too much for you? Well, how about just twenty-five pages a day? Shane Parrish writes:

> While most of us don't have the time to read a whole book in one sitting, we do have the time to read 25 pages a day. *Reading the right books, even if it's a few pages a day, is one of the best ways to ensure that you go to bed a little smarter than you woke up.*
>
> Twenty-five pages a day doesn't sound like much, but this commitment *adds up* over time. Let's say that two days out of each month, you probably won't have time to read. Plus Christmas. That gives you 340 days a year of solid reading time. If you read 25 pages a day for 340 days, that's 8,500 pages. 8,500. What I have also found is that when I commit to a minimum of 25 pages, I almost always read more. So let's call the 8,500 pages 10,000. (I only need to extend the daily 25 pages into 30 to get there.)
>
> With 10,000 pages a year, at a general pace of 25/day, what can we get done?
>
> Well, *The Power Broker* is 1,100 pages. The four LBJ books written by Robert Caro are collectively 3,552 pages. Tolstoy's two masterpieces—*War and Peace*, and *Anna Karenina*—come in at a combined 2,160. Gibbon's *The Decline and Fall of the Roman Empire* is six volumes and runs to about 3,660 pages. That's 10,472 pages.
>
> That means, in about one year, at a modest pace of 25 pages a day, you'd have knocked out 13 masterful works and learned an enormous amount about the history of the world. In one year!

That leaves the following year to read Shirer's *Rise and Fall of the Third Reich* (1,280), Carl Sandburg's *Six Volumes on Lincoln* (2,000), Adam Smith's *Wealth of Nations* unabridged (1,200), and Boswell's *Johnson* (1,300), with plenty of pages left to read something else.

This is how the great works get read: day by day, 25 pages at a time. No excuses . . .

The point of assigning yourself a certain amount of reading every day is to create a deeply held habit. The 25-pages-a-day thing is a habit-former! . . .

. . . Read what seems awesome and interesting to you now and let your curiosities grow organically. A lifelong interest in truth, reality, and knowledge will lead you down so many paths, you should never need to force yourself to read anything unless there is a very, very specific reason. (Perhaps to learn a specific skill for a job.)

Not only is this approach way more fun, but it works really, really well. It keeps you reading. It keeps you interested. And in the words of Nassim Taleb, "Curiosity is antifragile, like an addiction; magnified by attempts to satisfy it."

Thus, paradoxically, as you read more books, your pile of unread books will get larger, not smaller. That's because your curiosity will grow with every great read.

This is the path of the lifelong learner.[5]

This is compounding wisdom in action. This is how you become smarter. You must value your time very highly.

You've got to keep control of your time, and you can't unless you say no. You can't let people set your agenda in life.
—Warren Buffett

A Passion for Reading and Learning

The purpose of reading is not just raw knowledge. It's that it is part of the human experience. It helps you find meaning, understand yourself, and make your life better.

—Ryan Holiday

I read to increase knowledge. I read to find meaning. I read for a better understanding of others and myself. I read to discover. I read to make my life better. I read to make fewer mistakes.

To paraphrase David Ogilvy, reading and learning is "a priceless opportunity to furnish our mind and enrich the quality of our life."

Wherever I go, a book is not far behind. It might be on my phone or a physical copy, but a book is always close by. (I love printed books. I just find something so calming and peaceful about reading a paperback or hardcover book.) During my initial years in America, when I had to commute long distances to reach my workplace, I used to read books on my seat in the bus to ensure that not a single minute was wasted during my learning and development phase.

Finding time to read is easier than you might think. Waiting for a bus? Stop staring down the street and read. Waiting for a taxi? Read. On the train? Read. On the plane? Read. Waiting at the airport for your flight? Read.

Reading alone, however, isn't enough to improve your knowledge. Learning something insightful requires work. You have to read something above your current level. You need to find writers who are more knowledgeable on a particular subject than you are. This is how you become more intelligent. Reach out to and associate with people better than you and you cannot help but improve.

A lot of people confuse knowing the name of something with understanding it.

This is a good heuristic: Anything effortlessly digested means that you are reading for information. For example, the job of the news media is to inform us about day-to-day events, to entertain us, to reflect the public moods and sentiments of the moment, and to print stories that will interest us today and that we will want to read.

But that's exactly what creates problems for readers, who often succumb to the recency and availability biases that "news" creates. The same applies to social media. The feeds we take in are characterized by recency bias. Most of what we consume is less than twenty-four hours old. Rarely do we stop to ask ourselves questions about what we consume: Is this important? Is this going to stand the test of time for even a year?

As you grow older and become more mature, you realize that not everything deserves a response. This truth applies to most things in life and almost everything in the news.

We're surrounded by so much information that is of immediate interest to us that we feel overwhelmed by the never-ending pressure of trying to keep up with it all.
    —Nicholas Carr

The true scarce commodity of the near future will be human attention.
    —Satya Nadella

In an information-rich world, the wealth of information means a dearth of something else: a scarcity of whatever it is that information consumes. What information consumes is rather obvious: it consumes the attention of its recipients. Hence a wealth of information creates a poverty of attention and a need to allocate that attention efficiently among the overabundance of information sources that might consume it.

—Herbert Simon

In my view, studying old newspapers is a far more productive exercise than reading today's newspaper. (Buffett likes to call it "instructive art.") Morgan Housel writes:

> Every piece of financial news you read should be filtered by asking the question, "Will I still care about this in a year? Five years? Ten years?" The goal of information should be to help you make better decisions between now and the end of your ultimate goals. Read old news and you'll quickly see that the life expectancy of your goals is higher than that of the vast majority of headlines.[6]

Nassim Nicholas Taleb writes, in his book *Fooled by Randomness*, "Minimal exposure to the media should be a guiding principle for someone involved in decision making under uncertainty—including all participants in financial markets."[7] His key argument is that what is reported in the media is noise rather than information, but most people do not realize that the media is paid to get our attention.

The key lesson is that, in the pursuit of wisdom, we must read much more of what has endured over time (such as history or biographies) than what is ephemeral (such as daily news, social media trends, and the like). I agree with Andrew Ross, who says, "The smallest bookstore still contains more ideas of worth than have been presented in the entire history of television."[8]

All of the history of humankind is a short chapter in the history of biology. And all of biology is a short chapter in the history of the planet. And the planet is a short chapter in the history of the universe.

—Will and Ariel Durant

Will and Ariel Durant's work compresses five thousand years of history into one hundred pages of conclusions. It focuses on timeless truths, not on today's trends—the antithesis of social media. The book highlights the lessons of history, not the events that define it. It explains how all of life, from the simplicity of single-celled organisms to the complexity of humans, is governed by the laws and trials of evolution. The laws of biology double as the fundamental lessons of history. All beings are subject to the processes and trials of evolution. Only the fittest survive. Natural selection leads to better qualities being retained and passed along. The result is a constant cycle of improvement for the whole.

Always respect the old. Apply the "Lindy effect" to reading and learning. According to Nassim Taleb, "The Lindy effect is a concept that the future life expectancy of some nonperishable things like a technology or an idea is proportional to their current age, so that every additional period of survival implies a longer remaining life expectancy."[9] So, a book that has stood the test of time and survived fifty or one hundred or five hundred years and is still widely read because it contains timeless wisdom is expected to survive another fifty or one hundred or five hundred years for that very reason—that is, its wisdom is timeless.

> The man who doesn't read good books has no advantage over the man who cannot read them.
> —Mark Twain

One should read on varied topics, such as health and fitness, personal finance, investing, business, economics, decision making, human behavior, history, philosophy, self-awareness, and, of course, life. Reread the classics in these fields on a regular basis. Use the Lindy effect to your advantage. Also, share your latest book purchases with like-minded friends. It's a lot of fun to co-read and exchange insights.

Reading for understanding narrows the gap between reader and writer. How can we read better to bridge this gap?

How to Read a Book

The goal of reading determines how you should read. Although many people are proficient in reading for information and entertainment, few improve their ability to read for knowledge.

Mortimer Adler and Charles Van Doren have written the seminal book on reading. Their *How to Read a Book* provides the necessary skills to read anything. Adler and Van Doren identify four levels of reading: elementary, inspectional, analytical, and syntopical. Before we can improve reading skills, we need to understand the differences among these reading levels. They are discussed as levels because you must master one level before you can move to a higher level. They are cumulative, and each level builds on the preceding one.

Here is how Adler and Van Doren describe these four levels:

1. **Elementary reading.** This is the most basic level of reading as taught in our elementary schools. It is when we move from illiteracy to literacy.

2. **Inspectional reading.** This is another name for "scanning" or "superficial reading." It means giving a piece of writing a quick yet meaningful advance

review to evaluate the merits of a deeper reading experience. Whereas the question that is asked at the first level (elementary reading) is "What does the sentence say?" the question typically asked at this level is "What is the book about?"

3.   **Analytical reading.** Analytical reading is a thorough reading. This is the stage at which you make the book your own by conversing with the author and asking many organized questions. Asking a book questions as you read makes you a better reader. But you must do more. You must attempt to answer the questions you are asking. While you could do this in your mind, Adler and Van Doren argue that it's much easier to do this with a pencil in your hand. "The pencil," they argue, "becomes the sign of your alertness while you read."

Adler and Van Doren share the many ways to mark a book. They recommend that we underline or circle the main points; draw vertical lines at the margin to emphasize a passage already underlined or too long to be underlined; place a star, asterisk, or other symbol at the margin for emphasis; place numbers in the margin to indicate a sequence of points made in developing an argument; place page numbers of other pages in the margin to remind ourselves where else in the book the author makes the same points; circle keywords or phrases; and write our questions (and perhaps answers) in the margin (or at the top or bottom of the pages). This is how we remember the best ideas out of the books we read, long after we have read them—by making a book our own through asking questions and seeking answers within it. As Cicero said, "Nothing so much assists learning as writing down what we wish to remember."

4.   **Syntopical reading.** Thus far, we have been learning about how to read *a* book. The highest level of reading, syntopical reading, allows you to synthesize knowledge from a comparative reading of *several* books about the same subject. This is where the real virtue of reading is actualized.

Syntopical reading, also known as comparative reading, involves reading many books on the same subject and then comparing and contrasting the ideas, insights, and arguments within them. In syntopical reading, you create a latticework of the information in those books, along with your own life experiences and personal knowledge, to create mental models and new insights and form an understanding of the world that never quite existed before. This is the step that prepares the way for an original thinker to make a breakthrough.

It's a lot of fun to do this—to find connections between seemingly unconnected ideas from different disciplines. I cannot overemphasize the importance of this activity, because it has often led to many instances of serendipity and good fortune in my investing journey.

I usually read multiple nonfiction books in tandem. I pick the one that interests me the most at the time and read at least one full chapter. If it keeps my interest,

I keep going for another chapter. But if not, I'll jump to another book and read a full chapter. (It is harder to do this with fiction because you tend to lose the train of the plot and narrative.) I read this way because I start to see patterns across books about different topics. You may be reading one book on economics, one on business strategy, and another one on physics. Then, suddenly, something pops up that represents a common thread among those themes.

The past is not fixed. Yes, it is true. The past is not fixed. Reading can change this because a new book can make you aware of something incredible in an old book that you previously had not recognized. This is how knowledge compounds. Something you perceived to be of low value in an old book transforms into something of significant value, unlocked by another book in the future.

Therefore, no books are necessarily "the best." Usually, some combination of books, in unison, produce a big, nonlinear impact. Although many books may seem unrelated to one another, in reality they are all connected through some common threads. This realization creates a significant advantage, because it lets your interests pull you along, rather than forcing you to set a self-imposed deadline to finish a book. And if a book doesn't interest you, you just abandon it to save time and move on to something more interesting. Reading multiple books simultaneously, quitting those that are not engaging, and constantly picking up new ones is the antifragile approach to self-education.

In a 2017 interview, AngelList cofounder and CEO Naval Ravikant said, "I don't know about you, but I have very poor attention. I skim. I speed read. I jump around. I could not tell you specific passages or quotes from books. *At some deep level, you do absorb them and they become part of the threads of the tapestry of your psyche* [emphasis added]."[10] It is this development of the "tapestry of the psyche" that really matters a lot in becoming a wiser person over time.

How can we develop the same?

By starting early and taking advantage of the Matthew effect.

The Matthew Effect in Knowledge Acquisition

Imagine that you and Buffett are reading the latest issue of *The Economist* magazine. Who do you think will end up with greater insight at the end of this reading session?

The answer is obvious, isn't it? And for good reason.

Buffett is eighty-nine years old and, even at this age, he continues to be a relentless learning machine. He not only started learning early but also has been accumulating knowledge for more than three-quarters of a century.

The Matthew effect, in this context, refers to a person who has more expertise and thus has a larger knowledge base. This larger knowledge base allows that person to acquire greater expertise at a faster rate. So, the amount of useful insight that Buffett can draw from the same reading material would be quite high compared with most any other person, and again, Buffett would end up becoming smarter at a faster rate.

As you read increasingly more, your capacity to read and absorb more knowledge increases rapidly. During the initial days of inculcating my reading habit, I found it difficult to grasp the deep significance of many of the concepts in the books I read. Gradually, over time, I started discovering connections between the ideas that spread across different books. It is these connections that lead to the development of the "tapestry of the psyche," which in turn deepens our understanding of the big ideas coming from the key disciplines. This deep understanding makes the brain more efficient and smarter and better able to make sense of new information. None of us can know everything, but we can work to understand the big important models at a basic level across a broad range of disciplines so they can collectively add value in the decision-making process. Deep reading of the fundamentals enables us to understand the world for what it is. This is how we learn to reason from first principles.

First Principles Thinking

As to methods, there may be a million and then some, but principles are few. The man who grasps principles can successfully select his own methods. The man who tries methods, ignoring principles, is sure to have trouble.

—Harrington Emerson

When you first start to study a field, it seems like you have to memorize a zillion things. You don't. What you need is to identify the core principles— generally three to twelve of them—that govern the field. The million things you thought you had to memorize are simply various combinations of the core principles.

—John Reed

The best way to achieve wisdom is to learn the big ideas that underlie reality. . . . Even people who aren't geniuses can outthink the rest of mankind if they develop certain thinking habits.

—Charlie Munger

Five words separate the good from the great: flawless execution of the fundamentals. Boiling things down to their most fundamental truths, that is, to first principles (deconstructing), and then reasoning up from there (reconstructing) enables us to look at the world from the perspective of physics. This type of reasoning removes complexity from the decision-making process so that we can focus on the most important aspects that pertain to the decision at hand. Reasoning from first principles removes the impurity of assumptions and conventions. Instead, what remains is the essential information. First principles are the origins or the main concepts that cannot be reduced to anything else. Over two thousand years ago, Aristotle defined a first principle as "the first basis from which a thing is known." These are the fundamental assumptions that we know are true.

> When you have something that you know is *true*, even over the long term, you can afford to put a lot of energy into it.
> —Jeff Bezos

First principles thinking is a way of saying, "Think like a scientist." Scientists don't assume anything. They start with questions like "What are we absolutely sure is true?" or "What has been proven?" When Jeff Bezos started Amazon .com, in 1995, he clearly identified the first principles that would guide his business philosophy—that is, long-term thinking and a relentless focus on the customer rather than on the competition. This led Amazon to focus on things that don't change, such as customers' preference for low prices, fast delivery, and wider product selection, rather than on things that can and do change. Bezos has continued to focus relentlessly on these first principles until this date, and this line of thinking has made him one of the richest people in the world.

According to James Clear:

> In theory, first principles thinking requires you to dig deeper and deeper until you are left with only the foundational truths of a situation. Rene Descartes, the French philosopher and scientist, embraced this approach with a method now called Cartesian Doubt in which he would "systematically doubt everything he could possibly doubt until he was left with what he saw as purely indubitable truths."
>
> In practice, you don't have to simplify every problem down to the atomic level to get the benefits of first principles thinking. You just need to go one or two levels deeper than most people. Different solutions present themselves at different layers of abstraction.[11]

By focusing on the fundamental questions and then, while answering these questions, going two or three levels deeper by asking at every step "and then what?" we can arrive at the truth. This is the art of "reductionism." Less is more. When we remove the things that aren't truly representative of reality, we get closer to the ultimate truth. Michelangelo was once asked by the pope about the secret of his genius, particularly with regards to the statue of David, one of the greatest sculpting masterpieces of all time. Michelangelo responded by saying, "David was always there in the marble. I just took away everything that was *not* David."

Nassim Taleb calls this "subtractive epistemology." He argues that the greatest contribution to knowledge consists of removing what we think is wrong. We know a lot more about what is wrong than what is right. What does not work (i.e., negative knowledge) is more robust than positive knowledge. This is because it is a lot easier for something we know to fail than it is for something we know isn't so to succeed. Taleb dubs this philosophy "*via negativa*," employing a Latin phrase used in Christian theology to explain a way of describing God by focusing on what he is not, rather than on what he is. The absence of evidence doesn't qualify as the evidence of absence. In other words, just because all of the swans that have been observed to date are white, doesn't prove that all swans are white. One small observation (i.e., spotting a black swan) can conclusively disprove the statement "all swans are white" but millions of observations can hardly confirm it. Thus, disconfirmation is more rigorous than confirmation.

Elon Musk once referred to knowledge as a semantic tree: "Make sure you understand the fundamental principles, i.e., the trunk and big branches, before you get into the leaves/details or there is nothing for them to hang onto."[12] When you want to learn a new subject, first identify the fundamental principles and learn those in a clear and deep manner. Is there a way for us to do this effectively?

It turns out that, indeed, a simple way to do this exists.

It's simple but not easy.

The Feynman Technique

The Feynman technique, named after Nobel Prize–winning physicist Richard Feynman, is a great method for learning anything in a clear and deep manner and for improving retention.

The Feynman technique has four simple steps:

1. Pick and study a topic.
2. Take out a blank sheet of paper and write at the top the subject you want to learn. Write out what you know about the subject as if you were teaching it to someone who is unfamiliar with the topic—and not your smart adult friend but rather a ten-year-old child who can understand only basic concepts and relationships.

3. When you must use simple language that a child can understand, you force yourself to understand the concept at a deeper level and to simplify relationships and connections among ideas. If you struggle, you have a clear understanding of where you have gaps in knowledge. This is valuable feedback, because you have now discovered the edge of your mental capabilities. Knowing the limits of your knowledge is the dawning of wisdom.

4. Return to the source material, and then reread and relearn it. Repeat step 2 and compile information that will help you fill in those gaps in your understanding that you identified in step 3. Review and simplify further as necessary.

One sentence written by Feynman encapsulates the power of this technique. What started as a question about our existence has been translated into a single sentence that can be understood even by a middle-school student: "All things are made of atoms—little particles that move around in perpetual motion, attracting each other when they are a little distance apart, but repelling upon being squeezed into one another."[13]

Basically, Feynman says that if you know nothing about physics, the most essential scientific knowledge to understand is that everything is made up of atoms. In one simple sentence, Feynman conveys the foundational existence of our universe. Little wonder that he is widely regarded as one of the greatest teachers to have ever lived.

In a similar vein, consider Newton's law of gravity: the force of attraction between two bodies depends on their distance. Newton needed just a few pen strokes to express that thought mathematically. But from it, he showed why the planets move as they do, where comets fly, and even how high the tides flow. Later generations elaborated on this information, until we were able to send rockets, satellites, and humans into space. From Newton's earliest thought, the vast field of science and engineering grew to its present state.

To apply first principles thinking to the field of value investing, consider several fundamental truths. Understand and practice the following if you want to become a good investor:

1. Look at stocks as part ownership of a business.
2. Look at Mr. Market—volatile stock price fluctuations—as your friend rather than your enemy. View risk as the possibility of permanent loss of purchasing power, and uncertainty as the unpredictability regarding the degree of variability in the possible range of outcomes.
3. Remember the three most important words in investing: "margin of safety."
4. Evaluate any news item or event only in terms of its impact on (a) future interest rates and (b) the intrinsic value of the business, which is the discounted value of the cash that can be taken out during its remaining life, adjusted for the uncertainty around receiving those cash flows.

5. Think in terms of opportunity costs when evaluating new ideas and keep a very high hurdle rate for incoming investments. Be unreasonable. When you look at a business and get a strong desire from within saying, "I wish I owned this business," that is the kind of business in which you should be investing. A great investment idea doesn't need hours to analyze. More often than not, it is love at first sight.

6. Think probabilistically rather than deterministically, because the future is never certain and it is really a set of branching probability streams. At the same time, avoid the risk of ruin, when making decisions, by focusing on consequences rather than just on raw probabilities in isolation. Some risks are just not worth taking, whatever the potential upside may be.

7. Never underestimate the power of incentives in any given situation.

8. When making decisions, involve both the left side of your brain (logic, analysis, and math) and the right side (intuition, creativity, and emotions).

9. Engage in visual thinking, which helps us to better understand complex information, organize our thoughts, and improve our ability to think and communicate.

10. Invert, always invert. You can avoid a lot of pain by visualizing your life after you have lost a lot of money trading or speculating using derivatives or leverage. If the visuals unnerve you, don't do anything that could get you remotely close to reaching such a situation.

11. Vicariously learn from others throughout life. Embrace everlasting humility to succeed in this endeavor.

12. Embrace the power of long-term compounding. All the great things in life come from compound interest.

In addition to these fundamental truths, the value investing discipline has certain finer aspects that we come to realize and appreciate only with the passage of time and with experience:

Knowledge is overrated. Wisdom is underrated.
Intellect is overrated. Temperament is underrated.
Outcome is overrated. Process is underrated.
Short-term outperformance is overrated. Long-term adherence to one's investment philosophy is underrated.
Gross return is overrated. Stress-adjusted return is underrated.
Upside potential is overrated. Downside protection is underrated.
Maximization of returns is overrated. Avoidance of ruin is underrated.
Growth is overrated. Longevity is underrated.
Entry multiple is overrated. Exit multiple is underrated.
Price-to-earnings ratio is overrated. Duration of competitive advantage period is underrated.

Categorization of stocks into large cap, mid cap, and small cap is overrated. Categorization of businesses into great, good, and gruesome is underrated.

Being more frequently right than others is overrated. Being less wrong than others is underrated.

Forecasting is overrated. Preparation is underrated.

Confidence is overrated. Humility is underrated.

Conviction is overrated. Pragmatism is underrated.

Complexity is overrated. Simplicity is underrated.

Analytical ability is overrated. Personal behavior is underrated.

Having a high income level is overrated. Inculcating a disciplined saving habit is underrated.

Competition with peers is overrated. Helping our peers is underrated.

Large personal net worth is overrated. Good karma is underrated.

Talent is overrated. Resilience is underrated.

Being the best investor is overrated. Being the most authentic version of yourself is underrated.

CHAPTER 3

OBTAINING WORLDLY WISDOM THROUGH A LATTICEWORK OF MENTAL MODELS

Study the science of art. Study the art of science. Develop your senses—especially learn how to see. Realize that everything connects to everything else.

—Leonardo da Vinci

Any field you enter, from finance to engineering, requires some degree of specialization. Once you land a job, the process of specialization is only amplified. You become a specialist in certain aspects of the organization you work for. This approach, however, doesn't help solve problems. Because you don't know about the big ideas from the key disciplines, you start making decisions that don't take into account how the world really works. As in the story of the blind men and the elephant, you cannot see the whole picture. And investing is a liberal art that involves cross-pollination of ideas from multiple disciplines.

Marcel Proust said, "The real voyage of discovery consists not in seeing new sights, but in looking with new eyes." Multidisciplinary thinking is what allows us to see with new eyes.

Charlie Munger uses a latticework of mental models to make more rational and effective decisions. (Shane Parrish's summary compilation of the various mental models on the Farnam Street blog is an excellent resource to build up one's latticework.[1]) As the Chinese proverb goes, "I forget what I hear; I remember what

I see; I know what I do." Because the best way to learn something is by practicing it, we must routinely apply the mental models to different situations in our daily lives. One of Munger's favorite authors is Herbert Simon, who gave him the idea of mental models. Simon wrote in his autobiography, *Models of My Life*:

> The decision maker of experience has at his disposal a checklist of things to watch out for before finally accepting a decision. . . .
>
> If one could open the lid, so to speak, and see what was in the head of the experienced decision maker, *one would find that he had at his disposal repertoires of possible actions; that he had checklists of things to think about before he acted; and that he had mechanisms in his mind to evoke these, and bring these to his conscious attention when the situations for decisions arose* [emphasis added].[2]

In his book, *Charlie Munger: The Complete Investor*, Tren Griffin lays out Munger's path to worldly wisdom:

> Munger has adopted an approach to business and life that he refers to as worldly wisdom. Munger believes that by using a range of different models from many different disciplines—psychology, history, mathematics, physics, philosophy, biology, and so on—a person can use the combined output of the synthesis to produce something that has more value than the sum of its parts. Robert Hagstrom wrote a wonderful book on worldly wisdom entitled *Investing: The Last Liberal Art*, in which he states that "each discipline entwines with, and in the process strengthens, every other. From each discipline the thoughtful person draws significant mental models, the key ideas that combine to produce a cohesive understanding. Those who cultivate this broad view are well on their way to achieving worldly wisdom."[3]

Munger chose the latticework model to convey this idea of interconnectedness. We need more than a deep understanding of just one discipline—we need a working knowledge of many disciplines and an understanding of how they interact with each other.

Worldly Wisdom

In Munger's view, it is better to be worldly wise than to spend lots of time working with a single model that is precisely wrong. A multiple-model approach that is only approximately right will produce a far better outcome in anything that involves people or a social system.

—Tren Griffin

Munger would be what the Greek poet Archilochus called a fox.

Some 2,700 years ago, Archilochus wrote, "The fox knows many things, but the hedgehog knows one big thing." In the 1950s, philosopher Isaiah Berlin used that sentence as the basis for his essay "The Hedgehog and the Fox." In it, Berlin divides great thinkers into two categories: hedgehogs, who have one big overarching perspective on the world, and foxes, who have many different viewpoints. That essay, over time, has become a foundational part of thinking about the distinction between specialists and generalists.

Generalizing specialists have a core competency that they know a lot about. At the same time, they are always learning and have a working knowledge of other areas. Although a generalist has roughly the same knowledge for multiple areas, a generalizing specialist has one deep area of expertise and a few shallow ones. We have the option of developing a core competency while also building a base of interdisciplinary knowledge.

When Munger was asked at the 2017 Daily Journal Corporation meeting whether one should become a polymath or a specialist, his answer surprised a lot of people. Many people in the audience expected the answer to be obvious—of course he would recommend that people become generalists. But this is not what Munger said.

> I don't think operating over many disciplines, as I do, is a good idea for most people. I think it's fun, that's why I've done it. And I'm better at it than most people would be, and I don't think I'm good at being the very best at handling differential equations. So, it's been a wonderful path for me, *but I think the correct path for everybody else is to specialize and get very good at something that society rewards, and then to get very efficient at doing it. But even if you do that, I think you should spend 10 to 20 percent of your time [on] trying to know all the big ideas in all the other disciplines* [emphasis added].[4]

In Munger's comments, we find the underlying approach most likely to yield exponential results: specialize most of the time, but spend some time understanding the broader ideas of the world. That is how one attains worldly wisdom.

This approach isn't what most organizations and educational institutions advocate. Branching out into other disciplines outside one's core is not what generally is taught in academia. It is a project we have to undertake ourselves, by reading a wide range of books, experimenting with different subject areas, and drawing ideas from them. A true education should cultivate, above all, a sense of enjoyment about the process of thinking things through.

Munger talked about the importance of cultivating a broad-based general awareness during his 1995 speech at Harvard University: "Man's imperfect, limited-capacity brain easily drifts into working with what's easily available to it, and *the brain can't use what it can't remember* or what it is blocked from recognizing because it's heavily influenced by one or more psychological tendencies bearing strongly on it."[5]

Where do we get to learn these models from? We let history be our guide. If one way to ensure that we make poor decisions is to use a small sample size, we can reason that we should seek the biggest sample sizes we can.

What crosses most of history? Peter Kaufman, CEO of Glenair, board member of the Daily Journal Corporation, and editor of *Poor Charlie's Almanack*, has shared the answer in his "three-bucket" framework:

> Every statistician knows that a large, relevant sample size is their best friend. What are the three largest, most relevant sample sizes for identifying universal principles? Bucket number one is inorganic systems, which are 13.7 billion years in size. It's all the laws of math and physics, the entire physical universe. Bucket number two is organic systems, 3.5 billion years of biology on Earth. And bucket number three is human history, you can pick your own number, I picked 20,000 years of recorded human behavior. Those are the three largest sample sizes we can access and the most relevant.[6]

If we are to improve our learning, we should focus on things that change *slowly*. Kaufman's approach provides a framework of general laws that have stood the test of time—invariant, unchanging lenses that we can use to focus and arrive at workable answers. A foundational principle that aligns with the world and is applicable across the geologic time scale of human, organic, and inorganic history is compounding. Compounding is one of the most powerful forces in the world. In fact, it is the only power law in the universe that exists with a variable in its exponent. The power law of compounding not only is applicable to investing but also, and more important, can be applied to continued learning. The fastest way to simplify things is to spot the symmetries, or invariances—that is, the fundamental properties that do not change from one object under study to another. Munger explains:

> The models that come from hard science and engineering are the most reliable models on this Earth. And engineering quality control—at least the guts of it that matters to you and me and people who are not professional engineers—is very much based on the elementary mathematics of Fermat and Pascal . . .
>
> And, of course, the engineering idea of a backup system is a very powerful idea. The engineering idea of breakpoints—that's a very powerful model, too. The notion of a critical mass—that comes out of physics—is a very powerful model.[7]

But learning the big ideas from the key disciplines is not enough. We need to understand how these ideas interact and combine with each other, because this is what leads to "lollapalooza effects." Munger explains:

You get lollapalooza effects when two, three or four forces are all operating in the same direction. And, frequently, you don't get simple addition. It's often like critical mass in physics where you get a nuclear explosion if you get to a certain point of mass—and you don't get anything much worth seeing if you don't reach the mass.

Sometimes the forces just add like ordinary quantities and sometimes they combine on a break point or critical mass basis . . .

More commonly, the forces coming out of . . . models are conflicting to some extent. And you get huge, miserable trade-offs.

. . . You have to realize the truth of biologist Julian Huxley's idea that "Life is just one damn relatedness after another." So you must have the models, and you must see the relatedness and the effects from the relatedness.[8]

Commenting on Munger, Bill Gates once said, "He is truly the broadest thinker I have ever encountered."[9] Warren Buffett has said that Munger has "the best thirty-second mind in the world. He goes from A to Z in one move. He sees the essence of everything before you even finish the sentence."[10]

How is Munger able to do this?

Thinking

One of the advantages of a fellow like Buffett . . . is that he automatically thinks in terms of decision trees *[emphasis added].*

—Charlie Munger

The more models you have from outside your discipline, and the more you iterate through them in a checklist sort of fashion when faced with a challenge, the better you'll be able to solve problems.

Models are additive. Like building blocks. The more you have, the more things you can build, the more connections you can make between them, and the more likely you are to be able to determine the relevant variables that govern a situation.

And when you learn these models, you need to ask yourself under what conditions this tool will fail. That way, you're not only looking for situations in which the tool is useful but also for situations in which something interesting is happening that might warrant further attention.

We can improve our thinking process by taking out and devoting the necessary time for it. According to Tren Griffin,

Munger's breadth of knowledge is something that is naturally part of his character but also something that he intentionally cultivates. In his view, to know nothing about an important subject is to invite problems. Both Munger and Buffett set aside plenty of time each day to just think. Anyone reading the news is provided with constant reminders of the consequences of not thinking. Thinking is a surprisingly underrated activity. Researchers published a study in 2014 that revealed that approximately a quarter of women and two-thirds of men chose electric shocks over spending time alone with their own thoughts.[11]

Bertrand Russell rightly said, "Most people would rather die than think, and many of them do."

Without great solitude no serious work is possible.
—Pablo Picasso

One of the finest essays on learning how to think better is "Solitude and Leadership" by William Deresiewicz:

Thinking means concentrating on one thing long enough to develop an idea about it. Not learning other people's ideas, or memorizing a body of information, however much those may sometimes be useful. Developing your own ideas. In short, thinking for yourself. You simply cannot do that in bursts of 20 seconds at a time, constantly interrupted by Facebook messages or Twitter tweets, or fiddling with your iPod, or watching something on YouTube.

I find for myself that my first thought is never my best thought. My first thought is always someone else's; it's always what I've already heard about the subject, always the conventional wisdom. It's only by concentrating, sticking to the question, being patient, letting all the parts of my mind come into play, that I arrive at an original idea. By giving my brain a chance to make associations, draw connections, take me by surprise . . . You do your best thinking by slowing down and concentrating.[12]

Look at this generation, with all of its electronic devices and multitasking. I will confidently predict less success than Warren, who just focused on reading. If you want wisdom, you'll get it sitting on your ass. That's the way it comes.
—Charlie Munger

Munger has often credited his success to having a long attention span, that is, his ability to stay focused for an extended period of time. Munger is able to block out the world when he is thinking, which has provided him a great advantage in solving problems and developing ideas. Long attention spans allow for a deep understanding of subjects. When combined with deliberate practice, it helps us identify our leverage points and focus our energies on them.

As you can see, actual thinking is really hard work. It is why Henry Ford said, "Thinking is the hardest work there is, which is probably why so few people engage in it." The best ideas come to you in solitude. Introverts tend to be creative because, by spending more time alone, they are more susceptible to inspiration. Introverts are less susceptible to groupthink, and thus it is easier for them to go against the consensus.

Brilliant people aren't a special breed—they just use their minds differently. They practice certain habits of thinking that allow them to see the world differently from others. In their book *The 5 Elements of Effective Thinking*, Dr. Edward B. Burger and Dr. Michael Starbird outline some practical ways for us to improve our thinking:[13]

1. **Understand deeply.** When you learn anything, go for depth and make it rock solid. Any concept that you are trying to master is a combination of simple core ideas. Identify the core ideas and learn them deeply. This deeply ingrained knowledge base can serve as a meaningful springboard for more advanced learning and action in your field. Be brutally honest with yourself. If you do not understand something, revisit the core concepts again and again. Remember that merely memorizing stuff is *not* deep learning.

2. **Make mistakes.** Mistakes highlight unforeseen opportunities as well as gaps in our understanding. And mistakes are great teachers. As Michael Jordan once said, "I've missed more than nine thousand shots in my career. I've lost almost three hundred games. Twenty-six times, I've been trusted to take the game-winning shot and missed. I've failed over and over and over again in my life. And that is why I succeed." The takeaway is that we cannot come out with a correct solution on the first attempt. Start with a probable solution (hypothesis) and continue correcting the mistakes until you arrive at the right solution. Thomas Edison was famous for using this approach for his inventions. When he said that invention is 1 percent inspiration and 99 percent perspiration, the perspiration was the process of incrementally making mistakes and learning from them to make the next attempts apt to be closer to right. When Edison was asked how he felt about his countless failed attempts at making a light bulb, he replied, "I have not failed. I've just found ten thousand ways that won't work."

3. **Raise questions.** If you want to deepen your understanding, you need to raise questions. Do not be afraid to show your ignorance. If you do not understand, ask. The great philosopher Socrates would challenge his students, friends, and even enemies to make new discoveries by asking them uncomfortable, core questions, which often led to new insights.

4. **Follow the flow of ideas.** To truly understand a concept, discover how it evolved from simpler concepts. Recognizing that the present reality is a moment in a continuing evolution makes your understanding fit into a more

coherent structure. You cannot discover everything on your own. You need to use the existing idea and improve it. Edison was supremely successful at inventing product after product, exploiting the maxim that every new idea has utility beyond its original intent. He is credited with having said, "I start where the last man left off." More poignantly, he noted that "many of life's failures are people who did not realize how close they were to success when they gave up."

5. **Change.** You need to shrug off a lifetime's habit of accepting a relatively superficial level of understanding and start learning more deeply. You need to let go of the constraining forces in your life and let yourself fail on the road to success. You should question all of the issues you have taken for granted all those years. View every aspect of your world as a stream of insights and ideas. Be amenable to change. Each of us forever remains a work in progress—always evolving, ever changing. We're all rough drafts of the person we're still becoming.

Learning is a lifelong journey.

Munger's speeches and essays are filled with the thoughts of the great thinkers from many different domains. Munger reserves a lot of time in his schedule for reading and has read hundreds of biographies. He explains why he does so: "I believe in the discipline of mastering the best that other people have ever figured out. I don't believe in just sitting down and trying to dream it all up yourself. Nobody's that smart."[14]

Munger provides a compelling argument for spending more time thinking, reading, learning, and obtaining worldly wisdom. And, in today's digital age, there is no dearth of resources to further this endeavor.

The Internet is the best school ever created. The best peers are on the Internet. The best books are on the Internet. The best teachers are on the Internet. The tools for learning are abundant. It's the desire to learn that's scarce.

—Naval Ravikant

CHAPTER 4

HARNESSING THE POWER OF PASSION AND FOCUS THROUGH DELIBERATE PRACTICE

You are what your deepest desire is. As is your desire, so is your intention. As is your intention, so is your will. As is your will, so is your deed. As is your deed, so is your destiny.

—Upanishads

Take up one idea. Make that one idea your life—think of it, dream of it, live on that idea. Let the brain, muscles, nerves, every part of your body, be full of that idea, and just leave every other idea alone. This is the way to success.

—Swami Vivekananda

According to the Japanese, everyone has an *ikigai*—a reason for living. And according to the residents of the Japanese village with the world's longest-living people, finding it is the key to a happy life. Having a strong sense of *ikigai*—where passion, mission, vocation, and profession intersect—means that each day is infused with meaning.

Although there is no direct English translation, the word *ikigai* is thought to combine the Japanese words *ikiru*, meaning "to live," and *kai*, meaning "the realization of what one hopes for." Together these definitions create the concept of "a reason to live," or the idea of having a purpose in life (figure 4.1).

FIGURE 4.1 *Ikigai.*

Source: Thomas Oppong, "Ikigai: The Japanese Secret to a Long and Happy Life Might Just Help You Live a More Fulfilling Life," Medium, January 10, 2018, https://medium.com/thrive-global/ikigai-the -japanese-secret-to-a-long-and-happy-life-might-just-help-you-live-a-more-fulfilling-9871d01992b7.

When you can use your skills to make a difference in someone's life and get paid for it, that's a happy life. When you're passionate about it as well, that's a calling. The feeling is almost divine.

—Ed Latimore

The only way to deep happiness is to do something you love to the best of your ability.

—Richard Feynman

Your goal in life is to find out the people who need you the most, to find out the business that needs you the most, to find the project and the art that needs you the most. There is something out there just for you.

—Naval Ravikant

According to Gordon Matthews, professor of anthropology at the Chinese University of Hong Kong, how people understand *ikigai* can, in fact, often be mapped to two other Japanese ideas—*ittaikan* and *jiko jitsugen*. *Ittaikan* refers to "a sense of oneness with, or commitment to, a group or role," while *jiko jitsugen* relates more to "self-realization."

Self-realization is closely linked to the concept of self-actualization, best known in the field of psychology in the context of Abraham Maslow's hierarchy of needs. Self-actualized people are those who are fulfilled and are doing all that they are capable of. Maslow described the good life as one directed toward self-actualization, the higher need. Self-actualization occurs when you maximize your potential by doing your best. Maslow shared the names of those individuals he believed to be self-actualized, including Abraham Lincoln, Thomas Jefferson, and Albert Einstein, to elaborate the common characteristics of the self-actualized person. According to humanistic psychologist Albert Ellis, "self-actualization involves the pursuit of excellence and enjoyment; whichever people choose to desire and emphasize."[1] This focus on achieving excellence and enjoyment (even more than a focus on the realization of potential) prioritizes well-being and shows the relation between self-actualization and positive psychology.

Once we have discovered our calling in life, we need to embrace the power of *focus*.

> I fear not the man who has practiced 10,000 kicks once, but I fear the man who has practiced one kick 10,000 times.
> —Bruce Lee

> Give me six hours to chop down a tree and I will spend the first four sharpening the axe.
> —Abraham Lincoln

> Those who attain any excellence, commonly spend life in one pursuit; for excellence is not often gained upon easier terms.
> —Samuel Johnson

When Bill Gates met Warren Buffett for the first time, their host at dinner, Gates's mother, asked everyone around the table what they believed was the single most important factor in their success in life. Gates and Buffett gave the same one-word answer: "focus." Both men agree that relentlessly focusing on one specific passion leads to achievement. And that means pushing aside other ideas and interests until a goal is reached.

> Intensity is the price of excellence.
> —Warren Buffett

Buffett biographer Alice Schroeder writes about Buffett's intense focus: "He ruled out paying attention to almost anything but business—art, literature, science, travel, architecture—so that he could focus on his passion."[2] This shouldn't come as a surprise. Many of the highly successful people in the world attribute their success to a singular focus—a deep commitment to the pursuit of one main goal. Focus directs your energy toward your goals. The more focused you are, the more energy you put toward what you're working on.

Having the ability to focus on what is "important and knowable" is valuable in a world in which we are constantly bombarded with distracting and disparate ideas, information, and opinions. This has important implications for investors. Focus on those investments for which the *microeconomics* are going to dominate the outcome. This approach will allow you to call upon your accumulated experience in analyzing companies and industries and to utilize the same to your advantage. Fifty years ago, the best investors were the ones with an informational edge. Today, the best investors are the ones with a behavioral edge. As the speed of information dissemination in the markets and competition for short-term outperformance among money managers increased over the years, time horizons and patience levels significantly decreased. Today, an investor's edge is less about knowing more than others about a specific stock and more about the mind-set, discipline, and willingness to take a long-term view about the intrinsic value of a business.

Achievement is so ingrained in our culture that we often ignore the fact that gunning to maximize short-term productivity usually comes at the expense of slower but more consistent and durable long-term progress. We live in a society in which inactivity is often frowned upon, but part of our focus should be not just on doing but also on deeply understanding the parameters of what we need to do, now and in the future. Learning and understanding the upfront and changing parameters of the field in which you are participating will help you focus on the right place. As Albert Einstein said, "You have to learn the rules of the game. And then you have to play better than anyone else." These are incredibly powerful words in the context of focus. Buffett's genius is that he prioritizes learning so that he can have higher quality insights.

> Many people would see this as totally unproductive, but many of my best business solutions and money problem answers have come from periods of just sitting and thinking.
> —Warren Buffett

In a knowledge economy, learning and thinking are the best long-term investments you can make in your career. Learning and thinking determine our decisions, and those decisions, in turn, determine our results. Buffett spends the major part of his daily time reading and very little time actually taking action. He says, "In allocating capital, activity does not correlate with achievement. Indeed, in the fields of investments and acquisitions, frenetic behavior is often counterproductive."[3] Investing is a field in which success can flow from passively observing the world, reading, thinking, and doing nothing more than making an occasional telephone call. Most investors would perform better if they thought more and did less. One of the best hacks in the investment field is learning to be happy doing nothing.

Successful investing is a practical craft and is made up of heuristics: a tool kit of approximate, experience-based rules for making sense of the world. The rules are local rather than global and slowly change over time—they are sufficiently static to make experience valuable but sufficiently fluid to keep the craft interesting. Having a strong passion for lifelong learning is a durable competitive advantage for an investor. What differentiates successful investors from mediocre ones is passion. To be a truly passionate investor means you are always thinking about the future and the direction of the world. It means you are always enthusiastically observing everything around you. Investing isn't just a process of wealth creation; it is a source of great happiness and sheer intellectual delight for the truly passionate investor. It is great to be passionate in life, but it is wise to be so only for things that are under our control, or else we risk being dejected because of unfavorable outcomes. Value investors derive satisfaction from the mental process of investing and from the learnings embedded in the outcomes. Those who love the process end up with results naturally, unlike others who worship only outcomes.

> The only way to gain an edge is through long and hard work. *Do what you love to do, so you just naturally do it or think about it all the time, even if you are relaxing.* . . . Over time, you can accumulate a *huge* advantage if it comes *naturally* to you like this [emphasis added].
> —Li Lu

Buffett has always held the opinion that the people who discover their passion in life are lucky. His early passion for money management resulted in his studying, by age eleven, every book the Omaha Public Library had on investing, some of them twice.

In an interview with *Fortune* magazine in 2012, Buffett was asked how other people can "tap dance to work" the way he does. He provided the following answer: "Follow your passion. . . . I always tell college students to take the job that you would take if you were independently wealthy."[4] By doing that, the logic goes, you'll bring more energy to your work than anybody else does. There is power in passion.

"The truth is, so few people really jump on their jobs, you really will stand out more than you think," Buffett explains. "You will get noticed if you really go for it."[5]

As the well-known saying goes, "Choose a job you love, and you will never have to work a day in your life." You know that you are doing things right in your life when you go to bed at night and cannot wait to wake up and live the next day.

Instead of merely trying to live a long life, we should endeavor to infuse life into our lives. Too often, life appears short to us because we all seem to have so much to do. But the reality is that life is long if you know how to use it well.

> It is not that we have a short time to live, but that we waste a lot of it. Life is long enough, and a sufficiently generous amount has been given to us for the highest achievements if it were all well invested. But when it is wasted in heedless luxury and spent on no good activity, we are forced at last by death's final constraint to realize that it has passed away before we knew it was passing. So it is: we are not given a short life but we make it short, and we are not ill-supplied but wasteful of it. . . . Life is long if you know how to use it.
> —Seneca

Old too soon, wise too late. It is a sad irony that it often takes us a lifetime to learn to live in the moment. To just "be" in the moment. We put off "living happily ever after" for another year because we assume we have another year. We don't tell the ones we love how much we love them often enough because we assume there's always tomorrow. We ignore the warning of Socrates: "Beware the barrenness of a busy life." Having all the money in the world is pointless if you don't have the time or the health to enjoy it. In appendix A of this book, I share a beautiful poem written by David Weatherford, which I read a few years ago and continue to read from time to time. It has inspired me to work toward changing my life—from deferring living for tomorrow to trying to live today as happily as possible.

> We have two lives, and the second begins when we realize we have only one.
> —Confucius

When you find your North Star, that is, the most important thing that sets your life's course, you learn where you're headed. And that is such a good feeling. It is fine for your North Star to change over time. But whatever it is right now, let it guide you. Your North Star is highly meaningful and vital in a personal context, so aiming toward this beacon of light will bring great happiness to you every day.

Pursue your passion. You won't get this time back ever again. Life is but a pause between the first breath and the last. The only thing you can guarantee at somebody's birth is his or her death; everything else is unpredictable. They say life is a journey from B to D, that is, from birth to death. But what about the C that comes between B and D? It is choice. Our life is a matter of choices. Choose what makes you happy and your life will never go wrong. Some people die at age twenty-five but aren't buried until they are seventy-five. Some people aren't born until they are age twenty-five. Strive to be the latter.

> One day your life will flash before your eyes. Make sure it's worth watching.
> —Gerard Way

In 2004, Steve Jobs was diagnosed with pancreatic cancer and was informed that he only had a few weeks to live. This is what Jobs told the audience during his 2005 Stanford commencement speech:

> Remembering that I'll be dead soon is the most important tool I've ever encountered to help me make the big choices in life. Because almost everything—all external expectations, all pride, all fear of embarrassment or failure—these things just fall away in the face of death, leaving only what is truly important. *Remembering that you are going to die is the best way I know to avoid the trap of thinking you have something to lose. You are already naked. There is no reason not to follow your heart* . . . [emphasis added].
>
> Your time is limited, so don't waste it living someone else's life. Don't be trapped by dogma—which is living with the results of other people's thinking. Don't let the noise of others' opinions drown out your own inner voice. *And most important, have the courage to follow your heart and intuition* [emphasis added]. They somehow already know what you truly want to become. Everything else is secondary.[6]

Jobs was echoing the thoughts of Mark Twain, who said, "Twenty years from now you will be more disappointed by the things that you didn't do than by the ones you did do. So throw off the bowlines. Sail away from the safe harbor. Catch the trade winds in your sails. Explore. Dream. Discover."

Twain's quote reminds me of one of my favorite advertisements. It came from United Technologies. It runs:

> Most of us miss out on life's big prizes. The Pulitzer. The Nobel. Oscars. Tonys. Emmys. But we're all eligible for life's small pleasures. A pat on the back. A kiss behind the ear. A four-pound bass. A full moon. An empty parking space. A cracking fire. A great meal. A glorious sunset. Hot soup. Cold beer. Don't fret about copping life's grand awards. Enjoy its tiny delights. There are plenty for all of us.[7]

And therein lies the big life lesson for all of us: this moment is all that we have with us, and we need to prioritize things we want to do now. Take young children. They are in a natural state of happiness; they are neither stuck in the past nor living in anticipation of the future.

Enjoy the little things, for one day you may look back and realize they were the big things.

—Robert Brault

The best things in life are not things. They are experiences. What we truly treasure in the long run comes from experiences. Engaging experiences trump material objects when it comes to deriving lasting happiness. The pleasure derived from things is transitory, but the joy that comes from experiences is enduring. Don't chase things. Make memories. We are all on a journey. No one lives forever. Be generous to those who cross your path. Give to those who need. Touch hearts and spread happiness, hope, and optimism through your words and actions.

All our worries and plans about the future, all of the replays in our minds of the bad things that happened in the past is all in our heads (the human mind has a tendency to create issues out of nothing when it's idle). This worrying just distracts us from living fully right now. Let go of all that and instead focus on what you're doing right at this moment. You cannot reconstruct the framework of your reactions unless you deconstruct everything first, which you can only do by leaving things behind. Many events in life are outside our control. So we should just let it go and continue putting our best foot forward every day.

In his Stanford speech, Jobs shared the thought that would set the tone for the rest of his day: "For the past thirty-three years, I have looked in the mirror every morning and asked myself: 'If today were the last day of my life, would I want to do what I am about to do today?' And whenever the answer has been no for too many days in a row, I know I need to change something."[8]

These thoughts of Jobs are in alignment with the "regret minimization framework" espoused by Jeff Bezos.

When Bezos first considered starting Amazon, he was working for D. E. Shaw, one of the biggest quant-driven hedge funds on Wall Street. Today, in hindsight, his decision looks like a no-brainer, but at the time, no one would have considered it a prudent career move to leave a well-paying hedge fund job to start an online bookstore.

Mixing up ambition and genuine interest is a common phenomenon. Because of societal constraints, we never truly experience freedom. Hence, what we perceive as interest is often distorted by society's expectations and becomes what we think we should become, out of a fear based on beliefs.

Every big decision we make in life usually involves some sort of a trade-off. At times, we have to accept small regrets to avoid large ones later. Many people spend so much time worrying about the risks of taking action that they completely overlook the risks of failing to act. Sure, if you don't take any risk, there's no failure associated. No pain.

No pain? Really? Regrets will haunt you for the rest of your life. Failure hurts but passes quickly. Conversely, regret hurts forever. It's hard to look back and face the opportunities missed because of a lack of initiative. Failure doesn't hurt as much as witnessing how fear led us to mistrust our intuition. You only need to succeed once to unlock a new world of possibilities. Regret is in the nondoing. Many people are experts at success, but amateurs at failure. But not Bezos:

> The framework I found, which made the decision incredibly easy, was what I called—which only a nerd would call—a "regret minimization framework." So I wanted to project myself forward to age 80 and say, "Okay, now I'm looking back on my life. I want to have minimized the number of regrets I have." I knew that when I was 80 I was not going to regret having tried this. I was not going to regret trying to participate in this thing called the Internet that I thought was going to be a really big deal. I knew that if I failed I wouldn't regret that, *but I knew the one thing I might regret is not ever having tried* [emphasis added]. I knew that that would haunt me every day, and so, when I thought about it that way it was an incredibly easy decision.[9]

I love this framework because it doesn't involve a spreadsheet or a business plan. It has more to do with personal fulfillment and life goals.

Once we have understood the significant importance of passion and focus in life, how can we harness their power more effectively to achieve excellence in our respective fields?

By engaging in the process of deliberate practice.

Deliberate Practice

Many performance coaches and motivational gurus preach the mantra of "practice makes perfect." Ten thousand hours of practice, they say, is the key to world-class performance. Malcolm Gladwell popularized this idea in his bestselling book *Outliers*:

> The idea that excellence at performing a complex task requires a critical minimum level of practice surfaces again and again in studies of expertise. In fact, researchers have settled on what they believe is the magic number for true expertise: ten thousand hours. . . . Of course, *this doesn't address why some people get more out of their practice sessions than others do* [emphasis added]. But no one has yet found a case in which true world-class expertise was accomplished in less time. It seems that it takes the brain this long to assimilate all that it needs to know to achieve true mastery."[10]

Notice the statement that "this doesn't address why some people get more out of their practice sessions than others do." Practice alone doesn't make perfect. As James Clear says, "Motion does not equal action. Busyness does not equal effectiveness."[11]

In his book *Talent Is Overrated*, *Fortune* magazine editor Geoff Colvin highlights studies that show that greatness can be developed by any individual, in any field, through the process of what he calls "deliberate practice."[12] It is one of the big ideas from the science on human performance.

Deliberate practice is a highly structured activity with the specific goal of improving performance. It requires continuous evaluation, feedback, and a lot of mental effort.

Following are some of the key elements of deliberate practice:

1. **It's repeatable.** If you're a writer, you write a lot. If you are a musician, you know the importance of repeating your notes.
2. **It receives constant feedback.** Learning occurs when you get lots of feedback tied closely in time to decisions and actions. And deliberate practice constantly refers to results-based feedback. No mistakes go unnoticed. In fact, every error is a crucial piece of information for further improvement. The feedback can come from your observations or from a coach or mentor who notices the things that aren't always visible to you.
3. **It is hard.** Deliberate practice takes significant mental effort.
4. **It isn't much fun.** Most people don't enjoy doing activities that they're not good at. It's no fun to fail time and time again and to receive criticism about how to improve. Yet deliberate practice is designed to focus specifically on those things you are weak at, and this requires you to practice those skills repeatedly until you master them.

While practicing deliberately, you are at the boundary of your limits and knowledge, stretching out for a goal that is just a little out of reach. When you reach for something, the idea is pounded in even better.

Deliberate practice is all about having a blue-collar mind-set. In his book *The Little Book of Talent*, Daniel Coyle wrote:

From a distance, top performers seem to live charmed, cushy lives. When you look closer, however, you'll find that they spend vast portions of their life intensively practicing their craft. Their mind-set is not entitled or arrogant; it's 100-percent blue collar: They get up in the morning and go to work every day, whether they feel like it or not.

As the artist Chuck Close says, "Inspiration is for amateurs."[13]

Finding our calling in life, pursuing it with a strong passion and intense focus, and engaging in deliberate practice results in *ikigai*. Will Durant put it best when he said, "We are what we repeatedly do. Excellence, then, is not an act, but a habit."[14]

SECTION II

BUILDING STRONG CHARACTER

CHAPTER 5

THE IMPORTANCE OF CHOOSING THE RIGHT ROLE MODELS, TEACHERS, AND ASSOCIATES IN LIFE

I was lucky to have the right heroes. Tell me who your heroes are and I'll tell you how you'll turn out to be. The qualities of the one you admire are the traits that you, with a little practice, can make your own, and that, if practiced, will become habit forming.

—Warren Buffett

Good teachers, in any field, do far more than convey information; they pass along something of themselves.

—Peter Buffett

People who constantly strive to improve themselves usually have a role model. This is a crucial aspect in the journey of self-improvement. As creatures of comfort, we are reluctant to step out of our comfort zone, and we often lack the inner urge. Because many of us are motivated by examples, however, we come to realize that the drive to improve can sometimes be found among others—or, to be more precise, can be driven by others. Role models fill that position nicely, and having them in our lives is an indicator that we intend to embark on a path of self-improvement.

In his book *The Education of a Value Investor*, Guy Spier writes about the importance of find one's role models in life:

> There is no more important aspect of our education as investors, businesspeople, and human beings than to find these exceptional role models who can guide us on our own journey. Books are a priceless source of wisdom. But people are the ultimate teachers, and there may be lessons that we can only learn from observing them or being in their presence. In many cases, these lessons are never communicated verbally. Yet you feel the guiding spirit of that person when you're with them.[1]

Role models act as our motivational coach and as a source of daily inspiration in our lives. I have many role models, and every year, I discover new ones during the course of my journey. You may wonder how one learns from his or her role model. You need to read about the lives of these people, what they have accomplished over the years, and how they learned, and then learn from their experiences. Vicarious learning is valuable, as our personal experience and insight is but a tiny fraction of the total experience and insight of humankind.

Teachers open the door, but you must enter by yourself.
—Chinese proverb

The very instant when we come across our role model, we usually know it. The feeling we experience at that moment cannot be described in mere words; it can only be experienced. It is one of profound inspiration, motivation, and finding one's purpose in life.

Certain things you can do, or questions you can ask, will help you choose the most appropriate role models:

- Look for the people who achieved results similar to the ones you are trying to achieve.
- Look for people who have struggled with the same problems that you have in your life and try to understand how they overcame them.
- Find someone whose life story is so inspirational that it simply uplifts you and motivates you.
- If you have trouble staying motivated or inspired, look for someone who, by their very actions, inspires you in a specific way.
- If you lack discipline, look for role models who have plenty of it and who teach others how to adopt their discipline and dedication.

It really is up to you. First, you should clearly define exactly what you are looking for. After that, you can more easily identify your role models. As the saying goes, "When the student is ready, the teacher will appear."

No discussion of role models can ever be complete without mentioning our parents. Most of us have experienced the wide reach of their compassion. Years of daily care. Sleepless nights. Endless worrying about our well-being. Unconditional love. Moral support during tough times.

Always give time to your parents. We are so busy growing up that we often forget they are growing old. Parents usually don't ask that we spend time with them, but recognizing need is part of what makes one a person of value.

It is a wonderful feeling to care for our parents. We have many ways to do this. Showing appreciation for little acts. Spending time together. Making small gestures of love and affection. This is all most parents want from us. It is what gives them great happiness.

My noble mother taught me the virtues of honesty, kindness, and empathy. My dear father constantly motivated me to push my limits and to improve. He has been a great friend, philosopher, and guide and has given me the greatest gift anyone could give: he believed in me. I would like to make a special mention of my late maternal grandfather, who taught me the virtues of hard work. His eternal words of wisdom to me during my early teenage years had a profound and lasting impact on my life: "There is no alternative to hard work."

Throughout my childhood years, I was a weak student. I barely finished tenth grade. My scores were so abysmally low that it was a struggle for me to gain admission to a decent high school. It was only my subsequent awakening, driven by a major personal setback, that made me finally realize the virtues of hard work and determined effort, and that was the catalyst for my academic revival and professional career growth. And this is why I instantly related to legendary investor Arnold Van Den Berg's life, when I read his inspirational words:

> I always had this image of myself that I wasn't very smart, and the way I did in school proved that I wasn't. But: Once I realized that if you dedicate yourself and you commit yourself, you can learn anything. I will admit this: whatever I learn takes me three times as long as anybody else. But if I spend three times as much time as anybody else, then I'm equal. I can learn it, just give me more time, more books.[2]

Hang Out with People Better Than You, and You Cannot Help but Improve

In his 2002 shareholder letter, Warren Buffett, in his usual anecdotal way, narrated the story of Eddie Lampert. Eddie first lifted bats for the Chicago White Sox, and the White Sox went to the World Series that year. Later he switched to another team, and that team, too, won the title. And so on—wherever Eddie went, lady luck followed. While fame and fortune followed Eddie, Eddie didn't believe in his special powers. According to Buffett, "Eddie understood that how he lugged bats was unimportant; what counted instead was hooking up with the cream of those on the playing field. I've learned from Eddie. *At Berkshire, I regularly hand bats to many of the heaviest hitters in American business* [emphasis added]."[3]

We all can learn a deep lesson here: to be a winner, work with winners.

One of Berkshire's biggest strengths has been the group of managers running its subsidiaries and hitting home runs in the form of profitable growth with high rates of return. Many names come to mind: Ajit Jain, Greg Abel, Rose Blumkin, Gene Abegg, Tony Nicely, Ralph Schey, Chuck Huggins, and Stan Lipsey. Buffett and Charlie Munger's brilliance was to let managers of high caliber and integrity run their own businesses and then to stay out of their way. Both Buffett and Munger often joke that they delegate at Berkshire almost to the point of abdication.

> Nothing, nothing at all, matters as much as bringing the right people into your life. They will teach you everything you need to know.
> —Guy Spier

Surrounding yourself with smarter and better people provides a great education. You gain firsthand experience of their thought processes, how they prioritize (if you want to know someone's priorities in life, observe what they do between Friday evening and Monday morning), their value system, how they live each day, how they handle success and failure, and many other important things that textbooks cannot teach you. You get to experience a gravitational pull toward higher qualities.

It is better to be an average guy on a star team than a star on an average team. The former will be better for you in the long term; the latter is just an ego trip. For most of my professional and personal life, superior individuals made me feel uncomfortable. And so I would seek out people who made me feel like I fit in. This was clearly a wrong strategy. If you are the smartest person in the room, you are in the wrong room. It is wiser to be with better people and to be uncomfortable than to limit yourself to a mediocre circle just to feel comfortable. For instance, if it were not for the generous help and guidance of my smart investor friends and colleagues, then my personal portfolio would never have been able to perform as well as it did during the 2018–19 bear market in India. I give them a large part of the credit for my healthy portfolio returns to date and I hope to always keep learning from them throughout life. The people closest to you play an outsize role in your level of success or failure—so choose wisely. You are, after all, the average of the five people you associate with the most in your life.

Deserved Trust Is Earned

Of all forms of pride, perhaps the most desirable is a justified pride in being trustworthy.

—Charlie Munger

Trust lies at the heart of any relationship. In answer to the question "What is trust?" Jack Welch, the former chief of General Electric replied, "You know it when you feel it."[4] It is one of the simplest and best definitions of trust. We experience an echoing, anxious feeling when trust is not present. In such cases, we hesitate to take the next step. Conversely, when trust is present, we experience an open, connected feeling. Trust creates the foundation of all relationships, societies, organizations, nations, and our entire civilization. It is the oil that lubricates our entire economic and business system. Trust drives risk-taking, which leads to innovation and progress.

We build trust by being honest in our communications. By being authentic and sincere in both words and actions. By being transparent and admitting mistakes and sharing what we learn. By being reliable and fair in our dealings with others. Over time, as you build your network, put in your best efforts to constantly add value to others in your relationships and to build a seamless web of deserved trust (figure 5.1).

In his speeches, Munger often lists reliability as one of the essential traits for success. He explains that, although not many people can learn something like quantum mechanics, anyone can learn reliability. If you dedicate yourself to

FIGURE 5.1 Being trustworthy.

Source: Behavior Gap.

being reliable, that alone can overcome many failings or disadvantages you may have. Munger often applauds McDonald's for teaching millions of teenagers the importance of reliably showing up for work.

Woody Allen said that 80 percent of success in life is just showing up. Always reliably show up for the task entrusted to you. Never overpromise and under-deliver. Being unreliable will impair your career and friendships. If anything, underpromise and overdeliver. Trust is earned when actions meet words.

In his book, *Pebbles of Perception*, Laurence Endersen writes, "Our ability to choose is one of life's great gifts. We are the product of our choices. Good choices come from good character, and a few good choices make all the difference."[5]

Being reliable and trustworthy is one such choice.

CHAPTER 6

HUMILITY IS THE GATEWAY TO ATTAINING WISDOM

Acknowledging what you don't know is the dawning of wisdom.

—Charlie Munger

According to Confucius, real knowledge is knowing the extent of one's ignorance, and this sentiment has been expressed by many philosophers, in one form or another. Socrates, for example, put it quite bluntly when he said, "The only true wisdom is in knowing you know nothing." Only if we approach learning with an open mind can we truly educate ourselves.

The wiser we become, the more we realize how little we know. A lesser-known (and one of my all-time favorite) equation from Albert Einstein rings true: "Ego = 1 / Knowledge. More the knowledge lesser the ego, lesser the knowledge more the ego." The deeper one dives into any field, the more humble one generally becomes (also known as the Dunning-Kruger effect). By demonstrating intellectual humility and acknowledging what we don't know, we place ourselves into a beneficial position to learn more—thus, the dawning of wisdom. True expert knowledge in life and investing does not exist, only varying degrees of ignorance. This is not a problem to solve; it is simply how the world works. We cannot know everything, but we can work hard to become just about smart enough to make above-average decisions over time. That is the key to successful compounding. Ralph Waldo Emerson said, "Every man I meet is my master in some point, and in that I learn of him." Learning and accepting help from others creates value far beyond our individual capabilities. Look at every interaction as an opportunity to learn from the people you meet. You will be amazed at how quickly you grow and how much better you become, both as a professional and, more important, as a human being. A tree that wants to touch the sky must extend its roots into the earth. The more it wants to rise upward, the more it has to grow downward. Similarly, to rise in life, we need to be down to earth and humble.

> I was born not knowing and have had only a little time to change that here and there.
> —Richard Feynman

Always question what you think you know, and remember that every subject probably is more complex than we currently recognize. Such self-awareness creates a more accurate mental map of reality, which in turn results in adopting language that more closely reflects the nuances of the world. This is particularly true when we encounter absolutist words—such as "never" instead of "seldom," "all" instead of "many," and "always" instead of "usually" (even "etc." is a powerful reminder that we are leaving things out). A simple but effective way to remain self-aware is to add phrases like "seems to me" or "so far as I know" to these types of assertions.

You get the idea. We never can be fully sure.

Humility Is the Essence of Life

> *People couldn't believe that I suddenly made myself a subordinate partner to Warren. But there are people that it's okay to be a subordinate partner to. I didn't have the kind of ego that prevented it. There always are people who will be better at something than you are. You have to learn to be a follower before you become a leader. People should learn to play all roles.*
>
> —Charlie Munger

The more you reach out to and associate with individuals (whether younger or older) who are better and smarter than you are, the more you will learn and the faster you will improve. Humility is the gateway to attaining wisdom.

Humility. The constant desire to learn so that you can overcome ignorance. Open-mindedness to listen to what makes you uncomfortable. Humility—or lack of it—is reflected through your actions. Not asking. Not learning from others. All because you think you already know. Truly humble people do not experience any uneasy feelings when someone younger but more successful or knowledgeable than them shares advice. If you're truly happy and satisfied with the life you're leading, you'll be happy to see other people succeed. Don't make this life all about you. Be happy when other people are doing well and encourage their success. When you support others, it shows that you're not threatened by them because you are confident in your abilities.

Frank Wells was president of the Walt Disney Company from 1984 until his death in 1994. After Wells died, his son found a little piece of paper in his wallet that read "Humility is the essence of life." Later, it was discovered that Frank Wells had carried that note with him for thirty years.

We Never Can Be Fully Sure

Doubt is not a pleasant condition, but certainty is absurd.

—Voltaire

The quality of our lives is the sum of decision quality plus luck. We look to learn from the results of our decisions to improve. Our lives, however, are too short to collect enough data from our experiences to evaluate the quality of our decisions from the small set of results we experience.

We can only do so much to answer questions on our own. We are only exposed to the information we encounter, only live the experiences limited to our personal lives, and only think of the hypothesis that we can conceive of. As a result, it can be hard to know what reasons someone else could have for believing something different. The best cure for overconfidence in your beliefs is to constantly remind yourself that you have experienced less than a tiny fraction of a percent of what has happened in the world. This experience, however, ends up representing nearly 100 percent of how you believe the world works. People tend to believe in what they have personally seen, far more than what they read has happened to others. We are all biased by our personal history. Our installed beliefs are the result of our personal experiences in the past, and they shape our visual prism. If you have lived through hyperinflation or a severe bear market or were born in a poor family or have been discriminated against, you already believe in something that people who have not experienced those things never will. You likely also grossly overestimate the chance of those events happening again. Morgan Housel offers a helpful suggestion to help us better empathize: "Start with the assumption that everyone is innocently out of touch and you'll be more likely to explore what's going on through multiple points of view, instead of cramming what's going on into the framework of your own experiences. It's hard to do. It's uncomfortable when you do. But it's the only way to get closer to figuring out why people behave like they do."[1]

Becoming Rich Versus Staying Rich

Many people achieve success, but to sustain the same (and potentially build on it) over an entire lifetime requires humility, gratitude, and a constant learning mind-set. Becoming rich often becomes the biggest obstacle to staying rich. Winning big makes many of us feel invincible, and that feeling entices us to bet big on what worked for us in the recent past. This ends up creating a catastrophic event when the world changes or luck turns against us. Housel writes:

> It goes like this. The more successful you are at something, the more convinced you become that you're doing it right. The more convinced you are that you're doing it right, the less open you are to change. The less open you are to change, the more likely you are to tripping in a world that changes all the time.
>
> There are a million ways to get rich. But there's only one way to *stay* rich: Humility, often to the point of paranoia. The irony is that few things squash humility like getting rich in the first place.
>
> It's why the composition of Dow Jones companies changes so much over time, and why the *Forbes* list of billionaires has 60 percent turnover per decade. . . .
>
> Humility doesn't mean taking fewer risks. Sequoia takes as big of risks today as it did 30 years ago. But it's taken risks in new industries, with new approaches, and new partners, cognizant that what worked yesterday isn't what will work tomorrow.[2]

Absolute certainty never exists in the world of finance. Yet, on Wall Street, overconfidence is all-pervasive. Jason Zweig highlights the hubris of investors in his definitions of certainty and uncertainty in his book *The Devil's Financial Dictionary*:

> CERTAINTY. An imaginary state of clarity and predictability in economic and geopolitical affairs that all investors say is indispensable—even though it doesn't exist, never has, and never will. The most fundamental attribute of financial markets is uncertainty.
> UNCERTAINTY. The most fundamental fact about human life and economic activity. In the real world, uncertainty is ubiquitous; on Wall Street, it is nonexistent.[3]

Contrast the kind of egotism found on Wall Street with the humility of one of the greatest minds outside of finance, Richard Feynman. We should all learn from this great teacher, who humbly admits that nothing is ever certain: "We know that all our statements are approximate statements with different degrees of certainty; that when a statement is made, the question is not whether it is true or false but rather how likely it is to be true or false."[4]

Investing is no different. Approximate statements and different degrees of certainty require us to think probabilistically. The question is not "Will I be right or will I be wrong?" The question should be "What is the probability of this scenario versus another, and how does this information affect my assessment of value?" We must always leave room for doubt, even in those ideas that hold our highest conviction. Otherwise, we risk becoming complacent.

An attitude of knowing everything makes it difficult to learn anything. According to Feynman, before you begin any task, you first must *not* know the answer. We must begin by being uncertain about the answer. Otherwise, how can we learn? This may sound like common sense, but it is not so common in the world of finance.

Acknowledging that we do not know something is much more beneficial than having the incorrect answers. If we can be certain of one thing, it is that we can never be fully sure. We must learn to live with doubt and embrace uncertainty. We shouldn't feel anxious about not knowing things. Rather, we should welcome it. Because the realization of not knowing something is an opportunity to learn. In science, "I don't know" is not an indication of a failure but rather is a necessary first step toward enlightenment. As Feynman puts it,

The question of doubt and uncertainty is what is necessary to begin; for if you already know the answer there is no need to gather any evidence about it.

I have approximate answers and possible beliefs and different degrees of certainty about different things, but I'm not absolutely sure of anything and there are many things I don't know anything about.

The first source of difficulty is that it is imperative in science to doubt; it is absolutely necessary, for progress in science, to have uncertainty as a fundamental part of your inner nature. To make progress in understanding, we must remain modest and allow that we do not know. Nothing is certain or proved beyond all doubt. You investigate for curiosity, because it is unknown, not because you know the answer. And as you develop more information in the sciences, it is not that you are finding out the truth, but that you are finding out that this or that is more or less likely.

There are few absolute truths in investing. The best we can do is gather evidence as diligently as possible to assess the likelihood of various outcomes. We do this by connecting various pieces of the puzzle and trying to put them together in a way that makes sense. We are constantly exploring. We are constantly looking for new evidence—trying to find out more about what we know and to better understand what we don't know.

After we gather the evidence, we must study the same. What did we learn? What does that imply for our original hypothesis? How likely is it that we are correct? Are there other factors we failed to consider that may have led to different results or conclusions? Investors are often too anxious to jump to conclusions that support their original thinking. Confirmation bias is difficult to resist. Again, we should learn from Feynman:

> If we investigate further, we find that the statements of science are not of what is true and what is not true, but statements of what is known to different degrees of certainty: "It is very much more likely that so and so is true than that it is not true"; or "such and such is almost certain but there is still a little bit of doubt"; or, at the other extreme, "well, we really don't know." Every one of the concepts of science is on a scale graduated somewhere between, but at neither end of, absolute falsity or absolute truth. It is of great value to acknowledge ignorance.

Investors have a difficult time acknowledging the presence of uncertainty. But uncertainty remains the most fundamental attribute of financial markets. Living in an imaginary world of certainty can lead to potentially fatal mistakes in the real world of finance. The sooner we accept that we live in an uncertain world—that we don't have all the answers—the sooner we can begin trying to become wiser. This understanding is vital. Once accepted, it shapes our world-view and becomes a natural way of thinking. Incorporating uncertainty in the way we think about what we believe creates open-mindedness to alternative hypotheses, moving us closer to a more objective stance toward information that does not align with what we believe—that is truth seeking.

With respect to investing, intellectual humility is best illustrated through the concept of the circle of competence.

The Circle of Competence

I'm no genius, but I'm smart in spots, and I stay around those spots.

—Tom Watson Sr.

Warren Buffett has always advised investors to focus on operating only in areas they understand best. In HBO's documentary *Becoming Warren Buffett*, he compared his investing strategy to America's favorite pastime, referencing baseball legend Ted Williams's book *The Science of Hitting*, in which the all-star slugger emphasized the importance of knowing your sweet spot: "If he waited for the pitch that was really in his sweet spot, he would bat .400. If he had to swing at something on the lower corner, he would probably bat .235."[5]

The lesson for investors, Buffett says, is that we don't have to swing at every pitch: "The trick in investing is just to sit there and watch pitch after pitch go by and wait for the one right in your sweet spot. And if people are yelling, 'Swing, you bum!' ignore them."

Just as Williams only swung at pitches in his sweet spot, Buffett only invests in companies that are within his "circle of competence," a concept he described for the first time in his 1996 letter to shareholders: "What an investor needs is the ability to correctly evaluate *selected* businesses. Note that word 'selected': You don't have to be an expert on every company, or even many. You only have to be able to evaluate companies within your circle of competence. *The size of that circle is not very important; knowing its boundaries, however, is vital* [emphasis added]."[6]

This means that, as investors, we need to restrict ourselves only to those businesses whose long-term economics we can understand. For most investors, investing outside one's circle of competence is what often leads to big losses. One should not blindly chase "buzzing stocks" or get swayed by exciting "stories," "narratives," or "futuristic" concepts, because these kinds of businesses usually have unproven track records or they lack profitability and cash flow.

The key idea behind the circle of competence is not its size—the absolute number of businesses you can understand—but your awareness about its size—the kind of businesses you know you can understand.

It is not important how big that circle is. What matters is how well you have defined its perimeter. Investors who are intellectually honest and humble are always willing to admit their limitations and to stay within their area of expertise.

So, how do you find your circle of competence?

Instead of picking what you know, use the inversion technique, popularized by Charlie Munger, to create your circle of competence. Inspired by the German mathematician Carl Gustav Jacob Jacobi, Munger explains,

> Invert, always invert: Turn a situation or problem upside down. Look at it backward. What happens if all our plans go wrong? Where don't we want to go, and how do you get there? Instead of looking for success, make a list of how to fail instead—through sloth, envy, resentment, self-pity, entitlement, all the mental habits of self-defeat. Avoid these qualities and you will succeed. Tell me where I'm going to die, that is, so I don't go there.[7]

Try to know the things you don't know, and then draw a circle that keeps those things out. (This is very much what scientists do. They approach a problem and its solution by trying to prove it is false, not that it is true.)

In investing, risk comes from not knowing what you are doing. In fact, Buffett considers this to be one of the biggest risks in investing. So much so that he avoids using equity risk premiums to value stocks, confining himself only to those situations about which he is highly certain. Buffett uses the interest rate of long-term U.S. Treasury bonds to value stocks, except when he believes it is artificially low. During those times, he adds a few percentage points to his discount rate. He says, "I put a heavy weight on certainty. If you do that, the whole idea of a risk factor doesn't make sense to me. Risk comes from not knowing what you're doing." In a similar vein, Buffett adds, "We don't discount the future cash flows at 9 percent or 10 percent; we use the U.S. Treasury rate. We try to deal with things about which we are quite certain. You can't compensate for risk by using a high discount rate."[8]

At the 1998 Berkshire annual meeting, Buffett explained how he thinks about risk when evaluating any business:

> When we look at the future of businesses, we look at riskiness as being sort of a go/no-go valve. In other words, if we think that we simply don't know what's going to happen in the future, that doesn't mean it's risky for everyone. It means we don't know—that it's risky for us. It may not be risky for someone else who understands the business. However, in that case, we just give up. We don't try to predict those things. We don't say, "Well, we don't know what's going to happen. Therefore, we'll discount some cash flows that we don't even know at 9 percent instead of 7 percent." That is not our way to approach it.[9]

How does such strict adherence to his circle of competence greatly help Buffett in investing? He explains: "If we have a business about which we're extremely confident as to the business results, we'd prefer that its stock have high volatility. We'll make more money in a business where we know what the end game will be if it bounces around a lot."[10]

If you know things you don't know—your circle of incompetence—you will automatically get to what you do know—your circle of competence. Once you have defined your circle of incompetence, draw your personal circle, just as Buffett did. Buffett's investing process involves creating three lists of companies—in (simple and easy-to-understand businesses), out (difficult to understand), and too hard (so complex that it is not worth devoting any time to understanding them). Buffett once said that 99 percent of the stock ideas that came to him fell into the too hard category.

Just think about that for a minute. In Buffett, we have arguably the greatest investor who has ever lived admitting that he does not understand 99 percent of the businesses he comes across. The next time you feel you know it all, reflect deeply on that fact. A genuine and honest adherence to one's circle of competence is a deeply humbling experience. Let me share a personal example, to illustrate. In January 2018, I came across the most recent edition of *Indian Economy & Market* magazine, which contained investment thesis reports on "75 Hidden Gems," many of which had been written by my respected seniors and peers. I could properly understand only *one* name out of seventy-five. This is perfectly acceptable. Remember, it is not a competency if you don't know the edge of it. Venturing outside these edges is what gets investors into big trouble.

> Warren and I know better than most people what we know and what we don't know. That's even better than having a lot of extra IQ points. *People chronically misappraise the limits of their own knowledge; that's one of the most basic parts of human nature.* Knowing the edge of your circle of competence is one of the most difficult things for a human being to do. *Knowing what you don't know is much more useful in life and business than being brilliant* [emphasis added].
> —Charlie Munger

One sign of emotional intelligence is the ability to admit error. A mistake denied is a lesson not learned. Reflect deeply and objectively evaluate your performance. It is only through an honest self-assessment that an investor can discover his or her circle of competence. A key benefit of emotional intelligence is the intellectual honesty to view the world as it really is, not as one wants it to be, hopes it to be, or wishes it to be. My investing strike rate improved significantly once I acknowledged what I do not know and stayed within my circle of competence.

The basic idea behind the circle of competence is so simple it is embarrassing to say it out loud: when you are unsure and doubtful about what you want to do, do not do it.

If you can't find businesses within your circle of competence, don't hurriedly step outside that circle because of the fear of missing out, which is often the case in a bull market. Instead, spend time studying industries and companies outside your circle before crossing the boundaries. The biggest advantage of developing one's circle of competence over time is that different industries and types of companies are in favor at different stages of the market cycle. Having an expanded opportunity set at one's disposal to choose from can prove to be highly profitable at such times.

Again, it's not important how big your circle of competence is. What is critical is to clearly know where the edges are.

> It's not a competency if you don't know the edge of it.
> —Charlie Munger

Now you may well ask, "But how do I expand those edges so that I can enlarge my circle of competence?" There is a simple way to do it.

It's simple but not easy.

Read. A lot. That is the only way you can expand your circle of competence. For example, read a book called *Analyzing and Investing in Community Bank Stocks* and then read the annual reports of a few community banks. These are relatively easier to understand and value. Or pick an industry in which you have some expertise and begin reading the annual reports of the companies in that industry.

> I learned early in my career that if you read the annual reports, you've done more than 90 percent of the people on Wall Street. If you read the notes to the annual report, you've done more than 95 percent of the people on Wall Street.
> —Jim Rogers

In investing, the person that turns over the most rocks wins the game. There is no alternative to hard work. In life, relationships, business, or investing, nothing will work unless you do. And there is no intelligent reason for an investor to settle for an inferior track record in a marketplace filled with companies with outstanding fundamentals.

> I've always said that if you look at ten companies you'll find one that's interesting. If you look at 20, you'll find, two; if you look at 100, you'll find ten. The person that turns over the most rocks wins the game. . . . It's about keeping an open mind and doing a lot of work. *The more industries you look at, the more companies you look at, the more opportunity you have of finding something that's mispriced* [emphasis added].
> —Peter Lynch

Buffett once remarked:

> Back in 1951 Moody's published thick handbooks by industry of every stock in circulation. I went through all of them, thousands of pages, motivated by the hope that a great idea was just on the next page. I found companies like National American Insurance and Western Insurance Securities Company that nobody was paying attention to that were trading for far less than their intrinsic values. Last year we found a steel company on the Korean Stock Exchange that had no analyst coverage, no research, but was the most profitable steel company in the world.[11]

Buffett's story reminds me of a few of my experiences. Every day, I diligently review all of the corporate announcements on the Bombay Stock Exchange (BSE) website. It is a painstaking exercise for many, but for me, it is like an intellectual treasure hunt wherein I may strike gold at any time. Every day, I create numerous opportunities for serendipity to find me.

My personal investment opportunity set has significantly expanded over the years, with time and experience in the markets. Initially, it was restricted only to secular growth stocks at reasonable to expensive valuations. But now it covers multiple areas of the investment universe, including commodities, cyclicals, deep value, and spinoffs, as well as loss-making companies that are turning around, as reflected in slow, gradual changes (low contrast) in their improving balance sheet, working capital, margins, or a significant positive change in their industry dynamics. Instead of being restricted by my personal, biased views to a small opportunity set, as was the case during my early years, I am now able to invest in a variety of industries and situations, wherever I find mispricing of value and a highly favorable risk-and-return trade-off.

> Markets continually change. It also reminds me to look for investment opportunities in different markets, rather than keep going back to a well that is dry.
> —Robert Kiyosaki

No single strategy works all of the time and in every kind of market. That's why it's essential to build up one's investing arsenal to be able to hunt for value from within different areas.

Over the years, I have come to realize and appreciate just why this is critically important: a bull market is always going on, at all times, in some specific sectors of the stock market. For instance, even during the 2009–2013 bear market in India, consumer discretionary, pharmaceutical, and information technology companies created a lot of wealth for investors. New trends *always* emerge during a bear market—that's the period during which most investors are either waiting for their purchase price or are busy committing fresh sins by averaging the winning leader stocks bought during the previous bull market. (The number of retail investors in a sector tends to go up during its bullish phase, so, during the subsequent bear market for the sector, relentless selling usually occurs at every higher level, as old investors try their best to exit and rid themselves of bad memories.)

Where should we devote our limited time in life to achieve maximum success? Munger gives us the answer: "You have to figure out what your own aptitudes are. If you play games where other people have the aptitudes and you don't, you're going to lose. And that's as close to certain as any prediction that you can make. You have to figure out where you've got an edge. And you've got to play within your own circle of competence."[12]

The takeaway from Buffett and Munger is clear. If you want to improve your odds of success in life, business, and investing, then clearly define the perimeter of your circle of competence and operate only inside it. Over time, work to expand that circle, but never fool yourself about its current boundaries.

As Feynman says, "The first principle is that you must not fool yourself—and you are the easiest person to fool."

The following hypothetical conversation captures the essence of the dawning of wisdom.

> *Philosopher:* What are the three wisest words in investing?
> *Value investor:* "Margin of safety."
> *Philosopher:* Wrong.
> *Value Investor:* Then . . . ?
> *Philosopher:* "*I don't know.*"

CHAPTER 7

THE VIRTUES OF PHILANTHROPY AND GOOD KARMA

If you are in the luckiest 1 percent of humanity, you owe it to the rest of humanity to think about the other 99 percent.

—Warren Buffett

One of the important teachings of the *Bhagavad Gita* is to develop a trusteeship attitude toward material wealth. This keeps us humble and inculcates a sense of detachment in us. The process of creating wealth should motivate us to give our best, but the results should be surrendered for the betterment of humanity, after we have taken care of our needs. We are able to create wealth only with the help of others, so giving back also needs to be part of our planning.

If you are fortunate to have earned or inherited more than you need to live out your personal definition of a good life, you will have the opportunity and the responsibility to decide where and how to direct the surplus funds. Most individuals in this situation focus on two kinds of beneficiaries, both of which can be deeply meaningful: family members and philanthropic organizations, such as schools, colleges, hospitals, and religious organizations. The latter, giving back to society, is a highly noble activity. You can derive a great deal of happiness and personal fulfillment from the act of making a positive difference in other people's lives.

The best "value investment" of all is channeling money into goals that will make your life more valuable: drawing out your innate gifts to make yourself matter to other people and to make the world around you a better place.

—Jason Zweig

Blessed is the investor who uses his wealth to do good for others.

Charles Collier writes, in his guidebook on philanthropy *Wealth in Families*, that "according to Aristotle and his latter-day student, Thomas Jefferson, the 'pursuit of happiness' has to do with an internal journey of learning to know ourselves and an external journey of service of others."[1]

The meaning you give to wealth says a lot about you and the way you will be seen and remembered. That is why developing an environment of shared values with your family is so important. Devote time to introducing your will, sharing your values and feelings with those you love. This also may be an opportune time to ensure good things for others, after your death, by creating the appropriate provisions for future philanthropic activities in your formal will.

It may be your last opportunity to be heard and for your future wishes to be adhered to. Life is unpredictable.

On Maslow's needs hierarchy, self-transcendence ranks even higher than self-actualization and refers to the highest and most inclusive or holistic level of human consciousness. Self-transcendence can be experienced when we move beyond ourselves to see a greater fulfillment linked directly with serving the needs of others.

Givers greatly enjoy seeing the wealth they have created during their working lives come to life again by enabling good things to happen during their lifetimes for targeted causes that carry significant meaning to them. As the adage goes, "You can't take it with you." Givers derive great happiness from converting their financial resources into actions and values they truly care about (figure 7.1).

As a philanthropist, Warren Buffett is best known for giving billions of dollars to the Bill and Melinda Gates Foundation and for supporting the philanthropic work of his three children. He also generously gives to other groups, like the Glide Foundation, an antipoverty charity in San Francisco.

In philanthropy as in business, supporting the right people is more important than all other factors, according to Buffett: "When I buy businesses, it's the same as investing in philanthropy. I'm looking for somebody who will get the job done and is in synch with my goals. . . . You can have the greatest goals in the world, but if you have the wrong people running it, it isn't going to work. On the other hand, if you've got the right person running it, almost anything is possible."[2] Value for one's money is as important in philanthropy as it is in investing.

Notable philanthropists who Buffett admires include Andrew Carnegie, Peter Kiewit, and John D. Rockefeller.

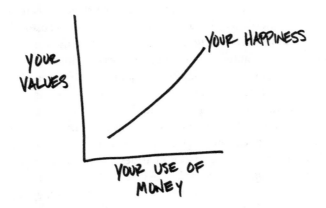

FIGURE 7.1 Giving and happiness.

Source: Behavior Gap.

"The problem of our age," Carnegie argued in an 1889 article in the *North American Review*, "is the proper administration of wealth."[3] The wealthy should use their riches to improve public facilities that would enable the deserving poor to help themselves, Carnegie said, because this kind of philanthropy is "best calculated to do . . . lasting good." Carnegie rose from being a penniless immigrant to become the wealthiest man in the world at his time. His vision was to create "an ideal state in which the surplus wealth of the few will become, in the best sense, the property of the many." After selling his steel empire for $500 million, Carnegie donated his wealth for the creation of schools, for a peace endowment, for New York's Carnegie Hall, and for the acquisition and installation of 7,689 church organs. But it was his keen support for library construction that became the most visible manifestation of his philosophy. Carnegie's philanthropy enabled the construction of 2,811 public libraries across the United States.

Kiewit grew his family's business from the twelfth-largest contractor in Omaha to one of the largest and most respected in the entire United States. Before he died, Kiewit directed that his personal estate should be used to establish a foundation to support public-purpose projects in Nebraska and western Iowa. The Peter Kiewit Foundation opened its doors in 1979 with a $150 million endowment, representing more than 90 percent of the fortune earned by Kiewit during his lifetime. Upon Peter Kiewit's death, Buffett shared his feelings: "Peter Kiewit made major deposits in society's bank . . . but his withdrawals have been few."[4] Kiewit gave generously while he was alive and gave away the majority of his net worth upon his death.

Rockefeller's charitable giving began with his first job, as a clerk, at age sixteen, when he gave 6 percent of his earnings to charity. By the time he was twenty, his charity exceeded 10 percent of his income. As Rockefeller's wealth grew, so too did his giving, primarily to educational and public health causes, basic science, and the arts. (He was reportedly influenced by a meeting in 1893 with Swami Vivekananda, who enlightened him on the virtues of helping the needy.)

We all can take a big lesson from Rockefeller's life. It is never too early to start giving and helping others. To make a difference in someone's life, you don't have to be brilliant, rich, or perfect. You just need to care. I did not want to deprive myself of the happiness from giving, so during my initial years in the United States, even when I was earning minimum wage as a front desk clerk at a hotel in San Francisco, I began donating to local charities, starting with small sums (as low as $10 in some cases when that was all I could afford at the time). It doesn't matter where you are, or if you have a little to give or a lot to give, something happens to your heart when you share with others. Something that changes you for the better.

> Love is doing small things with great love. It is not how much we do, but how much love we put in the doing. It is not how much we give, but how much love we put in the giving. To God there is nothing small.
> —Mother Teresa

Over time, as my wealth has increased, so too have my charitable contributions, and it gives me great happiness to put a smile on the face of those who are less privileged. I was delighted when a dear friend and I jointly won the bidding auction in November 2018 for the annual charity lunch with Mohnish Pabrai, the entire proceeds of which would go to benefit the Dakshana Foundation. Writing about and sharing my life's biggest learnings is my way of giving back to the investing community. Our goodwill compounds when we share with others. We should act as a funnel, not a sponge. As Charlie Munger so beautifully puts it, "The best thing a human being can do is to help another human being know more." In life, the winners also lose occasionally, but those who help others win can never lose. So always help others rise. This is how goodwill compounds over time.

Karma Is Like a Big Snowball

> You can't live a perfect day without doing something for someone who will never be able to repay you.
>
> —John Wooden

> The most meaningful way to succeed is to help other people succeed.
>
> —Adam Grant

Selflessly helping others in an unconditional manner, without expecting any favors in return, has great virtue. My sincere work ethic and helpful attitude toward my coworkers at my previous investment banking jobs encouraged them to share positive feedback about me when my current employer contacted them during the initial background checks conducted after my job interview. In addition, from time to time, my previous investment banking teammates generously helped me by imparting a solid understanding of the insurance and asset management industries in India from which many initial public offerings came during 2017 and 2018. This, in turn, helped me make better decisions about some of my existing holdings, which had a presence in insurance and asset management businesses.

> How you behave in one place, will help in surprising ways later.
> —Charlie Munger

Recall a key lesson from an earlier chapter: we should endeavor to constantly add value to others in our relationships, on our own initiative, without expecting anything in return. In September 2017, a senior investor (with whom I had previously spoken a couple of times) alerted me to some scuttlebutt about one of my portfolio companies being unable to pay its factory workers, and that it would default on the upcoming interest payment on its debt. This turned out to be a timely warning. Just a few days later, news broke in the media that this company was trying to defraud its lenders by artificially inflating its asset size, on its books of accounts, to get bigger loans from the banks. The stock promptly declined by almost 30 percent in the next few days.

Thanks to my senior's timely warning, I was able to exit the stock a few days earlier, at a handsome profit. When I called my senior to thank him and ask why he had helped me by sharing such sensitive information, these were his words: "Because you always used to share helpful company and industry data with me from time to time, even when I never asked you for it. You helped me then; I helped you now."

I believe this positive feedback loop always exists when you engage in the smallest of good acts for others. The acts tend to take a whole circle and return to bless you with positive things in your life. Karma is like a big snowball. Ask yourself, at the end of each day, "Did I do at least one good act to help someone today?" After that, thank the Almighty and your parents in your prayers for all that they have given to you in life. I do this ritual every day and it gives me great inner peace. No wonder Michael Jackson's song "Heal the World" has resonated so strongly with me ever since I first heard it many years ago.

CHAPTER 8

SIMPLICITY IS THE ULTIMATE SOPHISTICATION

Most geniuses—especially those who lead others—prosper not by deconstructing intricate complexities but by exploiting unrecognized simplicities.

—Andy Benoit

Life is really simple, but we insist on making it complicated.

—Confucius

Simplicity is the result of long, hard work, not the starting point. The ability to reduce something to its essence is the true mark of understanding. But one of the great ironies in life is that when the smartest minds generously share the secrets of their success with us, we ignore them, because they sound too basic and simple for us to appreciate.

"That's it? It can't be so simple!" we say, when we hear them giving us simple advice to achieve greatness.

Consider investing. When we read Warren Buffett's revelation of the only two rules of successful investing—"Rule number 1: Never lose money. Rule number 2: Never forget rule number 1"[1]—we protest, "Great thought, but is that it? It can't be so simple!"

Investing is simple, but not easy.
—Warren Buffett

In an interview with *Business Wire* in November 2011, Buffett said, "If you understand chapters 8 and 20 of *The Intelligent Investor* (Benjamin Graham, 1949) and chapter 12 of *The General Theory* (John Maynard Keynes, 1936), you don't need to read anything else and you can turn off your TV."[2] This advice from Buffett references two classics from the field of investing and economics.

Chapter 8 of Graham's book talks about not letting the mood swings of Mr. Market coax us into speculating, selling in panic, or trying to time the market.

Chapter 20 explains that, after careful analysis of a company's ongoing business and its prospects for future earnings, we should consider buying only if its current price implies a large margin of safety.

In chapter 12 of *The General Theory of Employment, Interest, and Money* ("The State of Long-Term Expectation"), Keynes remarks that most professional investors and speculators were "largely concerned, not with making superior long-term forecasts of the probable yield of an investment over its whole life, but with foreseeing changes in the conventional basis of valuation a short time ahead of the general public."[3]

Buffett took the simple but fundamental truths of investing from these three chapters quite seriously and applied them throughout his life, with a high degree of intensity, and it has made him one of the wealthiest individuals in the world.

Take a simple idea and take it seriously.
—Charlie Munger

The simple ideas with intensity of pursuit is what gets you to the promised land.
—Mohnish Pabrai

Buffett's key takeaway from *The Intelligent Investor* was this: If you eliminate the downside, then all that remains is the upside. After that, the key is to keep emotions in check and be patient. It really is that simple.

It's simple but not easy.

In the world of securities, courage becomes the supreme virtue after adequate knowledge and a tested judgment are at hand.
—Benjamin Graham

Many newcomers in the investing field consider *The Intelligent Investor* to be too dry and not "exciting" enough. It does not reveal any secrets to finding the next big multi-bagger, and it does not offer any shortcuts for making money quickly. But, as I have realized through my multiple readings of this book, it does build the character and steely resolve required to become a good investor. And character building, as compared with wealth building, is a much more difficult subject to read about and practice. (For the former, refer to Rudyard Kipling's poem "If" in appendix B.)

Mohnish Pabrai's book *The Dhandho Investor* is one of the more accessible books written on value investing. Just like Buffett, Pabrai has a gift for simplifying complex sounding ideas. In his book, he writes:

> Every business has an intrinsic value, and it is determined by the same simple formula. John Burr Williams was the first to define it in his *The Theory of Investment Value* published in 1938. Per Williams, the intrinsic value of any business is determined by the cash inflows and outflows—discounted at an appropriate interest rate—that can be expected to occur during the remaining life of the business. The definition is painfully simple. . . .
>
> Simplicity is a very powerful construct. Henry Thoreau recognized this when he said, "Our life is frittered away by detail . . . simplify, simplify." Einstein also recognized the power of simplicity, and it was the key to his breakthroughs in physics. He noted that the five ascending levels of intellect were, "Smart, Intelligent, Brilliant, Genius, Simple." For Einstein, simplicity was simply the highest level of intellect. Everything about Warren Buffett's investment style is simple. It is the thinkers like Einstein and Buffett, who fixate on simplicity, who triumph. The genius behind $E = mc^2$ is its simplicity and elegance.[4]

The Simplest Solution Often Tends to Be the Best

The grand aim of all science is to cover the greatest number of empirical facts by logical deduction from the smallest number of hypotheses or axioms.

—Albert Einstein

Occam's razor, named after fourteenth-century English logician William of Ockham, is a principle of parsimony, economy, or succinctness used in logic and problem solving. It states that among competing hypotheses, the hypothesis with the fewest assumptions should be selected. Other, more complicated solutions ultimately may prove to provide better predictions, but in the absence of differences in predictive ability, the fewer assumptions that are made, the better.

Investors should remember that their scorecard is not computed using Olympic-diving methods: *Degree-of-difficulty doesn't count* [emphasis added]. If you are right about a business whose value is largely dependent on a single key factor that is both easy to understand and enduring, the payoff is the same as if you had correctly analyzed an investment alternative characterized by many constantly shifting and complex variables.

—Warren Buffett

The way Buffett deals with difficult problems is to avoid them altogether. Unlike the figure skaters at the Olympics, we don't get extra points for higher degrees of difficulty in investing. Originality and complexity are not necessary or sufficient conditions for generating superior long-term returns. As investors, our job is simply to compound capital over time at the highest possible rate with the minimum amount of risk. We achieve this objective by seeking out undervalued stocks of companies within our circle of competence. Be completely indifferent to whether the market cap is large or small or to whether the company is relatively unknown or widely followed.

Investing is not about being original or creative; it is about looking for the greatest amount of value (for the price paid) with the least amount of risk. Putting in more time and effort does not guarantee better results in investing. Rather, it is more beneficial to do less and make fewer but better choices.

The more decisions you make, the less willpower you have. It's called decision fatigue. Focus on making fewer and better decisions. This allows you sufficient time to think about each decision deeply and reduces the chances of making a mistake. We should restrict ourselves only to those cases in which the investment decision looks like a no-brainer. As Charlie Munger says, "The goal of investment is to find situations where it is safe not to diversify."[5]

Look for simple businesses that require fewer assumptions and fewer hypothetical scenarios to work out and that do not require discounting cash flows from way out into the future to justify the investment. As Thomas Carlyle aptly put it, "Our main business is not to see what lies dimly at a distance, but to do what lies clearly at hand." In his 2004 letter, Buffett highlighted the importance of sticking to simple propositions:

> If only one variable is key to a decision, and the variable has a 90 percent chance of going your way, the chance for a successful outcome is obviously 90 percent. But if ten independent variables need to break favorably for a successful result, and each has a 90 percent probability of success, the likelihood of having a winner is only 35 percent. . . . Since a chain is no stronger than its weakest link, it makes sense to look for—if you'll excuse an oxymoron—mono-linked chains.[6]

It is important to identify and focus on the few key variables that really matter to an investment decision. This vastly simplifies the process and improves the probability of a successful outcome. The Occam's razor mental model is useful because it enables us to separate the long-term signal from the short-term noise and to calmly think through any investing decision. Yes, reading the annual reports, filings, press releases, and footnotes to the accounts is important, and occasionally, we will be able to dig out some extra detail that might give us an analytical advantage, but, in my view, understanding the big picture (the two to three key variables that really matter) is equally, if not more, important. Some of us may be average at business valuation but still can achieve above-average results by being able to better put the available information in the appropriate context, by remembering the big picture, and by being able to pinpoint the few factors that really matter to an investment.

In one of his lectures at Columbia University, Joel Greenblatt taught his students the importance of always keeping the big picture in mind: "Explain the big picture. Your predecessors failed over a long period of time. It has nothing to do about their ability to do a spreadsheet. It has more to do with the big picture. I focus on the big picture. Think of the logic, not just the formula."[7]

In investing, simplicity is the way to long-term success. Buffett says: "The business schools reward difficult complex behavior more than simple behavior, but simple behavior is more effective. . . . We haven't succeeded because we have some great, complicated systems or magic formulas we apply or anything of the sort. What we have is just simplicity itself."[8]

Simplicity is the art of thoughtful reduction. It is a systematic falsification of deeply held beliefs. Conan Doyle's fictional character Sherlock Holmes once said, "If you eliminate the impossible, whatever remains, however improbable, must be the truth." In contrast, complexity opens you up to far more possibilities and surprises, possibly in a harmful way.

Buffett has been emphasizing the idea of simplification for a long time. He wrote in his 1992 shareholder letter, "We try to stick to businesses we believe we understand. That means they must be relatively simple and stable in character. If a business is complex or subject to constant change, we're not smart enough to predict future cash flows. Incidentally, that shortcoming doesn't bother us."[9]

Munger agrees: "We have a passion for keeping things simple. If something is too hard, we move on to something else. What could be more simple than that?"[10]

Observe how Munger is able to greatly simplify the path to wealth creation: "Spend less than you make; always be saving something. Put it into a tax-deferred account. Over time, it will begin to amount to something. This is such a no-brainer."[11]

Intelligent people are drawn to complex solutions. Plenty of smart and highly educated people work in the world of finance. But that intelligence often comes at a cost, because smart people can more easily fool themselves into believing they have all the answers. That can get them into big trouble. As Albert Einstein said, "If you can't explain it simply, you don't understand it well enough."

According to William James, "The art of being wise is the art of knowing what to overlook." This is true not just for business problems but for people as well.

As Buffett cautions, "You can't make a good deal with a bad person."[12] This is precisely the philosophy he has followed in his business and personal life. He has chosen to work only with people he admires and trusts. As a result, he has rarely had to deal with nasty problems created by bad people.

Although Occam's razor is a useful mental model, it should not be seen as a substitute for empirical testing. It relies on subjective assessment of simplicity and looks for approximate or "good enough" solutions to the problems at hand (also known as "satisficing"). It is not a rule. It is more of a guide or a suggestion.

Sherlock Holmes would look for the simplest, most natural explanation for a case, but he also believed in not oversimplifying complex matters, especially when dealing with systems involving complicated interactions.

Similarly, Albert Einstein believed in the power of simplicity, but he also understood its limitations: "Everything should be made as simple as possible, but no simpler."

For example, the reason for the popularity of the price-to-earnings (P/E) ratio is its simplicity and accessibility. A ratio of 20× simply means that a company is available at a market capitalization that is twenty times its annual earnings. In other words, the stock price is trading at twenty times its earnings per share. The P/E ratio in isolation, however, tells us nothing about the business's capital intensity, cash flow generation, management quality, or balance sheet strength, or about the expected duration of its competitive advantage period. There's a lot more to making money in the stock market than just looking at P/E ratios. (Every investor should diligently study the white papers titled "What Does a Price-Earnings Multiple Mean?" and "The P/E Ratio: A User's Manual" by Michael Mauboussin and Epoch Investment Partners, respectively.[13])

Three Steps to Simplification

Complexity is about tactics; simplicity is about systems. Tactics come and go but an overarching philosophy about the way the world works can help you make better decisions in multiple scenarios. Simple doesn't go out of style but complex does.

—Ben Carlson

The first step in simplification is to avoid wasting time on things that are unknowable and unimportant. Before attacking a problem, ask whether it is important and worth solving. Buffett explains, "There are two questions you ask yourself as you look at the decision you'll make. (A) Is it knowable? (B) Is it important? If it is not knowable—as you know, there are all kinds of things that are important but not knowable—we forget about those. And if it's unimport-ant, whether it's knowable or not it won't make any difference. We don't care."[14]

Which way the interest rates will move, what the stock market is going to do next, where the economy is headed, and so on, are all important but unknowable.

The second step for simplification is focus. When we try to accomplish too many things simultaneously, we end up doing all of them poorly. Attention is a scarce resource that gets depleted throughout the day. Yet, we act as if it can be divided unlimitedly with no negative consequence. Decision-making is more effective when we focus on one thing at a time. Multiple research studies have shown, time and again, that the human brain is not optimized for multi-tasking, especially when one is working on complicated and unfamiliar tasks. One of the hardest things to do in life is to avoid good opportunities so that you have time to devote to great opportunities—and having the wisdom to know the difference.

Buffett's secret to success is his intense focus—instead of doing more, he does less. He once told his personal airplane pilot, Mike Flint, that Flint needed to do three things to reach his goals. The first was to write down his top twenty-five goals. The second was to circle the top five most important ones. Finally, he should separate the top five goals into a separate list—and put goals six through twenty-five on a "not-to-do" list. Buffett concludes by stating: "Everything you didn't circle just became your 'avoid at all cost list.' No matter what, these things get no attention from you until you've succeeded with your top 5."[15]

We have so many things in our life that we want to do. Who wouldn't want to succeed at twenty-five different things? But when we chase after twenty-five things at once, that's when we run the risk of becoming a jack-of-all-trades but a master of none. Our society rewards excellence and specialization. You need to excel at only a few chosen skills. And this is why Buffett's "not-to-do list" is so helpful. Items six to twenty-five on your list are probably all important things that you care about. But when it comes to items one to five, items six to twenty-five are a distraction. Spending time on secondary priorities is the reason we have twenty half-finished projects instead of five completed ones. As the Pareto principle states, "80 percent of your results come from 20 percent of your activities." Focus on the top 20 percent of activities and deprioritize the bottom 80 percent.

The not-to-do list concept is similar to the primary idea behind Gary Keller and Jay Papasan's book *The ONE Thing*. It debunks the theory that multitasking is the path to success. Instead, ask yourself, "What is the most important thing I can do today? What is the one thing that would make everything else in my life either easier or unnecessary?"

> The difference between successful people and very successful people is that very successful people say no to almost everything.
> —Warren Buffett

When you say no, you are saying no only to one option. When you say yes, you are saying no to every other option. So be careful to what and to whom you say yes. This choice eventually will shape many things in your life. Every day we have the opportunity to make choices and shape our future; every day is the first day of the rest of our lives.

The third step for simplification is to reason backward. Instead of trying to arrive directly at the solution, begin by eliminating the options that are not correct. You get an enormous advantage by narrowing your problem space. You can then focus your time and attention on the more productive areas.

> Let's be honest. We don't know for sure what makes us successful. We can't pinpoint exactly what makes us happy. But we know with certainty what destroys success or happiness. This realization, as simple as it is, is fundamental: Negative knowledge (what not to do) is much more potent than positive knowledge (what to do).
> —Rolf Dobelli

To make good investing decisions, you need to actively look for reasons *not* to buy the stock in question. Invert, always invert. Simplifying helps us make better decisions by breaking down complex problems into component parts. For example, I ask four inverted questions whenever I am looking at a stock. These questions break the mind-set of trying to find supportive bullish reasons and force me to actively seek out disconfirming evidence.

1. *How can I lose money?* versus *How can I make money?* If you focus on preventing the downside, the upside takes care of itself.
2. *What is this stock not worth?* versus *What is this stock going to be worth?* If you can identify the floor price or a cheap price for a stock, it's far easier to make profitable decisions.
3. *What can go wrong?* versus *What growth drivers are there?* Rather than focusing just on the growth catalysts, think probabilistically, in terms of a range of possible outcomes, and contemplate the possible risks, especially those that have never occurred.
4. *What is the growth rate being implied by the market in the current valuation of the stock?* versus *What is my future growth rate assumption?* A reverse discounted cash flow fleshes out the current assumptions of the market for the stock. We can then compare the market's assumptions with our own and make a decision accordingly.

Good investors demonstrate the flexibility to completely change their opinions if necessitated by the facts. They don't hope they will be right; they keep evaluating why they might be wrong. A good source for disconfirming evidence (from which I have greatly benefited) is the analysis provided by vigilante investors on social media. These investors tend to express bearish or skeptical commentary on almost every single company they review. Another useful source for disconfirming evidence is short-seller or negative reports on the stocks I am contemplating buying or those on which I am bullish. Seth Klarman has spoken in the past about the benefit of this source of information:

> From our experience, much long-oriented analysis is simplistic, highly optimistic, and sloppy. Short-sellers, by going against the long-term tide of economic growth and the short-term swells of public opinion and margins calls, are forced to be crackerjack analysts. Their work product is usually top-notch and needs to be. Short-sellers shouldn't be reviled or banned; most should be celebrated and encouraged. They are the policemen of the financial markets, identifying frauds and cautioning against bubbles. In effect, they protect the unsophisticated from predatory schemes that regulators and enforcement agencies don't seem able to prevent.[16]

Simplicity as a Way of Life

> *It is very simple to be happy, but it is very difficult to be simple.*

—Rabindranath Tagore

> *To attain knowledge, add things every day; to obtain wisdom, remove things every day.*

—Lao Tzu

Have you ever considered that there are way too many things that you need to evaluate day after day? Too many news items, too many questions, too many possessions, too many options for everything, too many stocks from which to choose, too many investment products that too many financial advisers want you to buy.

If that is the case with you, what you need to bring peace to your life is *minimalism*.

Minimalism is basically an extension of simplicity—you not only take things from complex to simple but also try to get rid of anything that is unnecessary. Few things in life really matter. Because few things matter, we must think carefully about what really matters to us and then commit our time primarily to those things. That way, we will remain focused on what matters rather than chasing the new thing, which probably will not really matter. The goal is not to have the fewest number of things but to have the optimal number of things.

Practicing minimalism has brought peace and simplicity to my life. I cherish it for the time it has freed up for me to focus on those aspects that are more meaningful to me—giving more time to my family, friends, personal health, and learning activities.

From traveling with less personal luggage, eating less junk food and sugar, and using fewer apps on my mobile phone to having fewer stocks in my portfolio, I have embraced minimalism as a way of living. I already can see the immense benefits of clarity, focus, and efficiency that this has brought to my life. To me, minimalism is about living with less stress. The fact that it saves money is just an added benefit.

Do you hold more than fifty stocks, spread across multiple brokerage accounts? I urge you to simplify. Have you invested in more than ten different mutual fund schemes? I urge you to simplify. Have you invested in numerous "investment plans" whose "original purpose" was to provide life and health insurance? I urge you to simplify. Have you, over time, piled up loads of defunct, useless stuff on your office desk or at your home? I urge you to simplify. Clearing the clutter from the various aspects of our lives reduces decision fatigue and sharpens our focus on what we really want to achieve.

There is no path to peace. Peace is the path.
—Mahatma Gandhi

Minimalism in life isn't a destination to reach, it is the path to follow.
Practicing and adopting minimalism as a way of life is simple.
It's simple but not easy.
You cannot become a minimalist overnight. But, as Lao Tzu said, "A journey of a thousand miles begins with a single step."

The parable of the Mexican fisherman and the American banker is one of my favorite stories and contains an important life lesson. It is habitual for most of us to build incessantly and forget that the endgame should really be happiness and a fulfilling life. It is equally easy to overlook all the goodness we are surrounded by today.

It doesn't take a lot of money to have a truly wealthy life, but it does take financial independence, which gives us control over our time. This is the important topic that we will address in the next chapter.

CHAPTER 9

ACHIEVING FINANCIAL INDEPENDENCE

It is difficult to get a man to understand something, when his salary depends on his not understanding it.

—Upton Sinclair

Whose bread I eat, his song I sing.

—Charlie Munger

Truth is hard to assimilate when it is opposed by interest. You cannot really understand how the world truly works unless you have financial independence. Once you achieve this state, it changes everything. It enables you to look at reality in a truly unbiased manner. Aim to achieve financial independence at the earliest time. That is when you will start seeing the world as it really is. It is difficult to think and act long term unless you are financially independent. Financial independence doesn't mean you don't work, just that you don't need to. It removes the internal distraction of unpredictable employment.

The goal of financial independence is to stop depending on others (bosses, clients, a schedule, a paycheck). True wealth is measured in terms of personal liberty and freedom, not monetary currency. Money alone does not signify independence. Control over time does. The only definition of success is to be able to spend your life in your own way.

Is there a way for us to achieve financial independence?

As it turns out, there is indeed a simple way to do it.

It's simple but not easy.

It requires a lot of hard work, sacrifice, discipline, and patience.

> When I was young, I read *The Richest Man in Babylon*, which said to *underspend your income and invest the difference* [emphasis added]. Lo and behold, I did this and it worked.
>
> —Charlie Munger

The first step to financial independence is to live within your means. In Charles Dickens's classic *David Copperfield*, he wrote, "Annual income twenty pounds, annual expenditure nineteen six, result happiness. Annual income twenty pounds, annual expenditure twenty pound ought and six, result misery."[1]

This was written in 1849, and it is just as true today—and will remain so forever.

Underspend your income to the maximum extent possible. Avoid taking on any debt for discretionary consumption. Cook at home. Buy clothes only on sale. Learn to cherish frugality. Read *The Way to Wealth* by Benjamin Franklin, *The Richest Man in Babylon* by George Clason, *The Millionaire Next Door* by Thomas Stanley and William Danko, and *Rich Dad Poor Dad* by Robert Kiyosaki. Always pay yourself first. Spend on yourself only what is left after you have made an investment. Never depend on a single source of income; make an investment in yourself and learn a new skill to create a second source. Avoid get-rich-quick schemes. Invest wisely by learning from the great investors. When you finally achieve financial independence, you will truly appreciate the value of money because of all the sacrifices you made in the past.

Building wealth over time has less to do with your income levels or investment returns and more to do with your savings discipline. As Peter Lynch says, "In the long run, it's not just how much money you make that will determine your future prosperity. It's how much of that money you put to work by saving it and investing it."[2] Wealth is the accumulated savings, over time, that is left over after you are done spending from your income. Because you can build wealth without a high income but have no chance without any savings, it is pretty obvious which one deserves a higher priority.

To me, money represents freedom and independence and not a means to engage in conspicuous consumption. Spending beyond a modest level of materialism is mostly a reflection of one's ego. One of the most effective ways to increase your savings is to raise not your income but your humility.

A friend once asked me, "Why make all that money so you can save it?" to which I replied, "Why spend all that money so you need to earn it again?"

If money were the true measure of wealth, every rich person would be happy. But we know this is not true. Money can't buy a loving family, good health, integrity, ethics, humility, kindness, respect, character, or a clear conscience. The most important things in life are priceless, and, in my view, those are the true measures of wealth. Lasting happiness is achieved by living a meaningful life—a life filled with passion and freedom in which we grow as individuals and contribute beyond ourselves. Growth and contribution are the bedrocks of happiness. Not stuff. In his book *The Geometry of Wealth*, Brian Portnoy describes wealth as "funded contentment," that is, the ability to underwrite a meaningful life in which purpose and practice are thoughtfully calibrated.[3] Wealth derives its real meaning from a personal definition of our inner values.

Savings is a hedge against life's inevitable setbacks. Savings confers on us options and flexibility, the ability to wait, and the very possibility to participate in the rare superlative opportunities that may present themselves during one's lifetime. But the most important reason for saving is personal freedom and control over time. This allows us to devote more attention to the meaningful aspects of our lives, such as relationships, creative pursuits, health, and philanthropy.

Personal freedom allows us sufficient time to think. Making good decisions requires quiet time alone in our heads to think through a problem from multiple points of view.

Uninterrupted personal time is life's most valuable limited resource. Several notable creators, including Bill Gates and Mark Zuckerberg, regularly take "think weeks" to invigorate their thinking and to allow their minds to wander. They often advocate the value of taking time off specifically to relax and clear one's head. Taking a whole week off to focus on our thinking process may sound like a farfetched scenario, but this is possible once we achieve financial independence. Only then can we engage in frequent pauses, self-reflection, and a calm distillation of thoughts, patterns, and wisdom. (This is essential. As investors, we tend to spend too much time reading about what others think or are investing in. As a result, we spend too little time on introspection.) Quiet freedom is exotic. Freedom is like income that cannot be taxed. Value investors who achieve financial independence in their thirties or forties spend the rest of their lives doing something that they love: learning more about the world.

Benjamin Franklin frequently wrote about the virtues of frugality and a strong work ethic. He was aware that "lost time is never found again," and he pursued financial independence to make sure he gained back as much time as possible. He testified that more than 90 percent of his writing was "the gleanings I had made of the sense of all ages and nations." Franklin studied the past so that he could gain more freedom in his present.

By building a print shop into a successful business, Franklin was able to retire at the age of forty-two. What is truly inspirational is his attitude toward building wealth. Here was a man who accumulated a vast fortune by the age of forty-two, but he didn't concern himself with accumulating money for money's sake. In a letter to his mother, Franklin wrote, "I would rather have it said, 'He lived usefully,' than, 'He died rich.'"

Franklin lived usefully and put himself into the position to give away his fortune throughout his life.

The *Way to Wealth*, published in 1758, is a summary of Benjamin Franklin's advice from *Poor Richard's Almanack*, published from 1733 to 1758. It's a compilation of proverbs woven into a systematic ethical code advocating industry and frugality as a "way to wealth," thereby securing personal virtue. Franklin's advice is just as relevant today as it was more than 260 years ago. He advocated work ethic, industry, and enterprise in one's daily affairs: "But dost thou love life, then do not squander time, for that's the stuff life is made of."

Franklin believed everyone should contribute to society and that we should enthusiastically approach each day as we make those daily contributions. In his eyes, life embodied a community of people working together for the common good. It is why he believed in "We, the people" and advocated that "if we are industrious we shall never starve; for, at the working man's house, hunger looks in but dares not enter."

The eldest Founding Father of the United States was also a firm advocate of the virtues of frugality: "If you would be wealthy . . . think of saving as well as of getting: the Indies have not made Spain rich, because her outgoes are greater than her incomes."

For Franklin, frugality and a strong work ethic were necessary character traits for building wealth.

> Benjamin Franklin was able to make the contribution he did because he had [financial] freedom.
> —Charlie Munger

During his interactions with the audience at the University of Michigan's Ross School of Business, in 2017, Charlie Munger shared an overview of his early years and how he personally achieved financial independence before really getting involved in business with Warren Buffett. In a blog post, Jonathan Ping discussed how Munger emulated his role model Benjamin Franklin's virtues:

- **Munger was not born into exceptional wealth.** He wanted to go to Stanford as an undergraduate, but his father encouraged him to go to the University of Michigan, because it was still an excellent school but was more affordable. Munger dropped out after only one year, in 1943, to serve in the U.S. Army Air Corps.

- **Military service, then law school.** After World War II, Munger took college courses on the GI Bill and eventually went to Harvard Law School. He got accepted even though he had never earned an undergraduate degree.
- **Successful law career.** Munger successfully practiced real estate law until he achieved about $300,000 in assets. This equaled ten years of living expenses for his family at the time (he had a wife and multiple kids). At this point, he started doing real estate development at the same time. When this took off, he stopped practicing law.
- **Successful real estate development.** When Munger achieved about $3 million to $4 million in assets, he wound down his real estate development firm. He was now "financially independent."
- **Decision to become a "full-time capitalist."** This last stage is what led him to his current status as a billionaire philanthropist. Along with his work with Buffett at Berkshire, Munger was the chairman of Wesco Financial, which also grew to be a conglomerate of various wholly owned businesses, along with a carefully run stock portfolio. Wesco Financial eventually became a wholly owned subsidiary of Berkshire Hathaway.

Using Munger's life as a blueprint, we can observe a pathway toward achieving financial independence:

- **Work hard, get an education, develop a valuable skill.** Munger didn't start Facebook from his dorm room or trade cryptos in high school. He served in the military, earned a law degree, and went to work every day for years. At this point, work means exchanging your time for money, but hopefully at a good hourly rate.
- **Use that work career and save up ten times your living expenses.** Munger dutifully saved as much as he could from his salary, while supporting his family and kids. You probably won't need ten times that amount if you don't have a family to support, but you should still plan for the future and target this level of savings.
- **To accelerate wealth accumulation, you can take some risk and start some sort of business.** You need something that scales, something that is not paid by the hour or the month. Munger pursued real estate development. If you look at people who got wealthy quickly, nearly all of them owned businesses of some type. Still, there are no guarantees. You need to believe that a reasonably calculated strategy based on sound and sensible principles will work. As Steve Jobs once remarked, "You can't connect the dots looking forward; you can only connect them looking backwards. So you have to trust that the dots will somehow connect in your future. You have to trust in something—your gut, destiny, life, karma, whatever." In short, you need to have faith.

- **At some point, your investments will earn enough passive income to support your living expenses.** This is when you achieve financial independence. It doesn't matter what you do during the day, because you earn enough money while you are sleeping. Many people choose to continue along one of the paths above: (1) employee-based career, (2) active business management, or (3) actively managing their investments.[4]

Munger's life teaches us that just showing up every day and chipping away at it, one small block at a time, eventually yields great dividends. Dogged, incremental progress over a long period of time is the key to success, and this, in essence, is what compounding is all about.

Spend each day trying to be a little wiser than you were when you woke up. Discharge your duties faithfully and well. Step by step you get ahead, but not necessarily in fast spurts. But you build discipline by preparing for fast spurts. . . . Slug it out one inch at a time, day by day. At the end of the day—if you live long enough—most people get what they deserve.
—Charlie Munger

We can learn a lot by observing Munger's actions. He was not a huge risk-taker. He grew his wealth gradually and never exposed his family to possible ruin. He worked hard for a long time and became extraordinarily rich and famous only later in his life. He primarily wanted to be independent, "and just overshot."

The Journey to the First Million

Making the first million dollars is often considered to be the hardest, because you don't know how to do it and because you don't know if you can do it. Once you have made $1 million, you know you can do it and you even know how to do it. This is why a self-made millionaire who loses all his money because of an unfortunate event can become a millionaire again.

Many people who are considered successful don't accumulate a million dollars, and it is not because they don't earn enough to do so. It is simply because they lack discipline. Society glamorizes a consumption-laden lifestyle, and most people follow this path, spending on non-necessities that drain earnings, leaving little in the form of savings. The journey to the first million starts with the very first dollar in savings, and then another, and so on. It is not the first million dollars that is the hardest, it is the first dollar. The most difficult part is getting started.

During my savings and wealth accumulation phase, I was willing to work as hard as I could, for as many hours as I possibly could, to reach this important milestone of the first million. I was trying to save every single dime that

I could during this endeavor. I never lost sight of Benjamin Franklin's teaching: "Beware of little expenses; a small leak will sink a great ship."

More important, I was constantly investing in myself. I was ferociously intense about learning as much as I possibly could, every day. Once a certain level of critical mass in portfolio value was achieved, compound interest took over and proceeded to amaze me with its magic.

Today, even after achieving financial freedom, I continue to work in a job because I want to, not because I need to. I do it because I just love the work I get to do every day, and I feel a sense of joy in doing what I love and loving what I do. Today, I get a deep sense of fulfillment when I look back at the memories of my challenging times and sacrifices in the past, which eventually helped me earn my first million dollars of profits from investing.

Benjamin Franklin laid down the way to wealth for all of us when he said, "The way to wealth is as plain as the way to market. It depends chiefly on two words, industry and frugality; that is, waste neither time nor money, but make the best use of both. Without industry and frugality nothing will do; with them, everything."

Resist Stepping on the Hedonic Treadmill

I saw that it was the artificial needs of life that made me a slave; the real needs of life were few.

—William James Dawson

Great wealth often inflicts a curse on its owners. It's called the "hedonic treadmill," and its function is to continually move the goalpost of your financial dreams, completely extinguishing the joy you thought you would get from having more money, once you attain it. People are constantly running on the hedonic treadmill; as they make more money, their expectations and desires rise in tandem, which results in no permanent gain in happiness.

Economist Richard Easterlin measured the life satisfaction of Americans in 1946 and 1970 and came to the conclusion that material progress was not reflected in increased life satisfaction. This revelation was termed the Easterlin paradox. Once one's basic needs have been met, incremental financial gain contributes nothing to happiness. This is because, in our minds, wealth is always relative, not absolute.

A research study posed the following question: Which new employee would be happier, the person making $36,000 in a firm where the starting salary is $40,000 or the one making $34,000 where the average is $30,000? Almost 80 percent said $34,000 would make them happier.[5]

We want what we want until we want some more. A process called "hedonic adaptation" determines that we quickly become accustomed to most things in our lives. As a result, experienced happiness is often fleeting. We may have x and think this should be sufficient to live a happy life, but when we see others who have $2x$, we think that would make us happier. And then we raise the bar to $3x$, $4x$, or $10x$. This is a sure path to lifelong misery, even if one eventually becomes monetarily rich. Very often, as Dave Ramsey points out, "We buy things we don't need with money we don't have to impress people we don't know."[6] We want to look good over doing good. Consequently, we make choices based on optics, defensibility, and so on. This typically results from not having a strong sense of self and from seeking external validation. As Benjamin Franklin said, "It is the eyes of others and not our own eyes that ruin us. If all the world were blind except myself I should not care for fine clothes or furniture." Acquired material objects do not necessarily improve your life. Desiring them is indicative of some social, emotional, or psychological gap that you need to work on. Don't confuse pleasure with happiness. Pleasure is short-lived, and modern corporations have convinced most people that the only way to be happy is through the pursuit of pleasure. The longer you stay on the hedonic treadmill, the more it will break you down emotionally, so get off of it, quickly.

The book *Classics: An Investor's Anthology* features an essay about P. T. Barnum that quotes Barnum on the tendency for individuals to step on the hedonic treadmill:

> Thousands of men are kept poor, and tens of thousands are made so after they have acquired quite sufficient to support them well through life, in consequence of laying their plans of living too expensive a platform. . . .
>
> Prosperity is a more severe ordeal than adversity, especially sudden prosperity. "Easy come, easy go" is an old and true proverb. Pride, when permitted full sway, is the great undying cankerworm which gnaws the very vitals of a man's worldly possessions, let them be small or great, hundreds or millions. *Many persons, as they begin to prosper, immediately commence expending for luxuries, until in a short time their expenses swallow up their income, and they become ruined in their ridiculous attempts to keep up appearances, and make a "sensation"* [emphasis added].[7]

Seneca also shared his thoughts on the futile attempts to maximize one's monetary worth rather than one's happiness:

> Epicurus says: "Contented poverty is an honorable estate." Indeed, if it be contented, it is not poverty at all. *It is not the man who has too little, but the man who craves more, that is poor* [emphasis added]. What does it matter how much a man has laid up in his safe, or in his warehouse, how large are his flocks and

how fat his dividends, if he covets his neighbor's property, and reckons, not his past gains, but his hopes of gains to come?

Do you ask what is the proper limit to wealth? It is, first, to have what is necessary, and, second, to have what is enough.[8]

Morgan Housel recommends a solution to the hedonic treadmill problem: "The solution, particularly after basic needs are met, is actively seeking contentment with what you have. That doesn't mean you stop saving, stop putting in effort, stop sacrificing. It means you come to terms with the idea that the outcome isn't a fountain of happiness. So if you're going to grind, you better damn well enjoy the process."[9]

Housel's words remind me of one of the most profound thoughts I have ever encountered on the subject, from George Lorimer: "It's good to have money and the things that money can buy, *but it's good, too, to check up once in a while and make sure that you haven't lost the things that money can't buy* [emphasis added]."

Never measure life by your possessions. Measure it by the hearts you touched, the smiles you created, and the love you shared. Love people and use things, because the opposite never works. Love is caring without an agenda. Love isn't something we fall into; it's someone we become.

CHAPTER 10

LIVING LIFE ACCORDING TO THE INNER SCORECARD

To be yourself in a world that is constantly trying to make you something else is the greatest accomplishment.

—Ralph Waldo Emerson

The path to true success is through authenticity.

—Guy Spier

According to Warren Buffett, there are two kinds of people in life: those who care what people think of them, and those who care how good they really are.

Buffett always remains true to himself and never compromises on his values. He has never cared about luxurious possessions, and he still lives in the modest house he bought for $31,500 in 1958. As an investor, Buffett thinks entirely for himself and invests only according to his personal investment philosophy. During 1999, in the midst of the Internet bubble, Buffett was being humiliated by some of the leading financial commentators of the time and Berkshire's stock price was getting hammered. But Buffett always kept in mind what he had been taught by his father—that the only scorecard that counts is your inner scorecard.

In December 1999, *Barron's* put Buffett on its cover with the headline "Warren, What's Wrong?" The accompanying article said Berkshire had "stumbled" badly. Buffett was facing a kind of negative press like nothing he had ever experienced. Many longtime value investors who followed Buffett's style had either shut down their firms or given in and bought technology stocks. Buffett did not. What he called his inner scorecard—a toughness about personal decisions that had infused him for as long as anyone could remember—kept him from wavering, and he steadfastly adhered to his long-held principles. He never forgot his teacher Ben Graham's words: "In the short run, the market is a voting machine, but in the long run, it is a weighing machine."[1]

Don't live a life based on approval from others. Be authentic—act in accordance with who you are and what you believe in, or one day your mask will fall off. If Buffett was living by the standards others followed, he would not have been able to maintain the firm independence of mind that has helped him avoid many financial bubbles and the subsequent personal misery. It is a significant lesson for all investors. A contrarian isn't one who always takes the opposite path just for the sake of it. That is simply a conformist of a different sort. A true contrarian is one who reasons independently, from the ground up, based on factual data, and resists pressure to conform.

If, in your heart, you know who you really are and that the choice you made was absolutely right, then the criticism of others should be considered and analyzed to see whether it truly has any merit, but it should not be given permission to belittle what you are trying to achieve. Let your life be guided by internal principles, not external validation. Self-respect beats social approval. Every time. We are not perfect, nor should we pretend to be, but we always should endeavor to be the best version of ourselves.

Buffett's operating principles during the Buffett Partnership years provide many lessons for fund managers—and all those who should always occupy the high ground in the interest of their clients.

The Buffett Partnership Years

In 1956, when he was just twenty-five years old, Warren Buffett formed Buffett Partnership Ltd. with $105,100 in capital and seven limited partners: his mother, sister, aunt, father-in-law, brother-in-law, college roommate, and lawyer. He charged no management fee, took 25 percent of any gains beyond a cumulative 6 percent, and agreed to personally absorb a percentage of any losses. You will rarely find such an equitable fee structure in the investment management industry today.

By 1969, $100,000 invested in the Buffett Partnership in 1957 would have become $1,719,481. If you had invested the same amount in the Dow, it would have grown to only $252,467. For more than a decade, Buffett achieved a compound annual return of 24.5 percent, net of fees (29.5 percent before fees). The compound annual return of the Dow over the same time, with dividends, was 7.4 percent.

And yet, despite all this success, Warren Buffett announced to his limited partners, in May 1969, that he would be *closing down* the Buffett Partnership.

Buffett was young, he was having extraordinary success, and he was having to actually turn away investors.

Why did Warren Buffett decide to close down his investment partnership in 1969?

Because he possessed certain virtues. Honesty. Sincerity. Integrity. Authenticity.

In January 1967, after a decade of incredible results, Buffett warned his limited partners to temper their expectations: "The results of the first ten years have absolutely no chance of being duplicated or even remotely approximated during the next decade."[2]

In October 1967, Buffett explained to his investors why he didn't think he would be able to achieve the same results:

Such statistical bargains have tended to disappear over the years. . . .

. . . When the game is no longer being played your way, it is only human to say the new approach is all wrong, bound to lead to trouble, etc. I have been scornful of such behavior by others in the past. I have also seen the penalties incurred by those who evaluate conditions as they were—not as they are. Essentially I am out of step with present conditions. *On one point, however, I am clear. I will not abandon a previous approach whose logic I understand (although I find it difficult to apply) even though it may mean foregoing* [sic] *large and apparently easy profits to embrace an approach which I don't fully understand, have not practiced successfully and which, possibly, could lead to substantial permanent loss of capital* [emphasis added].[3]

In January 1969, even after the Buffett Partnership's best year ever, Warren Buffett continued to stand his ground: "At the beginning of 1968, I felt prospects for BPL performance looked poorer than at any time in our history. . . . We established a new mark at plus 58.8 percent versus an overall plus 7.7 percent for the Dow, including dividends which would have been received through the ownership of the Average throughout the year. This result should be treated as a freak like picking up thirteen spades in a bridge game."[4]

In May 1969, Buffett said he was running out of good investment ideas. He said he could take some chances and gamble with his investors' money so that he could go out a hero, but he refused to do so.

Finally, in October 1969, Warren Buffett closed the Buffett Partnership.

In his final letter, Buffett wrote his partners a ten-page explanation of why he recommended tax-free municipal bonds—even offering to sit down with each of them individually to explain the rationale, as well as to make the actual purchases for them. For those who wished to continue to invest in stocks, he said, "I feel it would be totally unfair for me to assume a passive position and deliver you to the most persuasive salesman who happened to contact you early in 1970."[5]

Buffett recommended his clients invest with his Columbia classmate Bill Ruane, not because he was the best investor Buffett knew other than himself, but because Buffett viewed him as a person with high integrity and moral character. (Remember, most of Buffett's limited partners were his relatives and close friends.) According to Buffett, Ruane was "the money manager within my knowledge who ranks the highest when combining the factors of integrity, ability and continued availability to all partners."

Bill Ruane turned out to be a legendary investor in his own right, and his Sequoia Fund returned 289.6 percent over the next decade, versus 105.1 percent for the S&P 500. Later on, Ruane would be included as one of the superinvestors in Buffett's speech titled "The Superinvestors of Graham-and-Doddsville," delivered in May 1984 at Columbia Business School.

Throughout his early partnership years, Buffett embodied what Peter Kaufmann referred to during the 2018 Daily Journal Corporation meeting as the "five aces" of money management (figure 10.1).

Fund managers (who, in essence, are operating in a fiduciary role for their clients) should view themselves first and foremost as risk managers. As such, they should follow the key principles of prudent insurance underwriting, outlined in Buffett's 2001 shareholder letter:

> They accept only those risks that they are able to properly evaluate (staying within their circle of competence) and that, after they have evaluated all relevant factors including remote loss scenarios, carry the expectancy of profit. . . .
>
> They limit the business they accept in a manner that guarantees they will suffer no aggregation of losses from a single event or from related events that will threaten their solvency. They ceaselessly search for possible correlation among seemingly-unrelated risks.[6]

Charlie Munger has always admired his protégé Li Lu for his work ethic and high integrity as a trusted steward of capital. To understand why, one needs only to listen to what Lu told the students at the Guanghua School of Management in China, in October 2015:

> Establish an awareness of fiduciary duty. What are fiduciary duties? You must treat every dollar of client money as though it were the fruit of your own parents' labor, saved up piece by piece over a lifetime of diligence and thrift. Even if it's not much, it took years of struggle and sacrifice to accumulate. If you can

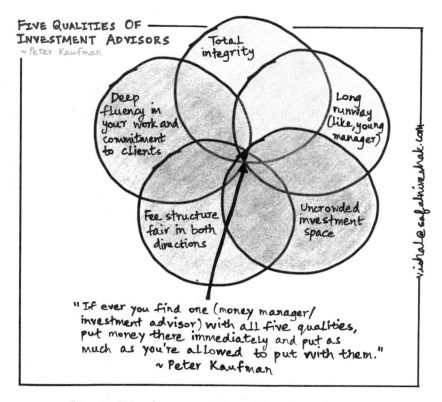

FIVE QUALITIES OF INVESTMENT ADVISORS
~ Peter Kaufman

Total integrity

Deep fluency in your work and commitment to clients

Long runway (like, young manager)

Fee structure fair in both directions

Uncrowded investment space

" If ever you find one (money manager/investment advisor) with all five qualities, put money there immediately and put as much as you're allowed to put with them."
~ Peter Kaufman

vishal@safalniveshak.com

FIGURE 10.1 "Five Qualities of Investment Advisors" by Peter Kaufman.

Source: "Charlie Munger on Bitcoins, Banking, AI, and Life," *Safal Niveshak* (blog), February 17, 2018, https://www.safalniveshak.com/charlie-munger-bitcoins-banking-life/.

understand the responsibility this entails, then you can start to understand the meaning of fiduciary duty.

I think the concept of fiduciary duty is innate: people either have it or they don't.[7]

Never forget your moral responsibility to the individuals and families who entrust you with their life's hard-earned savings. When the perma-bull inside you urges you to engage in risky strategies or to eke out the final few points of a rampant bull market where there could be a quick 20 percent upside along with a potential 50 percent downside, think about the man or lady who worked on the checkout line at Walmart for years to put something aside for his or her retirement. How would it affect their retirement dreams and life aspirations if you lost half their money? How would they feel if they knew what you were doing? How would *you* feel if you were fully aware about what you were doing?

An outer scorecard, which many people have, asks, "What will people think of me? Will they judge me by the way I dress or the way I look or the car I drive?"

But the inner scorecard, which is much more important, asks, "Am I doing the right things? Am I treating people correctly? Is this working for me as an individual?"

It's what Rose Blumkin, the Nebraska Furniture Mart founder, stood for, and she lived her life under one single motto: "Sell cheap and tell the truth."[8]

The inner scorecard is the inner set of criteria and standards by which a person judges her- or himself. In contrast, the outer scorecard is an external, comparative picture of self-worth predicated on the judgments of others. There is a clear parallel here between the inner scorecard and the concept of intrinsic value and between the outer scorecard and the concept of market value. Benjamin Graham had talked about this very parallel in *The Intelligent Investor*:

> Have the courage of your knowledge and experience. If you have formed a conclusion from the facts and if you know your judgment is sound, act on it—even though others may hesitate or differ. *You are neither right nor wrong because the crowd disagrees with you. You are right because your data and reasoning are right* [emphasis added].[9]

Focusing on his inner scorecard and living life in a principled manner has worked for Buffett. He has always believed in the dictum "Honesty is the best policy." Buffett has always taken the high road, and it has paid off very well. For instance, he could have saved billions by moving his reinsurance operations' tax domicile to a tax-advantaged jurisdiction, as many of his competitors did, but he didn't. His independent spirit infuses every aspect of his life. This includes his diet, which mostly revolves around burgers and Cherry Coke.

In the late 1980s, when the U.S. savings and loan (S&L) companies were using accounting tricks to create capital out of thin air, they were heading toward a crisis of widespread bankruptcies that would destroy depositor savings, require a taxpayer bailout, and result in a furious public backlash. Munger, who was chairman and CEO of Berkshire's S&L operation, Wesco Financial, foresaw that Wesco's better behavior wouldn't prevent it from being tainted by association. He not only cut back Wesco's lending but also took an extreme stand to distance Wesco from the other S&Ls by resigning from the U.S. League of Savings Institutions, in a letter in which he likened the trade association to metastasizing cancer cells and called its lobbying practices "flawed, indeed disgraceful."[10] It was a step that only a person who was willing to be detested by an entire industry could take. The move paid off when the S&L crisis erupted and Wesco's reputation was left completely unscathed. It was Munger's action of high integrity during the 1980s' S&L crisis that set Berkshire on its path to being held up as the moral exemplar of corporate America.

What Buffett, Munger, and a lot of other people who have been successful in life (true success, not measured by money) have in common is that they strive for a happy and fulfilling life. Not just getting rich. Not just trying to get famous. But living a truly satisfying existence with full integrity and helping others around them achieve the same.

Bernie Madoff achieved great admiration and wealth over the duration of his Ponzi scheme, but was he happy? He made it clear, after he had been caught, that he wasn't. Here was a guy who had all the admiration in the world, an external scorecard showing an A+. But what happened when he lost it all? He heaved a sigh of relief. According to *New York* magazine, "For Bernie Madoff, living a lie had once been a full-time job, which carried with it a constant, nagging anxiety. 'It was a nightmare for me,' he told investigators, using the word over and over, as if he were the real victim. 'I wish they caught me six years ago, eight years ago,' he said in a little-noticed interview with them."[11]

Shane Parrish writes, "The little mental trick is to remember that success, money, fame, and beauty, all the things we pursue, are merely the numerator! If the denominator—shame, regret, unhappiness, loneliness—is too large, our 'Life Satisfaction Score' ends up being tiny, worthless. Even if we have all that good stuff! . . . It's so simple. This is why you see people that 'should be happy' who are not. Big denominators destroy self-worth."[12]

Adam Smith addressed this issue more than two centuries ago in his book *The Theory of Moral Sentiments*. He said that even though we desire to be loved by others, at the end of the day, we experience happiness only when we are successful according to our inner scorecard. We derive true joy from our achievements only when we feel we truly deserve it. We can't just receive praise. We must *be* praiseworthy. We can't just be loved. We must *be* loveable.

To get what you want, *deserve* what you want. Trust, respect, and admiration need to be *earned*. As Munger says:

> It's such a simple idea. It's the golden rule so to speak. *You want to deliver to the world what you would buy if you were on the other end.* There is no ethos, in my opinion, that is better for any lawyer or any other person to have. By and large the people who have this ethos win in life, and they don't win just money, not just honors. *They win the respect, the deserved trust of the people they deal with, and there is huge pleasure in life to be obtained from getting deserved trust* [emphasis added].[13]

The idea of living one's life according to the inner scorecard is closely linked to the concept of the "Kantian fairness tendency," discussed by Munger in his essay *The Psychology of Human Misjudgment*: "Kant was famous for his 'categorical imperative,' a sort of a 'golden rule' that required humans to follow those behavior patterns that, if followed by all others, would make the surrounding human system work best for everybody."[14]

I look at this as the law of the higher good, of treading the high moral ground, of taking the road less traveled, of being the better people. Buffett and Munger have exemplified this behavior in their daily dealings for the past many decades, and their goodwill has compounded in an exponential manner over the years.

We must look at individual situations from our civilization's point of view rather than the viewpoint of any single individual, including ourselves. If we behave in a way that encourages lies and deceit, or if we tolerate such systems, we will ruin our civilization. If we don't punish the concerned individual, even if that person is us, the idea that it is okay to do minor unethical deeds once in a while will spread because of incentive effects and social proof ("Everyone is doing it, so it's okay."). It is our duty to act as moral exemplars and to inspire others to do the same.

> When I was an officer in the military, we had a rule called Conduct Unbecoming an Officer. It was not specific, but it said there were certain ways to behave as an example for others. . . . *If you rise high in a corporation or elsewhere in life, you have a duty to be an exemplar—you have a duty to take less than you deserve, to set an example* [emphasis added].
> —Charlie Munger

Ultimately, you want to be at peace with yourself, able to face the mirror every day. As the saying goes, "There is no pillow so soft as a clear conscience." We should not pay mere lip service to our role models in life; we should embody them in words, action, and spirit. Over the course of our lives, we will face difficult situations in which being truthful is painful up front. Following the path of righteousness during such times delivers enormous rewards in the long run. Our goodwill compounds exponentially over time when we live life according to the inner scorecard.

Again, Munger shares some great thoughts:

> I think the best single way to teach ethics is by example. And that means if you take in people who demonstrate in all their daily conduct a good ethical framework, I think that has enormous influence on the people who watch it. But if your ethics slip and people are rewarded [nevertheless, then] it cascades downward. Ethics are terribly important, but best taught indirectly by example. If you just learn a few rules by having ethics taught in school so they can pass the test, it doesn't do much. *But if you see people you respect behaving in a certain way, especially under stress, that has a real impact* [emphasis added].[15]

The principle of reciprocity states, "Treat others the way you would like them to treat you" and "Do unto others as you would have done unto you." Character is how you treat others when you have the upper hand and no one is watching. Over the long term, "what goes around comes around." Karma is a like a big snowball. So, acting in an ethical manner with everyone is the most honorable way to lead one's life. Our world's moral fabric would be completely transformed if all of humanity imbibed, as a way of life, Seneca's golden words: "Cherish some man of high character, and keep him ever before your eyes, living as if he were watching you, and ordering all your actions as if he beheld them."[16]

CHAPTER 11

THE KEY TO SUCCESS IN LIFE IS DELAYED GRATIFICATION

Someone's sitting in the shade today because someone planted a tree a long time ago.

—Warren Buffett

If you're glued together and honorable and get up every morning and keep learning every day and you're willing to go in for a lot of deferred gratification all your life, you're going to succeed.

—Charlie Munger

People who arbitrage time will almost always outperform. The first order thought of instant gratification is a crowded path, ensuring mediocre results at best. Delayed gratification, which requires second order thinking, is less crowded and more likely to get results.

—Shane Parrish

In the 1960s, Walter Mischel, an American psychologist specializing in personality theory and social psychology, conducted a famous experiment at Stanford University's nursery school. In the experiment, now widely known as the Stanford marshmallow experiment, four- and five-year-olds were presented with a difficult choice. They could eat one treat—a marshmallow—immediately, or they could wait fifteen minutes more and be rewarded with two marshmallows.

Over the next forty years, the children were included in follow-up studies. It was found that the children who were willing to delay gratification and waited to receive the second marshmallow ended up having higher SAT scores, lower levels of substance abuse, lower likelihood of obesity, better responses to stress, better social skills as reported by their parents, and better scores on a range of other life measures.

In other words, the experiment demonstrated the virtues of delayed gratification—doing what is hard now rather than doing what is easy. Over time, this builds up the muscle of discipline, strengthens one's skills and capabilities, and compounds into a much greater level of success and satisfaction than taking the easier path.

Charlie Munger has always been a big proponent of delayed gratification. He has emphasized the importance of patience and being prepared to act at scale when great opportunities arise. These are rare and fleeting, so we need to be patient, prepared, and decisive to seize them. Munger has shared an inspiring example. He had been reading *Barron's* magazine for more than fifty years and found only one actionable idea in it. It was a cheaply valued auto parts company (the name is widely speculated to be Tenneco), which he bought at $1 per share and sold a few years later at $15 per share, earning him $80 million in profits. Munger then gave Li Lu the $80 million and Lu turned this into $400 million. Through just two investments, Munger turned a few million into $400 million. This example illustrates the significance of extreme patience, deferred gratification, and displaying strong decisiveness at the right moment. It is why Munger has said, "It takes character to sit there with all that cash and do nothing. *I didn't get to where I am by going after mediocre opportunities* [emphasis added]."[1]

> The only way to win is to work, work, work, work, and hope to have a few insights.
> —Charlie Munger

How much insight does one need in a lifetime to be a successful investor? Not much, as Warren Buffett explains:

> I could improve your ultimate financial welfare by giving you a ticket with only twenty slots in it so that you had twenty punches—representing all the investments that you got to make in a lifetime. And once you'd punched through the card, you couldn't make any more investments at all. Under those rules, you'd really think carefully about what you did, and you'd be forced to load up on what you'd really thought about. So you'd do so much better.[2]

Munger repeatedly brought up the topic of deferred gratification during the 2017 Daily Journal Corporation meeting. He talked about how most investors are looking for a quick buck, but the best investors defer their gratification for much larger gains that come later, in the distant future.

Long-term investors look for management teams that are willing to defer gratification. These teams are focused on building a durable economic franchise. They are focused on the longevity of the business. They are willing to forgo near-term earnings to increase long-term value. Let's look at the compound interest formula and view it in a way that helps us think about building long-term value:

$$a = p * \left(1 + \left(\frac{r}{100}\right)\right)^n \qquad (19.1)$$

where a = accumulated future value, p = principal or present value, r = rate of return in percentage terms, and n = number of compounding periods.

All too often, management teams focus on the r variable in this equation. They seek instant gratification, with high profit margins and high growth in reported earnings per share (EPS) in the near term, as opposed to initiatives that would lead to a much more valuable business many years down the line. This causes many management teams to pass on investments that would create long-term value but would cause "accounting numbers" to look bad in the short term. Pressure from analysts can inadvertently incentivize companies to make as much money as possible off their present customers to report good quarterly numbers, instead of offering a fair price that creates enduring goodwill and a long-term win–win relationship for all stakeholders. The businesses that buy commodities and sell brands and have strong pricing power (typically depicted by high gross margins) should always remember that possessing pricing power is like having access to a large amount of credit. You may have it in abundance, but you must use it sparingly. Having pricing power doesn't mean you exercise it right away. Consumer surplus is a great strategy, especially for subscription-based business models in which management should primarily focus on habit formation and making renewals a no-brainer. Most businesses fail to appreciate this delicate trade-off between high short-term profitability and the longevity accorded to the business through disciplined pricing and offering great customer value. The few businesses that do understand this trade-off always display "pain today, gain tomorrow" thinking in their daily decisions.

Let's look at two contrasting examples. On one hand, we have Valeant Pharmaceuticals, which buys lifesaving drugs for rare diseases from innovative companies but then resorts to predatory pricing. The financial metrics might appear attractive, but a parasitic relationship of extracting value from customers (rather than adding value to them) usually ends up destroying shareholder value at some point in the future. On the other, we have companies like Amazon, led by Jeff Bezos, who says, "We've done price elasticity studies, and the answer is always that we should raise prices. We don't do that, because we believe—and we have to take this as an article of faith—that *by keeping our prices very, very low, we earn trust with customers over time, and that that actually does maximize free cash flow over the long term* [emphasis added]."[3]

Some companies are willing to look past maximizing short-run focused *r* and instead focus on maximizing long-term focused *n* to create maximum long-term stakeholder value and happy customers. Amazon, Nebraska Furniture Mart, Costco, and GEICO are prominent examples. As they have grown larger over time and have achieved economies of scale, they have continued to share those benefits with customers in the form of lower prices and to provide more value for their customers. This not only makes for delighted customers, who then spend more money with those companies, but also makes those businesses harder to compete with over time, because they have the rare ability to defer gratification in lieu of long-term benefits. Consider the following quotes from Bezos that reflect the culture of long-term thinking at Amazon:

A dreamy business offering has at least four characteristics. Customers love it, it can grow to very large size, it has strong returns on capital, *and it's durable in time—with the potential to endure for decades* [emphasis added]. When you find one of these, don't just swipe right, get married.[4]

Percentage margins are not one of the things we are seeking to optimize. It's the absolute dollar free cash flow per share that you want to maximize, *and if you can do that by lowering margins, we would do that* [emphasis added]. So if you could take the free cash flow, that's something that investors can spend. Investors can't spend percentage margins.[5]

[Selling at low prices creates] a virtuous cycle that leads *over the long term* to a much larger dollar amount of free cash flow, *and thereby to a much more valuable Amazon.com* [emphasis added].[6]

When forced to choose between optimizing the appearance of our GAAP [generally accepted accounting principles] accounting and *maximizing the present value of future cash flows* [emphasis added], we'll take the cash flows.[7]

Some of the best insight on the virtues of delayed gratification in creating long-term intrinsic value comes from studying Buffett's comments on GEICO's customer acquisition costs over the years:

In 1999, we will again increase our marketing budget, spending at least $190 million. In fact, there is no limit to what Berkshire is willing to *invest* in GEICO's new-business activity, as long as we can concurrently build the infrastructure the company needs to properly serve its policyholders.

Because of the first-year costs, companies that are concerned about quarterly or annual earnings would shy from similar investments, no matter how intelligent these might be in terms of building *long-term value*. Our calculus is different: *We simply measure whether we are creating more than a dollar of value per dollar spent—and if that calculation is favorable, the more dollars we spend the happier I am* [emphasis added].[8]

At GEICO, for example, we enthusiastically spent $900 million last year on advertising to obtain policyholders who deliver us *no immediate profits*. If we could spend twice that amount productively, *we would happily do so though short-term results would be further penalized* [emphasis added].[9]

Buffett views these expenditures, which put pressure on reported earnings in the short term, as long-term value creating *investments*. In owner-related business principle number 6 of the Berkshire owner's manual, he states, "Accounting consequences do not influence our operating or capital-allocation decisions. When acquisition costs are similar, we much prefer to purchase $2 of earnings that is not reportable by us under standard accounting principles than to purchase $1 of earnings that is reportable."[10]

Noted value investor Thomas Russo has often talked about companies that have "the capacity to suffer," or the capacity to reinvest to build long-term competitive advantage at the cost of depressed short-term reported earnings. Usually, these companies have an ownership structure that keeps activist investors at bay. Usually, some individual or entity has enough control to adhere to a strategic path and build a long-term economic franchise without bothering too much about short-term profitability. Growing a business in a new market requires high upfront costs. These higher costs depress current earnings, which negatively affect the stock price in a shortsighted market. Most early upfront costs beyond production and distribution are put toward converting people into lifetime consumers as their income grows. Significant advertising and promotion is needed initially to maintain early market presence before a company sees growth in market share or profits. That process takes time and requires a lot of patience, which most management teams do not have. That nagging itch from shareholders, employees with stock options, and the management's net worth measurements cause companies to make a little compromise here, hold back on some needed investment there, to feed the earnings machine, pacify Wall Street, and prop up the stock price. Just scratch that itch a little bit. It will feel so much better.

But once scratched, does the itch ever go away? This is doubtful. Companies end up getting entangled in the endless game of managing analyst expectations. By bowing to these expectations, they become complicit, and then it is hard to exit.

They begin playing the earnings management game to avoid the short-term hit that's likely to follow. Or they think it could threaten their tenuous hold on strategic control. Or they fear they may lose their jobs if Wall Street declares that the earnings are in a secular decline. Management teams that are influenced easily by short-term-oriented shareholders, like an activist, tend to focus on activities that drive short-term results at the expense of long-term success.

In the most recent edition of the book *Valuation: Measuring and Managing the Value of Companies*, the authors write, "We've found, empirically, that long-term revenue growth—particularly organic revenue growth—is the most important driver of shareholder returns for companies with high returns on capital. We've also found that investments in research and development (R&D) correlate powerfully with positive long-term total returns to shareholders." At the same time, the book also notes that "in a survey of 400 chief financial officers, two Duke University professors found that fully 80 percent of the CFOs said they would reduce discretionary spending on potentially value-creating activities such as marketing and R&D in order to meet their short-term earnings targets."[11]

Most managers are not willing to suffer upfront pain. So they focus on short-term results, which contributes to underinvestment in brand building, R&D, and other long-term growth initiatives, which in turn eventually leads to long-term pain. They cut current costs to prop up current earnings, rather than spend more now to gain much more later. Consequently, they hurt their chances of long-term success.

It is important to align your personal values with that of your investment. Buffett and Munger are masters of practicing delayed gratification, and unless you, as a partner in Berkshire Hathaway, are equally willing to delay gratification, you will end up as a frustrated shareholder.

Buffett is happy to forgo current profits for GEICO to acquire additional policyholders, but he is also willing to increase expenditures and their concurrent charges against earnings if warranted, because he always focuses on total lifetime value of every customer. When a business has a high ratio of lifetime value to customer acquisition costs, it's rational to invest as much as possible in acquiring new customers. That is how Buffett thinks about advertising dollars spent on profitable customer acquisition by GEICO: in net present value terms.

In the insurance business, Berkshire Hathaway not only will happily forgo business and market share in the absence of profitable underwriting opportunities but also, in specific instances, will incur underwriting losses that hit the bottom line in the current year. In exchange, they acquire float that will produce income for many years in the future. What could be worse? All of the expenses are currently recognized, and all of the income will be recognized only in future years as the float produces investment earnings. This is delayed gratification in the extreme.

The question in all of these cases is this: Are you, as a shareholder, willing to give the same commitment to delayed gratification that Buffett and Munger practice? If not, you may want to revisit your participation in this security and in other securities with similar long-term-minded management teams. Keep in mind that only by resisting the marshmallows today will you receive the whole box of See's truffles tomorrow.

Investors generally overlook businesses that are doing things that will create significant incremental earnings one to two years from now because they don't want to wait that far out. Investors often shun businesses that are investing for the future and currently are suffering from low initial margins in those new initiatives (because capacity gets utilized only over time) because the earnings growth is back-ended. Even if they execute well, they will see little "reported" earnings growth for the next four to eight quarters and may even see a decline resulting from incremental depreciation and poor initial margins (because of low capacity utilization). Even if they are expected to experience an exponential jump in earnings growth after that, the stock markets generally do not initially increase the market value of these businesses. They do re-rate them, however, around the time when the earnings growth is clearly visible.

As investors, we get an edge over competition if we pick these companies and have the patience and conviction to hold them. Although these businesses are clearly undervalued on a longer-term basis, it is psychologically challenging to invest in them and even more so to hold on to them. These difficulties result in a lack of investors and the subsequent mispricing of these stocks, because the price discovery is weak when investors' attention on these stocks is low.

Capitalizing on businesses that operate on a long-term timeline of value creation is possible only if we operate with a long-term view as well. When you focus on long-term outcomes, expect to be frequently misunderstood in the short term. This is true not only in business and investing but in life and relationships as well. To invest in companies with "the capacity to suffer," we must be willing to suffer along with them. In other words, we need a high tolerance for short-term pain.

> You must buy on the way down. There is far more volume on the way down than on the way back up, and far less competition among buyers. It is almost always better to be too early than too late, but you must be prepared for price markdowns on what you buy.
> —Seth Klarman

A money manager must have the resilience to suffer through periodic bouts of underperformance. During 1999, Russo was invested in high-quality businesses like Nestlé, Heineken, and Unilever, among others. They were terribly out of favor relative to the speculative forces that were driving the market at the time. Russo's fund was down 2 percent for the year and the Dow was up 27 percent. During the early part of the following year, he was down 15 percent and the market was up by 30 percent. Russo was able to stay the course because he had the capacity to suffer. The same can be said of his investors at the time. This is why the success of an investment manager is as much about his or her ability to vet prospective clients as it is to say no to the wrong type of investment idea.

Equity investing is like growing a Chinese bamboo tree. We should have passion for the journey as well as patience and deep conviction after planting the seeds. The Chinese bamboo tree takes more than five years to start growing, but once it starts, it grows rapidly to eighty feet in less than six weeks. As prominent blogger Anshul Khare once aptly remarked, "In the initial years . . . compounding tests your patience and in later years, your bewilderment."[12]

Peter Lynch's investing experiences share a symbolic resemblance to the inspiring bamboo tree story: "The stocks that have been most rewarding to me have made their greatest gains in the third or fourth year I owned them."[13] Stocks can stay cheap for longer than we expect and then may be repriced much more quickly than we expect.

We should judge our businesses based on their operating results, not on the volatility of their stock prices. The stock market is focused on the latter, but investing success is based on the former. If the management team executes, the stock eventually follows. In fact, not getting immediate returns on our existing high-quality growth stocks builds antifragility. Patience plays a critical role during such times. For instance, Berkshire Hathaway's stock has delivered a CAGR of ~21% over the past 42 years (as of October 2019). But if you bought it in 1997, you would have had to wait five years before you saw any positive return on the stock. Similarly, investors in Adobe (which, as of October 2019, has delivered a CAGR of ~24% since its IPO in August 1986) had to undergo a period of thirteen years (2000–2013) during which they made nil return on its stock. Investing is hard. Very hard.

It pays to have a long-term view. But a long-term investment horizon must be married with an investment process willing to continually question the core investment thesis. Investors should exercise active patience, that is, diligently verifying their original investment thesis and doing nothing until something materially adverse or negative emerges. All too often, when a stock doesn't work out as planned, we call it a "long-term investment." When we spend a lot of time getting to know a business and its management team before investing, as we investors often do, it becomes difficult to change our mind. Investors don't want to feel like all that time was wasted learning things that they didn't act upon. We gain an advantage over time by staying intellectually honest while studying new ideas and existing holdings, and only investing in the few in which we think the odds are significantly in our favor. Investors tend to become complacent and stop questioning their existing holdings when their stock prices are going up. They resume analyzing in detail only when the prices start falling. Don't analyze your holdings only when they fall. Just because the stock price of an existing holding is going up doesn't necessarily mean that nothing negative is happening in its business.

An Investor's Biggest Edge

If you want to make money in Wall Street you must have the proper psychological attitude. No one expresses it better than Spinoza the philoso- pher . . . Spinoza said you must look at things in the aspect of eternity.

—Benjamin Graham

To make money in stocks, you need to have vision to see them, courage to buy them and patience to hold them. Patience is the rarest of the three.

—Thomas Phelps

An investor who can hold on in the face of all of the advice and temptations to ensure a profit by selling an existing position demonstrates a quality of mind quite out of the ordinary.

Embracing deferred gratification is what leads to the single biggest edge for an investor. Human nature makes it difficult to utilize this edge. This diffi- culty is the very reason the edge exists, and because human nature will never change, this edge is a durable one for those who possess the right temperament to capitalize on it. Bezos referred to the source of this edge when he said, "If everything you do needs to work on a three-year time horizon, then you're competing against a lot of people. But if you're willing to invest on a seven-year time horizon, you're now competing against a fraction of those people, because very few companies are willing to do that. Just by lengthening the time horizon, you can engage in endeavors that you could never otherwise pursue."[14]

The ability to have a long-term orientation is now a bigger advantage than ever before. Fifty years ago, the average holding period for stocks on the New York Stock Exchange was seven years. Today it is barely four months. The short-term mind-set that is all-pervasive in the market creates irrational buying and selling for all sorts of reasons that have everything to do with the short-term direction of the stock but nothing to do with the long-term value of the business. Because the financial community has an ever-increasing focus on the next quarter, a long- term orientation is a structural competitive advantage for an investor, and one that is likely to strengthen over time as we experience information, data, and noise overload driven by technological innovations and social media. The very fact that most of the talent and resources on Wall Street are focused on competing in the short-term arena of the next few quarters is what leads to a big opportunity for those who can look three to five years out and quietly consider the bigger picture. Such a long-term orientation helps identify the few key variables that really matter, and those variables are rarely (if ever) the consensus estimates for next quarter's EPS or the decimal point accuracy of the reported margins. Capitalizing on others' desire to avoid volatility is what makes this strategy work.

Clients tend to demand constant success and have little patience for short-term underperformance, and this means that fund managers risk losing both assets under management and their jobs (also known as "career risk") if they do not intensely focus on the next month, quarter, or perhaps year at the most. Such clients obviously don't understand that the only three types of investment performance are bad, net good but occasionally bad, and always good but fraudulent.

This impatient mind-set of clients and the resultant pressure on fund managers to beat their benchmarks every quarter lead to excessive churning of portfolios and high frictional costs. This, in addition to high expense ratios, causes most active fund managers to fail to beat their respective benchmarks. S&P Dow Jones Indices, the "de facto scorekeeper of the active versus passive investing debate," in its *SPIVA U.S. 2018 Scorecard*, highlighted this fact (table 11.1).[15]

In other words, over a period of fifteen years, only one in twelve large-cap managers, one in fourteen mid-cap managers, and one in thirty-one

TABLE 11.1 **Percentage of U.S. equity funds outperformed by benchmarks, 2018**

Report 1: Percentage of U.S. Equity Funds Outperformed by Benchmarks

Fund category	Comparison index	1-Year (%)	3-Year (%)	5-Year (%)	10-Year (%)	15-Year (%)
All Domestic Funds	S&P Composite 1500	68.83	81.49	88.13	84.49	88.97
All Large-Cap Funds	S&P 500	64.49	78.98	82.14	85.14	91.62
All Mid-Cap Funds	S&P Mid Cap 400	45.64	74.29	79.88	88.03	92.71
All Small-Cap Funds	S&P Small Cap 600	68.45	84.35	89.40	85.67	96.73

Source: Aye Soe, Berlinda Liu, and Hamish Preston, *SPIVA U.S. 2018 Scorecard*, S&P Dow Jones Indices, Year-End 2018, https://www.spindices.com/documents/spiva/spiva-us-year-end-2018.pdf, https://www.spglobal.com/_assets/documents/corporate/us-spiva-report-11-march-2019.pdf.

small-cap managers were able to outperform their benchmark index. Institutions with access to the best brains and talent deliver such mediocre performance because they suffer from an obsessive desire to avoid volatility.

The significant importance of staying power that comes from a patient investor base with a long-term mind-set similar to that of the money manager is brought out by the highly successful but volatile track record, over the long term, of John Maynard Keynes (table 11.2) and Charlie Munger (table 11.3) during their fund management years.

As long as the odds are in our favor and we're not risking the whole company on one throw of the dice or anything close to it, we don't mind volatility in results. What we want are the favorable odds.

—Charlie Munger

TABLE 11.2 Investing track record of John Maynard Keynes, 1928–1945

	Annual Percentage Change	
Year	Chest Fund (%)	UK Market (%)
1928	0.0	0.1
1929	0.8	6.6
1930	−32.4	−20.3
1931	−24.6	−25.0
1932	44.8	−5.8
1933	35.1	21.5
1934	33.1	−0.7
1935	44.3	5.3
1936	56.0	10.2
1937	8.5	−0.5
1938	−40.1	−16.1
1939	12.9	−7.2
1940	−15.6	−12.9
1941	33.5	12.5
1942	−0.9	0.8
1943	53.9	15.6
1944	14.5	5.4
1945	14.6	0.8
Average Return	13.2	−0.5
Standard Deviation	29.2	12.4

Source: John F. Wasik, Keynes's Way to Wealth (New York: McGraw-Hill, 2013).

TABLE 11.3 Investing track record of Charlie Munger, 1962–1975

Year	Munger Partnership (%)	Dow Jones (%)	S&P 500 (%)
1962	30.1	−7.6	−8.8
1963	71.7	20.6	22.6
1964	49.7	18.7	16.4
1965	8.4	14.2	12.4
1966	12.4	−15.8	−10.0
1967	56.2	19.0	23.8
1968	40.4	7.7	10.8
1969	28.3	−11.6	−8.2
1970	−0.1	9.7	3.6
1971	25.4	9.8	14.2
1972	8.3	18.2	18.8
1973	−31.9	−13.1	−14.3
1974	−31.5	−23.1	−25.9
1975	73.2	44.4	37.0
Total Return	1156.7	96.2	102.6
Annual Return	19.8	4.9	5.2
Volatility	33.0	18.5	17.7

Source: Janet Lowe, *Damn Right* (Hoboken, NJ: Wiley, 2003).

Dealing with this interim volatility is the price of admission, but it is one that few market participants are willing to pay, and that is precisely why having a patient mind-set, focusing on long-term compound annual growth rate (CAGR) instead of yearly returns, and embracing volatility leads to significant financial rewards. This is time arbitrage in action.

One of the fertile hunting grounds in the markets for practicing time arbitrage is in the area of qualified institutional placement (QIP). A company's stock price performance is usually negative for many months immediately following a QIP. This is because the prevailing institutional demand for the company's stock gets absorbed in the QIP. Management teams drive up the stock price before the QIP by promising the moon to investors during their road show presentations. As a result, for many months after the QIP, the stock does not react to any good news, because it has already been discounted. Another point that triangulates the J-curve is that it takes time for the newly infused capital to earn the same return on equity (ROE) as the seasoned invested capital. As a result, the lower post-QIP ROE imposes an additional drag on the stock price.

Invest in businesses where you can play the long-term game with like-minded people. Investing is a long-term game. The more time you give it, the lower the odds of disappointment. As of September 2019, the range of stock market returns as measured by the S&P 500 in any given year since 1950 (using data supplied by JP Morgan research) has been from +47 percent to −37 percent, but over any 5-year period that range is +28 percent to −3 percent.[16] For any given 20-year period, the range of returns contracts still further to +17 percent to +6 percent. In short, since 1950, there has never been any 20-year period when investors did not make at least 6 percent per year in the stock market. Although past performance is no guarantee of future returns, history shows that the longer the time frame, the greater are the odds of earning a satisfactory return.

> The longer you can extend your time horizon, the less competitive the game becomes, because most of the world is engaged over a very short time frame.
> —William Browne

Keynes referred to our tendency to get swept up by short-term thinking as animal spirits, "a spontaneous urge to action rather than inaction, and not as the outcome of a weighted average of quantitative benefits multiplied by quantitative probabilities."[17] Markets often overreact to negative but short-term company-specific events that have a negligible impact on long-term intrinsic value. Critical thinking is always difficult, but it's almost impossible when we are scared. There's no room for facts when our minds are occupied by fear. Once fear about one aspect gets into the minds of people, they can't see other things some distance away. (As an illustrative example, one should study why Bandhan Bank's stock was locked in a 20 percent lower circuit on October 1, 2018.) During those times, focusing on the long term provides a behavioral edge and helps investors avoid making hurried mistakes when the amygdala in their brain triggers a fight-or-flight response. (We are emotional first and logical second. We are designed that way. Automatic processing originates in the evolutionarily older parts of the brain, also known as the "lizard brain," whose constituents include the cerebellum, the basal ganglia, and the amygdala. The deliberative mind operates out of the prefrontal cortex, which is part of the frontal lobe.) In his book *Seeking Wisdom*, Peter Bevelin writes, "It is a natural tendency to act on impulse—to use emotion before reason. The behaviors that were critical for survival and reproduction in our evolutionary history still apply today."[18]

Hyperbolic Discounting

Neuroscience has shown that the human brain processes value over different time periods inconsistently. We are short-term demanding and long-term inattentive. Our brain is hardwired for immediate rewards. Since people first began investing, they have been searching for a magic formula for instant wealth. It is human nature to seek instant gratification, and the market is dominated by individuals who simply do not want to wait for much larger rewards several years down the line. As a result, many investors end up engaging in "hyperbolic discounting," heavily discounting the distant but large cash flows of high-quality businesses by applying high equity risk premiums, and they end up with much lower estimates of intrinsic business value than otherwise would have been the case. Consequently, even though those businesses may be fairly valued in the short term, they end up becoming grossly undervalued on a long-term basis. Professor Sanjay Bakshi illustrated this anomaly in his seminal October 2013 white paper on how quality businesses frequently end up getting mispriced by the market.[19] (Any stock that has compounded at 15 percent to 20 percent for decades was, by definition, undervalued by the market for long periods of time.)

The Way to Wealth

> *Investing is forgoing consumption now in order to have the ability to consume more at a later date.*
>
> —Warren Buffett

The path to lasting wealth is deferred gratification, savings, and compound interest. Develop the habit of saving in such a way that you enjoy your present reasonably well and also ensure a bright future tomorrow. Save enough so that you are able to live a better lifestyle in the future than you are living today. Reducing your desires has the same effect as increasing your wealth, but with no downside risk. Being content in life and having fewer needs enables you to be happy in any situation. And that is real wealth and freedom. It is why Epictetus said, "Self-sufficiency is the greatest of all wealth. Wealth consists not in having great possessions, but in having few wants."

When you save and invest prudently, the benefits are deferred—but crucially, they are also compounded. The U.S. retirement system greatly rewards those who defer gratification. Claiming social security at age seventy leads to 76 percent higher inflation-protected benefits compared with claiming at age sixty-two.

Resist instant gratification. Embrace delayed gratification.

> Wealth, in fact, is what you don't see. It's the cars not purchased. The diamonds not bought. The renovations postponed, the clothes forgone and the first-class upgrade declined. It's assets in the bank that haven't yet been converted into the stuff you see.
>
> —Morgan Housel

Simple steps can help you cut your costs. You can cook your own food, buy goods on discount, turn down the heat during the winter and wear a sweater at home, and eliminate any spending not 100 percent necessary. Learn to cherish frugality. It will be the steppingstone to your financial freedom. I feel proud of the fact that I did not buy a single expensive item during my first three years of living in America, and even after getting a high-paying job, I used to walk to and from my office every day (except the snowy winter days) to save money on cab rides. During my initial years in the United States, as a hotel clerk working for minimum wage (I used to check-in guests, help them with their luggage, and occasionally wash dishes in the kitchen), I bought used books to save money. Today, I cherish those memories.

During his interview with Jason Zweig, in September 2014, Munger remarked that few people have the deferred gratification gene: "It's waiting that helps you as an investor, and a lot of people just can't stand to wait. *If you didn't get the deferred-gratification gene, you've got to work very hard to overcome that* [emphasis added]."[20]

Why did Munger say this?

To understand the deep reason behind it, we need to travel back many centuries in time. In his book *Sapiens*, Yuval Harari explains the "gorging gene" theory:

> We need to delve into the hunter-gatherer world that shaped us, *the world that we subconsciously still inhabit.*
>
> Why, for example, do people gorge on high-calorie food that is doing little good to their bodies? Today's affluent societies are in the throes of a plague of obesity, which is rapidly spreading to developing countries. It's a puzzle why we binge on the sweetest and greasiest food we can find, until we consider the eating habits of our forager forebears.
>
> In the savannahs and forests they inhabited, high-calorie sweets were extremely rare and food in general was in short supply. A typical forager 30,000 years ago had access to only one type of sweet food—ripe fruit. If a Stone Age woman came across a tree groaning with figs, the most sensible thing to do was to eat as many of them as she could on the spot, before the local baboon band picked the tree bare. The instinct to gorge on high-calorie food was *hard-wired into our genes* [emphasis added].
>
> Today we may be living in high-rise apartments with over-stuffed refrigerators, but our DNA still thinks we are in the savannah. That's what makes us spoon down an entire tub of Ben & Jerry's when we find one in the freezer and wash it down with a jumbo Coke.[21]

All specific human cravings are modern manifestations of broad evolutionary desires. The deep-rooted desire to gorge on all available sweet fruit out of fear of losing it to the local baboon remains within us even today. We gorge on the food we know is bad for us and chase the stocks we understand may be very risky for us. This is because we fear missing out on the instant gratification we may get from consuming and buying them.

If we are not born with the deferred gratification gene, is there no way to inculcate it?

As it turns out, this problem has a simple solution.

It's simple but not easy.

It requires a tremendous amount of patience, consistency, dedication, and a deep conviction in the power of compounding.

One Small Step at a Time

One Small Step Can Change Your Life: The Kaizen Way by Robert Maurer is one of my favorite books. It talks about the power of compounding small daily positive actions. This small book talks about the big idea of *kaizen*, which is Japanese for "taking small steps for continual improvement."

The difference between those who fail and those who succeed is the courage to act—repeatedly. Most people, when faced with change, will feel at least some element of fear. Very often that fear can get in the way of actually making the change. The idea of kaizen is to make such small changes in your life that your brain doesn't even realize that you are trying to change and therefore doesn't get in the way. Kaizen is a neat mental hack that helps us bypass our brain's fear response.

In his book, Maurer talks about six strategies that can help us bring about big changes in our life over a period of time:

1. Asking small questions
2. Thinking small thoughts
3. Taking small actions
4. Solving small problems
5. Giving small rewards
6. Recognizing small moments

Start Small . . . Really Small . . . Even Smaller

Usually, if we try to tackle a big life change all at once—like completely cutting out sugar or learning to invest in the stock market or inculcating a reading habit—it might work for a while, but we will give up soon.

This is because the big changes trigger the brain's subconscious fears, which end up hindering us.

So, taking small, incremental steps is the way to get past that and succeed.

For instance, when it comes to investing in the stock market, we overwhelm ourselves with big questions like "How can I pick the best stock for my portfolio?" or "How will I ever become a successful investor when others have failed?"

Instead, use kaizen and focus on small questions like "What little step could I take today toward learning how to pick stocks effectively?"

If you want to form the habit of reading one annual report a day, start with reading one page of an annual report a day, then increase it to two pages, then three, and so on.

Kaizen is how I learned to use the treadmill effectively in the gym when I first started trying to lose weight. The very thought of briskly walking non-stop for thirty minutes on high-incline mode seemed impossible to me, and

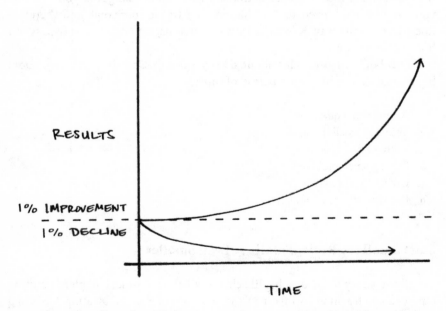

1% BETTER EVERY DAY

1% worse every day for one year. $0.99^{365} = 00.03$

1% better every day for one year. $1.01^{365} = 37.78$

FIGURE 11.1 The effects of small habits compound over time. For example, if you can get just 1 percent better each day, you'll end up with results that are nearly 37 times better after one year.

Source: James Clear, *Atomic Habits* (New York: Avery, 2018), used by permission of the author.

I did not want to even try. But then I started with slow walking on low incline for five minutes a day, then six minutes at a slightly faster speed on a slightly higher incline after some time, then seven minutes at a slightly faster speed on a slightly higher incline, and so on. Eventually, I reached my target duration, speed, and incline level.

The idea is to make it simple, habitual, and fun. And nobody can say they don't have an extra minute a day, right?

You see, big, bold actions like lofty New Year's resolutions often get us initial results, but they don't take into account things like fear or mental resistance.

The smaller steps, however, get us to the desired goal because they can be incorporated more easily into our daily life. Small steps make delaying gratification easier and sustainable.

So, whether it is quitting a bad habit or forming a good one, the idea is to start small, very small, and then to build on it over time (figure 11.1). As the saying goes, "If we are facing in the right direction, all we have to do is keep on walking."

In the challenging journey of pursuing financial independence, a supportive partner plays a crucial role. Delaying gratification means sacrifice, and investors' spouses tend to embrace their partner's dream as their own. It is these shared long-term goals that keep their home warm and comfortable during any of those initial tough years. I have nothing but utmost respect and admiration for such genuine relationships of care, affection, and true love.

SECTION III

COMMON
STOCK INVESTING

CHAPTER 12

BUILDING EARNING POWER THROUGH A BUSINESS OWNERSHIP MIND-SET

Investing is most intelligent when it is most businesslike.

—Benjamin Graham

Warren Buffett has shared great insights on having a business ownership mind-set in his 1977 letter to shareholders:

Our experience has been that pro-rata portions of truly outstanding businesses sometimes sell in the securities markets at very large discounts from the prices they would command in negotiated transactions involving entire companies. Consequently, bargains in business ownership, which simply are not available directly through corporate acquisition, can be obtained indirectly through stock ownership. When prices are appropriate, we are willing to take very large positions in selected companies, not with any intention of taking control and not foreseeing sell-out or merger, but with the expectation that excellent business results by corporations will translate over the long term into correspondingly excellent market value and dividend results for owners, minority as well as majority....

We invested $10.9 million in Capital Cities Communications during 1977....

Capital Cities possesses both extraordinary properties and extraordinary management. And these management skills extend equally to operations and employment of corporate capital. To purchase, directly, properties such as Capital Cities owns would cost in the area of twice our cost of purchase via the stock market, and direct ownership would offer no important advantages to us. While control would give us the opportunity—and the responsibility—to manage operations and corporate resources, we would not be able to provide management in either of those respects equal to that now in place. In effect, we can obtain a better management result through noncontrol than control. This is an unorthodox view, but one we believe to be sound.[1]

Once a strong foundation is created for a business, owners don't work for money. Rather, money works for them. As an investor, your money is working for you 24/7. You are becoming wealthier with each passing second, alongside the increasing intrinsic value of your businesses. Tick, tick, tick.

An investor builds earnings power through a business ownership mind-set. Investing in publicly listed businesses is a great way to passively reap most of the major benefits of running one's own business, without being exposed to the disproportionate risks emanating from the usual vagaries of directly running a business. Such a passive approach offers multiple benefits:

1.   **The possibility of partly owning a business with a small investment corpus.** For a person coming from the middle class, capital is usually a big limitation to starting a business. This is not to say that if a person has a great idea, he or she will not find the needed capital to fund it. Often, however, this is the most challenging part of starting a business.

Suppose someone wants to set up a small-scale chemical factory in the state of West Bengal, India. The minimum initial equity contribution required may be of the tune of approximately INR 10 million, or about US$140,000. This might mean investing one's entire life savings in a single venture, which may or may not work out. Alternatively, that person could invest just a fraction of this amount and own part of Vinati Organics, the world's largest manufacturer of isobutyl benzene (IBB) and 2-acrylamido 2-methylpropane sulfonic acid (ATBS). It would take years, if not decades, to replicate its global market leadership from scratch. If one looks at return on capital employed, Vinati generates returns in excess of 30 percent. Thus, even with a smaller ticket size, an investor could generate better returns on capital employed than could have been obtained, in most cases, from a privately owned chemical factory.

2.   **Minimizing risk through diversification.** An investor can enjoy part ownership of ten to fifteen of the best businesses in existence at any time. Diversification reduces the risk of losing capital entirely, which could happen, for any unfortunate or unforeseen reason, if you own only one business. Because

one's capital is spread across various businesses, this mitigates idiosyncratic (individual company–specific) risk. No matter how well you may know your stocks, every business has unknown risks. Few can know about a Satyam, an Enron, or a Ricoh India in advance. Diversification also protects investors from the risk of ruin as a result of a natural calamity or any other significantly adverse development in one or two businesses.

Take the example of the April 2015 earthquake in Nepal. Had I been directly running and managing only a single business operating in that location, I could have been potentially wiped out, or it would have taken a long time to recoup my losses in the form of general insurance proceeds (if the business was covered by it at all). In contrast, even though the plant belonging to one of my portfolio companies, Hester Biosciences, was disrupted by that earthquake, I was able to comfortably weather the storm, because at the time, my portfolio consisted of many other businesses that were not affected at all. Sometimes, factors like currency depreciation or rising interest rates hurt some of our portfolio companies while benefiting others, so that the overall impact is muted. Most notably, if we invest in a diversified portfolio of good businesses, then most of the time the tailwinds pushing a few businesses forward will compensate for the headwinds pushing back the others, thus protecting us from permanent loss of capital.

3. **Access to top-notch managers to run the business.** When investing in the stock market, an investor gains access to top-notch managerial talent free of cost. Investors are given an opportunity to ride in the passenger seat next to people who have complementary skills that are specific to them, and this has significant value. (This is also known as "sidecar investing.") As an investor in the company, these skills are made available to us at zero cost, but the benefits we derive can be enormous. In contrast, when running a private business, access to people with such skills can be prohibitively expensive, and hence the odds of making extraordinary returns are significantly lower.

4. **Buying business ownership on your own terms.** This is what Graham was referring to when he talked about an investor's "basic advantage." It is important to choose our battles wisely, and we should choose those for which the odds of winning are clearly in our favor. Life often does not give us an opportunity to choose our battles, but the stock market gives us the invaluable flexibility of choosing not only the battle we want to fight but also, in many cases, the battleground and the timing of the fight as well.

Human beings are a messy living compilation of a multitude of cognitive and behavioral biases, especially when it comes to matters related to money. The auction-driven nature of the stock market, which is a heady cocktail of swirling human emotions and sentiments, makes it the perfect place to look for pockets of periodic irrational behavior, which is sometimes extreme to the point of being ludicrous. Greed and fear are always present in abundance in the market, and the most recent marginal opinion, not long-term intrinsic value, determines the present stock price. This sets a perfect stage for getting incredible bargains that no private business owner in a sane state of mind would ever offer.

For a businessperson, the stock market is the best place to look at buying businesses at substantial discounts or selling them at staggering premiums. The biggest advantage for an individual investor is the option to calmly wait until identifying a business that is available at a significant discount to intrinsic value. In a private transaction, this simply is not possible. Just imagine what would happen if you offered to buy a growing and highly profitable business at less than the amount of cash sitting on the books. You most likely would be thrown out the door. As an investor in the stock market, however, you may get opportunities to invest in such cash bargains during one's lifetime.

5.   **Opportunity to shoot rare, fast-moving elephants.** That which is rare is considered valuable. In the past, I gained access through the stock market to Bharat Financial Inclusion's low-cost leadership in India's microfinance industry, Eicher Motors's coveted Royal Enfield franchise, Can Fin Homes's pristine asset quality, HEG's strongly guarded proprietary technology in graphite electrodes, Bhansali Engineering Polymers's leadership position in India's acrylonitrile butadiene styrene (ABS) market, and CCL Products's deeply entrenched relationships with coffee makers worldwide. Today, the stock market has given me part ownership of Bajaj Finance's, CreditAccess Grameen's, SBI Cards's, and Aavas Financier's deep expertise in consumer finance, rural microfinance, digital payments, and affordable housing finance, respectively; Bandhan Bank's, AU Small Finance Bank's, and Ujjivan Small Finance Bank's emerging banking franchises; PSP Projects's strong project execution skills; HDFC Life's product innovation capabilities; HDFC Asset Management Company's robust free cash flow generation; Vinati Organics's global market leadership in ATBS and IBB; Dixon Technologies's economies of scale in consumer electronics manufacturing; and Hester Biosciences's global low-cost advantage in Peste des petits ruminants vaccines.

6.   **The invaluable flexibility of a quick and smooth exit.** Even if you are running a sole proprietorship, it takes a lot of time to complete all the closing formalities and to wind up the business. The process is far more cumbersome if it is a private limited company. All of the compliance requirements must be met until every account is settled and money has been distributed to all stakeholders. If the business involves more than one partner, the matter is further complicated if any of them want to continue the business while

you want to exit. When investing in a stock, however, even though you are a part owner of the business, you can exit your entire holding (for any urgent or personal reason) with the click of a mouse, and the entire sale proceeds will be deposited in your bank account in a matter of days. This flexibility and ease of exit is extremely useful, when, in your judgment, the business is going downhill with no turnaround in sight, the management shows a lack of integrity, or you simply have found a much more profitable alternative in which to invest.

Stocks Closely Resemble Bonds

In a 1977 *Fortune* article, Buffett explained how stocks closely resemble bonds.[2] An understanding of the finer nuances of his teachings on this topic enable us, as part owners of a business and one of the two primary providers of capital (bondholders and shareholders), to appreciate the subtle similarities between the two components of enterprise value (i.e., debt and equity).

1. **Coupon.** A company's equity coupon is the owner earnings it generates. Our job as investors is to ascribe a value to those coupons. A portion of the coupon is handed out as a dividend. The investor is free to do what he wants with that cash, but the remaining portion of the company's earnings is retained within. The amount of earnings a company retains from year to year is left to the company's discretion. Earnings retention is one of the lesser appreciated marvels of capitalism. It provides anyone with a brokerage account and some patience cheap access to the productive power of a business (or an entire market economy, if investing in a total market index fund).

2. **Maturity.** Stocks are meant to be perpetual and do not have an obvious maturity date. Businesses are going concerns, which means they are intended to last forever. Creative destruction, however, has ensured that few companies in history have been able to survive forever. In fact, most companies have extinguished their stock well before infinity. But the timing of these events can never be known in advance with certainty. So, although businesses exist under the assumption of operating forever, the reality is that their stocks have uncertain maturity dates.

3. **Par value.** The par value of a stock is the book value of its equity. This is an accounting value that approximates the value of a business to its shareholders if it were to stop operations immediately—that is, it does not account for future growth. It is the difference between what a company owns (assets) and what that company owes to others (liabilities). Buffett has cautioned investors not to confuse book value with intrinsic value: "Of course, it's per-share intrinsic value, not book value, that counts. Book value is an accounting term that measures the

capital, including retained earnings, that has been put into a business. Intrinsic value is a present-value estimate of the cash that can be taken out of a business during its remaining life. At most companies, the two values are unrelated."[3]

Buffett's insights are valuable because they remind us that stocks are not just pieces of paper but fractional ownership stakes in real businesses. They are a claim to a piece of a business's profits, which grows as the business invests in productive activities, executes well, and generates returns.

The sheer delight that we as passionate investors experience whenever any of our portfolio companies signs up a new client, wins a landmark contract, completes the execution of an order before the stipulated time, embarks on a promising expansion, or receives recognition for corporate excellence is something that cannot be described. It has to be felt from within.

Be passionate about the business but dispassionate about the stock. Celebrate the big successes of your businesses and reflect on failures. A true feeling of ownership gives an investor the conviction to hold. When you think like a business owner, you no longer view stocks as pieces of paper or buy them with "target prices" in mind. Instead, you view stocks as part ownership in a business and you want to savor the journey alongside the promoters. As companies grow larger and more profitable, their stockholders share in the increased profits and dividends. Invest for the long term. Live fully today.

Every day, millions of hardworking people around the world are doing great things at so many companies.

As investors, we are thankful.

CHAPTER 13

INVESTING BETWEEN THE LINES

Perhaps 90 percent of our shares are owned by investors for whom Berkshire is their largest security holding, very often far and away the largest. Many of these owners are willing to spend a significant amount of time with the annual report, and we attempt to provide them with the same information we would find useful if the roles were reversed.

—Warren Buffett

When we start researching an investment idea, the first thing we want to know is whether the business is sound and profitable. We read the company's annual report for numbers like net income, debt, cash flow, profitability, ratios, and the like. We assume that these "audited" numbers must be accurate and authentic. But even Enron's and Satyam's numbers were "certified" by auditors, and both of them ended up as big accounting scandals and corporate frauds. (In general, be extra diligent with firms that have convoluted structures, such as a large number of subsidiaries and cross-holdings.)

As an investor, how do we know that the management is telling us the truth? And how does an honest CEO communicate with the shareholders in a manner that establishes trust?

Laura Rittenhouse, in her book *Investing Between the Lines*, attempts to answer these questions.[1] She offers clues to separate the facts from the fluff in annual reports, corporate communications, and quarterly earnings calls.

Through the ideas in her book, Rittenhouse helps us cut through the noise and enables us to better decode CEO communication.

Capital Stewardship

If we do the right things, the stock price will take care of itself, and our share-holders will be rewarded.

—Jim Sinegal

Companies that are focused on stewarding investor capital tend to deliver superior returns over time. Rittenhouse writes, "As an investor, your goal is to find businesses which are run by leaders who steward capital and are accountable for their words and actions. Capital Stewardship reveals whether a CEO's actions are based on attitudes of being entrusted with or entitled to investor capital."

To check for the presence of capital stewardship, look for clues related to the following topics in shareholder letters, annual reports, and other executive communications:

- **Capital discipline.** CEOs who are good capital allocators typically offer commentary about returns on investment, on invested capital, and on assets. The strength or weakness of a CEO's capital discipline is expressed in the commentary about book value or market value. Ask these questions while reading the annual report commentary: Is capital allocation discussed explicitly and rationally? Are words consistent with actions? Are actions and words consistent over time?
- **Cash flow.** Recurring cash flows are crucial for long-term sustainability of a business. This is why many investors like to invest in stocks of small-ticket consumer nondurables, which are purchased almost as a matter of habit and whose consumption cannot be indefinitely delayed. (For this very reason, within cyclical industries, consumable-oriented businesses enjoy higher valuations than capex-oriented ones, which have a long replacement cycle.) Given its importance, investors might expect every shareholder letter to include commentary on operating and free cash flow. But most letters fail to report on this aspect. Look for CEOs who place a great deal of emphasis on cash flows and communicate about it in a clear manner. Also look at a company's balance sheet and cash flow statement to see whether the cash flow numbers listed in those financial statements match with the numbers in the CEO's communication.

- **Operating and financial goals.** Meaningful financial goal statements indicate that a CEO is serious about efficient capital allocation. Instead of stating goals as platitudes, such as "our goal is to delight all our customers," effective CEOs provide meaningful context around quantifiable goal statements. Ask yourself: What are the CEO's incentives? How does the CEO get paid? Is there a return-on-investment component? Look for CEOs and insiders who have low salaries and high stock ownership, as they get rich only when shareholders get rich.

CEOs who publish meaningful financial and operating goals and focus on capital discipline, cash flow, and balance sheet health are exemplars of capital stewardship.

Candor

Candor is the language of trust, and it means being authentic with your words. As Warren Buffett puts it, "We will be candid in our reporting to you, emphasizing the pluses and minuses important in appraising business value. Our guideline is to tell you the business facts that we would want to know if our positions were reversed. We owe you no less."[2]

Buffett exemplifies the pinnacle of candor in CEO communication with shareholders. He quantifies not only the accounting cost of his errors but also their opportunity cost. In his 2014 letter, he wrote:

> Berkshire paid $433 million for Dexter and, rather promptly, its value went to zero. GAAP [generally accepted accounting principles] accounting, however, doesn't come close to recording the magnitude of my error. The fact is that I gave Berkshire stock to the sellers of Dexter rather than cash, and the shares I used for the purchase are now worth about $5.7 billion. As a financial disaster, this one deserves a spot in the Guinness Book of World Records.[3]

The easiest way to test for candor is to invert the problem and test for the absence of candor. How can we test for the absence of candor in an executive communication? Rittenhouse writes:

> When Rittenhouse Rankings analyzes a shareholder letter, we start reading with a red pencil or pen in hand and use it to underline clichés such as "employees are our greatest assets," "our future is bright," "advancing momentum," and "we aim to create shareholder value." This kind of meaningless jargon and platitudes diminishes our understanding of the business and our trust in the leadership.

When we finish coding a communication, we look back at the pages. If we see more red than black ink on the pages, we put a company on probation. We dig further to examine the company's accounting and its marketplace claims. This was certainly true of Enron, whose 2000 shareholder letter offered the following linguistic anesthesia:

"Our talented people, global presence, financial strength and massive market knowledge have created our sustainable and unique businesses. EnronOnline will accelerate their growth. We plan to leverage all of these competitive advantages to create significant value for our shareholders."

In one short paragraph, Enron introduced six popular CEO clichés: Talented people, Global presence, Market knowledge, Financial strength, Leverage competitive advantages, Significant value for our shareholders.

Each "competitive advantage" is an important business concept, but so many generalities are meaningless to the reader. Not only do these clichés fail to inspire trust, but they should cause a prudent investor to wonder what the company might be hiding.

Investors who read between the lines and look for the absence of candor can spot companies like this that may be headed for trouble.[4]

It's not that the content CEOs write in their letters and other communication is difficult to understand. Sometimes the content is deliberately written in a way not to be understood. "Restructuring" is one of the more abused words we hear from CEOs who have made highly expensive blunders in the past and now want to get back on track only to make more such blunders in the future. "One-time" restructuring expenses often turn out to be perpetual. Sadly, investors never receive even a small apology from the CEOs and executives responsible for such costly mistakes.

Most annual reports and other such financial disclosures are written not to inform readers but rather to protect the provider of the information. That's because most issuers of equities, debt, and other financing instruments are apprehensive that, if they communicated in plain simple English, someone might actually understand just what was at stake. Just imagine if an investment banker said, or an initial public offering (IPO) prospectus read, "You could lose all your money if you buy this."

Rittenhouse has coined an acronym for the absence of candor: FOG, or "fact-deficient, obfuscating generalities." Investors who find a fogged-over communication (presence of clichés, jargon, and hyperbole) need to ask, "Does the CEO not understand the business, or does he or she *not* want owners to understand it?"

When we read something full of jargon and clichés, we often presume that we are not smart enough to understand it, and we underappreciate our personal judgment. Rittenhouse writes, "Is it because we fear our vulnerability in relation to leaders whom we must trust? To imagine that they would injure us to advance their self-interest is disturbing, even frightening. Instead, we choose to doubt ourselves."

If you feel that you are not smart enough to understand what's written in the corporate communications, then don't worry. This is not your problem. It is the management's responsibility to write the letter in a manner that can be easily comprehended by the average reader.

To evaluate the quality of the management, you don't need privileged access to insider information. The secret is right in front of you—in black and white—in the words of every shareholder letter, annual report, and other corporate correspondence. Once you learn how to read between the lines in the corporate communications, you can make a better assessment about management quality and their intentions.

Remember, analyzing words is just as important as analyzing numbers.

CHAPTER 14

THE SIGNIFICANT ROLE OF CHECKLISTS IN DECISION-MAKING

Checklist routines avoid a lot of errors. You should have all this elementary [worldly] wisdom and then you should go through a mental checklist in order to use it. There is no other procedure in the world that will work as well.

—Charlie Munger

A fair amount of research has been done in the past that suggests the immense value of checklists. We tend to be overconfident about our capabilities. A checklist can remind us that we are not infallible, that we do make mistakes, and that we should not be too sure about our decisions.

Use the following general principles when devising a checklist:

- Good checklists are brief, precise, efficient, and easy to use even under difficult conditions. They do not try to spell out everything and they provide reminders of only the critical and most important steps.
- Bad checklists are vague, imprecise, too long, hard to use, and try to spell out every single step.
- Checklists should be confirmed: perform jobs/tasks from memory and experience, but then stop, run the checklist, and confirm that everything was done correctly.

- Checklists should be reviewed: carry out tasks as they are checked off.
- Checklists should include some deal-breaker questions as well as other questions that may require trade-offs.

Investing in stocks is not as complex as doing a medical surgery or flying an airplane, but checklists still play an important role. In one of her past interviews, Alice Schroeder discussed Warren Buffett's use of "disqualifying features" as one of his checklist items:

> Typically, and this is not well understood, his way of thinking is that there are *disqualifying features* to an investment. So he rifles through and as soon as you hit one of those it's done. Doesn't like the CEO, forget it. Too much tail risk, forget it. Low-margin business, forget it. *Many people would try to see whether a balance of other factors made up for these things. He doesn't analyze from A to Z; it's a time-waster* [emphasis added].[1]

Charlie Munger has often been credited with popularizing the use of checklists in investing. In *Poor Charlie's Almanack*, Peter Kaufman summarized Munger's investing principles (risk, independence, preparation, intellectual humility, analytic rigor, allocation, patience, decisiveness, change, and focus) in a checklist form. This is a must-read for all investors.

It's not the answers that make you good in the investing business; it's the questions you ask. Ask the right questions; you'll get valuable answers. Do the initial groundwork. A prudent investor never purchases ownership in a company without conducting the necessary due diligence. Learn about the company and its competitors (both listed and unlisted) from company websites, filings, and information on the Internet. Read the past ten years' worth of annual reports, proxies, notes and schedules to the financial statements, and management discussion and analysis (check for changes in tone and industry outlook) and observe the recent trends in insider shareholding.

Accounting is the language of business, and a basic understanding of its fundamentals is essential for investors. Because accounting is a double-entry system, even a false entry needs to be matched by an offsetting number. If one of the three accounting statements—income statement, cash flow, and balance sheet—is falsified, traces will show up in the other two. Everything must add up arithmetically, even if the company is fraudulently misclassifying key figures. A simple triangulation exercise will help you spot accounting shenanigans in time. For example, if net income receives too much attention, study the inventories and receivables on the balance sheet. When analyzing the quarterly or semiannual results of any company, investors always should first check the balance sheet for any red flag items before even taking a look at the income statement.

After you have concluded the initial groundwork, study the following parameters in a checklist fashion.

1. Income Statement (Profit and Loss Account) Analysis

Sales growth. The higher sales growth is, the better (provided it is profitable). Over the long term, stock returns are highly correlated to sales growth as margins revert to the mean. Organic growth driven by internal accruals is most desirable. Be cautious of high growth driven primarily by big-ticket acquisitions.

Gross profit margin. Focus on the trend over the years. If it is fluctuating a lot in a cyclical manner, then it means that the company does not have pricing power over its customers and is not able to pass on increases in raw material cost. On the contrary, if it is high *and* stable or improving over the years, then the company in question may have an economic moat. Dig deeper in such cases (as well as when a company's operating margins are much higher than that of its industry peers).

Interest income (usually shown as "other income"). Check the cash and investments figure on the balance sheet. If the interest income is not at least equal to the bank's fixed deposit return, then analyze it deeper to see where the company has invested its cash.

Interest expense. A low-interest expense or a high-interest coverage ratio in isolation should never be taken at face value. Always check whether the company has been *capitalizing* the interest cost. Multiply the total debt figure by the prevailing rate of interest for similarly rated corporations and compare that figure with the total interest expense number used in the calculation of the interest coverage ratio.

Employee cost. In fraudulent companies, the reported figure may be grossly out of line when evaluated against the existing number of employees stated in the company filings or on the website.

Other expenses. Several miscellaneous expenses are aggregated under this heading, which makes for a rich conduit for leakage. A sharp rise in "other expenses" in a depressed market or slowing economy could point to money being siphoned off.

Taxes. The tax payout ratio should be near the standard corporate tax rate. If it is low, then check whether the company has accumulated losses from the past or if it is enjoying tax incentives from operating out of a special economic zone or other tax-advantaged jurisdictions.

Net profit margin. The higher this margin is, the better. Be wary of companies that show high sales growth with declining profit margins. Companies that chase growth at the cost of profitability usually do not create sustainable wealth for shareholders.

2. Cash Flow Analysis

Cash flow from operating activity (CFO). The higher the CFO is, the better. Compare the CFO with net profit over the years to see whether the funds are getting stuck in or released from working capital.

Capital expenditure (capex). Compare capex with the CFO to see whether the company can fund its capital expenditures from its operating cash flow. Companies that show high sales growth without much capex potentially could be capital-light compounders.

Total debt. The lower the debt is, the better. High debt (for nonfinance businesses) signifies living beyond one's means. Avoid companies that heavily depend on the kindness of strangers.

Cash balances. Very high cash levels in companies that do not pay dividends should be viewed with caution. The cash shown on the balance sheet may be fictitious.

Free cash flow (FCF). This is the discretionary surplus that can be distributed to reward shareholders. The higher the proportion of FCF out of the CFO, the better. If FCF is negative and the dividend is always funded by debt, then the investor should not take any comfort from a high dividend yield. If a company is not ever able to generate FCF, then it may be the equivalent of a perpetual Ponzi scheme, wherein it simply robs Peter to pay Paul. Remember, intrinsic value is derived from the cash that can be taken out of a business during its lifetime. When a company reports profits but bleeds cash, believe the cash. Always. The most common symptoms of falsified earnings are negative free cash flow accompanied by rising debt, increasing shares outstanding, and bloating in receivables, inventory, noncurrent investments, and intangibles.

3. Return Ratios Analysis

Self-sustainable growth rate (SSGR). This represents the debt-free, SSGR potential of a company. Companies growing at a higher rate than SSGR are using more resources than their inherent operations can generate, and they experience increasing debt levels. An SSGR higher than the sales growth rate is desirable.

Profit before tax/average net fixed assets. The higher this ratio is, the better. A company should earn more on its tangible assets (as well as tangible equity and capital employed) than the bank's fixed deposit rate.

Pretax return on tangible equity. The higher the pretax return is, the better. Tangible equity is calculated by subtracting intangible assets and preferred equity from the company's book value. Be cautious of companies for which the high return on equity figure is being primarily driven by higher leverage.

Return on capital employed. The higher this return is, the better. This is calculated as earnings before interest and taxes, divided by capital employed.

4. Operating Efficiency Analysis

Net fixed asset turnover ratio. The higher this ratio is, the better. A high ratio shows that the company sweats its fixed assets in an efficient manner.

Receivables days. The lower the number of days, the better. A higher number means that the company is giving customers a longer credit period to generate sales. In case of fictitious sales, in which cash is not received from customers, the number of receivables days will be constantly increasing.

Inventory turnover ratio. The higher this ratio is, the better. Lower inventory turnover means that the company is accumulating a lot of inventory (which might become obsolete later).

5. Balance Sheet Analysis

Net fixed assets. Look for sharp increases in this figure on the balance sheet. These increases signify that the company has completed a capex program, which could drive higher sales and profits in the future.

Capital work in progress. Look for sharp increases in this figure on the balance sheet. These increases signify that the company is currently undertaking a capex program, which may be on the verge of completion.

Share capital. Ideally, the share count should be constant over the years, or it should decrease because of buyback. An increase in share capital that is not due to bonus shares represents a dilution of existing shareholders. Keep in mind that stock splits and bonuses affect only the liquidity of a stock, not its intrinsic value.

Debt-to-equity ratio. The lower this ratio is, the better. Check for off–balance sheet exposures like underfunded pension liabilities, disputed legal claims, non-cancelable operating leases, and contingent liabilities like corporate guarantees for loans taken by promoter-owned group entities. Test the debt serviceability through interest coverage (earnings before interest and taxes/interest) and FCF. A company may have a low debt-to-equity ratio but still face financial stress if the cash is insufficient to meet the near-term payment obligations.

6. Management Analysis

Study the background and credentials of promoters and search the Internet for any corporate governance issues. Use keywords like "fraud," "scam," "litigation," "investigation," and the like.

Management red flags include exorbitant salaries, perks, and commissions (most worrisome if paid during a period of losses); a high percentage of insider holdings being pledged; promoters merging their weaker privately owned companies into their publicly listed company; engaging in significant related-party transactions; appointing relatives who lack adequate qualifications; using aggressive accounting practices; frequently changing auditors; changing the company name to include buzzwords from the hot sectors currently in high demand; and engaging in overly promotional activities, such as quoting broker reports for its revenue or profit guidance and issuing frequent but meaningless press releases and announcements. A hard sell usually indicates that some form of financing is impending. (Show me a promoter who is obsessed with the company's stock price, and I'll show you a business that guzzles cash and constantly needs to raise money.) Always read the "Liquidity and Capital Resources" section in annual and quarterly Securities and Exchange Commission filings to assess the capital-raising needs of the business you are researching.

7. Munger's Psychological Checklist of the Standard Causes of Human Misjudgment

Bias from mere association. This bias automatically connects a stimulus with pain or pleasure. It includes liking or disliking something associated with something good or bad, and includes seeing situations as identical because they seem similar.

Underestimating the power of rewards and punishment. People repeat actions that result in rewards and avoid actions for which they are punished. If people don't have to pay for a benefit, they tend to overuse it. After a success, we become overly optimistic risk takers. After a failure, we become overly pessimistic and risk averse. This happens even in cases in which success or failure was merely a result of chance. We do not improve the man we hang; we improve others by him. Tie incentives to performance. Ensure that people share both the upsides and downsides. Make them understand the link between their performance, their reward, and what you want to accomplish. Reward individual performance, not effort or length of time in the organization.

Underestimating bias from one's own self-interest and incentives. Persuade others by asking them questions that highlight the consequences of their actions. Appeal to interest, not to reason.

Self-serving bias. This bias encourages an overly positive view of our abilities or being overly optimistic. Successes always draw far more attention in the media than failures. The more we think we know about a subject, the less willing we are to use other ideas. We solve a problem in a way that agrees with our method of expertise. Always ask, "How might I be wrong?"

Self-deception and denial. When we practice denial, we engage in a distortion of reality to reduce pain. This includes wishful thinking. As Demosthenes said, "What a man wishes, he will believe."

Bias from consistency and commitment tendency. This bias causes us to remain consistent with prior commitments and ideas, even in the face of disconfirming evidence. This includes confirmation bias—that is, looking for evidence that confirms our beliefs and ignoring or distorting disconfirming evidence to reduce the stress from cognitive dissonance. We tend to double down on our failed efforts because of the sunk cost fallacy. The more time or money we spend on something, the less likely we are to abandon it. When we have made an investment, we tend to seek evidence to confirm that we made the right decision and to ignore information that shows we made the wrong one. As Buffett has said, "What the human being is best at doing is interpreting all new information so that their prior conclusions remain intact."[2]

The more publicity a decision receives, the less likely it is that we will change it. Rigid convictions are more dangerous enemies of truth than lies. It is better to be right than to be consistent. Calibration requires an open-minded consideration of diverse points of view and exploration of alternative hypotheses.

You are more likely to be right if you try to prove yourself wrong. You should hold and explore conflicting possibilities in your mind while steadily advancing toward what is likely to be the truth, based on what you learn along the way. If you find yourself in a hole, stop digging. To admit you are wrong means you are wiser today than yesterday. The greatest enemy of truth is the innate desire to win every argument. Learning is what happens when you end up justifiably agreeing with people who disagree with you. Welcome criticism when you see it is sincere, founded on knowledge, and given in a spirit of helpfulness. Growth requires a steadfast commitment to pivot and adapt. Be open-minded and always triangulate your thesis with people who see things differently from you. By engaging them in thoughtful disagreement, you will gain a better understanding of their reasoning and allow them to stress test your thoughts. In this way, you will raise your probability of being right. Remember, you are looking for the right answer, not merely the best one that you can come up with on your own. Just try to be right—it doesn't matter if the right answer comes from someone else. As Karl Popper said, "The aim of an argument, or of a discussion, should not be victory, but progress." Focus on understanding, not on agreement or disagreement. Judgment follows understanding, not vice versa.

Bias from deprival syndrome. This strong reaction comes when something we like and have (or have almost obtained) is (or threatens to be) taken away or lost. It includes desiring and valuing more of what we can't have. People respond to immediate threats. Anything that happens gradually tends to get ignored. If compliance practitioners want a person to take a risk, they try to make him feel as if he is behind.

Status quo bias and do-nothing syndrome. This bias keeps things the way they are. It minimizes effort and supports a preference for default options. Our unconscious mind rules our behavior. Our senses send our brains roughly 11 million bits of information per second—vastly more than our conscious processing capacity, which maxes out at an estimated fifty bits per second. Research studies show that this bias could be due to the fact that challenging mental activities require more of the body's basic fuel, glucose. When we avoid hard thinking, we save mental energy. We are programmed to be lazy and are naturally inclined to follow the path of least resistance, that is, doing what is easy rather than doing what is required.

Impatience. When we are impatient, we value the present more highly than the future.

Bias from envy and jealousy. People will do many things to feel loved. They will do all things to be envied.

Distortion by contrast comparison. This bias involves judging and perceiving the absolute magnitude of something not by itself but rather based only on its difference from something else when presented closely in time or space or from some earlier adaptation. This includes underestimating the consequences of gradual changes over time (low contrast).

Bias from anchoring. When we anchor, we overweigh certain information (often arbitrary and meaningless) as a reference point for future decisions.

Overinfluence from vivid or recent events. Always back up "stories" with facts and numbers. Many times, the data refutes the anecdotes, but people still prefer to believe the latter. People's minds usually don't change with data when the subject matter is an emotional or political issue for them.

Omission and abstract blindness. When we experience this bias, we see only stimuli we encounter or that grabs our attention, and we neglect important missing information and the abstract. Today, millions of people did not win the lottery. We don't see the quiet losers. We don't see those who didn't predict well. Missing information doesn't draw our attention. This bias includes inattentional blindness.

Bias from reciprocation tendency. We repay in kind what others have done for or to us. This bias includes favors, concessions, attitudes, and information sharing.

Bias from overinfluence by liking tendency. We believe, trust, and agree with people we know and like. This includes bias from excessive desire for social acceptance. It also includes bias from disliking—our tendency to disagree with people we don't like, even though they may be right. A good person can make a bad argument. A bad person can make a good argument. Judge the argument, not the person. Practice intellectual integrity.

Bias from overinfluence by social proof. We imitate the behavior of "similar others." This bias includes crowd folly. When all are accountable, no one is accountable.

Bias from overinfluence by authority. We tend to trust and obey perceived authorities or experts.

Sense making. When we construct explanations that fit an outcome, we may act too quickly to draw sound conclusions, thinking events that have happened were predictable in advance. In hindsight, everything seems obvious. Always assess the quality of previous decisions in the context of the time at which they were made.

Reason respecting. We often comply with requests merely because we have been given a reason. If you always tell people why, they will consider it more important and they will be more likely to comply. People are moved more by what they feel than by what they understand.

Believing first and doubting later. It can be easy to believe what is not true when in a distracted state.

Memory limitations. This causes us to remember selectively and wrongly. This bias includes influence by suggestions.

Do-something syndrome. We may be prone to take some action just for the sake of being active.

Mental confusion from say-something syndrome. We often feel a need to say something when we have nothing to say. As the saying goes, "Better to remain silent and be thought a fool than to speak and remove all doubt."

Emotional arousal. It is easy to make hasty judgments under the influence of intense emotions. This includes exaggerating the emotional impact of future events.

Mental confusion from stress, physical or psychological pain, or the influence of chemicals or diseases.

During the research process, conduct an honest emotional self-check. Write down how you are feeling as well as the main reason you want to buy the stock in question. Are you buying just because of the large amount of research and effort you have put into the stock? Are you reluctant to accept differing opinions?

Resist the urge to buy first and study later. Avoid buying just because others are buying the stock and making a lot of money off of it. Do not fall prey to the fear of missing out. Switch off the television and social media. If necessary, take a break and clear your mind.

Checklists are a systematic way to engage the rational brain, and, for investors, they can be highly effective vaccines against what Guy Spier calls the "cocaine brain": "You go into the greed mode. . . . Neuroscientists have found that the prospect of making money stimulates the same primitive reward circuits in the brain that cocaine does."[3]

The ideal checklist is subjective and it varies from individual to individual. A borrowed or outsourced checklist is not recommended. Every investor needs to build his or her own checklist based on personal experiences, knowledge, and previous mistakes. A checklist created in this manner would be most useful. Munger agrees: "You need a different checklist and different mental models for different companies. I can never make it easy by saying, 'Here are three things.' You have to derive it yourself to ingrain it in your head for the rest of your life."[4]

At the end of the day, an investor should be self-aware and have a clear understanding of what he or she is trying to achieve. In his book *Seeking Wisdom*, Peter Bevelin writes, "Doing something according to pre-established rules, filters and checklists often makes more sense than doing something out of pure emotion. But we can't have too many rules, filters or items without thinking. *We must always understand what we're trying to accomplish* [emphasis added]."[5]

Along with checklists, we have another valuable tool to improve our decision-making skills.

A journal.

CHAPTER 15

JOURNALING IS A POWERFUL TOOL FOR SELF-REFLECTION

Observe all men; thy self most.

—Benjamin Franklin

It is wisdom to know others. It is enlightenment to know one's self.

—Lao Tzu

If most of us remain ignorant of ourselves, it is because self-knowledge is painful and we prefer the pleasures of illusion.

—Aldous Huxley

A significant part of human memories is mostly fiction. We form false memories quite easily. Our subconscious brain tends to distort certain events before storing them in the form of memories. Many research studies have supported the idea of selective memory. The human brain is a meaning-making machine. It is always optimizing and conserving energy by extracting the gist of everything. When we observe anything, our brain immediately tries to glean the meaning of what we see. For most people, this meaning is personal. Memory generally is a product of our preconceived notions and personal biases, that is, what makes sense to us and how that belief fits into our picture of the world. Any information that conflicts with this subjective interpretation is discarded by the brain's grey matter. In other words, our minds are drawn to what feels true, not to what is necessarily so. Every time we pull out a piece of information from memory, we get back a summary that has a lot of missing details. To comprehend that piece of memory, our brain regenerates some part of it on the fly by imaginatively filling in the missing details with stuff that seems plausible, whether or not it actually happened. This reconstruction of any piece of memory happens not just once but every time we access it. When we remember something, we are simply pulling up a number of false details. Maybe we are even adding new errors with each act of recall. The presence of this feedback loop in memory reconsolidation compounds the problem over time. We tend to remember the things we want to remember and forget the things we would rather forget. As a result, a significant part of our memories is self-distorted fiction.

Making effective decisions is a complicated affair, but that is our primary task as investors. Our job is to make decisions. And yet very few of us think about how we engage in decision-making. Confusing actual experience with a false memory of it can be a big deterrent to learning from our past investing outcomes. And if we are not learning effectively from our past experiences, we cannot improve our process to make better decisions. Because of narrative fallacy, hindsight bias, and imperfect memory, it is almost impossible to recall with 100 percent accuracy the reasons why we made a particular decision in the past. Our brain fools us by presenting a distorted picture of the circumstances under which we made the decision, which leads to the wrong conclusion about why a stock turned out to be a mistake or a success.

We often struggle to improve our decision-making skills because we rarely receive feedback on the quality of our decisions. Good decisions do not guarantee success, but bad ones almost always lead to failure. The way to test the quality of our decisions is to test the process by which we make them. There is a simple way to do this.

It's simple but not easy.

Implementing it requires a great deal of humility and intellectual honesty.

Carry a notebook and track all of your important decisions.

A decision journal helps you collect accurate and honest feedback on what you were thinking when you made decisions. This feedback helps you realize when you were just plain lucky. Sometimes things work out well for very different reasons than we initially envisaged. The key to understanding the limits to our knowledge is to check the results of our decisions against what we thought was going to happen and why we thought it was going to happen.

This feedback loop is incredibly important, because the mind won't provide it on its own. We don't know as much as we think we know. We are fooled into thinking that we understand something when we do not, and we have no means to correct ourselves. Our minds revise history to preserve our view of ourselves. The story that we tell ourselves conjures up a linear cause-and-effect relationship between a decision we made and the actual outcome. The best cure for this cognitive malfunction is a decision journal.

Maintain a journal that contains your original investment thesis at the time you made the purchase as well as the rationale for making the sale. As Robert Heinlein writes, "man is not a rational animal; he is a rationalizing animal."[1] After the fact, everything seems obvious; in hindsight, fundamental analysis of any event can be reconstituted and is always brilliant. A journal is the most objective way to remain true to yourself and to avoid hindsight bias. More important, it helps you continuously learn from your mistakes, and these insights will be your greatest teachers in life, business, and investing. The significant intrinsic value of learning from one's personal mistakes (and, even more important, learning vicariously from others' mistakes) over an investing lifetime is grossly underestimated.

Planning Fallacy and the Critical Role of a Premortem

Overly optimistic forecasts of the outcome of projects are evident everywhere. This bias, a phenomenon in which predictions about how much time or cost will be needed to complete a future task display an overly optimistic view, is called "planning fallacy," a term coined by Daniel Kahneman and Amos Tversky. Planning fallacy occurs when plans and forecasts assume a best-case scenario and ignore the base rates of similar cases in the past. This, in turn, leads to significant time and cost overruns.

What causes people to succumb to the planning fallacy? The "inside view," according to Kahneman and Tversky, is the culprit here. The inside view is that which we all spontaneously adopt to assess future prospects. When our intuitions pertain to probability and statistics, we shouldn't trust them. We tend to focus on specific circumstances and to search for evidence within the small world of our personal experiences, a phenomenon known as availability bias. When we have information about an individual case, we rarely want to know the statistics of the reference class to which the case belongs. We tend to forecast based on the information in front of us (availability bias again). We do not consider the succession of possible events that could cause the task to drag on longer. In other words, we ignore the very existence of unknown unknowns.

According to Kahneman, taking an outside view is a way to break the over-confidence illusion created by planning fallacy. To take an outside view is to take your attention away from your specific case and focus it toward a class of similar cases. Check the statistics of success and failure rates of similar cases in the past. If you want to know how something is going to turn out for you, look at how it turned out for others in similar situations in the past—the base rate.

> The best investors make a habit of putting procedures in place, *in advance* [emphasis added], that help inhibit the hot reactions of the emotional brain.
> —Jason Zweig

Getting exactly what we planned for is a nonevent for our brain activity. So, if we are mentally prepared for the worst-case scenario and have a contingency plan ready to cope with it, we will be far less susceptible to overreacting and making costly mistakes under sudden stressful conditions. As legendary Chinese general Sun Tzu aptly put it, "Battles are won [or lost] *before* they are fought." A premortem is an investigation of a bad outcome, but before it happens. We tend to bask in an optimistic view of the future and overestimate the probability of favorable outcomes. A premortem tempers this innate bias.

In investing, conducting a premortem lets us take appropriate corrective action in a timely manner in the future. Before you buy a stock, visualize that a year has passed from the date of your purchase and that you have lost money on your investment, even in a steady market. Now, write down on a piece of paper what went wrong in the future. This "prospective hindsight" technique forces you to open up your mind, to think in terms of a broad range of outcomes, to consider the outside view, and to focus your attention on those potential sources of downside risk that did not intuitively come to your mind the first time you thought about buying a stock. Visualizing a range of scenarios for variables outside of one's control also helps investors make better decisions for individual position sizing and portfolio construction.

Many investors do postmortems and glean lessons from decisions made, but a premortem begins by assuming that a decision has failed and then asks why. Think about what can go wrong before making the investment, and keep evaluating it as time passes. Avoid compounding in reverse. To make money, you need to have money. In other words, to maximize profits, you have to minimize losses. You must focus on capital preservation above all else. Value investors always think about the potential downside risks first when evaluating a potential investment. Even the father of value investing, Benjamin Graham, emphasized return of capital and placed it before return on capital in his definition of investing: "An investment operation is one which, upon thorough analysis, promises safety of principal and an adequate return. Operations not meeting these requirements are speculative."[2]

When making an investment, always ask, What can go wrong? What will be my reaction if those things do go wrong? What are the risks? How likely are the risks? How big are the risks? Can I bear them if they come true? When making decisions under conditions of uncertainty, always think in terms of consequences (and "consequences of consequences"), and not just in probabilities. As Benjamin Franklin wrote in *Poor Richard's Almanack*, "He that builds before he counts the cost, acts foolishly; and he that counts before he builds, finds he did not count wisely."

Writing Is a Medium for Increased Self-Awareness, Understanding, and Happiness

I spent ten dollars on a journal in late 2014, and I consider it to be one of the best value investments I ever made. Since that day, I have been keeping track of my investing decisions and subsequent developments in a journal. This habit has helped me a lot in learning about myself and improving as both an investor and an individual. I receive a lot of valuable feedback and use it to correct my biases. I also have maintained a personal archive of the media commentary and investor behavior during various episodes of market panic between 2015 and 2019. I find that it is highly beneficial to refer to this information whenever the market undergoes its periodic steep corrections. Human behavior in the markets has not really changed much over time.

The process of structuring our thoughts into a journal entry brings clarity to our thinking. Journaling by hand reduces the possibility of hindsight bias. It is hard to look at your own writing and deny your previous thoughts. A periodic review is an important part of the process. This is how you start getting better. Realizing where you make mistakes, why you make them, and what the common mistakes are that you tend to make all can help you improve over time. Whenever the outcome of a past decision is known, revisit your decision journal. Odds are, you will discover some surprises. In many of the favorable outcomes, you'll commonly find that the original reasoning wasn't right. Outcomes distort our thinking a lot. Unless you are humble and intellectually honest, you will end up taking the wrong lessons from favorable outcomes. It is not intuitive to honestly recall how the events unfolded, especially after getting a favorable result. We may be right a lot of the time, but it may well be for the wrong reasons. This self-realization can be humbling. It is also how we learn and improve.

Writing, apart from being a communication tool, is a thinking tool, too. It is almost impossible to write one thing and simultaneously think something else. When you force your hand to write something, it channels your thoughts in the same direction. Journaling turns out to be not just a tool for thinking but also a highly effective medium for focusing our thoughts. The more you write, the more precision of thought you build. Writing is a thinking exercise, and it acts as a shield against the rusting of our mind. It is also a useful tool for retaining what we read, and it deepens our understanding.

An added benefit of journaling is that it deepens commitment. The very act of writing things down deepens our resolve to make good things happen in our lives. It is like a personal declaration that acts as a constant motivator.

Journaling has therapeutic benefits, too. Writing aids self-reflection, which is a great way to ease any unhappiness in our lives. Writing also improves our memory, because we remember more when we write down our thoughts and learnings.

Stephen King says, "Writing is magic, as much the water of life as any other creative art. The water is free. So drink."[3]

Write, make better decisions, and be happier.

CHAPTER 16

NEVER UNDERESTIMATE THE POWER OF INCENTIVES

Never, ever, think about something else when you should be thinking about the power of incentives.

—Charlie Munger

If you want to persuade, appeal to interest not to reason.

—Benjamin Franklin

My main life lesson from investing: self-interest is the most powerful force on earth, and can get people to embrace and defend almost anything.

—Jesse Livermore

Never ask anyone for their opinion, forecast, or recommendation. Just ask them what they have—or don't have—in their portfolio.

—Nassim Nicholas Taleb

To know what people really think, pay regard to what they do, rather than what they say.

—René Descartes

W
e do that for which we are rewarded and avoid that for which we are punished. Incentives are at the root of most of the situations we face, and yet we often fail to account for them. The behavior we observe is usually the result of incentives we do not observe. Incentives carry the power to distort our behavior and blind us to reality. In his book *Pebbles of Perception*, Laurence Endersen writes:

> We can only see a situation with true clarity when we take the time to carefully consider *the interests at hand*. And we understand it even better when we consider how the situation might be different if the underlying interests were different. . . .
>
> Incentives matter greatly—underestimate them at your peril. *People will navigate the shortest path to the incentive* [emphasis added]. The curious among us will pay particular attention to incentives, monetary or otherwise.[1]

The iron rule of life is that you get what you reward for. People follow incentives the way ants follow sugar. Rewards as a valuable psychological tool have been part of the academic vocabulary since the mid-twentieth century, when behavioral psychologist B. F. Skinner articulated his philosophy of "positive reinforcement," a way to shape behavior through reward systems. Skinner's experiments in operant conditioning and behaviorism are his biggest contributions to the field of psychology. Operant conditioning can be summarized as follows: a behavior is followed by a consequence, and the nature of the consequence modifies the organism's tendency to repeat the behavior in the future.

It is imperative that we think deeply about the incentive systems we create, because ignoring the second- or third-order effects of an incentive system often leads to unintended consequences, also known as the Peltzman effect. Endersen writes, "An example is monetary rewards offered to help exterminate unwanted animals such as rats and snakes. What authorities failed to foresee was that people would start to breed the rats and snakes."

It not only is important to have symmetrical incentives but also is crucial to not allow gaming of the system. Human beings have the tendency to game systems for their benefit. It is better to miss rewarding a desirable behavior than to produce an incentive system that promotes cheating behavior, because bad behavior, once rewarded, is habit forming. And then it spreads. If we think carefully, we can observe the fact that incentive-caused bias and social proof create the lollapalooza of Gresham's law. Bad behavior drives out good behavior. As William Ophuls said, "As with Gresham's law in economics, bad values drive out good, so the moral currency is continuously debased."[2] This just goes to show how the interplay of multiple behavioral biases results in extreme irrational outcomes. It is why Charlie Munger recommends, "Anti-gaming features constitute a huge and necessary part of system design. Also needed in the system design is an admonition: dread." Incentives are not only financial but also include prestige, freedom, time, titles, power, and admiration. All of these are powerful incentives. And, according to Munger, few forces are more powerful than incentives:

> Almost everyone thinks he fully recognizes how important incentives and disincentives are in changing cognition and behavior. But this is not often so. For instance, I think I've been in the top 5 percent of my age cohorts almost all my adult life in understanding the power of incentives, and yet I've always underestimated that power. Never a year passes but I get some surprise that pushes a little further my appreciation of incentive superpower.[3]

Often, the solution to a behavior problem is to simply align the incentives with the desired goal. Munger shares his favorite case study from this context:

> In human affairs, what determines the behavior are the incentives for the decision maker.
>
> From all business, my favorite case on incentives is Federal Express. The heart and soul of their system—which creates the integrity of the product—is having all their airplanes come to one place in the middle of the night and shift all the packages from plane to plane. If there are delays, the whole operation can't deliver a product full of integrity to Federal Express customers.
>
> And it was always screwed up. They could never get it done on time. They tried everything—moral suasion, threats, you name it. And nothing worked.
>
> Finally, somebody got the idea to pay all these people not so much an hour, but so much a shift—and when it's all done, they can all go home. Well, their problems cleared up overnight.[4]

Lessons from Berkshire Hathaway for Structuring Incentives in Organizational Settings

Capital allocation is a CEO's most important job. How he or she allocates capital is what determines the value created for the business and its shareholders in the long run. Many CEOs fail in allocating capital because of their incentive structure, which is aligned to what they can do in the short term rather than what they should do for the long term. This is why Munger says, "Perhaps the most important rule in management is to get the incentives right."[5]

In theory, stock options should align the interests of managers with shareholders. But as Yogi Berra said, "In theory, there is no difference between practice and theory. In practice, there is."

Two aspects of stock options make them an ineffective way to incentivize management. First, they are a capital cost. For a manager with a fixed price option, retained earnings are "free-of-cost" capital. Second, managers do not bear any downside risks, but shareholders do. So it is more like a free lottery ticket for managers.

In his 1996 letter, Warren Buffett explained Berkshire Hathaway's incentive compensation principles. It is widely regarded as the blueprint for how organizations should design incentive and compensation structures:

> Goals should be (1) tailored to the economics of the specific operating business; (2) simple in character so that the degree to which they are being realized can be easily measured; and (3) directly related to the daily activities of plan participants. As a corollary, we shun "lottery ticket" arrangements, such as options on Berkshire shares, whose ultimate value—which could range from zero to huge—is totally out of the control of the person whose behavior we would like to affect. In our view, a system that produces quixotic payoffs will not only be wasteful for owners but may actually discourage the focused behavior we value in managers.[6]

It is important to study the business, understand its key value drivers, and then bind the incentives with those value drivers, as Buffett has done with GEICO: "The bonuses received by dozens of top executives, starting with Tony, are based upon only two key variables: (1) growth in voluntary auto policies and (2) underwriting profitability on 'seasoned' auto business (meaning policies that have been on the books for more than one year)."[7]

How does Buffett ensure that he gets the incentives right for his managers so that they send all their excess capital to Berkshire Hathaway headquarters? He does this by linking it directly to their compensation and to areas under their control:

> In setting compensation, we like to hold out the promise of large carrots, but make sure their delivery is tied directly to results in the area that a manager controls. When capital invested in an operation is significant, we also both charge managers a high rate for incremental capital they employ and credit them at an equally high rate for capital they release.
>
> The product of this money's-not-free approach is definitely visible at Scott Fetzer. If Ralph can employ incremental funds at good returns, it pays him to do so: His bonus increases when earnings on additional capital exceed a meaningful hurdle charge. But our bonus calculation is symmetrical: If incremental investment yields sub-standard returns, the shortfall is costly to Ralph as well as to Berkshire. The consequence of this two-way arrangement is that it pays Ralph—and pays him well—to send to Omaha any cash he can't advantageously use in his business.[8]

Skin in the Game

A system is responsible in proportion to the degree that the people who make the decisions bear the consequences.

—Charles Frankel

An example of a really responsible system is the system the Romans used when they built an arch. The guy who created the arch stood under it as the scaffolding was removed. It's like packing your own parachute.

—Charlie Munger

The presence of misaligned incentives results in perverse outcomes. But when you align incentives of everyone in both positive and negative ways, you create a system that takes care of itself. Thinking about the incentives of others is necessary to creating win–win relationships. Munger often says that people respond most strongly to what they view as their incentive or disincentive. Nassim Taleb considers incentives and disincentives a better risk management tool than popular statistical methods like value at risk. Incentives encourage desirable behavior. Disincentives prevent them.

Almost four thousand years ago, King Hammurabi of Babylon laid out one of the first sets of laws. The Code of Hammurabi is among the oldest translated writings and consists of 282 laws, most of them concerning punishment. Taleb and George A. Martin describe law 229 of Hammurabi's Code as "the best risk management rule":

> The Hammurabi rule marks the separation between an agent's interests and those of the client, or principal, she is supposed to represent. This is called the agency problem in the social sciences. Often closely associated is the problem of moral hazard, wherein an actor has incentive to behave in an economically or socially suboptimal manner (e.g., overly risky) because she does not bear all of the actual and/or potential costs of her action. . . . The Hammurabi rule solves the joint agency and moral hazard problem by ensuring that the agent has sufficient non-diversifiable risk to incent the agent to act in the joint interest of the agent and the principal.[9]

This moral principle is exactly what Seth Klarman refers to in his book *Margin of Safety*:

> You probably would not choose to dine at a restaurant whose chef always ate elsewhere. You should be no more satisfied with a money manager who does

not eat his or her own cooking. It is worth noting that few institutional money managers invest their own money along with their clients' funds. The failure to do so frees these managers to single-mindedly pursue their firms', rather than their clients', best interests.[10]

Misaligned Incentives Often Result in Perverse Outcomes

Early in the history of Xerox, Joe Wilson, who was then in the government, had to go back to Xerox because he couldn't understand how their better, new machine was selling so poorly in relation to their older and inferior machine. Of course when he got there, he found out that the commission arrangement with the salesmen gave a tremendous incentive to the inferior machine.

—Charlie Munger

In most cases, complexity favors the seller, simplicity, the buyer. Any product with a fat commission will get pushed, no matter how toxic it is for the customer. Munger says, "Any time you create large differences in commissions where the guy gets X% for selling A, which is some mundane security, and 10 times X for selling B, which is something toxic, you know what's going to happen."[11]

Incentive-caused bias is so pervasive that it occurs in almost every profession. Outsider CEOs (as opposed to founders) in public companies avoid long-term value-creating investments and research and development, because their compensation is based on their meeting or beating quarterly street expectations. Lawyers make clients litigate more than necessary. Doctors prescribe expensive branded drugs instead of generics. Contractors engage in the gaming of "cost-plus" arrangements. Auditors overlook accounting irregularities. Credit rating agencies give high ratings to junk-grade instruments. Investment bankers price initial public offerings (IPOs) to extract maximum value for their clients, because that is the basis on which they get paid.

The real power of incentives is the ability to manipulate the cognitive process. An otherwise-decent individual may act immorally because he or she is driven by the perverse incentives prevailing in the system. When you work in a job for someone else, you could face the same problem. Because incentive-caused bias operates automatically, at a subconscious level, you may be fooled into believing that what is good for you is also good for the client. And so you may find yourself selling addictive and harmful products like tobacco and alcohol, or overpriced and sales-load-heavy insurance and investment products, just for the money. It is difficult to get rich on a salary because you get paid linearly for analyzing and solving a given problem in a job. But you get paid in an exponential manner for spotting and seizing opportunities as an investor, venture capitalist, or entrepreneur.

As investors, we can intelligently use the power of incentives to our advantage by recognizing certain subtle clues in the public markets. For example, if the existing private equity partners are not selling any stake during an IPO or the promoter purchases shares from the open market just ahead of the closure of the trading window before the quarterly results, we should sit up and take notice. If a promoter announces a rights issue at an unattractive price, it could be because he is aware of the strong growth prospects ahead and wants to deliberately discourage participation by minority shareholders and increase his ownership in the firm. Significant insider ownership in entrepreneur-backed companies helps align the incentives of the promoter with those of the minority shareholders. (One should prefer situations in which the promoter has his or her entire skin in the game in just one company rather than owning multiple listed or privately held entities.)

Never Ask the Barber Whether You Need a Haircut

Widespread incentive-caused bias requires that one should often distrust, or take with a grain of salt, the advice of one's professional advisor, even if he is an engineer. The general antidotes here are: (1) especially fear professional advice when it is especially good for the advisor; (2) learn and use the basic elements of your advisor's trade as you deal with your advisor; and (3) double check, disbelieve, or replace much of what you're told, to the degree that seems appropriate after objective thought.

—Charlie Munger

"All commissioned salesmen," said Munger, at the 1988 Wesco Financial annual meeting, "have a tendency to serve the transaction instead of the truth." Munger recommends that we should always reflect on the question "What is someone getting out of this?" The more the managers and brokers take, the less the investors make. As Buffett says, "For investors as a whole, returns decrease as motion increases."[12] Investors get what they don't pay for. Many investment advisers are actually disguised brokers or subbrokers, mutual fund distributors, and insurance policy sellers, whose objective is to maximize commissions and brokerage. Ensure that your adviser is "fee only," receiving no remuneration from any source other than you.

The fund management industry is meant to be a fiduciary business, but many money managers conduct their affairs as a marketing firm selling investments in the guise of an investment firm. Learn to distinguish between the two:

- A marketing firm overly advertises the track records of its hottest funds. An investment firm does not.
- A marketing firm creates new "sector" funds based on the latest fads—because they can sell them, not because they think they are good investments for clients. An investment firm does not.
- A marketing firm churns out "incubator funds," shuts down and buries those that do not perform well, and does mass advertising of the ones that survive. An investment firm does not.

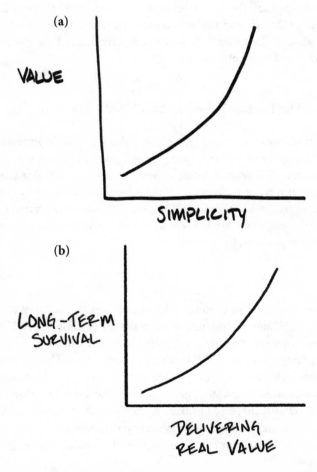

FIGURE 16.1 (a) Simplicity drives value, and (b) delivering value to clients ensures long-term survival and prosperity.

Source: Behavior Gap.

- An investment firm continually engages in client education on market volatility and explains how past performance is not representative of the future. A marketing firm does not.
- A small- and mid-cap-oriented investment firm closes the fund to new investors when it begins to incur excessive impact costs because of its bigger size, which precludes it from taking meaningful positions in smaller companies. A marketing firm does not.
- An investment firm passes on to clients its savings benefits in the form of reduced fees when its operating cost ratios improve with increasing assets under management. A marketing firm does not.

If investment firms focus on generating the best possible risk-adjusted returns and maintain an ongoing dialogue with clients regarding their process and philosophy in a clear manner, the rest should take care of itself. Keep it simple. Simplicity drives value, and delivering value to clients ensures long-term survival and prosperity (figures 16.1a and 16.1b).

Ultimately, the best way to overcome incentive-caused bias is to achieve financial independence, because this independence empowers you to see things as they really are. Only free people can be honest. Only honest people can be free.

Buffett captured the superpower of incentives in its full essence when he said: "I could end the deficit in five minutes. You just pass a law that says that any time there's a deficit of more than 3 percent of GDP, all sitting members of Congress are ineligible for re-election."[13]

I have nothing to add.

CHAPTER 17

ALWAYS THINK ABOUT THE MATH, BUT AVOID PHYSICS ENVY

Investing in stocks is an art, not a science, and people who've been trained to rigidly quantify everything have a big disadvantage.

—Peter Lynch

Math helps us evaluate when things make sense. And math is stable over time. It was true that two plus two equals four one million years ago and it will be true one million years from today. When we quantify and translate something into numeric form, we can make relevant comparisons and sound judgment calls by heeding the wise words of John Maynard Keynes: "It is better to be roughly right than precisely wrong."

At the height of the Internet bubble at the turn of the century, Warren Buffett embodied Keynes's wisdom:

When we buy a stock, we always think in terms of buying the whole enterprise because it enables us to think as businessmen rather than stock speculators. So let's just take a company that has marvelous prospects, that is paying you nothing now where you buy it at a valuation of $500 billion. . . . To deliver, let's assume that there's only going to be a one-year delay before the business starts paying out to you and you want to get a 10 percent return. If you paid $500 billion, then $55 billion in cash is the amount that it's going to have to be able to disgorge to you year after year. To do that, it has to make perhaps $80 billion, or close to it, pretax. Look around the universe of businesses in this world and see how many are earning $80 billion pretax, or $70 billion or 60 or 50 or 40 or even $30 billion. You won't find any.[1]

Note how Buffett uses extreme reductionism and "proof by contradiction" to greatly simplify an investing decision.

As investors, we do not need to endlessly strive for precision. Just being approximately right while having a good margin of safety is sufficient to get the job done. Remember, you don't need a weighing scale to know that a four-hundred-pound man is fat. Don't obsess over whether the business will earn $2 or $2.05 in the next quarter. Focus instead on finding a big gap between the current price and the value you have placed on long-term earning power using conservative estimates to create a large margin of safety, just in case your initial assessment is wrong. But don't invest in a situation in which a complicated financial model is required to justify a purchase. Keep things simple. Buffett thought PetroChina was worth $100 billion, and he could buy it at $37 billion.

You can engage in all sorts of elaborate analysis, but Buffett boils down everything to whether a big discrepancy exists between the current price and the estimated value, using conservative estimates, which gives him a large margin of safety.

Don't overweigh what can be counted and underweigh what cannot. Be wary of clinging to false precision in a complex world.

Not everything that counts can be counted, and not everything that can be counted counts.
—Albert Einstein

In his 2003 speech at the University of California, Santa Barbara, Economics Department, titled "Academic Economics: Strengths and Faults After Considering Interdisciplinary Needs," Charlie Munger said:

You've got a complex system and it spews out a lot of wonderful numbers that enable you to measure some factors. *But there are other factors that are terribly important, [yet] there's no precise numbering you can put to these factors.* You know they're important, but you don't have the numbers. Well, practically everybody (1) overweighs the stuff that can be numbered, because it yields to the statistical techniques they're taught in academia, and (2) doesn't mix in the hard-to-measure stuff *that may be more important* [emphasis added].[2]

When it comes to investing, precision has much less practical application than an investor would think. This tendency to look for precision where none exists is a human bias and is referred to by Munger, in the same speech, as "physics envy":

In *Poor Charlie's Almanack*, Peter Kaufman writes:

Charlie strives to reduce complex situations to their most basic, unemotional fundamentals. Yet, within this pursuit of rationality and simplicity, he is careful to avoid what he calls "physics envy," the common human craving to reduce enormously complex systems (such as those in economics) to one-size-fits-all Newtonian formulas. Instead, he faithfully honors Albert Einstein's admonition, "A scientific theory should be as simple as possible, but no simpler." Or in his own words, "What I'm against is being very confident and feeling that you know, for sure, that your particular action will do more good than harm. You're dealing with highly complex systems wherein everything is interacting with everything else."[3]

A monumental example of this problem is the efficient market theory, which assumes all market participants to be *Homo economicus* or Economic Human (i.e., perfectly rational beings, at least according to the economic definition). This theory is the outcome of trying to impose the discipline of a hard science on economics, which actually is not a hard science—it is a social science. Markets are all about human behavior, and while they are efficient at aggregating information and valuing data, they certainly are not rational. They are too complex and reactive to lend themselves to the kind of discipline that rules the hard sciences. Discontinuity, far from being an anomaly best ignored, is an essential ingredient of markets that sets finance apart from the natural sciences. According to Michael Mauboussin,

A complex adaptive system has three characteristics. The first is that the system consists of a number of heterogeneous agents, and each of those agents makes decisions about how to behave. The most important dimension here is that those decisions will evolve over time. The second characteristic is that the agents interact with one another. That interaction leads to the third—something that scientists call emergence: In a very real way, *the whole becomes greater than the sum of the parts.* The key issue is that you can't really understand the whole system by simply looking at its individual parts. . . .

. . . When you see something occur in a complex adaptive system, your mind is going to create a narrative to explain what happened—even though cause and effect are not comprehensible in that kind of system. Hindsight's a beautiful thing. . . .

. . . *Complexity doesn't lend itself to tidy mathematics in the way that some traditional, linear financial models do* [emphasis added].[4]

Value investors commonly joke that more fiction has been created using Excel than Word. Because of deeply ingrained confirmation bias, we do not need a spreadsheet to provide us with a "goal seek" function. This function is embedded in our brains. Personally, I have never opened a spreadsheet even once when making an investment decision. The most advanced technology I have ever used is a pocket calculator for basic math like addition, subtraction, multiplication, and division.

Extensive spreadsheets and complex quantitative software tools can be harmful to one's financial well-being. Tiny changes in input assumptions can dramatically change the estimate of intrinsic value, so bankers and deal consultants can engage in any level of wishful reverse-engineering that they deem convenient. (A discounted cash flow model remains the best strategic destination for all analysts where their imagination of price-to-earnings, price-to-book, and price-to-sales ratios or enterprise value multiples failed to reach.) As Benjamin Graham said, "The combination of precise formulae with highly imprecise assumptions can be used to establish, or rather to justify, practically any value one wishes."[5] Never underestimate the power of incentives.

The world cannot be understood without numbers. At the same time, it cannot be understood with numbers alone. Relying solely on complex quantitative analysis can divert our attention away from things that really matter. For example, spreadsheets cannot model trust, integrity, goodwill, reputation, or the execution capabilities of the management. Thus, due diligence always needs to have a softer, subjective side to it. Investing is part art and part science. Nuanced judgment is required.

Buffett says, "Price is what you pay. Value is what you get."[6] So we have to ensure that we do not pay more than the intrinsic value of a company. Now, this poses a challenge. We have to compare the price, which can be measured precisely, with an inherently imprecise estimate of value. Most investors attempt to do just that—they try to arrive at a "precise" number for intrinsic value. For instance, exact price targets in an analyst report, right down to the last decimal point, is a misleading anchor to cling to, because the preciseness of the target price number instills a false sense of confidence in readers. And this false confidence makes readers vulnerable to serious mistakes. It's a classic case of physics envy in action.

Over the years, I have come to appreciate the fact that investing is a field of simplifications and approximations rather than of extreme precision and quantitative wizardry. I also have realized that investing is less a field of finance and more a field of human behavior. The key to investing success is not how much you know but how you behave. Your behavior will matter far more than your fees, your asset allocation, or your analytical abilities. Even low-cost index funds won't be able to help you if you succumb to behavioral biases. Most of the time, the real risk is not in the markets but in our behavior. Emotional intelligence has a much bigger impact on the success or failure of investors than the college they attended or the complexity of their investment strategy. Most of the time, their high intellect works against them, because they become so sure of themselves and their abilities that they cannot change their mind. It is always a struggle to keep things simple in a complex world. That struggle is more pronounced for the highly educated people. The smarter you are, the better you are at constructing a narrative that supports your personal beliefs, rationalizing and framing the data to fit your argument or point of view. You may be smart, but not necessarily intelligent, because intelligence is the ability to arrive at accurate cause-and-effect descriptions of reality.

Buffett has often said that the calculation of intrinsic value is a challenge. In the Berkshire owner's manual, he said:

> The calculation of intrinsic value, though, is not so simple. As our definition suggests, intrinsic value is an estimate rather than a precise figure, and it is additionally *an estimate that must be changed if interest rates move or forecasts of future cash flows are revised* [emphasis added]. [7]

In his 2005 letter to investors, Buffett wrote, "Calculations of intrinsic value, though all-important, *are necessarily imprecise* and often seriously wrong. *The more uncertain the future of a business, the more possibility there is that the calculation will be wildly off-base* [emphasis added]."

And, in his 2000 letter, he wrote, "Using precise numbers is, in fact, foolish; *working with a range of possibilities is the better approach* [emphasis added]."[8]

As investors, we can use simple approximations under a range of different business scenarios to estimate our potential return from any single stock and then compare this with the expected return from existing passive instruments and from the alternative choices in our stocks' opportunity set to select the one with the highest expected return.

Thinking Forward and Backward

Whenever we try to solve problems and predict what is likely to happen or is likely to be true or false, we should think things through both forward and backwards. Here are some of Munger's thoughts on the subject:

"Think forwards and backwards—invert, always invert."
"Many hard problems are best solved when they are addressed backward."
"The way complex adaptive systems work and the way mental constructs work is that problems frequently get easier, I'd even say usually are easier to solve, if you turn them around in reverse."[9]

In his enlightening talk in July 1996 titled "Practical Thought on Practical Thought," Munger took up a case involving the turning of $2 million into

$2 trillion in 150 years. (Note: Numerical fluency helps a lot when working with big numbers. In this case, the seemingly huge $2 trillion figure translates into a compound annual growth rate of 9.64 percent. Compounding even at modest rates, when done over a long period of time, produces truly spectacular outcomes.) Although many great lessons can be gleaned from the transcript of this talk, the big idea that I took away was the fact that Munger does not think in terms of intrinsic value today, which is an imprecise number and often triggers a hornet's nest of debates regarding the discount rate to be used for valuing future earnings, or the perpetual growth rate (also known in finance parlance as "terminal growth rate") to use at the end of the explicit forecasting period. The latter is a critical point of contention today, when the longevity of businesses across industries is shrinking rapidly because of technological disruptions and the very concept of terminal value (which traditionally accounted for more than half the estimated intrinsic value of a business) is being questioned. An accelerating pattern of value migration is taking place away from outmoded business designs toward new designs that better satisfy customers' most important priorities. History suggests that many companies eventually will end up with a terminal value of zero. Always be conservative when making assumptions about terminal value.

In his talk, Munger teaches us how to think about arriving at a potential future value that we then can compare with the business's current market value to calculate expected return. In this case, we are forced to think in terms of the math implicit in our assumptions while arriving at potential future value. This method is popularly known in finance parlance as conducting a "reverse discounted cash flow" operation. (As you can see, inversion helps solve many problems in life.)

Let's take a simple hypothetical example to explain this process. Let's say we want to buy shares of Company X, whose current market value is $1 billion. For the sake of simplicity, we assume that there are no dividends, stock options, debt, or off-balance-sheet obligations. The business has owner earnings of $40 million and an assumed average annual growth rate of 10 percent for ten years (the explicit forecasting period in this example). This leads to a value of $104 million in owner earnings in year 10.

Let's assume that the market pays an average multiple of 15× on owner earnings for this type of business and that no valuation rerating or derating of the business occurs in the interim period. This gives us a market value of $1.56 billion in year 10. Compared with the current market value of $1 billion this gives us an implied yearly return of 4.5 percent.

Now simply compare this with the expected returns from the other investment opportunities available to you. If the expected return over the next ten years is not even equal to the yield on the top-rated sovereign bond, then it would be irrational to own this stock at the current price. A business may have great economic characteristics, but if the expected returns are greatly inferior when compared with existing alternatives, investors should avoid it.

Suppose we want to know under what scenario we could earn a 15 percent annual return from this stock. What assumptions would be required to hold true to achieve this—and, more important, are they reasonable?

A present market value of $1 billion and an annual return of 15 percent leads to $4 billion in market value in year 10. An exit multiple of 15× suggests owner earnings of $270 million in year 10. This implies an average annual growth rate of 21 percent in owner earnings (on the initial starting point of $40 million). A hypothetical profit margin of 15 percent suggests sales of $1.8 billion in year 10. This implies a 21 percent annual growth rate in sales for ten years. Now we can work with the various assumptions regarding required sales volume growth, trends in sales realization per unit, market share, and so on, and we can assess whether these are reasonable, given the past trends and track record of volume growth, pricing power, profit margins, market size, market share, and competitive advantage. We also can find out which factor has the greatest impact on future owner earnings (and thereby value) and under what circumstances it could change. We then could engage accordingly in a constructive "premortem" exercise.

To build in multiple redundancies to act as sources of margin of safety, we should always use conservative assumptions. We should avoid assuming future growth rates significantly in excess of historical growth rates (both long term and short term), use a reasonable exit multiple at the end of the explicit forecasting period, and apply the method only on stable business models.

The inherent advantages of thinking in terms of long-term expected return instead of a precise current intrinsic value are multifold. This approach forces the mind to think about future value drivers. It helps us determine the appropriate position sizing through an objective comparison of the competing investment alternatives available within our circle of competence. It helps us select only simple businesses whose future is relatively more predictable. We cannot apply this model to fast-moving technology businesses, but we can apply it to moated businesses that meet basic human needs and aspirations in a relatively unsaturated market with a long runway for growth. These businesses usually experience a slower rate of change in their business models.

The essence of this chapter is best summed up by Munger's words at the 1990 Berkshire annual meeting: "We never sit down, run the numbers out and discount them back to net present value. . . . *The decision should be obvious* [emphasis added]."[10]

CHAPTER 18

INTELLIGENT INVESTING IS ALL ABOUT UNDERSTANDING INTRINSIC VALUE

A general definition of intrinsic value would be that value which is justified by the facts—e.g., assets, earnings, dividends, definite prospects. In the usual case, the most important single factor determining value is now held to be the indicated average future earning power *[emphasis added]. Intrinsic value would then be found by first estimating this earning power, and then multiplying that estimate by an appropriate "capitalization factor."*

—Benjamin Graham, *Security Analysis*

The process of determining the intrinsic value of a business is an art form. You cannot follow rigid rules to plug data into a spreadsheet and hope that it spits out the value for you. Stocks are worth what people are willing to pay for them, and no shortcuts will give you an exact equilibrium value. Intrinsic value is a moving target that is constantly changing as fundamental data come out and investors update their "expectations" based on knowledge and past experience.

In the past, Warren Buffett has described intrinsic value as private owner value, the price that an informed buyer would pay for the entire business and its future stream of cash.

Thus, the intrinsic value of an asset is the sum of the cash flows expected to be received from that asset, over its remaining useful life, discounted for the time value of money and the uncertainty of receiving those cash flows.

If we carefully read Benjamin Graham's definition at the beginning of this chapter, it is interesting to note that he says that future earning power is "the most important single factor determining value."

So the main question we are trying to answer is this: What is the normalized earning power of the business? In other words, if I am a private buyer, how much cash will this business put in my pocket each year, after paying for the expenditures required to maintain my competitive position? What normalized owner earnings can I expect from this business?

It's Owner Earnings That Count

Buffett defined owner earnings in his 1986 letter as follows: "(a) reported earnings plus (b) depreciation, depletion, amortization, and certain other non-cash charges . . . less (c) the average annual amount of capitalized expenditures for plant and equipment, etc. that the business requires to fully maintain its long-term competitive position and its unit volume. (If the business requires additional working capital to maintain its competitive position and unit volume, the increment also should be included in (c).)"[1]

On Wall Street, the term "earnings" refers to net income or earnings per share (EPS) from the income statement. This is what most analysts latch onto and they succumb to availability bias. (They fail to heed Charlie Munger's warning: "There is nothing more dangerous than an idea if it's the only one you have.") Another widely used metric is earnings before interest, taxes, depreciation, and amortization (EBITDA), which, although a ubiquitous term on Wall Street, is a relatively new financial concept. (It was not until the leveraged buyout boom in the 1980s that EBITDA was widely adopted as a financial measure.) EBITDA, however, does not take into account real cash expenses like capital expenditure (capex), interest, and taxes.

For value investors, the earnings used for valuation purposes are the owner earnings. Net income and EPS are reported figures under accounting principles, but the actual cash that the business owner is able to finally take out is quite different. Owner earnings tell us how much cash comes into the business owner's pockets, which is meant to be actual, spendable cash, not inventory and receivables. This is why Buffett calls it owner earnings. Remember, buying a stock is buying a part ownership in a business.

Buffett's definition of owner earnings is widely regarded in the value investing community as the holy grail for understanding the true earning power of a company.

Note, however, the subtle omission in Buffett's definition.

Buffett started from reported earnings and then made some adjustments to arrive at owner earnings. But he did not adjust for outlays having a quasi-capex nature, such as advertising or research and development, which are generally treated as an expense in the profit and loss (P&L) statement before reported earnings are arrived at. So the first variable (reported earnings) in Buffett's equation is likely to be depressed in cases of businesses with emerging moats, that is, businesses that are investing in long-term value-creating initiatives that currently are being expensed in the income statement.

Investors should capitalize these types of expenditures and amortize them over a conservatively assumed economic life. Two conditions must be satisfied to warrant such an adjustment: volume growth and market share gains. Business analysts should treat any money spent that expands the size of the moat as an expenditure that delivers an enduring advantage—just like capex. Businesses that follow conservative accounting, however, treat all this money spent as an expense in the income statement. Such an adjustment, if made, will—in growing businesses in which such expenditures also are growing—result in owner earnings exceeding reported earnings. This is why accounting numbers should always be used only as a basic starting point for investment analysis.

In moated businesses where money is being spent on expanding the moat and where this adjustment is made, the correct number to use for determining intrinsic value is the owner earnings or economic earnings number. Discount that number back from the future to arrive at fair value.

Many times, conventional valuation measures based on reported earnings or accounting book values result in an optically high price-to-earnings or price-to-book ratio for a moated business, and investors end up making costly mistakes of omission because they find these businesses to be overvalued. But, as Buffett has said:

> Whether appropriate or not, the term "value investing" is widely used. Typically, it connotes the purchase of stocks having attributes such as a low ratio of price to book value, a low price-earnings ratio, or a high dividend yield. Unfortunately, such characteristics, even if they appear in combination, are far from determinative as to whether an investor is indeed buying something for what it is worth and is therefore truly operating on the principle of obtaining value in his investments. Correspondingly, opposite characteristics— *a high ratio of price to book value, a high price-earnings ratio, and a low dividend yield—are in no way inconsistent with a "value" purchase* [emphasis added].[2]

The key point is that for businesses that will grow their earnings even at a moderate pace, but for a very long time, the optically high price-to-earnings (P/E) multiples that deter many value investors in reality are pretty low. This means that if you buy a strong moated business at what appears to be a "full price based on current year earnings," you will end up compounding your money at a higher rate than the discount rate you used to arrive at that "fair price." The longer the competitive advantage period (CAP), the more likely a business is worth a lot more than what the market thinks. "Durability" of the moat is the key factor. The market tends to underappreciate companies that have really strong moats because the durability often allows for the company's runway to last longer than many expect. For long-term investing, the focus should be shifted from entry P/E multiples to duration of the CAP. And P/E multiples should be the result of the valuation exercise and not the cause. Evaluating accounting numbers from the right perspective is vital to succeeding as an investor.

For example, goodwill can reflect either having paid too much for an acquisition or enduring long-term intangibles whose value increases over time. Investors will have to figure this out, because the accountants won't. With that in mind, let us evaluate some of the important components of economic earnings, namely, maintenance capex and working capital.

My observation has been that the market always displays its wisdom and accords a lower valuation to companies with higher maintenance capex, which thus optically appear to be cheaper than their peers. One needs to derive the maintenance capex figure from the annual report, or get it from management during the conference calls or annual general meetings. (Always cross-check what management says with what they actually report.) Total capex is given in the investing section of the cash flow statement. All capex that is not growth capex must necessarily be maintenance capex. So if we can estimate growth capex, we can estimate maintenance capex. Sometimes it is obvious that almost all the capex is maintenance capex because of competitive pressures. For example, the functional equivalents of Buffett's shutdown of his textile mills are common in the business world, so do not take the accountants' definition of capex at face value. Accountants don't evaluate; they record transactions. They would rather show something as precise even if it is wrong. How a business transaction is recorded does not alter the event or its impact on value. Avoid availability bias by asking, "Is this expenditure likely to result in a sustainable rise in economic earnings in the future?"

This will not be the case if the margin or productivity gains have to be fully passed on to the customer; if capex is incurred to replace defunct machinery that will only help the company maintain its current earning power; if the industry is characterized by cutthroat competition or high rates of technological change or obsolescence that requires constant capex for protective reasons or just to keep up with the competition, which keeps inventing new technology applications, thus making old technology obsolete; or if historical cost accounting during highly inflationary periods results in underprovision of depreciation in the books. In all of these cases, the company in question makes no real profits. When we correctly treat the money spent on such frequent capex programs not as capex but as maintenance capex, we will figure out that, essentially, there are no owner earnings. And when there are no owner earnings, there is no value.

This will always hold true, even if the stock market value of such a business in the interim period touches billions of dollars. During such periods, the Keynesian beauty contest phenomenon is in force, with the investing public pricing shares based not on what they think their fundamental value is but rather on what they think everyone else thinks their value is or on what everybody else would predict the average assessment of value to be. This is a common phenomenon during sector- or asset-class-specific bubbles.

Bubbles are more of a social phenomenon than an economic or financial one. People crave the shared experience of being part of something exciting and new. The origin of these bubbles usually is grounded in a sound premise that eventually is overextended and taken too far. In other words, the essence of every bubble is strong fundamentals—euphorically extrapolated. Graham used to talk about how ideas that initially were sound eventually were carried too far on Wall Street: "You can get in way more trouble with a good idea than a bad idea, because you forget that the good idea has limits."[3]

Buffett explains how certain asset-heavy businesses with no owner earnings get into trouble when they begin to distribute out of restricted earnings:

> All earnings are not created equal. In many businesses—particularly those that have high asset/profit ratios—inflation causes some or all of the reported earnings to become ersatz. The ersatz portion—let's call these earnings "restricted"—cannot, if the business is to retain its economic position, be distributed as dividends. Were these earnings to be paid out, the business would lose ground in one or more of the following areas: its ability to maintain its unit volume of sales, its long-term competitive position, its financial strength. No matter how conservative its payout ratio, a company that consistently distributes restricted earnings is destined for oblivion unless equity capital is otherwise infused.
>
> Restricted earnings are seldom valueless to owners, but they often must be discounted heavily.[4]

In these kind of companies, debt issuance and equity dilution occur frequently. New investors keep pouring money into the firm but are never able to take anything out. And if any dividends are paid, they come not from operating cash flow but from the fresh fund infusions made by debt and equity investors. These companies are just recycling cash from new investors to old investors, which is the functional equivalent of a Ponzi scheme. In Berkshire's fiftieth annual letter, Buffett described these kind of companies:

> Business models based on the *serial issuances of overpriced shares*—just like chain-letter models—most assuredly redistribute wealth, *but in no way create it.* Both phenomena, nevertheless, periodically blossom in our country—they are every promoter's dream—though often they appear in a carefully crafted disguise.

The ending is always the same: Money flows from the gullible to the fraudster. And with stocks, unlike chain letters, the sums hijacked can be staggering.

At both BPL and Berkshire, we have never invested in companies that are hell-bent on issuing shares. That behavior is one of the surest indicators of a promotion-minded management, weak accounting, a stock that is overpriced and—all too often—outright dishonesty [emphasis added].[5]

Munger also has voiced his opinion on such businesses:

Benjamin Graham used to talk about a "frozen corporation"—a company whose charter prohibited it from ever paying out anything to its owners or ever being liquidated or sold. And Graham's question was, "What is such an enterprise worth?"

I do think that it's an interesting case because I think there is a class of business where the eventual "cash back" part of the equation tends to be an illusion. There are businesses like that—*where you just constantly keep pouring it in and pouring it in, but where no cash ever comes back* [emphasis added].[6]

The working capital component in the owner earnings definition is an important input in the valuation exercise. Any time a business requires additional capital (fixed or working) that will do nothing for rise in unit volume or market share, the money spent should be treated as an expense. When competitive conditions deteriorate, such required expenditures always go up. This increase is usually a warning signal of things to come. If bargaining power is permanently shifting from a business to its customers or suppliers, then the amount of working capital needed by the business just to stand its ground in terms of unit volume and competitive position will increase. That increase is (c) in Buffett's equation and should be treated as a charge against earnings.

Of course, when we do that in practice, then, in many cases, we will find that (c) exceeds (a) + (b), which means that there are no real earnings to speak of. And if there are no real earnings, then there is no real value, although the asset in question may enjoy fabulous market value for a while. As Buffett notes, "Value is destroyed, not created, by any business that loses money over its lifetime, no matter how high its interim valuation may get."[7] He closed his textile operations when he figured out that there were no owner earnings; he refused to throw good money after bad.

In *Security Analysis*, Graham, contrary to popular belief, actually spends a lot of time discussing future earnings—not what the business earned in the past but rather what we can expect the business to earn each year on average in the future. Graham was signaling that valuation is an art form. Determining the present value of all the future cash flows of a business involves looking at the various aspects of a business's DNA, including its capital intensity, business model durability, balance sheet strength, profitability, competitive position, future growth prospects, and management bandwidth, among other factors—all weighted and compared with the current price. Some businesses are easier to value than others. Predictability of cash flows is an important factor. Graham talked about this when he said that the security analyst must "use good judgment in distinguishing between securities and situations that are better suited and those that are worse suited to value analysis. Its working assumption is that the past record affords at least a rough guide to the future. The more questionable this assumption, the less valuable is the analysis."[8]

In other words, it is easier to value a business with stable operations and cash flows than a business with high volatility in its underlying operations every year. The intrinsic value is the sum of the present value of the cash flows during the explicit forecasting period and the present value of the terminal value. Less predictable cash flows need to be discounted at a higher rate. This leads us to the discussion regarding the appropriate starting point for the cost-of-capital number.

Both Buffett and Munger acknowledge that calculating a company's cost of capital is an inexact art that does not result in a precise estimate. This is reflected in their comments during the 2003 annual meeting:

> *Buffett:* Charlie and I don't know our cost of capital. It's taught at business schools, but we're skeptical. We just look to do the most intelligent thing we can with the capital that we have. We measure everything against our alternatives. I've never seen a cost of capital calculation that made sense to me. Have you Charlie?
>
> *Munger:* Never. If you take the best text in economics by Mankiw, he says intelligent people make decisions based on opportunity costs—in other words, it's your alternatives that matter. That's how we make all of our decisions. The rest of the world has gone off on some kick—there's even a cost of equity capital. A perfectly amazing mental malfunction.[9]

Taking a cue from Buffett and Munger, the S&P 500's long-term annual return of 9.7 percent during the twentieth century can be taken as a reasonably good proxy for an investor's long-term opportunity cost. Professor Bruce Greenwald often instructs students in his value investing class to "just use 10 percent. It close enough and it makes the math easy."[10] It is a reasonable assumption to use 10 percent as the starting estimate for the cost of capital when calculating a company's value. (Investors in countries outside the United States can use the long-term market returns of their respective countries as the starting point.) This can then be revised up or down, depending on the individual company's risk characteristics.

The best outcome that an investor can hope to achieve when it comes to appraising business values is to come up with a range of values and then wait for the market to offer a price that is significantly below the lower end of the range—this gives you both a margin of safety in the event your analysis is wrong and high returns on your investment if you are right. If you can understand the business well, it will be easy for you to quickly judge whether the stock is "obviously cheap" *or* "obviously expensive" based on a simple back-of-the-napkin calculation. *Security Analysis* discussed the concept of a range of value:

> The essential point is that security analysis does *not* seek to determine *exactly* what is the intrinsic value of a given security. It needs only to establish that the value is *adequate*—e.g., to protect a bond or to justify a stock purchase—or else that the value is *considerably higher or considerably lower* than the market price. *For such purposes an indefinite and approximate measure of the intrinsic value may be sufficient* [emphasis added].[11]

From this we can infer that Graham never intended for intrinsic value to be thought of as a single point estimate of value. Rather, he thought of it more as a concept of value. In fact, in the 1934 edition of *Security Analysis*, Graham discusses the flexibility of the concept of intrinsic value as "*a very hypothetical 'range of approximate value,' which would grow wider as the uncertainty of the picture increased.*"[12]

To deal with an inherently uncertain future, an investor needs to consider various possible scenarios when forecasting a company's future cash flows and calculating its intrinsic value. One could produce a range of potential intrinsic values by performing a sensitivity analysis in which the assumption about one or more of the future cash flow components varies over time. Each scenario will produce a different, discrete present value estimate that the investor can use to create a range of possible intrinsic values. The values closest to the central point represent the estimates that the investor believes have the highest likelihood (probability) of being the company's true intrinsic value, whereas the estimated values near each of the tails are the scenarios the investor believes are less likely to occur. The range of possible intrinsic values grows wider as uncertainty increases. A wide range of estimates may result from the fact that the timing, duration, magnitude, or growth of the company's cash flows are highly uncertain.

When the range of possible outcomes is wide, it is foolish to use scenario analysis and calculate estimates such as (a) base case $[x], probability 60 percent; (b) optimistic case $[x], probability 10 percent; and (c) pessimistic case $[x], probability 30 percent; and then come up with weighted average price of $[x] for the stock. That would be the functional equivalent of a six-foot-tall man who cannot swim trying to cross a river that has an average depth of five feet. He forgets that the range of depth is between four feet and twelve feet—and he would drown. Ignoring the range of possibilities is foolish. In businesses like oil, or any business that involves extracting stuff from below the earth's surface, that range can be huge.

Each business's economics is different. All earnings are not created equal. Ten dollars of earnings from a capital-light business like Moody's, with its low reinvestment requirements, is obviously worth a lot more than the same earnings figure from a capital-intensive business like General Dynamics, so investors should capitalize each of them differently. Investors have to look at each business's earning power, along with the future prospects of the business, to decide how much they are willing to pay to acquire that business's future cash flows.

Many entrepreneurs recognize that wealth creation is not a zero-sum game and that if they behave ethically, their businesses will enjoy a much higher valuation multiple than would be the case if they didn't. A high multiple stock does not just create a high valuation for the business; it also provides the management with a wonderful tool to grow inorganically through acquisitions, with lower equity dilution. When A acquires B for stock, it always means A is selling a stake in its business to acquire B.

Earnings are created by businesses, but earnings multiples are created by markets. Other things remaining unchanged, a business that is run in the interests of all stakeholders is worth more than one that is run solely in the interests of the controlling stockholders. Buffett has highlighted this important point in the past: "Investors should pay more for a business that is lodged in the hands of a manager with demonstrated pro-shareholder leanings than for one in the hands of a self-interested manager marching to a different drummer."[13]

Some Thoughts on Value Traps

The traditional "value investor" mentality of buying cheap securities, waiting for them to bounce back to "intrinsic value," selling and moving onto the next opportunity, is flawed.

In today's world of instant information and fast-paced innovation, cheap securities increasingly appear to be value traps; often they are companies ailing from technological disruption and long-term decline. This rapid recycling of capital also creates an enormous drag on our after-tax returns. In addition, by focusing on these opportunities, we incur enormous opportunity costs by not focusing instead on the tremendous opportunities created by the exceptional innovation S-curves we are currently witnessing.

—Marcelo Lima

Most of the time, switching from a high P/E stock to one with a low P/E proves to be a mistake. Value traps are abundant and all-pervasive. I have learned to respect the market's wisdom. Everything trades at the level it does for a reason.

High quality tends to trade at expensive valuation and junk or poor quality is frequently available at cheap (or the harmful "optically cheaper on a relative basis") valuation. It took me many years to learn this big market lesson: expensive is expensive for a reason and cheap is cheap for a reason.

In the stock market, prices usually move first, and the reported fundamentals follow. (For instance, for debt issued by listed companies, stock price behavior usually turns out to be a more accurate barometer for gauging the probability of default than ratings given by the credit rating agencies.) A plummeting stock price (in an otherwise steady market) often turns out to be an accurate harbinger of deteriorating fundamentals for a company. Think about this before you jump in to buy. Avoid investing in melting ice cubes. What appears to be cheap or relatively inexpensive can continue becoming cheaper if industry headwinds intensify. An irrational fall in price makes a stock cheaper. A rational fall in price makes a stock more expensive. Many of the high dividend-yield stocks in expensive markets eventually turn out to be value traps and destroy wealth. When you see a deep value stock suddenly break down on high volumes with no visible explanation, take notice. You are likely observing a value trap. Value traps are businesses that look cheap but actually are expensive. This could happen for a variety of reasons:

- **Cyclicality of earnings.** A low P/E stock may look cheap because the business is enjoying cyclically peak earnings, but the normalized P/E may not really be low if adjusted for cyclicality.
- **App risk.** A taxi company may look cheap based on past earning power, but that may have existed only until Uber arrived.
- **Bad capital allocation by the management.** The market may correctly be punishing a business by assigning a low multiple to its earnings because the managers keep burning cash in bad projects and there is no prospect of such misallocation being stopped.
- **Governance issues.** A business run by a crook may appear to be quite cheap relative to the large amount of cash reported on its books, until that cash is completely siphoned off. Give zero valuation to the cash held in the books of a business being run for social purposes or owned by shady promoters. Gains in intrinsic value often are not reflected in realized returns for investors because insiders channel the gains to themselves. Remember, human nature does not change. Crooks don't suddenly sprout a sense of fiduciary duty. Always keep Thomas Phelps's words in mind: "Remember that a man who will steal for you, will steal from you."[14] Avoid partnering with such forms of management even if it comes at the cost of missing an opportunity. The notional loss from not capitalizing on an opportunity can be made up any time, but the eventual realized loss from partnering with a crook is permanent and irrecoverable.

CHAPTER 19

THE THREE MOST IMPORTANT WORDS IN INVESTING

A margin of safety is achieved when securities are purchased at prices sufficiently below underlying value to allow for human error, bad luck, or extreme volatility in a complex, unpredictable and rapidly changing world.

—Seth Klarman

We can learn some important lessons from the past about the likely future returns for investors who pay exorbitant valuations for today's hot stocks. Let us dip into the past to canvass one moment of investor exuberance, the era of the Nifty Fifty, to see what the future may hold for today's current batch of high fliers. For those unfamiliar with the era of the Nifty Fifty, which reached its zenith in 1972, here is a description of the period by Professor Jeremy Siegel:

The Nifty Fifty were a group of premier growth stocks, such as Xerox, IBM, Polaroid, and Coca-Cola, that became institutional darlings in the early 1970s. All of these stocks had proven growth records, continual increases in dividends (virtually none had cut its dividend since World War II), and *high market capitalization. This last characteristic enabled institutions to load up on these stocks without significantly influencing the price of their shares.*

The Nifty Fifty were often called one-decision stocks: buy and never sell. Because their prospects were so bright, many analysts claimed that the only

TABLE 19.1 Returns of the Nifty Fifty, beginning June 1972

"Expensive" Nifty Fifty Stocks

Company	Symbol	Starting P/E	Subsequent Annualized Total Returns			
			10-year	20-year	30-year	40-year
McDonald's	MCD	85.7	1.75%	12.06%	11.53%	12.17%
Int'l Flavors & Fragrances	IFF	75.8	−5.24%	6.93%	5.50%	5.87%
Walt Disney	DIS	81.6	−3.78%	10.81%	9.40%	9.12%
Johnson & Johnson	JNJ	61.9	1.72%	10.48%	13.38%	10.62%
Coca Cola	KO	47.6	−6.93%	11.83%	11.52%	9.98%
Eli Lilly	LLY	46	−0.72%	8.26%	11.17%	7.99%
Merck	MRK	45.9	−0.23%	14.31%	13.11%	9.75%

Source: Lawrence Hamtil, "Price Is What You Pay; Value Is What You Get—Nifty Fifty Edition," *Fortune Financial* (blog), May 24, 2018, http://www.fortunefinancialadvisors.com/blog/price-is-what-you-pay-value-is-what-you-get-nifty-fifty-edition.

direction they could go was up. Since they had made so many rich, few if any investors could fault a money manager for buying them.

At the time, many investors did not seem to find 50, 80 or even 100 times earnings at all an unreasonable price to pay for the world's preeminent growth companies [emphasis added].[1]

Lawrence Hamtil of wealth management firm Fortune Financial calculated the returns of the expensive Nifty Fifty stocks over the next forty years, beginning from June 1972. Table 19.1 shows his findings.

According to Hamtil,

The lesson from this exercise, I believe, is that investors should always be conscious of starting valuation when placing their bets. *With few exceptions, eventually valuations that are simply too high will drift back down to more reasonable levels, often at the expense of poor intermediate-term performance. This appears to be true no matter how revolutionary the new business appears to be, and no matter how much potential you believe it has* [emphasis added]. Of course, if your conviction is such that you plan on holding your shares for multiple decades, valuation may indeed matter less to long-term returns, but that is assuming you follow through on your commitment. Over several years of subpar performance, that is much easier said than done.[2]

All fast growers eventually turn into stalwarts or slow growers. This painful transition can result in a lost decade for investors, during which time valuation derating causes the stock to remain flat or to trade sideways. Time and again, the market teaches us that a big difference exists between a great company and a great stock.

> For the investor, a too-high purchase price for the stock of an excellent company can undo the effects of a subsequent decade of favorable business developments.
> —Warren Buffett

> I conceive that a great part of the miseries of mankind are brought upon them by the false estimates they have made of the value of things, and by their giving too much for their whistles.
> —Benjamin Franklin

At times, the valuation of a stock we have held for a long time becomes so absurdly high that we should be able to sell it instantly, without any hesitation or doubt. But this type of sale is not mentally easy to execute, because the valuation expansion would have been accompanied by huge gains for the investor, leading to excessive greed and the subsequent tendency to debunk "traditional" measures of valuation.

Compounding at a moderate but steady rate of return over a long period of time is vastly superior to merely generating sharp outperformance for a year or two. Averages can be grossly misleading, so we should always use a geometric progression and look at compound annual growth rate (CAGR) if we want to understand returns the right way. An investor with 14 percent average annual return (20 percent, 40 percent, 20 percent, −50 percent, and 40 percent) over a five-year period underperforms someone with 9 percent average annual return if the latter is consistent every year. As of February 2018, only 5 percent of the listed Indian companies with at least INR 10 crores (~US$1.4 million) of net profit grew earnings by more than 20 percent CAGR over the preceding ten years. Against that, 55 percent of the companies had an earnings decline. Because earnings drive returns in the long term, it just goes to show how difficult it is to compound wealth by more than 20 percent on a sustainable basis. (Achieving a CAGR of 100 percent for a few years is commendable, but achieving a CAGR of 20 percent for six decades is what makes a Warren Buffett. He played the game for the longest time and became the biggest winner.)

Investing success is challenging over a long time period. A bull market year or two in between fools many market participants into thinking otherwise. It takes a fairly short time to learn how to make money, but it takes a lifetime to learn how to not lose it. A margin of safety in investing is necessary to avoid "compounding in reverse." A stable investor who earns 20 percent for two consecutive years comes out ahead of a flamboyant newcomer who earns 100 percent in a bull market year and loses 30 percent or more in the following year. (Most of the inexperienced investors realize this harsh math the painful way when junk stocks finally start crashing after a bull market, and only then do they begin to appreciate the significant importance of investing in quality.) One single year of a big loss can undo all the hard work and sacrifices of the past. Sample this. If you generate 15 percent return per year for two years but lose 15 percent in year 3, your CAGR is only 4.0 percent. If you make 15 percent per year for three years and then lose 15 percent in year 4, your CAGR is cut to 6.6 percent. And if you earn 15 percent per year for four years but lose 15 percent in year 5, your CAGR is cut to 8.3 percent. The difference becomes even more striking when considering larger absolute return figures. If you generate 30 percent return per year for two years but lose 30 percent in year 3, your CAGR is only 5.8 percent. If you make 30 percent per year for three years and then lose 30 percent in year 4, your CAGR is cut to 11.4 percent. And if you earn 30 percent per year for four bull market years but lose 30 percent in year 5, your CAGR is cut to 14.9 percent.

Buffett's adaptation of margin of safety for the masses follows:

Rule number 1: Never lose money.
Rule number 2: Never forget rule number 1.

When Brent Beshore asked Buffett about Berkshire's due diligence process, Buffett replied, "Price is my due diligence."[3] It was the clearest articulation of his investment philosophy. Buffett is extremely patient and disciplined and does not take a swing of the bat if any deal cuts too close with regards to the price paid versus the value received. Buffett's investment criterion is demanding. He will not buy a security until he sees an ample margin of safety, considered from multiple vantage points. The opportunity needs to be simply incredible.

When you pay low entry prices, you don't need many good things to happen for you to get a good return. Even if some bad news comes out about the company, because it already has been discounted, the stock price impact is limited. Conversely, if any good news emerges, you get a highly positive result.

There always seems to be a strong divide within the investing community between "deep value" (statistically cheap securities) and "growth at a reasonable price" (high-quality compounders). It is true that many investors do well by buying great businesses at fair prices and holding them for long periods of time, whereas other investors prefer to buy cheap stocks of average or mediocre quality and sell them when they appreciate to fair value, repeating the process over time as they cycle through multiple new opportunities.

The styles are different, but not as different as most people describe them to be. The tactics used are different, but the objective is exactly the same—that is, trying to buy something for less than what it's really worth, or trying to locate the low-risk fifty-cent dollars. Both strategies are just different versions of Graham's margin-of-safety principle.

Quality Increases the Margin of Safety Over Time

If you plan to hold a share for the long term, the rate of return on capital it generates and can reinvest at is far more important than the rating you buy or sell at.

—Terry Smith

The margin of safety can be derived from the gap between price and value, and it also can be derived from the quality of the business. For example, a business that can grow intrinsic value at a rate of 18 percent annually is worth much more than a business that is growing its value at 6 percent annually, all other things being equal. Because the higher-quality compounder is worth a lot more over a long-term holding period than the lower-quality business, the former offers a larger margin of safety.

The problem with investing only in statistically cheap securities (also known as "cigar butts") is that the underlying business's economic value gradually erodes with each passing day, making the investment a race against time. As investors, our goal should be to minimize the number of decisions and to reduce the potential for unforced errors. It is much more productive to be invested in businesses with growing intrinsic value over time, because it allows for a larger margin of error in case we are wrong and higher returns in case we are right.

In a 1975 article in *Financial Analysts Journal*, written by Charles D. Ellis and titled "The Loser's Game," Ellis talks about how the approach taken by good and bad tennis players is also seen in investing. In the article, Ellis cites a study done in a book called *Extraordinary Tennis for the Ordinary Tennis Player*, written by Simon Ramo. As the study showed, and as Ellis wrote in his article, "Professionals win points; amateurs lose points."[4]

This point on amateur tennis is similar to how many investors invest. Most wealth destruction happens as a result of unforced errors. If investors focused on reducing unforced errors instead of trying to hit the next home run, then their returns would improve dramatically. It is like the amateur tennis champion who wins because he or she has made the fewest mistakes but not necessarily the most forehand wins. In the view of Ellis, investing, like tennis, is a loser's game. The winners in the game come out with superior long-term results simply by making fewer mistakes. The losers end up with losses because they make the same mistakes repeatedly. No one can avoid making new mistakes, but the great investors repeat old mistakes less often.

The stock markets, in aggregate, have been a positive-sum game over the long term. With such a natural tailwind behind us, investing for the long term is a winner's game. One way to reduce unforced errors in investing is to carefully choose the businesses that we decide to own. Investors are better off with a few solid long-term choices than flitting from one speculation to another, always chasing the latest hot stock in the market. (Better to have a few good, long-term friends rather than changing your friends every week for short-term advantage.) The gap between price and value ultimately will determine our returns, but picking the right business is possibly the most important step in reducing errors. Improving pattern recognition skills increases the probability of successfully identifying the right businesses to invest in.

Without doubt, cigar butts as a category have the potential to outperform quality over a short holding period, but over the long term, companies with increasing intrinsic value over time are the clear winners. On balance, paying a high price for even a great business may not always work out well if you have to sell that business in one or two years. But if you plan to hold your stocks for longer periods of time—say, five years, ten years, or longer—then quality becomes "much more important" than cheap initial valuations when assessing margin of safety. This leads to an important conclusion: when investing in short-term opportunities like commodities, cyclicals, and special situations, pay greater attention to price and mean reversion, but when investing in long-term compounders, pay maximum attention to the quality of business and management above all else.

For example, buying a low-quality public sector bank in India at 30 percent to 40 percent of book value can work out well if and when the stock gets revalued to 100 percent of book value. But over ten- or fifteen-year periods or longer, paying even three times book value for a high-quality, well-managed franchise like HDFC Bank should deliver better results. (Between two lenders with similar levels of return on equity and growth, I would prefer the lender with a higher price-to-book valuation for two reasons: (1) growth capital in the future would be available at a lower equity dilution, and (2) a higher price-to-book valuation tends to signify important nondisclosed aspects like superior underwriting skills, robust internal processes, and better quality of the loan book.)

Having started out as Grahamites—which, by the way, worked fine—we gradually got what I would call better insights. And we realized that some company that was selling at 2 or 3 times book value could still be a hell of a bargain because of momentums implicit in its position, sometimes combined with an unusual managerial skill plainly present in some individual or other, or some system or other.

—Charlie Munger

For a Graham and Dodd investor, the margin of safety comes from a low price relative to asset value or from a high earning power relative to a AAA bond yield. There is less focus on the quality of the business or the management. For a Warren Buffett–Charlie Munger–Phil Fisher investor, the margin of safety comes from the ability of a business to deliver high returns on invested capital on a sustained basis over long periods of time, which in turn comes from a durable competitive advantage created by exceptional managers at the helm. These franchise-focused investors do not hesitate to pay up for quality in the form of an expensive multiple for current year earnings if they believe that the future earnings will be significantly higher.

The Graham and Dodd investor believes in mean reversion—that is, bad things will happen to good businesses and good things will happen to bad businesses. Buffett–Munger–Fisher investors invest in businesses with fundamental momentum, that is, a high probability of sustaining excess returns over long periods of time. These two ideologies often clash (mean reversion versus fundamental momentum) in the value investing community. For most businesses, mean reversion applies, but for some exceptional ones, it starts applying after a prolonged period of time, and until then, fundamental momentum applies. Although Benjamin Graham is widely renowned as a deep value investor, the profits from his single growth stock investment, GEICO, were more than all his other career investments combined. In 1948, Graham's investment partnership (Graham-Newman) purchased 50 percent of GEICO for $712,000. By 1972, this was worth $400 million. Graham had scored a Peter Lynchian five-hundred-bagger. He later wrote, "Ironically enough, the aggregate of profits accruing from this single investment decision far exceeded the sum of all the others realized through 20 years of wide-ranging operations in the partners' specialized fields, involving much investigation, endless pondering, and countless individual decisions."[5]

> Since stock markets typically value companies on the not unreasonable assumption that their returns will regress to the mean, businesses whose returns do not do this can become undervalued. Therein lies our opportunity as investors.
> —Fundsmith Equity Fund Owner's Manual

In a June 2013 research paper by Credit Suisse, the authors provided strong evidence supporting Buffett's philosophy of investing in successful companies with an established track record of delivering high owner earnings in relation to invested capital. (The authors used a proxy called "cash flow return on investment.") They looked at hundreds of firms from around the world, from 1993 to 2013, and at the beginning of each quarter starting from 1993, divided the universe into quartiles. "Q1−−" were firms in the poorest performance quartile and "Q4++" were the best-quality firms with the highest cash flow

TABLE 19.2

Transition Probability, %

		Ending Quartile			
		Q1: − −	Q2: −	Q3: +	Q4: ++
Starting Quartile	Q1: − −	**56**	27	11	6
	Q2: −	28	**40**	23	8
	Q3: +	13	28	**39**	20
	Q4: ++	9	12	28	**51**

Source: Credit Suisse, "Was Warren Buffett Right: Do Wonderful Companies Remain Wonderful?" *HOLT Wealth Creation Principles*, June 2013, https://research-doc.credit-suisse.com/mercurydoc?language =ENG&format=PDF&document_id=1019433381&serialid=*EMAIL_REMOVED*&auditid=1182867.

Note: The boldface numbers represent the probability of the firms remaining in their respective performance level quartiles over successive five-year periods.

return on investment. The researchers then determined the persistence, or stickiness, of cash flow return on investment by studying the historical transition between performance levels over successive five-year periods for each firm and came up with the findings detailed in table 19.2.

These results tell us a few things:

1. Operating performance is not random. Had it been random, all probabilities would have been closer to 25 percent. We find little evidence of mean reversion.
2. The best-performing firms had a 51 percent probability of remaining among the best-performing firms, and the worst-performing firms had a 56 percent probability of remaining the poorest performers.
3. Great businesses tend to remain great, or they become good businesses (combined probability of 79 percent). There was only a 9 percent chance that a great business would end up in the quartile of poorest performers.
4. Poor businesses tend to remain poor, or they become slightly better but still remain below average (combined probability of 83 percent). There was only a 6 percent chance that the weakest businesses would transition to the "best performers" category.

The authors of the study, Bryant Matthews and David Holland, conclude with the following summary:

Corporate profitability is sticky. Wonderful companies tend to *remain* wonderful, and poor companies tend to *remain* stuck in the mud. Our empirical evidence suggests that *sustainable corporate turnarounds are difficult to execute*. . . .

Companies in defensive industries exhibit more stickiness in corporate profitability than firms in cyclical industries. However the persistence in performance remains highly significant and thus the reputation of the business tends to remain intact regardless of industry. . . .

Firms with excellent profitability tend to outperform those with the worst return on capital. The outperformance improves if high-quality firms are purchased at a fair price [emphasis added].[6]

The key finding of this study was that, despite being recognized as successful businesses, the Q4++ category businesses continued to deliver outstanding investment results over the long term. But if markets were "efficient," this should not have happened. The prices of such stocks should have been bid up to the point at which buyers could not earn exceptional returns. But they did. Markets systematically underprice quality over long time periods.

This has been proven empirically not just in this study but in many others. Financial economist Robert Novy-Marx looked at New York Stock Exchange firms between 1963 and 2010 and at international firms between 1990 and 2009. He found the same persistence of high performance, not just in business fundamentals but also in stock market returns: "More profitable companies today tend to be more profitable companies tomorrow. Although it gets reflected in their future stock prices, the market systematically underestimates this today, making their shares a relative bargain—diamonds in the rough."[7]

Buffett's Evolution from Graham to Fisher

Buffett's gradual transition from being a deep value investor to one willing to "pay up for quality" can be best understood by studying the evolution in his thought process over the years, as expressed in the following quotes:

When a management with a reputation for brilliance tackles a business with a reputation for poor fundamental economics, it is the reputation of the business that remains intact.[8]

My own thinking has changed drastically from 35 years ago when I was taught to favor tangible assets and to shun businesses whose value depended largely upon economic Goodwill. This bias caused me to make many important business mistakes of omission, although relatively few of commission. . . .

Ultimately, business experience, direct and vicarious, produced my present strong preference for businesses that possess large amounts of enduring Goodwill and that utilize a minimum of tangible assets.[9]

It's far better to buy a wonderful company at a fair price than a fair company at a wonderful price. Charlie understood this early; I was a slow learner.

But now, when buying companies or common stocks, we look for first-class businesses accompanied by first-class managements.[10]

High quality always beats a bargain over time. Although there are certainly exceptions, in the long run, bargains never outperform solid investments. This simple yet profound principle can be applied to virtually every area of life. Crash diets, predatory pricing, dishonesty, and shortcuts can work well for a while, but they are never sustainable.

CHAPTER 20

INVESTING IN COMMODITY AND CYCLICAL STOCKS IS ALL ABOUT THE CAPITAL CYCLE

The risk of paying too high a price for good-quality stocks—while a real one—is not the chief hazard confronting the average buyer of securities. Observation over many years has taught us that the chief losses to investors come from the purchase of low-quality securities at times of favorable business conditions. The purchasers view the current good earnings as equivalent to "earning power" and assume that prosperity is synonymous with safety *[emphasis added]*.

—Benjamin Graham, *The Intelligent Investor*

I n 1955, Benjamin Graham had to testify on the state of the stock market before the U.S. Senate Committee on Banking and Currency. The following excerpt is from an exchange between Graham and the committee chair:

Chair: When you find a special situation and you decide, just for illustration, that you can buy for 10 and it is worth 30, and you take a position, and then you cannot realize it until a lot of other people decide it is worth 30, how is that process brought about—advertising, or what happens?
Graham: That is one of the mysteries of our business, and it is a mystery to me as well as to everybody else. We know from experience that eventually the market catches up with value. It realizes it in one way or another.[1]

Graham's response to the question regarding an undervalued stock rising to a level of fair valuation captures the essence of the process of mean reversion. But what causes this revaluation? For that, an understanding of the capital cycle is essential. A capital cycle is based on the premise that the prospect of high returns will attract capital (which results in intense competition), just as low returns repel it. The resulting ebb and flow of capital affects long-term returns for stockholders in what often are predictable ways—this is termed the capital cycle.

When investing in commodities and cyclicals, look for industries that are in a major down cycle and are starved for capital. This step should be followed by a detailed analysis of the fundamentals of individual companies and behavioral insights within the sector to uncover stocks that are selling at a significant discount to their intrinsic value. Next, conduct a stress test to check whether the short-listed companies have manageable debt and are capable of surviving another couple of years in a downturn. Then wait for a few companies in the industry to go bust or shut down some plants and initiate your buying activity after that happens, while pessimism levels are high. As the cycle starts turning, add more to your position.

Given the contrarian and long-term nature of the capital cycle approach to investing, this strategy entails firm variant perception and long holding periods. Such a disciplined and patient deep value investing approach enables investors to achieve high risk-adjusted returns when the cycle eventually turns.

According to financial historian and investment strategist Edward Chancellor, capital cycle investing is more profitable than strategies based on growth or value orientation. Chancellor's book *Capital Returns: Investing Through the Capital Cycle*, captures the essence of the capital cycle approach to investing.

Capital Cycle Red Flags

Even if we cannot actively monitor the changes in fixed assets in an industry, we can still look for signals of a capital cycle–related bubble. Chancellor gives several examples of such red flags:

- **Watch what investment banks are doing.** "Investment banks are the investor's enemy," Chancellor says.[2] Be wary of industries that are characterized by high levels of investment banking activities, such as mergers and acquisitions, initial public offerings (IPOs), and debt (especially high-yield) issuance. IPOs are a capital allocation decision that often represents a buildup of capacity in a company or industry. Chancellor says that the surge in junk-bond issuance by U.S. energy companies in 2016 was a sign that investors should have avoided the sector.

- **Beware of investor frenzy.** Early signs include thematic investor conferences and growing levels of industry coverage by analysts, news channels, business magazines, and newspapers.
- **Look out for high levels of capital investment in an industry.** This is the most direct sign of a capital cycle that is about to harm investors.
- **Monitor metrics such as assets, share count, debt issuance, the capital expenditure-to-depreciation ratio, and profitability (margins and return on capital).** Sharp growth in any of these metrics is a warning sign.

Chancellor says, "You don't need supply to increase to destroy returns; capital expenditures will do it." Carefully study the flow of capital into or out of an industry. Investors often do not pay attention to this movement. They simply extrapolate the demand based on recent experience and do not add up how much supply is coming on at the same time. It is difficult to precisely forecast demand, which is unknowable, and, given human nature, the projections tend to err on the optimistic side. Noted strategist Russell Napier has often remarked that analysts spend 90 percent of their time thinking about demand and only 10 percent thinking about the supply side, even though supply in most industries can be forecasted accurately through a number of readily available hard metrics and it takes quite a while for new supply to come online.

In the introduction to his book, Chancellor provides data to demonstrate the robustness of a capital cycle–based investment strategy. Citing research by Societe Generale's Andrew Lapthorne, Chancellor shows that annual returns of stocks from 1990 to 2015 have been nearly perfectly inversely correlated with asset growth. The more companies invest in assets, the worse the returns are for shareholders.

Academic research, Chancellor writes, "is edging toward the conclusion that the excess returns historically observed from value stocks and the low returns from growth stocks are not independent of asset growth." The key insight, according to Chancellor, is that when analyzing value versus growth, "it is necessary to take into account asset growth, at both the company and the sectoral level." He cites an academic paper that showed that the value effect disappears after controlling for capital investment.

What about investors who do not possess the required temperament to invest in and hold on to commodity and cyclical stocks during the prolonged period of a depressed cycle? The cycle for certain commodities and cyclicals, such as sugar, graphite electrodes, steel, hotels, and the like, usually lasts for a longer time than the cycle for other commodities and cyclicals. This gives investors sufficient time to enter a bit late and still make a lot of money during the remainder of the cycle. Many times, even after a big miss on earnings and a sharp cut in analyst estimates, a commodity or cyclical stock actually goes up after bad earnings. This is a typical sign of a company or industry bottoming out—when the stocks no longer go down after companies report bad news. Always remember Howard Marks's two rules:

Rule number 1: Most things will prove to be cyclical.
Rule number 2: Some of the greatest opportunities for gain and loss come when other people forget rule number 1.[3]

The Significance of Empathy in the Investing Discipline

Empathy is the ability to understand and share the feelings of another. It is useful for investors to possess this trait. Different market players are playing their game on the same field. You just need to keep playing your own game, regardless of the game others are playing. Never confuse your time frame with someone else's. A meaningful price level for a shorter-time-frame participant is often an irrelevant figure to someone planning to hold longer term.

Empathy opens our minds to different points of view and reveals certain aspects that might have escaped our attention earlier. In investing, it refers to looking at a business from the point of view of an analyst, a banker, a value investor, a customer, a supplier, and the society at large. Stepping into others' shoes enables us to analyze a situation in the appropriate context.

One of the best ways to gain an investing edge is by using our inherent capacity to empathize. A stock chart can tell you a great deal about what its current holders may be feeling. Think of a scenario with a price volume breakout on a stock from a longtime resistance of $150 that increases to $170. More trading volume means more new shareholders, who are created with an average cost basis higher than the old resistance level. These shareholders are going to be slow to sell if the stock drifts back down. More trading volume also means that many of the older shareholders, who had their average cost near the old resistance level, sold at a profit. They are likely to buy back the stock if its drifts lower.

Generally, the stronger the original resistance level was, the stronger the new support level will be. Many people who bought at $150 and sold at $170 experience a positive outcome, and they create a mental shortcut that associates buying the stock around $150 with a positive feeling. Therefore, $150 becomes a strong support level. In fact, at times, this association becomes so deep-rooted at the subconscious level that these investors end up ignoring facts like a deteriorating outlook for the company's fundamentals.

Over time, as an active and highly engaged investor, you develop what is known as a "feel" for the market. If a group of stocks from a single industry are all rapidly going up together at the same time for a few successive days in a row, then that is a strong signal that the fortunes of that industry may be turning around and should be investigated further. This scenario is even more significant if it happens amid overly negative sentiment for the sector in question. This is one of the best ways to identify inflection points in a sectoral trend that occur as an industry's fortunes are beginning to turn around. Most of the time, we observe that the stocks that are going up together so rapidly do not have any current earnings to support their valuations, but we generally realize only in hindsight that the market was an extremely smart discounting machine. It is why Gerald Loeb said, "The market is better at predicting the news than the news is at predicting the market." Always respect the wisdom of the collective. If a particular stock displays a price volume breakout to fifty-two-week/multiyear/all-time highs on large volumes, then that stock is a strong candidate to start researching. (In technical analysis parlance, if a stock's price rise is on low volumes, it may be topping out, and if the price remains range-bound on large volumes, it implies a distribution is being made. Chartists prefer a decrease in volume when a stock is in its consolidation phase.)

Time frame is important. All else being equal, a stock that has broken out of a multiyear trading range is more promising than a stock that has broken out of a one-year trading range. In the case of the former, many individuals who bought the stock years ago may have sold it a long time ago, out of frustration, and fewer people would be waiting to get back to break-even and to sell the stock at higher levels. Note that prices don't break out of a long-term range unless investors' expectations have changed. Someone is willing to pay a price that no one else has paid for a long time, and this is usually a sign that something major has changed in the underlying fundamentals of the company.

Nothing is more heartwarming for an investor to see than a new high for a stock against the backdrop of a strong earnings report and improving fundamentals. A stock going to a new high is typically a bullish event, because the market has eliminated the supply of all previous buyers who experienced a loss and were waiting to get out at even. A stock hitting a new high has no overhead supply to contend with and has much more of an open running field. Everybody has a profit; everybody is happy. In contrast, a stock near its fifty-two-week low has a great deal of overhead supply to work through and lacks upside momentum, because it is vulnerable to fresh bouts of selling by the old investors at every higher level.

Techno-Funda investors tend to believe in two key principles, in addition to strong earnings growth and industry fundamentals, when analyzing potential buys: first, stocks that show relative strength, that is, that go sideways or consolidate during significant market pullbacks, tend to outperform significantly during the subsequent market recovery; and, second, the first stocks that break out to new fifty-two-week highs after, or during, a major correction tend to become the leaders of the next rally. The beauty of the Internet and social media is that everyone has access to the best brains on the planet for a marginal cost.

The fifty-two-week high list is often a shortcut to the minds of smart investors. At any given time, the market has only a few great growth stories but hundreds of institutions want to own them. For these institutions, it's all about catching the next big thing, and price-to-earnings ratios are a secondary consideration. Trends persist because supply is limited—early buyers are not eager to sell, and plenty of new buyers would like to participate. There's always a scarcity of great growth stories, and markets love high growth.

Even if you do not end up investing in any of the breakout stocks, the positive takeaway from this exercise would be the fact that your mental database will have expanded by studying the annual reports, presentations, and conference call audio recordings and transcripts of the various companies in the industry. (Conference calls are a vital component of any serious investor's research activity list.) For truly passionate investors, researching new companies is just delightful and never gets old. The importance of insatiable intellectual curiosity, along with a deep passion for continuous learning, cannot be overstated in the investing profession. In investing, all knowledge is cumulative, and the insights we acquire by putting in the effort today often help us in a serendipitous way at some time in the future. Work hard today to let good luck find you tomorrow.

Opportunities in the stock market can spring to life on short notice. To take advantage of them, you must be prepared and ready to act. Make sure you properly allocate your time playing offense as well as defense. Playing defense means monitoring the companies you already own, and playing offense means scanning the other thousands of listed companies for new and superior ideas. There's a lot of truth to the expression "The harder I work, the luckier I get." If you spend many weeks and months evaluating a business and end up discarding the name after doing all the work, it is not a waste of time. This time is very well spent. You gain insight about the business, which you put in your mental data bank, which in turn alerts your subconscious when a similar or related opportunity is presented the future, because you know the background and the context and can assess it faster. Our results today are the fruits of the hard work done in the past.

Buffett was reading Bank of America and IBM reports for decades before he ever bought a share. Similarly, the work that I am doing today may not pay off immediately. But I am confident that it is going to pay off at some crucial time in the future, as has happened many times in the past, when a unique insight seemingly fired up in my mind out of nowhere, driven by my accumulated experiences, helped me to connect the dots in a rapid manner. Successful investing is all about "connecting the dots"—finance is just one of the many small dots. In a way, investing is like chess. The novice knows how the pieces move. The amateur knows a few openings. But it takes a grand master to appreciate how it all comes together.

My Tryst with Commodity Investing

In late 2015, the sugar stocks in India started rallying together as a group, and many of them were undergoing big multiyear price volume breakouts. I had never invested in a commodity stock until this point and had restricted myself to secular growth stocks. I was highly biased against commodities, based on my reading about the past experiences of most investors in this category. (John Maynard Keynes identified my problem: "The difficulty lies not so much in developing new ideas as in escaping from old ones.") Many of my respected peers were recommending sugar stocks to me at the time as a highly promising investment opportunity. I decided to come out of my comfort zone and try my hand in commodity stock investing for the first time.

After studying many companies in the sugar sector, I bought shares of Balrampur Chini, in May 2016. I was excited about this selection, as the company was widely regarded as having the most efficient operations and the best balance sheet in the entire industry. What transpired over the next several months, however, left me completely perplexed. Although the stocks of loss-making sugar companies with bad balance sheets kept increasing rapidly, Balrampur Chini went nowhere. Eventually, in November 2016, I sold it out of frustration, at a loss of 7 percent.

Thus, my first tryst with commodities ended on an unsuccessful note. But, in my eyes, this entire experience had served a much bigger purpose. It had opened my eyes to the strong return potential of commodity investing. Thankfully I did not behave like Mark Twain's cat after a bitter experience: "We should be careful to get out of an experience only the wisdom in it, and stop there, lest we be like the cat that sits down on a hot stove-lid. She will not sit down on a hot stove-lid again but also she will never sit down on a cold one anymore."

For many months after this episode, the reason I had not succeeded with Balrampur Chini remained an intriguing mystery. I had picked the industry's leading company and it had turned out to be the biggest laggard. My dismal performance amid such a rapid appreciation of peer stocks in the same industry had ignited a tremendous zeal and curiosity, and I began enthusiastically scouring the commodities universe for opportunities.

This journey of discovery soon led me to an industry unlike any other that I had ever witnessed before (figure 20.1). It led me to an investment operation that soon taught me many significant lessons about commodity investing and about the critical significance of understanding the supply side. It led me to an experience in which I was finally able to conquer many of my personal biases. It led me to a development in my life that exemplified the virtues of lifelong learning and to never give up when in doubt. It led me to the game-changing investment that taught me the huge importance of individual position sizing,

Gautam Baid
@Gautam__Baid

A multi-year fundamentals-driven bull market in the graphite electrodes industry worldwide is underway.Make the most of this big opportunity

> **Niraj Shah** ✔ @_nirajshah
> Spotlight @BloombergQuint
> HEG
> Jefferies on HEG
> Target price - 1050...

7:14 PM - 13 Sep 2017

FIGURE 20.1 The game-changing investment operation.

Source: Gautam Baid (@Gautam_Baid), "A multi-year fundamentals-driven bull market in the graphic electrodes industry worldwide is underway," Twitter, September 13, 2017, https://twitter.com/Gautam__Baid/status/908152062638096385.

significantly bolstered my returns profile, and catapulted me to within touching distance of financial independence.

The two listed graphite electrode stocks in India, Graphite India and HEG, had begun their ascension in unison from June 2017 onward and were experiencing big multiyear price volume breakouts. When you truly embrace lifelong learning, Lady Luck and serendipity eventually reward you in a big way. A few years earlier, I had read Safal Niveshak's blog post of 2012 on Graphite India, and I had developed a basic understanding of the industry. This prior knowledge, in turn, helped me research the industry much more efficiently in 2017. In investing, all learning is cumulative, and nothing goes to waste. Upon further study, the industry prospects looked strong, and, true to my blueprint, I bought shares of Graphite India in August 2017. I chose it over HEG for the following reasons:

- Graphite India had a net cash balance sheet, whereas HEG was highly leveraged.
- Graphite India had a larger capacity than HEG, so it would benefit more from rising prices.
- Graphite India was profitable even during the difficult times, whereas HEG was experiencing huge losses.

How could I lose? I had ticked off all the boxes on my commodity-investing checklist. Buy the highest quality company with the best balance sheet in the sector and you will make a killing during a cyclical upturn.

Except that, once again, things turned out horribly wrong. Graphite India actually declined in price over the first two weeks of my purchase, whereas HEG shot up almost 50 percent, from INR 470 to INR 690!

Making a mistake is unavoidable in life, but losing hope, becoming despondent, and living with your errors is a choice. This time I refused to take it lying down. When you do not understand something, simply roll up your sleeves, put your head down, and get to work. Be a learning machine. I immediately read Sam Zell's book *Am I Being Too Subtle?* which drilled the core fundamental concepts of demand and supply into my mind. I also reread Edward Chancellor's book *Capital Returns* as well as the excellent chapter on commodity investing in Parag Parikh's book *Value Investing and Behavioral Finance*. The right book at the right time will speak to you in a way that the right book at the wrong time just won't. I had previously read Chancellor's and Parikh's books in 2016. I did not appreciate them at the time. I read them again in 2017, and they changed my life.

I generally underline my favorite text in a book and write my personal notes about the key learning points on the side of the pages as I read them, and I keep referring to them from time to time. Always read, reread, and reflect on your learnings from the books you read. When you read them more than once, you will notice that, with the passage of time, because of your accumulated personal and vicarious experience, you are able to obtain additional and new insights from the same book.

You start developing pattern recognition.

Before proceeding to describe what happened next, I would like to spend some time discussing intuition.

Harnessing the Power of Intuition to Our Advantage

You need a certain amount of intelligence, but it's wasted over a certain level. After that it's more about intuition *[emphasis added].*

—Stanley Druckenmiller

First of all I trust my own instinct, *experience that I gained over years and* feeling *[emphasis added] when the moment is right for buying shares. That is what one calls intuition.*

—Alisher Usmanov

I've been reading IBM's annual report every year for fifty years. This year I saw something that sort of clicked [emphasis added].

—Warren Buffett

Self-awareness is vital to improving as an investor. For some investors, an intuition of danger is actualized into physical changes. George Soros would sense something was wrong with his investments whenever he felt acute back pain. He was self-aware enough to recognize negative emotions as some sort of warning signal. As investors, we should recognize sharp emotions as alarm bells. Dismissing these feelings could be a big mistake. Don't just blindly reverse course every time you get a strong feeling. Rather, treat these feelings as catalysts to analytically reevaluate your existing position. Investment decisions begin with gut feelings but always should be safeguarded with logic and hard data.

The role of intuition is grossly underrated in the investing profession, but we can harness it effectively to our advantage if we work at it. Contrary to what many people believe, intuition is not some sort of magical sixth sense. This emotion arises from pattern recognition. Time may not always bring wisdom, but it does provide experience, which in a pinch, can be a substitute for wisdom. The firefighter in Malcolm Gladwell's intriguing story in *Blink* had many years of experience in his field. The expertise, gained from his experience, trained his subconscious to come to expect certain patterns.[4]

Likewise, Warren Buffett's intuition did not develop overnight. It is the result of many years and decades of experience and study. Buffett does not begin his investment process by comparing a bunch of possible investment alternatives. And he does not use quantitative screening tools. Instead, he "intuitively" gravitates toward a company he finds interesting and understands. He then analyzes the company, its industry, and its valuation to determine whether the investment makes sense. If it does not, he moves on to the next company his intuition leads him to analyze. If this potential investment seems attractive, Buffett again relies on his intuition with regard to the management's competence and trustworthiness. He also utilizes his gut instinct with regard to position sizing, judging individuals, and sensing danger. For example, he doesn't assess that one investment should be worth X amount based on analytics alone. A meaningful portion of that decision is based on intuition.

Visualization exercises are a great way for investors to develop intuition. When an investor conducts a premortem and imagines an investment failing and tries to visualize all the possible reasons for the loss, he or she develops intuition about what negative developments to watch for. Investors who have a better idea of what can go wrong with their individual businesses are better prepared for the future. This self-awareness empowers them to sell on time while others are still evaluating the unexpected (for them) developments.

When multiplied over many trades and compounded over many years, this minor advantage leads to material outperformance.

I gained many valuable lessons on commodity investing during my extensive study of the field in 2017:

- Well-managed low-cost commodity producers usually do not generate higher returns. High-cost producers do, because they show a higher percentage gain in profitability. This is highly counterintuitive for most investors.
- A commodity up-cycle lifts all the players in the industry. This is where the low base effect becomes essential. It is relatively easier to improve earnings before interest, taxes, depreciation, and amortization (EBITDA) margins from 5 percent to 10 percent than from 20 percent to 40 percent. This is why the laggards score over the leaders. This makes their stocks go up much faster. In investing, always focus on delta, that is, on the rate of change in earnings growth and its underlying quality.
- When comparing commodity stocks and deciding which one to buy, evaluate them in terms of enterprise value (EV) to installed capacity. HEG was cheaper than Graphite India on this metric.
- Most of the time, sector leaders move up first and become expensive. Then the attention turns to the secondary players in the industry. Investors begin to realize that these secondary players are cheaper, and they bid them up.
- For loss-making companies with sizeable revenues and a low market cap-to-sales ratio, even a small improvement in profit margin adds a significant number to the profit value. In addition, loss-making companies usually have sizeable tax loss carryforwards from the previous down-cycle, resulting in lower taxes and high net profits during the up-cycle. Newbie investors extrapolate these temporary supernormal profit numbers into infinity, and they chase these stocks at close to their peak earnings. You will hear analysts (and sometimes even renowned investors) say, "This time it's different, and it is a structural long-term change in the industry dynamics, which should drive sustainably-higher valuation multiples." During boom times for any commodity, people forget how horrible the past down-cycle was and how horrible the future one will be, too.
- Commodity stocks are valued on an EV/EBITDA multiple, not on price-to-earnings. Investors in commodity stocks need to shift focus away from the profit-and-loss statement to a balance sheet–driven approach. When looking at a commodity stock, debt is one of the most important items to look at, as it has a significant impact on earnings (because of the tax shield on interest payments) and on market cap during an up-cycle. As operating cash flows improve, debt falls, and EBITDA rises for the highly leveraged players, the entire debt reduction amount flows to the equity side of the enterprise value equation and market cap rises sharply. Some companies use the favorable

business conditions to refinance their debt at more favorable terms and lower rates of interest, giving a material boost to their earnings per share.

- Instead of looking at just the total installed capacity, pay attention to existing capacity utilization and room for excess capacity to take advantage of the higher selling prices in an up-cycle. Operating leverage is powerful in these situations. HEG was operating at a lower capacity utilization than was Graphite India. Keep in mind that operating leverage cuts both ways. Those who accurately identify it end up winning big, and those who misunderstand it end up losing big.

- In a commodity up-cycle, the integrated players with captive power or raw material linkages are the biggest beneficiaries. HEG had access to captive power and had cogeneration power capacity of 77 megawatts.

- Never ignore the power of incentives. Align your interests with those of the insiders. HEG's promoter was continuously buying shares from the open market in August and September 2017. Generally, this is a good method to identify the turning point in an industry's fortunes. The promoters of many companies start increasing their ownership (through preferential allotment or by issuing warrants to themselves), together, at around the same time, just ahead of a broad-based recovery in their industry.

- Some agricultural commodities, like sugar, are highly water intensive. In those cases, be on the lookout for deficient monsoons, particularly back-to-back ones. This leads to a sharp decline in output. This is what happened in India's sugar sector in 2015. Sometimes, even within a country, the rainfall distribution is highly uneven, leading to water shortage in certain geographies.

- Check whether prices are determined domestic or international. Also check whether any restrictions have been placed on the import and export of the commodity. Sometimes government intervention in the form of antidumping duties or minimum import prices also acts as a good support for selling prices. A profitable timing of entry in such cases is exactly when the government imposes such duties or protectionist measures and deems them to be in force for a period of five years or more (rather than just for a single year).

- When many companies start announcing capacity expansions, it is a good signal to reevaluate one's thesis, or to exit. This is because commodity producers tend to engage in the misallocation of capital, or "diworsification" initiatives, around the peak of a cycle. They act consistently with what Peter Lynch calls the "bladder theory" of corporate finance: "The more cash that builds up in the treasury, the greater the pressure to piss it away."[5]

- Commodity stocks are not long-term investments. They generate alpha in portfolios in a short period of time, driven by a combination of financial and operating leverage, and you exit them not on peak reported earnings but when the expectations of margin improvement peak out. A good time to begin planning your exit from a commodity industry is when the government decides to curb its profitability. This usually coincides with the period during which the industry starts becoming obscenely profitable, and the cycle approaches its peak. For example, by the time government intervention in India's sugar industry began in 2017, smart investors already had made hundreds of percentage points of returns on many sugar stocks and had begun to offload their big winners onto the greedy latecomers to the party.

- Selective opportunistic plays in commodities often arise between the start of the Chinese winter (when many plants shut down because of smog issues) and the beginning of summer (when the plants resume production).
- Commodity investing is highly challenging and counterintuitive, as stocks can hit fifty-two-week lows even while posting record high earnings. Stocks react less to reported earnings and more to supply dynamics and expectations of margin improvement having peaked out. Commodity stocks typically embark on the inevitable decline from their peak when the markets expect earnings to peak out or decline after a couple of quarters. Once you get a sense that this is happening, do not wait to observe the next quarterly results. Exit while the market is still obliging. Be highly alert and have a firm risk management discipline.
- *When only a single firm in the entire industry is profitable, then the commodity in question may be at or near the bottom of the cycle.*

In the future, when a set of facts similar to those of a typical capital cycle start becoming visible, our experienced judgment, that is, our intuition, will help us recognize the pattern in a timely manner (figure 20.2). It will simply "feel" right.

Charlie Munger has said,

Experience tends to confirm a long-held notion that being prepared, on a few occasions in a lifetime, to act promptly in scale, in doing some simple and logical thing, will often dramatically improve the financial results of that lifetime. A few major opportunities, clearly recognizable as such, will usually come to one who continuously searches and waits, with a curious mind, loving diagnosis involving multiple variables. And then all that is required is a willingness to bet heavily when the odds are extremely favorable, using resources available as a result of prudence and patience in the past.[6]

Powered by Munger's words of wisdom, I allocated a big portion of my portfolio to HEG at INR 700. I also added more to my position over the next few weeks following my purchase. Why? Because the severe supply deficit was expected to persist for a long time (figure 20.3).

On December 19, 2017, a media report announced that the Indian government was planning to impose an export duty on graphite electrodes from India.

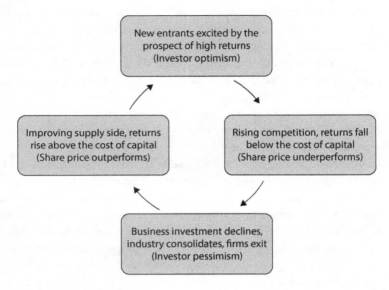

FIGURE 20.2 The capital cycle.

Source: Edward Chancellor, *Capital Returns* (Basingstoke: Palgrave Macmillan, 2016).

Graphite electrode shortage could last five years plus: Jefferies

The graphite electrode shortage could last five years or more, investment bank Jefferies said in a report Wednesday after spending time with management of Japanese producer Tokai Carbon.

Related podcast:
Electrodes, changing trade flows top of mind for many in steel

Jefferies said 10% of needle coke output is now being directed to the lithium-ion sector and anode material production requires the same facilities as graphite electrode production. It also said Hurricane Harvey had taken some needle coke capacity offline.

The natural growth in electric arc furnace-based output at the expense of blast furnace production, led by a drive to reduce pollution, would trigger stronger demand for electrodes, Jefferies said.

FIGURE 20.3 A severe supply deficit was projected for the graphite electrodes industry.

Source: Colin Richardson, "Graphite Electrode Shortage Could Last Five Years Plus: Jefferies," S&P Global, October 12, 2017, https://www.spglobal.com/platts/en/market-insights/latest-news/metals /101217-graphite-electrode-shortage-could-last-five-years-plus-jefferies.

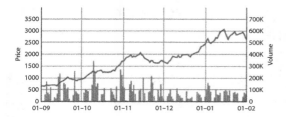

FIGURE 20.4 HEG stock price from September 1, 2017, to February 1, 2018.

Source: "HEG Ltd.," BSE India, September 1, 2017, to February 1, 2018, https://www.bseindia.com/stock-share-price/heg-ltd/heg/509631/.

FIGURE 20.5 A great investment outcome.

Source: Gautam Baid (@Gautam_Baid), "From 700 to 2620 in just months, it has been a wonderful journey in HEG," Twitter, February 1, 2018, https://twitter.com/Gautam__Baid/status/959131998685032448.

Despite my best efforts, I was unable to gauge the impact of this move on the economics of HEG, so I put a deep stop loss in place on the stock on the morning of India's Union Budget, February 1, 2018. The stop loss was triggered intraday (see figures 20.4 and 20.5), although the government had introduced only an enabling provision to impose the export duty in the future. In any case, in my view, the stock was now fairly priced at my assumed selling price of $10,000 per metric ton. (GE prices had shot up from $2,350 per metric ton in April 2017 to $10,000 per metric ton by January 2018.)

Making more than 270 percent in less than five months on such a big allocation within an already enlarged portfolio was a life-changing experience for me. I was now on the cusp of realizing my dream of achieving financial freedom.

But it did not stop there. It never does, when you are truly dedicated to the passionate pursuit of lifelong learning (figures 20.6 and 20.7).

On March 5, 2018, I came across a news report that graphite electrodes were being sold in the Indian market at $14,500 per metric ton and that the supply situation was becoming even tighter (figure 20.6). When the facts change, change your mind. I immediately repurchased HEG at INR 2,700, this time with half the percentage allocation that I had at the time of exit (figure 20.7). In one single go, I was able to conquer a host of personal biases that had affected me since the beginning of my investing career—anchoring bias, commitment and consistency bias, and status quo bias. This is why the HEG investment will always be special to me. It was a significant step forward in my evolution toward rationality.

I finally exited HEG at a profit of 64 percent shortly after the company's first quarter FY2019 results announcement in August 2018 (according to my assessment at the time, margin improvement had finally peaked for HEG, as higher needle coke contract prices would start taking effect after a few months),

 **Nigel D'Souza**
@Nigel__DSouza

Good news for Graphite Electrode producers like HEG & Graphite

VARDHMAN SPECIAL STEELS tells
@CNBCTV18Live @CNBCTV18News
*Prices of graphite electrodes +6x In last 1 yr
*Graphite Electrode Price/tn is at 14500$/tn
(Rs.950 to Rs.1000/kg)- This is higher dan
analyst estimates

10:40 PM - 5 Mar 2018

FIGURE 20.6 Update on the selling prices of graphite electrodes in the Indian market.

Source: Nigel D'Souza (@Nigel_DSouza), "Good news for graphite electrode producers like HEG & Graphite," Twitter, March 5, 2018, https://twitter.com/Nigel__DSouza/status/970896905399144448.

 **Gautam Baid**
@Gautam__Baid

Thanks for sharing this update Nigel. Re-entered HEG today after seeing this data point. I was pencilling in a selling price of $10,000 in my estimates. Looks like there is some good upside still remaining "even if" the Indian government imposes an export duty sometime this year.

> **Nigel D'Souza** @Nigel__DSouza
> Good news for Graphite Electrode producers like HEG & Graphite
>
> VARDHMAN SPECIAL STEELS tells @CNBCTV18Live @CNBCTV18News
> *Prices of graphite electrodes +6x In last 1 yr

11:51 PM - 5 Mar 2018 from Salt Lake City, UT

FIGURE 20.7 When the facts change, change your mind.

Source: Gautam Baid (@Gautam_Baid), "Thanks for sharing the update Nigel," Twitter, March 5, 2018, https://twitter.com/Gautam__Baid/status/970914649045479425.

resulting in a compounded total profit of more than 350 percent on my initial invested capital in this company's stock.

This is the power of compounding good investing decisions in action. This outcome was driven entirely by the sheer intensity of the pursuit of lifelong learning on the part of an individual with average intellect. The pursuit of knowledge enabled me to overcome my initial limitations in understanding a given subject matter. Learning never stops when you are truly passionate. You are constantly in the process of challenging yourself and operating near the edge of your limits. This is what deliberate practice is all about. Over time, these additional small gains that you manage to squeeze out of individual securities during your journey add up to a significant amount when compounded multiple times over. They really do. In my investing experience to date, I have not yet had even one "ten-bagger," a much-hallowed achievement among investors. But I did not require that level of a big individual stock success story to achieve financial freedom. Multiplicative compounding of smaller multibaggers many times over helped me realize my dream. I experienced *the joys of compounding*. (I always kept this simple math in my mind: "Ten thousand dollars. Two ten-baggers. Millionaire.") For a successful investing career, what matters is the long-term compound annual growth rate in overall portfolio value with the least possible risk, not the number of stocks it took you to achieve it.

My Early Beginnings with Investing in Cyclicals

During the past few years, my circle of competence gradually expanded to cover cyclicals like infrastructure and construction. I gained important insight during this period while studying a company named Dilip Buildcon: when it comes to the infrastructure and construction sectors, the market rewards the stocks of only those companies that have strong execution capabilities and a healthy balance sheet that can support fundraising for the execution of future order wins. This very insight eventually helped me identify PSP Projects in 2018.

I had erroneously ignored PSP during its IPO in May 2017 because of stereotyping bias. Investors generally do not perceive the construction industry to have good standards of corporate governance and this industry regularly incurs time and cost overruns. But PSP Projects (named after its founder Prahaladbhai Shivrambhai Patel) was a clear exception. The company enjoyed a stellar reputation for timely and high-quality execution in its hometown of Ahmedabad, India. This, in turn, had led to regular repeat business from its key clients. Since its inception in 2009, PSP had executed thirteen projects for Cadila Healthcare and its affiliates, six projects for Torrent Pharmaceuticals and its affiliates, and four projects for Nirma and its affiliates. The company also had executed many marquee projects for the government, including portions of the

Sabarmati Riverfront in Ahmedabad and renovation of the Gujarat Legislative Assembly building. In its 2017 annual review of Indian operations, Peri Group, one of the world's largest manufacturers of formwork and scaffolding, mentioned twenty-five marquee projects for which their formworks were used by contractors, and it singled out PSP for having "excellent capabilities."

In November 2017, PSP won a project valued at INR 1,575 crore (US$225 million), to construct the Surat Diamond Bourse in Gujarat, amid stiff competition from much larger and well-established peers. This single project was expected to add annual revenues at a run rate equivalent to the current run rate of the entire company. More important, the successful completion of this project would give PSP's reputation for executing large-scale projects a big boost and would catapult PSP into the league of larger constructors like L&T and Shapoorji, in a field in which competition is limited to five or six players. It also would help PSP win similar projects outside its home territory of Ahmedabad in the future. In essence, the addressable opportunities for PSP were expected to expand manifold over time.

PSP's revenues, operating profit, and net profit had grown at a compound annual growth rate of 18 percent, 34 percent, and 38 percent, respectively, from FY2012 to FY2017, and it maintained a debt-free balance sheet and strong return ratios (average return on equity of more than 35 percent). On the basis of its current order book and its vastly improved prospects for large-size order wins in the future, healthy growth rates were expected over the medium to long term. In addition to these factors, the reading of a January 2018 *Outlook Business* article on PSP by Bhavin Shah further boosted my conviction in the company. In that article, Shah highlighted some important points.[7]

PSP had the lowest receivables days among its peers, and its three-year average was just twenty-nine days, compared with 128 for its peers. Along with advances received for mobilization (which supports twenty to twenty-five days of execution), PSP, in effect, was able to run its operations on a negative carry mode (about forty days of negative cash conversion cycle). This, in turn, helped PSP keep its suppliers happy, as reflected in its creditor days of seventy-five days, compared with 124 for its peers. Instead of ordering large quantities of materials, PSP ordered just enough material to continue the work. As a result, it was able to maintain inventory for fewer than five days, against an industry average of fifty to ninety days. This was exceptional working capital management. (As investors, we make our money off the income statement, but we survive off the balance sheet. A cooked-up income statement eventually sinks in the quicksand of the balance sheet. A bull market merely delays the inevitable for such companies.)

In addition to commodities and cyclicals, another section of the market often provides great opportunities for alpha generation.

Spinoffs.

CHAPTER 21

WITHIN SPECIAL SITUATIONS, CAREFULLY STUDY SPINOFFS

Special situations are the happy hunting grounds for the simon-pure analyst who prefers to deal with the future in terms of specific, measurable developments *[emphasis added] rather than general anticipations.*

—Benjamin Graham

Under the pen name "Cogitator," Benjamin Graham wrote several articles for *The Analysts Journal.* He penned a seminal article on special situations in the fourth quarter 1946 issue, in which he wrote, "In the broader sense, a special situation is one in which a particular development is counted upon to yield a satisfactory profit in the security even though the general market does not advance. In the narrow sense, you do not have a real 'special situation' unless the particular development is *already under way* [emphasis added]."[1]

Graham concluded the article by summing up the essence of a special situation as "an expected corporate (not market) development, within a time period estimable in the light of past experience."[2]

During one of the meetings Mohnish Pabrai had with Charlie Munger, Munger explained that an investment operation would do exceedingly well to focus on three things:

1. Carefully look at what other great investors are doing. This includes following their 13F filings.
2. Look at "cannibals," or companies that are buying back huge amounts of their own stock.
3. Carefully study spinoffs.

The very fact that Munger singled out a specific category for a special situation (i.e., spinoffs) is enough to make any serious investor take note.

I was able to better appreciate and understand Munger's keen endorsement for spinoffs when I learned about their high base rates of success.

A global study conducted by consulting firm The Edge and accounting firm Deloitte looked at 385 global spinoffs from January 2000 to June 2014 involving parent companies with a market cap of $250 million or more. To qualify, transactions needed to be pure spinoffs, with shareholders of parent companies receiving shares of newly listed companies. The study found that the worldwide asset class of spinoffs generated more than ten times the average gains of the MSCI World Index during their first twelve months independent of the parent.[3]

The best performance came from the consumer, health-care, utility, and energy sectors. Importantly, value creation did not depend on economic growth or company coverage by analysts. On average, two out of ten spinoffs were either acquired or taken private within two years.

In India, the performance of spinoffs is even more remarkable. SBI Capital analyzed 154 spinoff transactions in India during the 2002–2016 period and showed how spinoffs outperformed the broader market indices across market cycles. Their study showed spinoffs generating an average excess return over the market index (Sensex) of around 36 percent.[4]

Investors often receive a blanket piece of advice like "Never add to a losing position" or "Do not ever average on the downside" or "Avoid catching a falling knife." I simply recommend this: always think it over.

A profitable opportunity often arises when a promising but small-size company demerged from a large-size parent is listed and has residual institutional holding. During its initial weeks and months of trading, you often observe forced selling by institutions that cannot hold the new stock in their portfolios because of certain rigid institutional mandates, such as being allowed to invest only in certain sectors or restrictions on market cap, and you end up with sizeable paper losses on your existing holding of the demerged company's shares.

Whenever someone sells in desperation, they tend to sell cheap. As a buyer, I love to be on the opposite side of such trades in which the other party is being forced to liquidate holdings at any price, regardless of underlying value. The time to buy is when those investors are in a hurry to dump shares at any price. These institutions submit the relevant declarations and bulk deals information to the exchanges on the same day that these large trades are executed. Keeping track of these filings in a diligent manner is the key to investment success in such situations.

Spinoffs represent live case studies on time arbitrage, in which the patient investor is paid for merely waiting and letting the procedural formalities take their due course. A demerger process in India typically involves a sequence of six steps: (1) board approval, (2) stock exchange approval, (3) secured and unsecured creditors' and shareholders' approval, (4) National Company Law Tribunal final approval, (5) record date announcement by the board, and (6) listing of the demerged entity.

Some of the most profitable demerger opportunities arise when the listed conglomerate entity trades at a low valuation multiple. The demerged entities, however, would have traded at a far higher multiple once separated, which sometimes is based on completely different valuation parameters than the currently listed parent entity. (Having a sound understanding of both the relative valuations and the different metrics used for valuing the various kinds of businesses in the stock market gives the diligent investor a significant advantage in spinoffs.) The sum of the parts is often more than the whole. At times, a lot more. This happens in those situations in which a loss-making business is spun off from the parent company and then sandbagged with most of the former's debt. The parent company's valuation multiple, net profit, and market cap go up because of enhanced profitability and a stronger balance sheet. At the same time, the loss-making business gets some market cap based on multiples like price-to-sales ratio or EV/EBITDA (the enterprise value to earnings before interest, taxes, depreciation, and amortization).

Seth Klarman, Joel Greenblatt, and Peter Lynch have discussed spinoffs in great detail in their past works.

Spinoff companies often do not publicize the attractiveness of their business and undervaluation of their stock as they prefer to initially fly under the radar. Klarman explains that this is "because management often receives stock options based on initial trading prices; until these options are, in fact, granted, there is an incentive to hold the share price down. Consequently, a number of spinoff companies make little or no effort to have the share price reflect underlying value."[5]

Klarman states that the parent company also can represent an attractive investment opportunity in certain cases. He frequently recommends spinoffs as a fertile ground for finding attractive investments. In a 2009 speech at the Ben Graham Center for Investing, Klarman said, "Spinoffs are an interesting place to look because there's a natural constituency of sellers and there's not a natural constituency of buyers."[6]

Joel Greenblatt is the most widely known proponent of investing in spinoffs. In his seminal book on special situation investing, *You Can Be a Stock Market Genius*, Greenblatt dedicates a full seventy-six pages to a discussion of spinoffs.

Greenblatt quotes a Penn State study that found spinoffs outperform the market by 10 percent per year. If you assume that the market will return 10 percent, then, theoretically, you can make 20 percent per year by just blindly buying spinoffs. What if you selectively choose which spinoffs to invest in? You potentially could exceed 20 percent.

Next, Greenblatt discusses five reasons why a parent may spinoff a subsidiary:

1. Usually, conglomerates trade at a "conglomerate discount." By separating the unrelated businesses, management can "unlock" value. In other words, the sum of the parts is greater than the whole.
2. To separate a "bad" business from a "good" business.
3. To realize value for a subsidiary that can't easily be sold.
4. To recognize value while avoiding a large tax bill that would become due if the parent company pursued a sale instead of a spinoff.
5. To resolve a regulatory hurdle. For instance, a company may be in the process of being acquired. It may need, however, to spin off a subsidiary to address antitrust concerns.

Another reason why spinoffs do so well, as Greenblatt explains, is "because capitalism, with all its drawbacks, actually works."[7] Once a spinoff is complete, its management is freed from the bureaucracy of the parent and is empowered to make changes that will create shareholder value, because if management owns a significant portion of the spinoff's stock, they will benefit directly. Greenblatt writes, "A strategy of investing in the shares of a spinoff or parent company should ordinarily result in a preselected portfolio of strongly shareholder-focused companies." By proceeding with a spinoff, a management team makes a strong statement that it cares about shareholder returns.

Next, Greenblatt explains how to pick the best spinoffs and shares the characteristics he looks for:

1. **Institutions don't want it (and their reasons don't involve the investment merits).** In addition to the reasons outlined so far, it is common for the spinoff entity to be loaded up with debt or cash. Loading up the spinoff is a way for the parent company to transfer these assets and liabilities in a tax-free manner. Understanding what the post-spinoff balance sheet looks like helps investors better analyze its potential performance. Greenblatt talks about how the presence of leverage can result in asymmetrical payoffs:

Say what you will about the risks of investing in such companies, *the rewards of sound reasoning and good research are vastly multiplied when applied in these leveraged circumstances.* Tremendous leverage would magnify our returns if spinoff turned out, for some reason, to be more attractive *than its initial appearances indicated* [emphasis added].

2. **Insiders want it.** Always obtain a sound understanding of the incentives management has for performance within the spinoff. Greenblatt uses management incentives as his top metric when evaluating a spinoff:

Insider participation is one of the key areas to look for when picking and choosing between spinoffs—for me, the most important area. Are the managers of the new spinoff incentivized along the same lines as shareholders? Will they receive a large part of their potential compensation in stock, restricted stock, or options? Is there a plan for them to acquire more? When all the required public documents about the spinoff have been filed, I usually look at this area first.

The management team of the parent company is generally more interested in managing a larger business, so if they decide to move to a smaller company wherein they receive a healthy stock-based compensation, investors should definitely dig further. Another situation worth studying is when the management of the demerged entity announces a buyback soon after listing but refrains from participating in the buyback in order to increase its stake.

3. **A previously hidden investment opportunity is created or revealed.** Greenblatt writes, "This could mean that a great business or a statistically cheap stock is uncovered as a result of the spinoff." Always study and evaluate how *both* the parent and the spinoff will look after the spinoff transaction. This is because the post-spinoff opportunity may not reside exclusively in the demerged entity. Greenblatt says, "The point is that looking at a parent company that is about to be stripped clean of a complicated division can lead to some pretty interesting opportunities." As investors, we have the option to take a position in the parent, the spinoff, or both, depending on which is the more profitable course of action.

In other words, if the management of the spinoff starts trumpeting its bright prospects immediately after the spinoff's listing, take it as a signal that the management is not looking to meaningfully hike its stake in it.

Greenblatt recommends studying the relevant Securities and Exchange Commission (SEC) filings to check whether the spinoff's management will have a substantial option package. He writes, "In a situation where management's option package is substantial, it may be a good idea to establish a portion of your stock position *before* [emphasis added] management becomes incentivized to start promoting the new spinoff's stock."

Always study insider incentives. A way to do that is to pull out the spinoff's Form 10-12B filing (in the United States, this is the document that the parent company files with the SEC before the separation) and search for "executive compensation." There, we should be able to learn how many shares of the spinoff are reserved for the new management and employee incentives. For example, a spinoff may have the following in its Form 10-12B: "The aggregate number of shares that may be issued pursuant to incentive awards under the Equity Plan is the sum of X shares." Then, simply calculate what percentage of the spinoff's total shares outstanding these shares represent.

In his investing classic *One Up on Wall Street*, Peter Lynch speaks highly about the merits of spinoffs. He begins by saying, "Spinoffs often result in astoundingly lucrative investments."[8]

Lynch believes parent companies do not want to spin off divisions that could fail, as this would reflect poorly on the parent. He writes, "Once these companies are granted their independence, the new management, free to run its own show, can cut costs and take creative measures that improve the near-term and long-term earnings."[9]

Spinoffs receive little attention from Wall Street, are usually misunderstood, and thus are mispriced by investors. All this bodes well for future returns.

TABLE 21.1 First-year performance of spinoffs in the United States with heavy insider buying within a week of being spun off, 2001–2011

Spinoffs	Year	1st Year Return	S&P 500	Beat S&P 500?
GNW	2004	46.92%	6.71%	Yes
HSP	2004	22.62%	6.90%	Yes
LYV	2005	87.45%	11.32%	Yes
AMP	2005	36.42%	14.18%	Yes
THI	2006	39.96%	16.12%	Yes
SBH	2006	15.90%	5.71%	Yes
MWA	2006	−3.10%	17.76%	No
PCX	2007	−18.21%	−41.57%	Yes
TDC	2007	−20.97%	−28.00%	Yes
PM	2008	−23.53%	−38.63%	Yes
HI	2008	−26.57%	−35.93%	Yes
MJN	2009	74.49%	33.67%	Yes

Source: "Look at All These Spinoffs Beating the Market," *Old School Value* (blog), July 6, 2011, https://www .oldschoolvalue.com/blog/special_situation/look-at-all-these-spinoffs-beating-the-market.

Lynch recommends looking for spinoffs with insider buying, as this will confirm the management's belief in the spinoff's long-term potential: "If you hear about a spinoff, or if you're sent a few fractions of shares in some newly created company, begin an immediate investigation into buying more. *A month or two after the spinoff is completed, you can check to see if there is heavy insider buying among the new officers and directors. This will confirm that they, too, believe in the company's prospects* [emphasis added]."[10] Remember, insiders may sell for many reasons, including personal ones. But insiders have only one reason to buy their own stock: they believe it will go up. A particularly strong insider buying signal is what is known as a cluster-buy. This occurs when three or more insiders from a management team make open-market purchases within a short period of time. (Pay special attention when you see a chief financial officer buying stock from the open market. It's generally not in their DNA to think like an owner.)

Value investor Jae Jun of Old School Value studied the first-year performance of all the spinoffs in the United States between 2001 and 2011 that had heavy insider buying within a week of being spun off. The findings were remarkable: all but one of the spinoffs beat the market index performance by a wide margin (table 21.1).[11]

The key takeaway from this chapter: apart from strongly incentivized management, the initial forced selling in spinoffs often leads to some attractive opportunities.

SECTION IV

PORTFOLIO MANAGEMENT

CHAPTER 22

THE HOLY GRAIL OF LONG-TERM VALUE INVESTING

Leaving the question of price aside, the best business to own is one that over an extended period can employ large amounts of incremental capital at very high rates of return *[emphasis added]. The worst business to own is one that must, or will, do the opposite—that is, consistently employ ever-greater amounts of capital at very low rates of return.*

—Warren Buffett

A core test of success for a business is whether every dollar it invests generates a market value of more than that amount for the shareholders. Warren Buffett calls this the one-dollar test, and he explains it in his 1984 letter, "Unrestricted earnings should be retained only when there is a reasonable prospect—backed preferably by historical evidence or, when appropriate, by a thoughtful analysis of the future—that for every dollar retained by the corporation, at least one dollar of market value will be created for owners. This will happen only if the capital retained produces incremental earnings equal to, or above, those generally available to investors."[1]

When Buffett talks about a dollar of retained capital creating a dollar of market value (he prefers to apply this test on a five-year rolling basis), he is talking about a dollar of intrinsic value. His implication is that the stock market will be a fairly accurate judge of intrinsic value over time. (A simple way to do a quick one-dollar test is to compare the change in beginning and ending market value of a company over a period of time to the change in its beginning and ending retained earnings values.) Basically, Buffett is saying that the market, over time, will reward those companies that create high returns on the dollars they keep (by giving them a higher valuation multiple) and will punish those companies whose retained dollars fail to earn their keep (by giving them a lower valuation multiple).

According to Charlie Munger,

> Over the long term, it's hard for a stock to earn a much better return than the business which underlies it earns. If the business earns 6 percent on capital over 40 years and you hold it for that 40 years, you're not going to make much different than a 6 percent return even if you originally buy it at a huge discount. Conversely, if a business earns 18 percent on capital over 20 or 30 years, even if you pay an expensive looking price, you'll end up with a fine result.[2]

The math behind Munger's assertion is easy to follow. An 18 percent return on invested capital (ROIC) over a multidecade period will dominate a 6 percent ROIC in terms of shareholder returns. Simple.

It's simple but not easy.

One of the biggest challenges in investing is determining the competitive advantage of a business and, more important, the durability and longevity of that advantage.

Competitive advantage is defined as a company's ability to generate "excess returns," that is, ROIC less cost of capital. A sustainable competitive advantage is defined as a company's ability to generate excess returns over an extended period of time, which requires barriers to entry to prevent competitors from entering the market and eroding the excess returns. This, in turn, enables excess returns on invested capital for long periods of time (also known as the competitive advantage period, CAP). Growing firms with excess returns and longer CAPs are more valuable in terms of net present value. The value of a company's CAP is the sum of the estimated cash flows solely generated by these excess returns, discounted for the time value of money and the uncertainty of receiving those cash flows.

In a 1999 interview with *Fortune*, Buffett highlighted "moats" as the main pillar of his investing strategy: "The products or services that have wide, sustainable moats around them are the ones that deliver rewards to investors."[3] In his 2007 letter, Buffett wrote what is considered by many to be the seminal piece on competitive advantage and value creation in which he discussed great, good, and gruesome businesses.[4]

For an increase in earnings to be evaluated properly, it always should be compared with the incremental capital investment required to produce it.

Great businesses are those with an ever-increasing stream of earnings with virtually no major capital requirements. They produce extraordinarily high returns on incremental invested capital. The truly great businesses are literally drowning in cash all the time. They tend to earn infinitely high return on capital as they require little tangible capital to grow and are driven by intangible assets such as a strong brand name with "share of mind," intellectual property, or proprietary technology. Great businesses typically are characterized by negative working capital, low fixed asset intensity, and real pricing power.

Negative working capital means that customers are paying the company cash up front for goods or services that will be delivered at a later date. This is a powerful catalyst for a growing company, as the customers are essentially financing the company's growth through prepayments. Best of all, the interest rate on this financing is zero percent, which is tough to beat. Negative working capital is common in subscription-based business models in which customers pay up front for recurring service or access. Because revenue is recognized when the service is performed, which is after the cash comes in, these businesses typically have operating cash flow that exceeds net income.

Low fixed asset intensity can be analyzed by comparing annual sales to net property, plant and equipment, or capital expenditures. In the franchisor business model, the franchisor collects a royalty from franchisees in exchange for the use of the brand name, business plan, and other proprietary assets. The overall system grows as franchisees supply the capital to build new locations, enabling the franchisor to increase revenue and earnings without deploying additional capital. This business model is great if it can be scaled up, because it is capital light and throws off lots of free cash flow by simply leveraging the brand-name equity of the franchisor. This is why Buffett says, "The best business is a royalty on the growth of others, requiring little capital itself."[5] Firms that outsource their core manufacturing activities while focusing on design, marketing, and branding efforts also have low fixed asset intensity.

If the business provides a product or service that is differentiated, has high switching costs, or is critical to customers (while constituting a minuscule percentage of overall cost), it may be able to consistently raise prices at levels exceeding inflation. This method is the simplest way to grow earnings without additional capital, because the flow-through margins on price increases are usually quite high. Companies such as Bloomberg and See's Candies have long histories of raising prices at or above inflationary rates, and Buffett considers this to be one of the most important variables when analyzing a business: *The single most important decision in evaluating a business is pricing power* [emphasis added]. If you've got the power to raise prices without losing business to a competitor, you've got a very good business."[6]

Great businesses are rare, scarce, and thus valuable. They are usually given rich valuation multiples by the market when longevity of growth is predictable with a high degree of certainty. Indeed, longevity of growth is becoming increasingly scarce in today's world, which is characterized by rapid pace of change. The average time a company spent in the S&P 500 in the 1960s was about sixty years. Today, the average is barely ten years. Fewer than 12 percent of the Fortune 500 companies in 1955 were still on the list sixty-two years later in 2017, and 88 percent of the companies in 1955 had either gone bankrupt or had merged with (or were acquired by) another firm. If they still exist, they have fallen from the top Fortune 500 companies (as ranked by total revenues).[7] This is Joseph Schumpeter's "creative destruction" at its very best.

The market places a heavy weight on certainty. Stocks with the promise of years of predictable earnings growth tend to go into a long period of overvaluation, until such time that they are no longer able to grow earnings in a steady manner. Predictability of long-term growth matters more to the market than the absolute rate of near-term growth, so a stock that promises to grow earnings at 50 percent for the next couple of years, with no clarity thereafter, is given a lower valuation multiple by the market than a stock that has slower but highly predictable growth for a much longer period. Consistent growth increases valuation; consistent disruption decreases valuation. The longevity of growth is always given a greater weight by the market than the absolute rate of growth, so you often will notice stocks with 12 percent to 15 percent predictable earnings growth for the next ten to fifteen years getting current year price-to-earnings (P/E) multiples of 40× to 50×. This phenomenon perplexes most new investors, but with experience, they come to appreciate the finer nuances of the market and respect its wisdom. The expensive, high-quality secular growth stocks tend to remain at elevated valuations for extended periods of time because investors in such stocks generally are willing to sit out periods of high valuation until earnings catch up. Markets provide disproportionate rewards to companies that can promise years of sustainable earnings growth.

The principle of scarcity premium applies to the number of high-growth stocks available in an individual sector as well as in the overall market. A business with a perceived sustainable growth rate of 30 percent to 35 percent often ends up getting a 40× to 50× P/E (or an even higher valuation that generally keeps expanding throughout the entire duration of the bull run, as long as the high growth expectations are intact) if only a few companies in the market are able to achieve such high growth rates. In contrast, a business growing at 20 percent may not get more than 15× to 20× P/E if many 20 percent growers are available. (This is why looking at the P/E-to-growth ratio, also known as PEG ratio, in isolation can result in suboptimal return outcomes.)

When growth becomes scarce, the market breadth narrows, and demand–supply dynamics take over. During bearish phases, investors want certainty of growth (whereas during bullish phases, they are ready to take a leap of faith). During such periods of uncertainty, the market's focus becomes extremely narrow, and valuations of the select few high-quality growth stocks in the market keep expanding until their growth rate remains at above-average levels relative to the majority of the stocks in the market. (Most investors remain in denial during this phase, as these expensive stocks keep becoming more expensive.) When growth finally starts decelerating, the valuation derating begins. The actual threat to a bull market stock is not excessive valuation but a sharp correction in its growth expectations by the investor community, because valuations remain expensive and then become excessive until such time as the company delivers above-average rates of growth. Markets love uninterrupted rates of high growth and accord rich valuations to companies that can convince the market that they have the ability to consistently deliver above-average rates of growth over longer periods of time.

Investors with a bias against high P/E stocks miss some of the greatest stock market winners of all time. Over ten years or more, a high P/E company that's growing earnings per share at a much faster rate eventually will outperform a lower P/E company growing at a slower rate. This will be true even if some valuation derating occurs in the interim period for the former. If it comes to a choice between a 15 percent grower at 15× P/E and a 30 percent grower at 30× P/E, investors always should choose the latter, particularly when longevity of growth is highly probable.

As investors, we constantly try to identify "emerging moats" so that we benefit not only from the initial high growth years of the company but also from the subsequent valuation rerating as well. An example would be a lower-margin and working-capital-intensive business-to-business (B2B) company transitioning into a higher-margin business-to-consumer (B2C) company with superior terms of trade. Even if we miss the initial high growth phase but can identify these emerging moat businesses during their intermediate stages, a lot of wealth is created over time.

Good businesses are those that require a significant reinvestment of earnings to grow and produce reasonable returns on incremental invested capital. Many businesses fall in this put-up-to-earn-more category.

Gruesome businesses are those that earn below their cost of capital and still strive for high growth, even though that growth requires significant sums of additional capital and destroys value. These businesses usually are highly capital intensive and are subject to rapid technological obsolescence. They never make any real economic profits because they are subject to the "Red Queen effect"—that is, they keep investing more and more capital just to keep pace with competition and to remain at the same starting position, or they stop investing in new technology and are obliterated. (Debt, intense competition, and high capital intensity together make for a deadly concoction.) Buffett describes them best: "The worst business of all is the one that grows a lot, where you're forced to grow just to stay in the game at all and where you're reinvesting the capital at a very low rate of return. And sometimes people are in those businesses without knowing it."[8]

Consequently, the managements of these businesses often mindlessly mimic their competitors after falling prey to what Buffett calls the "institutional imperative." They are not aware that they are constantly trying to run up a down escalator whose pace has accelerated to the point at which upward progress has halted. They are blindsided by the rapid growth rate at an industry level and fail to heed Benjamin Graham's warning: "Obvious prospects for physical growth in a business do not translate into obvious profits for investors."[9]

Buffett learned this valuable insight from his teacher very well. In his 1999 interview with *Fortune*, he said, "The key to investing is not assessing how much an industry is going to affect society, or how much it will grow, but rather determining the competitive advantage of any given company and, above all, the durability of that advantage."[10] The next time an analyst or so-called market expert touts the rapid growth rate of any industry as a justification for investing in the stocks within that industry, watch out. When all else is equal, a higher ROIC is always good. The same can't be said for growth. Investing is all about individual stocks and their economic characteristics. If you want to participate in the high growth rate of an industry that is characterized by poor profitability, do so indirectly through an ancillary industry that has better economics and lower competition (the best-case scenario would be if it's a monopoly business and the sole supplier to all the players in the primary industry). For example, the organized luggage industry in India (characterized by moderate competition) could be used as a proxy to profit from the high traffic growth of airlines (characterized by hypercompetition).

Buffett sums up the discussion in his 2007 letter with a great analogy: "To sum up, think of three types of 'savings accounts.' The great one pays an extraordinarily high interest rate that will rise as the years pass. The good one pays an attractive rate of interest that will be earned also on deposits that are added. Finally, the gruesome account both pays an inadequate interest rate and requires you to keep adding money at those disappointing returns."[11]

> We prefer businesses that drown in cash. An example of a different business is construction equipment. You work hard all year and there is your profit sitting in the yard. We avoid businesses like that. We prefer those that can write us a check at the end of the year.
> —Charlie Munger

Recall Buffett's definition of the best business to own. I love the business Munger talks about, which cuts me a check every year from its owner earnings. Ideally, however, I am looking for a business that will forgo sending me a check because it has attractive internal reinvestment opportunities. In other words,

I prefer a business that not only produces high returns on invested capital but also consistently reinvests a large portion of its earnings at similarly high returns. This is the holy grail of long-term value investing. At this point, a business has achieved true internal compounding power, which is the product of two factors: return on incremental invested capital and the reinvestment rate. This compounding power leads to huge value creation over time.

This phenomenon was discovered almost a century ago by Edgar Lawrence Smith and was subsequently brought to the attention of the mainstream investment community by John Maynard Keynes, who, in May 1925, reviewed Smith's book *Common Stocks as Long Term Investments*. Keynes stated, "[This is] perhaps Mr. Smith's most important point . . . and certainly his most novel point. Well-managed industrial companies *do not*, as a rule, distribute to their shareholders the whole of their earned profits. In good years, if not in all years, they retain a part of their profits and put them back in the business. Thus, there is an element of *compound interest* [emphasis added] operating in favor of a sound industrial investment."[12]

The two big ideas are reinvested profit and compound interest. Typically, "compounding machines" enjoy a niche positioning or some durable competitive advantage that allows them to achieve high returns on capital for a long time. The key to investing in these reinvestment moats lies in the conviction that the runway ahead for growth is long and that the competitive advantages that produce those high returns will sustain or strengthen over time. When I look at high-ROIC businesses, I am really looking for return on incremental invested capital (ROIIC), that is, the return a business can generate on its incremental investments over time. The growth of a company's intrinsic value depends on the returns it can earn on its incremental invested capital. Whether growth is good or bad is contingent on ROIIC. For companies that have a large spread between ROIIC and cost of capital, high growth is good and adds a lot of value. All things being equal, for such companies, faster growth translates directly into a higher P/E multiple. The value of high-ROIIC companies is extremely sensitive to changes in perceived rates of growth.

Investors tend to confuse ROIIC with ROCE (return on capital employed) or ROIC. ROIIC less cost of capital drives value creation. Even though legacy moat businesses with established franchises and low or no growth opportunities may have high return on invested capital, if you purchase their stock today and own it for ten years, it is unlikely that you will achieve exceptional returns. In this case, the company's high ROIC reflects returns on prior invested capital rather than on incremental invested capital. In other words, a 20 percent reported ROIC today is not worth as much to an investor if no more 20 percent ROIC opportunities are available to reinvest the profits. Mature legacy moat businesses with good dividend yields may preserve one's capital, but they are not great at compounding wealth.

I prefer businesses that grow intrinsic value over time. This type of growth provides us with a margin of safety not just in the valuation but also in the gap between price and intrinsic value, which widens over time as the business value continues to grow. If two businesses (Company A and Company B) have the same current ROIC of 20 percent, but Company A can invest twice as much as Company B at that 20 percent rate of return, then Company A will create much more value over time for its owners than Company B. Both of these companies will show up as businesses that produce 20 percent ROIC, but one is clearly superior to the other. Company A can reinvest a higher portion of its earnings, and thus it will create a lot more intrinsic value over time. The longer you own Company A, the wider the gap grows between Company A's and Company B's investment result.

I cannot emphasize this critical fact enough: although valuation is more important over shorter time periods, quality along with growth is much more important over long time periods (seven to ten years and longer). The longer you hold a stock, the more the quality of that company matters. Your long-term returns will almost always approximate the company's internal compounding results over time. It is far more important to invest in the right business than it is to worry about whether to pay 10× or 20× or even 30× for current-year earnings. Many mediocre businesses are available at less than 10× earnings that lead to mediocre results over time for long-term owners. The intrinsic value of quality business increases over time, thus increasing the margin of safety in the event of a stagnant stock price. This is a pleasant situation because it creates antifragility for an investor. In contrast, if a business is shrinking its intrinsic value, time is your enemy. You must sell it as soon as you can, because the longer you hold it, the less it is worth.

Time is the friend of the wonderful company, the enemy of the mediocre.
   —Warren Buffett

The bitterness of poor quality remains long after the sweetness of low price is forgotten.
   —Benjamin Franklin

The best stocks will always seem overpriced to a majority of investors.
   —Gerald Loeb

An astonishing anomaly is that these superlative reinvestment moat opportunities often hide in plain sight. Most investors shun them at first glance, citing expensive current valuations, and end up overlooking the long-term power of internal compounding. The math behind choosing the right business is compelling.

TABLE 22.1 Comparison of investment results

	Reinvestment Corporation	Undervalued Corporation
Current Earnings Power	$100	$100
Beginning Multiple	20×	10×
Current Valuation	$2,000	$1,000
Percent of Earnings Reinvested	100%	50%
Returns on Retained Earnings	25%	10%
Cumulative Dividends*	$0	$629
Year-10 Earnings Power	$931	$163
Year-10 Multiple	15×	15×
Year-10 Valuation	$13,970	$2,443
Total IRR**	21.5%	13.6%
Multiple on Original Investment	7.0×	3.0×

Note: IRR = internal rate of return.
*Assumes all earnings not reinvested are distributed as dividends.
**Pretax IRR, factoring in tax rates, will only further the advantage of Reinvestment Corp.
Source: Saber Capital Management.

Let's consider two investments and observe which yields better results over a ten-year horizon (table 22.1). The first business, Reinvestment Corporation, has the ability to deploy all of its retained earnings at a high rate because of its strong reinvestment moat. Of course, the market acknowledges this likelihood, and the entry price is fairly high, at 20× earnings, leading most deep value investors to scoff. Conversely, Undervalued Corporation is a typical Graham cigar butt—that is, a steady business with a good dividend yield selling for only 10× earnings. Assume that, over time, both companies will be valued in line with the market, at 15×.

> This is the most nuanced and misunderstood aspect of investing: a fair price may be *a lot more* than you would think *if profitable reinvestment really can take place* [emphasis added].
> —Tom Gayner

> What is most important . . . is that stocks are not bought in companies where the dividend pay-out is so emphasized that it restricts realizable growth.
> —Phil Fisher

When businesses treat equity capital as gold, even those with limited internal compounding growth opportunities can create significant shareholder value through disciplined capital allocation. If excess free cash flow cannot be reinvested, then look for sound capital allocation that might result in dividends or value-accretive buybacks and acquisitions. Henry Singleton of Teledyne Technologies was an exemplary capital allocator. He would issue shares to acquire cheaper companies when his company's stock was trading at expensive P/E multiples of 40x to 50x, and when his stock P/E was in single digits, he would repurchase stock. It is smart capital allocation to raise equity at a low dilution when the shares are trading at steep valuations.

To create significant shareholder value, absolute size of the firm does not matter. Profitability matters. Businesses can achieve high returns through high profit margins. Capital efficiency matters. Businesses with a modest level of margins can achieve attractive returns through high asset and inventory turnover. In both cases, it is the growth in intrinsic value per share that ultimately matters. In the long term, the change in the market value tends to approximate the change in the intrinsic value of the enterprise plus any value added from capital allocation decisions.

ROIC can be calculated as owner earnings divided by invested capital, in which invested capital equals working capital (excluding excess cash) plus net property, plant, and equipment. Certain long-term value-creating expenditures are not always categorized as capital investments but are expensed on the income statement—things like advertising expenses or research and development (R&D) costs. To be accurate, you would need to know what portion of advertising is needed to maintain current earning power (akin to maintenance capex). The portion above that number would be similar to growth capex, which should be included in capital employed. R&D could be thought of in the same way.

Investing is part art, part science, but over the long term, investing in businesses that earn high returns on incremental invested capital significantly improves the probability of achieving above-average returns. Finding a great business that does all of the heavy lifting for you while you passively let value compound is about as good as it gets. These businesses give long-term investors the joys of averaging upward on improved prospects and superior execution, which is akin to giving a bonus to your best-performing employees for exceeding expectations. After all, the promoters of our investee companies are working around the clock to create wealth for us. I have a simple overarching belief that makes me joyfully average upward in the great businesses that I own. Over the coming decades, trillions of dollars are going to be added to India's gross domestic product (GDP). The nation's best-managed companies, with proven ability to scale up operations, will capture the bulk of this upcoming wealth creation boom in India's stock market, assuming the market-cap-to-GDP ratio (also known as the "Buffett indicator") approximates 100 percent over time.

When looking for moated businesses, those with a sustained history of high returns on equity (without much leverage) or high returns on capital are a good starting point. Note that I mentioned the starting point, and not the final point. What ultimately determines investment returns is the future trajectory of the return ratios, margins, balance sheet, and working capital situation of a company, and not the current numbers or ratios in absolute terms. (Wayne Gretzky's famous words are apt in this context: "I skate to where the puck is going to be, not where it has been.")

You might ask: How does one determine whether the attractive returns of the past will continue in the future? In his 1987 letter, Buffett shared his insights on businesses that are built to last:

> The *Fortune* champs may surprise you in two respects. First, most use very little leverage compared to their interest-paying capacity. Really good businesses usually don't need to borrow. Second, except for one company that is "high-tech" and several others that manufacture ethical drugs, the companies are in businesses that, on balance, seem rather mundane. Most sell non-sexy products or services in much the same manner as they did ten years ago (though in larger quantities now, or at higher prices, or both). The record of these 25 companies confirms that *making the most of an already strong business franchise, or concentrating on a single winning business theme, is what usually produces exceptional economics* [emphasis added].[13]

In terms of percentages, the high-quality compounder category likely will have fewer errors—that is, fewer permanent capital losses—than the "statistically cheap" securities category. This doesn't mean one will do better than the other, as a higher winning percentage doesn't necessarily mean higher returns. But if you want to reduce "unforced errors," or losing investments, it is more beneficial to focus on high-quality businesses. As an investor, life feels so pleasant when you are invested in high-quality compounders. Buffett advises:

> Your goal as an investor should simply be to purchase, at a rational price, a part interest in an easily understandable business whose earnings are virtually certain to be materially higher five, ten and twenty years from now. Over time, you will find only a few companies that meet these standards—so when you see one that qualifies, you should buy a meaningful amount of stock. . . . Put together a portfolio of companies whose aggregate earnings march upward over the years, and so also will the portfolio's market value.[14]

A few years back, I randomly came across a sample table of stock returns while browsing the Internet (table 22.2). This was the moment of awakening that made me finally realize the true power of Buffett's insight. It sparked

TABLE 22.2 Comparison of stock returns, 2008 and 2013

Stock/Index	Current Market Price, January 2008	Current Market Price, January 2013	Percentage Return
BSE SENSEX	21,000	19,650	−6%
Hawkins	230	2,350	922%
ITC	110	287	161%
Titan Industries	77	281	265%
HDFC Bank	340	684	101%
Reliance Communications	780	73	−91%
Reliance Capital	2,800	495	−82%
DLF	1,080	225	−79%
HDIL	900	106	−88%
GMR Infra	125	20	−84%

Source: Indianwallstreet (blog), https://indianwallstreet.wordpress.com/2013/01/02/sensex-at-21000-in-2013-making-sense-of-the-sensex/.

an illumination, an enlightenment, an oceanic feeling. Something akin to the one that sent Archimedes jumping out of the tub shouting, "Eureka!"

Consider that $20,000 invested in the great businesses (Hawkins, ITC, Titan, and HDFC Bank) appreciated almost five times, to $100,000, in five years, while the same money in the gruesome businesses (Reliance Communications, Reliance Capital, DLF, HDIL, and GMR Infra) experienced brutal destruction and would have been worth only $3,000.

This led me to one of the biggest findings in my investing journey: great businesses created a lot of wealth even when measured from the top of the previous bull market to close to the end of the subsequent bear market. To achieve big wealth creation, an investor had only to hold on to them in a disciplined manner during the turbulent times in the stock market and stay the course. Liquidity and sentiment drive the market index in the short term, whereas individual company earnings drive stock prices in the long term. Great businesses create enormous wealth over long holding periods across market cycles, even in the midst of negative macro headlines about high inflation, rising interest rates, geopolitical tensions, weak macroeconomic data points, and political uncertainty. Gruesome businesses eventually destroy wealth, irrespective of whether the news is positive or negative.

Sample this. The Dow Jones Industrial Average was 874.12 on December 31, 1964, and 875.00 on December 31, 1981. Nearly zero change in seventeen long years. Yet Buffett compounded his capital at more than 20 percent compound annual growth rate during this period. Investing is about identifying great businesses with high-quality earnings growth and capital allocation and firmly holding on to them as long as they exhibit these characteristics. The stock markets do not really matter over the long run when you invest in such businesses and, most important, stay the course.

Tying It Together: ROIC with Competitive Advantage and Capital Allocation

Critically evaluating the durability of competitive advantage and how capital allocation affects shareholder value can create a variant perception when selecting equities for long holding periods.

—Pat Dorsey

Combining the key insights from this chapter, we arrive at investing nirvana: long-term ownership of competitively advantaged businesses with significant reinvestment potential, managed by excellent capital allocators and shareholder-friendly management teams.

Competitive Advantage

The guiding principle of value creation is that companies create value by using capital they raise from investors to generate future cash flows at rates of return exceeding the cost of capital (the rate investors require as payment). The faster companies can increase their revenues and deploy more capital at attractive rates of return, the more value they create. The combination of growth and return on invested capital (ROIC) relative to its cost is what drives value. Companies can sustain strong growth and high returns on invested capital only if they have a well-defined competitive advantage. This is how competitive advantage, the core concept of business strategy, links to the guiding principle of value creation [emphasis added]. The corollary of this guiding principle, known as the conservation of value, says anything that doesn't increase cash flows doesn't create value.

—Timothy Koller

Companies that produce high returns on capital generally do so in one of two ways: by earning above-average profit margins or by turning over their capital quickly. This is essentially the crux of the DuPont analysis: Return on invested capital = Owner earnings ÷ Sales × Sales ÷ Invested capital.

Businesses achieve high returns on capital through an advantage either on the consumer side (high profit margins) or on the production side (high capital turnover). The smaller the business, the harder it is to have competitive advantage separated and independent from the owner or promoter. (In small companies, the P/E that matters most is the "promoter entrepreneur." The younger the company, the more the investing process becomes an art and less of a science.)

Capitalism is brutal. Excess returns attract competition. Only a few rare businesses enjoy excess returns for many years by creating structural competitive advantages or economic moats.

An extended period of excess returns increases business value. Competitive advantages stem from various sources, including intangible assets, such as brands, patents, and licenses; switching costs; network effects; or low-cost advantages.

Intangible Assets

Some brands are ubiquitous and widely trusted. Think Budweiser, Tide, and Maggi. They lower search costs for consumers and offer psychological advantages. They make prospective customers switch from a system 2 type of slow, reasoned, reflective thinking to a system 1 type of fast, automatic, reflexive thinking through mental association and Pavlovian conditioning. Some brands (such as Rolex or Rolls-Royce) create positional value, while others (such as Nielsen Holdings or Gartner) confer legitimacy.

Although positional and legitimacy brands are based on strong social consensus, the incumbent brands, which merely lower search costs through traditional shelf-space distribution advantages, are much more vulnerable to threats from disruptive online startups. Challenger brands, such as Dollar Shave Club or the Craft Beer Co., do not require a change in social consensus to deliver high value to new users (as they cut out the intermediary and avoid the typical retail markup). Moreover, the use of social media platforms has dramatically reduced the cost of reaching a mass market. Companies can gain scale much more quickly and acquire new customers more cheaply. In addition to these upstarts, Amazon poses a constant threat. As Jeff Bezos famously quipped, "Your margin is my opportunity."

Some companies (such as Apple) simply offer a product or service that is far superior to their competitors' products, and other companies offer a product or service of quality similar to their competitors' products but simply are better at telling a story about that product (such as Tiffany & Co.). Businesses that primarily depend on marketing a story are much more vulnerable to shifting consumer behavior. (The most devastating substitutes cost less and have at least one feature that is superior.) Branding has historically served a few key purposes: to guarantee minimum assured product quality and to allow people to express their identity in a social context. Brands prospered in an environment of information scarcity, in which an asymmetrical relationship developed between customers and companies. Signs are clear, however, that this trend is coming to an end. Brands must be authentic, because very few veils remain between a business and the public. Everything is on the record all the time in today's information age. In a highly connected and well-informed world, value to the customer is the most important thing to consider when analyzing a company.

Another intangible asset is patents. Patents confer legal monopolies (in the case of innovator companies), and a basket of patents is preferable to an overdependence on a single patent. Some regional or national monopolies have a product that customers have difficulty avoiding, something like a toll road. (Buffett often has talked about his love for toll roads in a figurative manner, such as newspapers in one-newspaper towns.) Likewise, licenses and regulatory approvals confer legal oligopoly status through regulatory fiat (as is the case with ratings agencies).

Switching Costs

Switching costs come in many forms and may be explicit (in the form of money and time) or psychological (resulting from deep-rooted loss aversion or status quo bias). These costs tend to be associated with critical products (such as Oracle's SAP software) that are so tightly integrated with the customer's business processes that it would be too disruptive and costly to switch vendors, or with products that have high benefit-to-cost ratios (such as Moody's).

Network Effects

The network effect advantage comes from providing a product or service that increases in value as the number of users expands, as with Airbnb, Visa, Uber, or the National Stock Exchange of India. This functions as a strong moat as long as pricing power is not abused and the user experience does not degrade. Creating a two-sided network such as an auction or marketplace business requires both buyers and sellers, and each group is going to show up only if they believe the other side will be present as well. Once this network is established, it becomes stronger as more participants from either side engage. As more buyers show up, more sellers are attracted, which in turn attracts more buyers. Once this powerful positive feedback loop is in place, it becomes nearly impossible to convince either the buyer or the seller to leave and join a new platform. This kind of business actually becomes stronger as it grows and displays accelerating fundamental momentum. Look at Airbnb's strong two-sided network as an example of a business model that greatly benefits from positive feedback loops (figure 22.1).

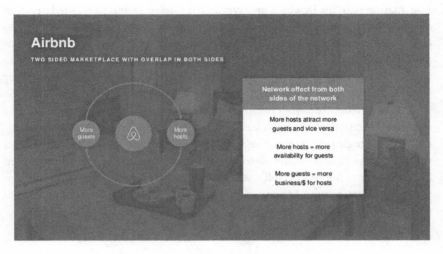

FIGURE 22.1 The strong network effect enjoyed by Airbnb.

Source: "Airbnb TWOS: Network Effects," SlideShare, March 7, 2016, https://www.slideshare.net/a16z
/network-effects-59206938/34-AirbnbT_W_O_S_I.

Low-Cost Advantages

Low-cost advantages stem from various sources, including process, scale, niche, and interrelatedness.

Process. Advantage accrues when a company creates a cheaper way to deliver
a product, which cannot be replicated easily, as with Inditex, GEICO, or
Southwest Airlines.

Scale. Advantage accrues when a company spreads fixed costs over a large base,
as do Costco and Nebraska Furniture Mart. Relative size in a market matters
more than absolute size in isolation.

Niche. Advantage accrues when a company dominates an industry with high
minimum efficient scale relative to total addressable market, as with Wabtec
Corporation or Spirax-Sarco Engineering.

Interrelatedness of new initiatives with existing lines of business. Companies gain an advantage when their product lines or business segments are
interrelated and reinforce each other (as with Hester Biosciences). Saurabh
Madaan of Markel Corporation refers to this as the "octopus model."[15]
Phil Fisher has talked about this source of competitive advantage in the
past: "The investor usually obtains the best results in companies whose
engineering or research is to a considerable extent devoted to products
having some business relationship to those already within the scope of
company activities."[16]

Low-cost producers can sell their product or service at a lower margin than competitors and still operate profitably, because of the large volume of customers. A good example of a low-cost producer is GEICO, the direct seller of automobile insurance to Americans. GEICO has the lowest operating costs in its industry, primarily because it sells directly to its customers instead of hiring insurance agents. Buffett has often talked about GEICO's cost advantage over its competitors as a strong moat: "Others may copy our model, but they will be unable to replicate our economics."[17] The more customers that buy from a low-cost producer, the more its cost advantage moat widens over time, creating a "flywheel" that accelerates as the business grows.

Culture as a Moat

We have discussed the traditional sources of competitive advantages, but a much-underappreciated source of a sustainable and difficult-to-replicate competitive advantage is culture. Culture is best epitomized by such companies as Berkshire Hathaway, Amazon, Costco, Kiewit Corporation, Constellation Software, and Markel Corporation, to name a few.

To illustrate the critical significance of an organization's culture, consider this: from 1957 to 1969, Buffett did not mention the word "culture" even once in his letters; from 1970 to 2017, he has mentioned the word more than thirty times. Businesses with a strong culture focus on delivering a great customer value proposition and communicating about the same more effectively than their competitors do. To create strong value propositions, firms should ask customers what they want to achieve and how they measure success and failure. (Instead, too many firms still ask customers what they want. Customers are not experts on the solution.)

As investors, we look for those companies that are fanatically obsessed with the well-being of their customers and that empathize with them more than their competitors do. Culture matters to long-term investors because it empowers the company's employees to do their day-to-day tasks slightly better than the company's competitors do theirs. Over time, these little advantages compound into much larger advantages, which can persist far longer than conventional wisdom expects.

The answer to the question, "What will widen the company's moat?" should always drive management's strategy. For Amazon, it is improving customer experience. For Costco and Nebraska Furniture Mart, it is sharing scale economies. For Uber, it is increasing availability of vehicles with well-trained drivers. For Facebook, it is driving user engagement.

When investing in businesses that are widening the moat, with the passage of time, these businesses invariably turn out to be much cheaper than what would have resulted from our initial valuation work.

High absolute market share (think General Motors) is not a moat. Great technology products (think GoPro), absent customer lock-in, is not a moat, as commoditization and disruption are inevitable. Hot products (like Crocs) can generate high returns for a short period of time, but sustainable excess returns make a moat. When assessing the moat of any business, simply ask yourself how quickly a smart competitor with unlimited financial resources could replicate it. If your competitors know your success secret and still can't copy it, you have a strong moat.

> One question I always ask myself in appraising a business is how I would like, assuming I had ample capital and skilled personnel, to compete with it.
> —Warren Buffett

Capital Allocation

Capital allocation is the bridge between intrinsic business value and shareholder value. If a company has high-return investment opportunities internally, it should reinvest heavily. Maturing companies, however, often continue to invest despite declining or low returns on capital. (Aging is tough for companies as well as for people.) These companies should instead return capital via dividends or share buybacks. Dividends are important not only for the obvious reason of the use of idle cash but also because they act as a discipline—for a company to pay a dividend, the profits have to be real. Remember, dividends are not necessarily good if they are funded poorly (sometimes management takes on debt just because shareholders expect dividends) or if they are paid out in lieu of investing in high-net-present-value projects and represent a large opportunity cost.

Share buybacks always should be driven by an objective assessment of intrinsic value, but many times, they are done to offset stock option dilution and *manage* reported earnings per share. Note that buybacks do not create value; they simply redistribute wealth among shareholders. Buybacks transfer wealth from ongoing shareholders to former shareholders, if executed above intrinsic value, and vice versa.

Often, management teams that engage in empire building destroy value through extravagant merger and acquisition (M&A) deals. Always check to see whether company size, measured in terms of total revenues, with no mention of profitability, is a factor in management compensation. Managers who are paid handsomely to misallocate capital will do so. Incentives matter.

> I will tell you a secret. Deal-making beats working. Deal-making is exciting and fun, and working is grubby. Running anything is primarily an enormous amount of grubby detail work and very little excitement, so deal-making is kind of romantic, sexy. That's why you have deals that make no sense.
> —Peter Drucker

The simple M&A rule of thumb is this: the bigger the deal size and the less similarity between buyer and target, the more likely the deal will destroy value. During the M&A mania of 1982, Buffett remarked that, in many of these deals, "managerial intellect wilted in competition with managerial adrenaline. *The thrill of the chase blinded the pursuers to the consequences of the catch* [emphasis added]."[18] Big-ticket (often touted as "transformational") M&As have low base rates of success, whereas smaller, tuck-in, or bolt-on acquisitions that share similar areas of activity have higher base rates of success. In general, M&As have a higher chance of creating value when they represent a core element of strategy and when management has a track record of disciplined and value-accretive M&A. Firms in this category are rare. Think Berkshire Hathaway, Fairfax Financial, Markel Corporation, and Constellation Software.

Above all, the truly exemplary capital allocators act as trustees for shareholders. These individuals demonstrate rationality and complete emotional detachment when making decisions.

When capital is deployed in ways that amplify value, shareholders benefit from both increased intrinsic business value and from value-accretive actions. Value compounds for shareholders. (William Thorndike's book *The Outsiders* has done a fantastic job of detailing some notable management teams with a talent for capital allocation.[19])

Great capital allocators can compensate for a lack of competitive advantage (as with Buffett's textile mill), and a great competitive advantage can compensate for poor capital allocation, including value-destroying M&A (as with Microsoft).

To sum up, quantitative data usually are priced in. Qualitative insight, however, is less efficiently priced. Schools can't teach what they can't grade. Thus, things that aren't quantifiable or easily evaluated become niche opportunities. In my view, qualitative analysis is more important than quantitative analysis because quantitative data, like the analyst reports, is often a lagging indicator. By the time you see it in the financial statements, it is too late. The time to evaluate quality is before the price action starts and not after it.

Making the correct qualitative judgment about a business, including the long-term sustainability of its success attributes, is more important than the entry valuation over a long-term holding period. Within reason, you can survive overpaying for a growing high-quality franchise. If you have to go wrong, go wrong on valuation but not on quality.

It seems fitting to end this chapter with Buffett's views on the topic of quantitative versus qualitative investing:

> Interestingly enough, although I consider myself to be primarily in the quantitative school (and as I write this no one has come back from recess— I may be the only one left in the class), *the really sensational ideas I have had*

over the years have been heavily weighted toward the qualitative side where I have had a "high-probability insight." This is what causes the cash register to really sing. However, it is an infrequent occurrence, as insights usually are, and, of course, no insight is required on the quantitative side—the figures should hit you over the head with a baseball bat. *So the really big money tends to be made by investors who are right on qualitative decisions but, at least in my opinion, the more sure money tends to be made on the obvious quantitative decisions* [emphasis added].[20]

CHAPTER 23

THE MARKET IS EFFICIENT MOST, BUT NOT ALL, OF THE TIME

The stock market is a giant distraction to the business of investing.

—John Bogle

In Berkshire Hathaway's 1987 annual letter to shareholders, Warren Buffett discussed the concept of Mr. Market:

In my opinion, investment success will *not* be produced by arcane formulae, computer programs or signals flashed by the price behavior of stocks and markets. *Rather an investor will succeed by coupling good business judgment with an ability to insulate his thoughts and behavior from the super-contagious emotions that swirl about the marketplace* [emphasis added]. In my own efforts to stay insulated, I have found it highly useful to keep Ben's Mr. Market concept firmly in mind.[1]

When Buffett refers to the "ability [of an investor] to insulate his thoughts and behavior from the super-contagious emotions that swirl about the marketplace," he is highlighting the critical importance of a sound temperament. Buffett has always ranked temperament higher than intellect as a prerequisite for successful investing.

It is easy in the world to live after the world's opinion; it is easy in solitude to live after our own; but the great man is he who in the midst of the crowd keeps with perfect sweetness the independence of solitude.

—Ralph Waldo Emerson

Don't let exuberant markets get to your head. Don't let pessimistic markets get to your heart. Volatility of the mind is far riskier than volatility of the stock price, and an objective mind is key to investing success. Remember, disruptions may be accelerating, but human nature and investor psychology have not changed in centuries. As the saying goes, "Don't throw the past away; you might need it some rainy day." Be an ardent student of the history of human behavior during times of utter panic as well as periods of extreme exuberance. This approach will enable you to stay the course during such times and adhere to Napoleon's definition of a military genius: "The man who can do the average thing when all those around him are going crazy." Your lifetime achievement as an investor will be determined primarily by how you conduct yourself during the occasional periods of extreme market behavior.

Benjamin Graham had said, "Basically, price fluctuations have only one significant meaning for the true investor. They provide him with an opportunity to buy wisely when prices fall sharply and to sell wisely when they advance a great deal. At other times he will do better if he forgets about the stock market and pays attention to his dividend returns and to the operating results of his companies."[2] Read, reread, and reflect on this timeless piece of wisdom by Graham. If you can just adhere to these words throughout your investing career, you are bound to succeed. This advice is what Buffett was referring to when he shared the secret to becoming rich in the stock market: "I will tell you how to become rich. Close the doors. *Be fearful when others are greedy. Be greedy when others are fearful* [emphasis added]."[3]

Mr. Market's Mood Swings Affect All Sections of the Market

An important paradox applies to small companies: they are less well researched and yet easier to research. Compared with larger companies, the accounts are simpler, the management is more accessible, and the business segments are few. The market often misprices small-cap companies, as they are relatively illiquid and often ignored by the bigger participants.

When it comes to blue-chip stocks, many investors have a common bias that reminds me of the "bystander effect" seen in the Kitty Genovese murder. (No one who witnessed the crime called the police because they all thought someone else would.) Many investors avoid looking at the widely followed large-cap stocks because they assume that everyone else does. These investors

TABLE 23.1 Top 10 largest companies in S&P 500, as of October 11, 2019

Company	Ticker	Current Market Cap (billions)	52 Week Low	52 Week High	Percent Change (High/Low)	Change in Market Value (billions)
Apple	AAPL	$1,052	142	235	65.5%	$420
Microsoft	MSFT	$1,048	94	142	51.1%	$366
Amazon	AMZN	$844	1307	2036	55.8%	$361
Google	GOOG	$823	970	1289	32.9%	$221
Facebook	FB	$511	123	209	69.9%	$245
Berkshire Hathaway	BRK-B	$510	186	224	20.4%	$93
Visa	V	$373	122	187	53.3%	$146
JPMorgan Chase	JPM	$371	91	120	31.9%	$93
Johnson & Johnson	JNJ	$342	121	149	23.1%	$74
Walmart	WMT	$335	86	120	39.5%	$97
Average Percent Change High/Low					44.3%	
Average Change in Market Value (U.S. dollar billions)						$212

Source: John Huber of Saber Capital Management.

assume that such stocks must be fully priced and that they lack the possibility of having an edge.

The astonishing reality, however, is that the ever-present characteristics of greed and fear focus on short-term thinking, lack of patience, and the innate desire for instant gratification among market participants frequently lead to stock prices of even the large-cap blue-chip companies temporarily becoming grossly out of line with their underlying intrinsic value (table 23.1).

Looking at these figures, it is remarkable that even with market volatility being at all-time lows for much of this period, mega-cap stocks—the ten of the largest, most widely followed companies on the planet—still saw an average of a 45 percent gap between their fifty-two-week high and low prices.

Buying cheap and selling dear is always a good strategy, and Mr. Market keeps offering us plenty of opportunities to do so, even with durable, established, and widely followed businesses. Peter Lynch calls these companies "stalwarts." They are the big companies without a lot of high growth potential. Occasionally, however, you can buy them at a discount and sell them after a 30 percent to 50 percent rise, which largely comes from the valuation multiple reverting back to the mean, as opposed to the business value increasing. Always remember: stock prices randomly fluctuate every day, sometimes wildly on either side, but business value changes very slowly. Therein lies the big opportunity. Focusing on what is moving is part of our evolutionary instincts. This explains why market participants focus more on stock prices, which keep bobbing around, than on business values, which change quite slowly.

How to Think About Market Conditions at Any Point in Time

Bull markets typically are fueled by cheap liquidity and usually come to an end with a sharp spike in interest rates. Buffett has shared important insights on the significant impact of interest rates on valuations:

> In economics, interest rates act as gravity behaves in the physical world. At all times, in all markets, in all parts of the world, the tiniest change in rates changes the value of every financial asset. You see that clearly with the fluctuating prices of bonds. But the rule applies as well to farmland, oil reserves, stocks, and every other financial asset. And the effects can be huge on values.[4]
>
> The rates of return that investors need from any kind of investment are directly tied to the risk-free rate that they can earn from government securities. So if the government rate rises, the prices of all other investments must adjust downward, to a level that brings their expected rates of return into line. . . .
>
> In the case of equities or real estate or farms or whatever, other very important variables are almost always at work, and that means the effect of interest rate changes is usually obscured. Nonetheless, the effect—like the invisible pull of gravity—is constantly there.
>
> In the 1964–81 period, there was a tremendous increase in the rates on long-term government bonds, which moved from just over 4% at year-end 1964 to more than 15% by late 1981. That rise in rates had a huge depressing effect on the value of all investments, but the one we noticed, of course, was the price of equities. So there—in that tripling of the gravitational pull of interest rates—lies the major explanation of why tremendous growth in the economy was accompanied by a stock market going nowhere.[5]

Buffett reminds us to always evaluate data in the appropriate context: "Stocks are high, they look high, but they're not as high as they look."[6] For example, the high price-to-earnings (P/E) ratio of the U.S. markets in 1921 should not have been concerning, because corporate profits were highly depressed and at a cyclical low. The slightly lower but still high P/E in 1929 is the one that should have been worrisome, because it was based on peak margins and earnings.

If any theme in the narratives of past financial crises is recurring, it's the sudden withdrawal of market liquidity. In an interview with *Barron's* in 1988,

Stanley Druckenmiller highlighted the critical importance of liquidity for bull markets:

> The major thing we look at is liquidity, meaning as a combination of an economic overview. Contrary to what a lot of the financial press has stated, looking at the great bull markets of this century, *the best environment for stocks is a very dull, slow economy that the Federal Reserve is trying to get going* [emphasis added].[7]

Investors usually step up their efforts during a bear market, because of the tense environment, and they tend to become complacent during a bull market. Instead, dream big, manage risk, and intensify your efforts during a bull market to achieve financial independence early in life. When you are lucky to experience a bull market, ensure that it makes a big difference to your life. Make the most of a bull market to earn. Make the most of a bear market to learn.

At this point, you may well ask, "But how does one identify a bull market?"

This is how John Templeton has described bull markets: "Bull markets are born on pessimism, grow on skepticism, mature on optimism, and die on euphoria."[8]

This is how Howard Marks defines the three stages of a bull market: "Fortunately, one of the most valuable lessons of my career came in the early 1970s, when I learned about the three stages of a bull market: the first, when a few forward-looking people begin to believe things will get better, the second when most investors realize improvement is actually underway, and the third, when everyone's sure things will get better forever."[9]

And this is how Ivaylo Ivanov, author of Ivanhoff.com, describes the three stages of a typical bull market:

Typical market uptrends go through three main sentiment stages:

1. **"What bull market? The fall is right around the corner."**
   Most of the signs of an uptrend are already here—money is leaving defensive names in order to chase higher yield, breadth is improving, correlation and volatility decline substantially. Despite of that [*sic*], many people don't believe the rally and prefer to short "overbought" names, only to get squeezed by the tidal wave of monstrous accumulation.
   The fastest price appreciation happens in stage 1 and stage 3.

2. **Acceptance stage**
   More and more people gradually warm up to the idea that we are in an uptrend and the market should be considered "innocent until proven guilty." Stocks have been going up for a while and the minor dips were short lived.
   Between stage 2 and stage 3, there is usually a deeper market pullback, which tests the resilience of the rally, shakes weak hands out and allows for

new bases to be formed. The deeper pullback is used as a buying opportunity by institutions, which missed the initial stages of the rally, and their purchases push the market to new highs.

3. **Everything will go up forever**

During stage 1, most people are skeptical, because the market has just come from a high-correlation, mean-reversion environment and most are unwilling to see the ensuing change in market character. In stage 2, investors gradually turn bullish for the simple reason that prices have been going up for a while. Analysts and strategists are also turning bullish in an attempt to manage their career risk. In the third stage, most market participants are ecstatic, not only because prices have been going up for a while, but because they personally have managed to make a lot of money. Everything seems easy, the future looks rosy and complacency takes over proper due diligence.[10]

Initial public offerings (IPOs) are an effective indicator of market senti-ment. During stage 1, good companies come out with IPOs at cheap valuations. During stage 2, good companies come out with IPOs at expensive valuations. And during stage 3, bad companies (many of which do not even have any earnings) come out with IPOs at ludicrous valuations and still are heavily over-subscribed by retail investors, whose surging presence in the markets is a late cycle indicator. Very high levels of margin funding in the primary and second-ary markets is a predominant characteristic of the final blowout phase of a bull market (during which the already overvalued bull market sector leaders' stock prices go parabolic and double or treble in a matter of a few months, to a point at which their absurd valuations can no longer be justified even by the greatest use of any imagination). After this point, a bear market ensues, during which time common stocks are returned to their rightful long-term owners. This is when Charles Mackay's saying comes true: "Men, it has been well said, think in herds; it will be seen that they go mad in herds, while they only recover their senses slowly, one by one."[11]

The quality of investor portfolios is another valuable indicator of the prevail-ing market psychology. As a bull market matures, many investors tend to move their portfolios from high-quality stocks with steady growth and high return on equity to cheaper but higher-growth stocks with poor management quality and inferior return ratios, and then to commodities and cyclicals, and then to turn-around situations that are currently loss-making, and then to microcaps with limited track records of operations, and finally to highly leveraged companies with projections of rapid revenue growth. At this point, the bull market usually tops out, and at the end of the euphoric phase, most investor portfolios have only junk left in them. (Only when the tide goes out do you discover who's been swimming in momentum.) During the bear market that follows, both quality and junk stocks fall hard. The former eventually bounce back in the subsequent recovery, whereas the latter stay low for many years, until the next bull run takes over. Only after going through the pain of a couple of such cycles can an investor resist the incessant urge to move down the quality ladder and chase quicker returns. The greatest learnings always come from a bear market, and these lessons bear fruits for an entire lifetime. Never let a bear market go to waste. A bear market teaches the reality of the harsh math behind compounding in reverse with fraudulent management teams or weak business models. This is when we realize the deep wisdom in Andy Grove's words, "Bad companies are destroyed by crisis, good companies survive them, great companies are improved by them."[12] And this is the catalyst for the transformational phase when investors can take huge strides and begin to rebuild their portfolios to include strong high-quality businesses. The key then is to not succumb to greed in the future bull markets.

You may have noticed that all of these bull market definitions are completely subjective. They don't say that bull markets are over once we hit certain predefined valuation targets or market sentiment survey levels.

The best investors are willing to humbly admit that market cycles do not exhibit any certainty or predictability. On this topic, you should completely ignore the so-called market experts, talking heads, and macro forecasters. It is impossible to know exactly when a market cycle will end, because the pendulum can swing too far in either direction. The challenging aspect of risk management in the stock market is that you can only approximately and qualitatively evaluate the extent of risk but can never precisely time the trigger that will cause this risk to play out. Former Federal Reserve chair Alan Greenspan's highly publicized "irrational exuberance" comments were made in 1996, but the tech bubble popped only in March 2000. John Maynard Keynes rightly said, "Markets can remain irrational longer than you can remain solvent."

For every data point on stock ownership or investor sentiment that shows stocks are overvalued or undervalued, a logical-sounding corresponding counterargument exists. Any time you see a data set or a single data point attempting to define the current stage of the stock market, treat it with skepticism. Markets are driven by emotion. And sentiment, existing only in the minds of human beings, is subject to abrupt change without any notice. (The market is characterized by meta-randomness. Stocks are conditionally random on news. News is conditionally random on people. People are conditionally random on moods. Moods are conditionally random on mind-set.) Trillions of moving parts are involved, so it is simply impossible for a single variable or even a handful of variables to tell us exactly when the good or bad times will end.

It is easy to make logical arguments with data, but far harder to convince someone to forget their feelings. If investors experience an extreme economic or stock market event in the first decade of their career, they tend to obsess over it repeating for their lifetime. We have been inundated with crash calls since 2009. (Much of this is due to recency bias, because we have witnessed or experienced in the past twenty years two of the most widely documented crashes in market history.) Many intelligent arguments explain why the bull market should have ended. It just hasn't mattered until now. And it never will. The stock market will always be totally unpredictable, because it is a complex adaptive system. (George Soros's reflexivity theory suggests that markets cannot possibly discount the future because they do not merely discount the future but rather also help to shape it. Reflexivity is, in effect, a two-way feedback mechanism in which reality shapes the participants' thinking and the participants' thinking shapes reality, in an unending loop.)

Investors spend too much time trying to determine which year the current market setup resembles. Is this 1999 all over again? Is it just like 2007? How about 1987, or better yet, 1929? (Fun fact: if you check Twitter during times of sharp market movements on either side, you will observe people posting images or data drawing parallels between the current market situation and past extremes.) Investor actions are shaped by their most recent experiences, so 2020 is just like 2020. The only constant is that investor emotions shape market behavior, especially over shorter time frames. This is why Templeton, Marks, and Ivanov all use market psychology to describe bull markets and not long-term, cyclically adjusted, P/E ratios. (The cyclically adjusted P/E ratio, commonly known as the CAPE ratio or Shiller P/E, is a valuation measure typically applied to the S&P 500 and is defined as price divided by the moving average of ten years of earnings, adjusted for inflation.)

Market cycles are impossible to call with any precision. The best we can do is use the process of elimination to identify where we are not. As Howard Marks aptly put it, "You can't predict. You can prepare."[13]

As of today, most investors are well past the pessimism and skepticism stages (except for those who have been wrong the entire way up). Improvement is under way. There is no blood in the streets. There are no babies being thrown out with the bathwater. It is not the time to get greedy.

Do these conditions mean it is time to sell all your stocks because of the huge gains made since March 2009?

Whether or not to sell depends on an investor's time horizon, which is the primary determinant of how risk is perceived and experienced. The more time you have, the less risk you bear. Patience is a great equalizer of cycles in the financial markets. Time in the markets with good businesses, not timing the markets, drives wealth creation. This is what Peter Lynch was referring to when he said these golden words: "The real key to making money in stocks is not to get scared out of them."[14] Low- and negative-return years are a routine part of the investing game. You have to be present in this game for a long time to win. The key is to avoid getting thrown out midway because of reckless decisions. We cannot control the direction of the market or what returns it will give, but we can control some essential aspects of the investing process (figure 23.1).

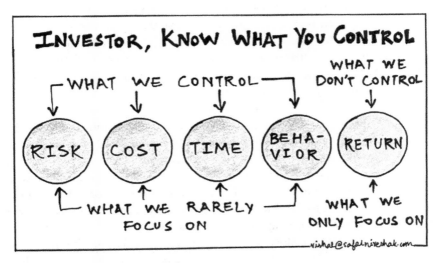

FIGURE 23.1 What investors control.

Source: "Dealing with Stock Market's Moments of Terror," *Safal Niveshak* (blog), February 5, 2018, https://www.safalniveshak.com/dealing-stock-markets-moments-terror/.

Bull markets eventually come to an end. As Buffett has said, "Bull markets can obscure mathematical laws, but they cannot repeal them."[15] Stocks go down sharply, and we experience a bear market. These things are to be expected. When it happens is up to Mr. Market and no one else. I repeat, no one else. A phenomenon usually holds true, however: before a full-blown bear market occurs, it generally is preceded by a vertical market rise of significant proportions. Otherwise, what we experience is simply the random periodic process of corrections. (Intensify your research activity during times of correction, as most of your demotivated competition will want to just "wait it out.") A big bear market needs to be preceded by complete euphoria, a major *unexpected* negative dislocation, and a complete drying up of liquidity. The 2008 bear market happened because financial institutions were going bankrupt. The market was euphoric (India's Nifty index went up 7× between 2003 and 2007), and liquidity dried up completely (credit markets froze after the collapse of Lehman Brothers).

How can excessive booms and busts take place so frequently in an efficient market whose primary foundation is rooted in the combined assumptions of utility-maximizing behavior, market equilibrium, and stable preferences? The answer is found in what Daniel Kahneman describes as the "availability heuristic" (one of the most insidious and potent cognitive biases):

People tend to assess the relative importance of issues by the ease with which they are retrieved from memory—and this is largely determined by the extent of coverage in the media. Frequently mentioned topics populate the mind even as others slip away from awareness. In turn, what the media choose to report corresponds to their view of what is currently on the public's mind. It is no accident that authoritarian regimes exert substantial pressure on independent media. Because public interest is most easily aroused by dramatic events and by celebrities, media feeding frenzies are common.[16]

Availability errors are a common source of folly in human reasoning. Whenever a memory turns up high in the results list of the mind's search engine for reasons other than frequency—because it is recent, vivid, gory, distinctive, or upsetting—people tend to grossly overestimate its likelihood. Because of the extreme media emphasis on either side, widespread greed feeds on greed and widespread fear feeds on fear. When prices move up or down sharply, they tend to create self-reinforcing loops. And this leads to the consequent boom-and-bust cycles wherein stock prices are completely dislocated from underlying business values. During these times, investors should always heed Buffett's advice: "The less prudence with which others conduct their affairs, the greater the prudence with which we should conduct our own affairs." He continues, "During such scary periods, you should never forget two things: First, *widespread fear is your friend as an investor*, because it serves up bargain purchases. Second, *personal fear is your enemy* [emphasis added]."[17]

Markets oscillate between extreme optimism and pessimism, which is why it is so useful to have a "reverse discounted cash flow frame of mind." Invert, always invert. Stock prices sometimes fall to such extremely low levels that the earnings of the next three to four years alone add up to the current market cap. Conversely, sometimes stock prices go to such extremely high levels that even a high earnings growth rate for a decade would not produce earnings sufficient to justify a future value large enough to make a commitment today. Thinking in terms of a reverse discounted cash flow analysis to evaluate stocks during such periods helps investors make better decisions.

Mr. Market is a delightful opponent to play against, because even in general market conditions, he lets investors capitalize on the mispricings that result from his prejudices and constant tendency to paint all stocks within a group with the same brush. In other words, Mr. Market often resorts to blanket categorization, or what Kahneman has referred to as the unnecessary negative connotation associated with "stereotyping":

> Stereotyping is a bad word in our culture, but in my usage it is neutral. One of the basic characteristics of System 1 is that it represents categories as norms and prototypical exemplars. This is how we think of horses, refrigerators, and New York police officers; we hold in memory a representation of one or more "normal" members of each of these categories. When the categories are social,

these representations are called stereotypes. Some stereotypes are perniciously wrong, and hostile stereotyping can have dreadful consequences, but the psychological facts cannot be avoided: stereotypes, both correct and false, are how we think of categories.[18]

Consider the following notable examples of how biased Mr. Market frequently gives patient investors many opportunities:

1. Grossly undervaluing moated businesses on a long-term basis by focusing on accounting earnings instead of owner earnings and normalized long-term earning power. In these cases, the economic earnings generally exceed the accounting earnings, even though the accounting P/E ratio looks optically high.
2. Overlooking a "hidden champion" that is a critical part of the value chain in a commodity industry and that consistently exhibits high gross margins that are stable over time, indicating pricing power.
3. Not giving the long rope to an entrepreneur who is a learning machine, even after he has rectified his past mistakes and has taken a series of value-creating initiatives.
4. Totally bypassing serial acquirers as a broad category, even though few companies have a proven long-term track record of successful value-accretive M&A deals.
5. Completely shunning IPOs even when they pertain to great businesses being offered at cheap valuations during a bear market, citing the various oft-stated cons of IPOs, like the timing option for the sale being in the hands of insiders, the presence of many buyers and only a handful of sellers, and the incentive for merchant bankers to act in the insiders' best interests by "managing" the IPO in a way that maximizes the amount of money raised with the issuance of the fewest shares possible. (Some notable red flags include a company name change just before the IPO to reflect a currently fancied sector; a sudden jump in sales or profitability in the year of or immediately preceding the IPO and inconsistent growth in prior years; the primary objective of the IPO being "to meet working capital requirements"; or the IPO being issued at peak multiples on peak earnings near the top of the industry cycle.) Note that IPOs of sunrise businesses that have few to no listed peers tend to command a scarcity premium.
6. Exhibiting reluctance to invest in great businesses available at reasonable valuations just because they have large absolute stock prices.
7. Lacking the ability to delay gratification and ending up heavily discounting the distant future cash flows of companies that currently are undergoing a large expansion program and consequently experiencing depressed reported earnings in the near term because of the significant initial operating expenses incurred amid low-capacity utilization.

8. Stereotyping a promoter with an extravagant salary as unethical, even though the opportunity cost of not siding with certain intelligent fanatics may be high when the various aspects specific to the investment situation at hand are considered in totality.
9. Labeling an entire industry as untouchable and completely ignoring the exceptional performers within it.
10. Getting confused between risk and uncertainty, which results in significant mispricing in certain cases. Risk is the potential for permanent loss of capital or purchasing power, whereas uncertainty refers to an unpredictable range of possible outcomes. In these situations, it ultimately boils down to the price. Just because a company's future is highly uncertain or unknown at present, this does not mean an investment in it is risky. In fact, some of the best investment opportunities are highly uncertain but have minimal risk of permanent capital loss.
11. Throwing out the baby with the bathwater. This is a common occurrence in spinoffs and bankruptcy situations. Abruptly mispriced opportunities keep arising in the financial markets from time to time. Always be alert.
12. Separating a given company's bonds into two buckets—high risk and low risk— based on certain "labels." Sometimes, a company's "junior" bonds are issued at a high interest rate at a time when the same entity's "senior" bonds are offering a low interest rate. Investors should heed Graham's words of wisdom in such cases: "If *any* obligation of an enterprise deserves to qualify as a creditworthy investment, then *all* its obligations must do so. Stated conversely, if a company's junior bonds are not safe, its first-mortgage bonds are not creditworthy either. For, if the second mortgage is unsafe, the company itself is weak, and generally speaking there can be no creditworthy obligations of a weak enterprise."[19]

Successful investing in these various situations is all about having people agree with you—later. The alignment between price and value can be greatly distorted by psychological and technical factors in the short term. As Graham said, "In the short run, the market is a voting machine, but in the long run, it is a weighing machine."[20] Ironically, to generate alpha, investors need the markets to be efficient—eventually. The market needs to realize that it has made an error and then to correct it. Otherwise, mispricings would persist forever, and in such a market, no one could reliably outperform.

Market Efficiency and the Wisdom of Crowds

Information is not a single big thing that's locked in a safe. It exists in bits and pieces scattered around the world. Everybody has a little piece of the total information available. If information is widely scattered and diffuse, then no single individual is going to have much information relative to the total. In fact, regardless of how smart or informed a person is, any given individual has only a fraction of the information available to the entire market at any point in time. The function of the markets is to aggregate that information, evaluate it, and incorporate it into prices. Through the wisdom of crowds and the power of efficient markets, the current price of a security swiftly reflects the market's collective assessment of the likelihood of possible, plausible, and probable future events. (To understand and appreciate the incredible information-gathering capability of the stock market, study Michael Maloney and J. Harold Mulherin's famous case analysis titled "The Complexity of Price Discovery in an Efficient Market: The Stock Market Reaction to the Challenger Crash."[21]) Don't let the markets become your master, however; a collective loss of sensibility can result when herd mentality takes over. Knowing when the market is being brilliantly rational and when it is being ludicrously irrational is learned from experience and an extensive study of financial history.

The wisdom of crowds aggregation process in the market generates an "accurate" answer by transferring (partial) domain-specific knowledge from individuals to the collective. A popular example of the wisdom of crowds phenomenon is the analysis of a 1906 ox-weighing contest, written by Sir Francis Galton, titled "Vox Populi."[22] Three key tenets of market efficiency pertain to information, and the wisdom of crowds implements those tenets under six conditions. For each of the following, only a sufficient or threshold number of investors, not all, is required for the condition to hold.

1. **Dissemination.** Information must be available and observed.
2. **Processing.** The group must have an adequate amount of domain-specific knowledge in the form of facts or expertise, the crowd must be diverse, and investors must act independently.
3. **Information.** Investors should not face significant impediments to trading; otherwise, estimates of value will not be expressed, aggregated, and incorporated into the stock price; and individuals must have incentives to give estimates that they believe are true.

When these conditions are met, the crowd produces an accurate answer and it will be next to impossible for the individual to beat the collective.

When I read James Surowiecki's book *The Wisdom of Crowds*, I finally learned to recognize the significance and deeper meaning of trading volumes. When in doubt about a stock after a sudden sharp move on either side, look at the volumes. The collective wisdom of the market will guide you in the right direction most of the time. Knowledge compounds over time. As new neural connections are formed in our brains, through both direct and vicarious experience, a latticework of mental models starts to develop. Keep learning every day to constantly nurture and nourish this vibrant latticework. You never know when you will experience a big "eureka" moment. (Always note such findings immediately. You may not be able to recall them at a later date.) Any one of these findings could help you earn handsome profits during a sudden fortunate phase in your investing journey. Continuously work toward creating opportunities for serendipity to find you at the unlikeliest of times and places in your life.

CHAPTER 24

THE DYNAMIC ART OF PORTFOLIO MANAGEMENT AND INDIVIDUAL POSITION SIZING

Diversification is the best way to admit you have no idea what's going to happen in the future. It's how you prepare a portfolio for a wide range of future possibilities and admit your own infallibility.

—Ben Carlson

Many articles, books, and white papers on investing recommend having a highly diversified investment portfolio. The reality, however, is that all you are doing in this case is swapping one type of risk for another. You are exchanging company-specific risk (unsystematic risk), which may be quite low, depending on the type of company in which you invest, for market risk (systematic risk). Risk hasn't been reduced, it simply has been transferred from one form to another. Diversification of investments is touted as reducing both risk and volatility. Although a diversified portfolio indeed may reduce your overall level of risk, it also may correspondingly reduce your potential level of reward. The more extensively diversified an investment portfolio, the greater the likelihood is that it, at best, mirrors the performance of the overall market.

Because many investors aim for better-than-market-average investment returns, it is important to have a clear understanding of diversification versus concentration in portfolio choices. Some level of diversification should be considered in constructing an investment portfolio, but it should not be the main driver. The primary focus of an investment operation should always be on putting together a portfolio that is best suited to meet the personal life goals and financial needs of the individual. The only benchmark any investor should care about is whether they're on track to reach the goals they set up their portfolio to achieve in the first place. From my readings over the years, I have gleaned the following thoughts about diversification versus concentration.[1]

Overdiversification tends to result in mediocre performance . . .

The academics have done a terrible disservice to intelligent investors by glorifying the idea of diversification. Because I just think the whole concept is literally almost insane. It emphasizes feeling good about not having your investment results depart very much from average investment results.
 —Charlie Munger

The appeal of a concentrated portfolio is that it is the only chance an investor has to beat the averages by a noteworthy margin.
 —Frank Martin

because the benefits of diversification start diminishing beyond a certain point.

Statistical analysis shows that security-specific risk is adequately diversified after fourteen names in different industries, and the incremental benefit of each additional holding is negligible.
 —Mason Hawkins

Two things should be remembered, after purchasing six or eight stocks in different industries, the benefit of adding even more stocks to your portfolio in an effort to decrease risk is small, and overall market risk will not be eliminated merely by adding more stocks to your portfolio.
 —Joel Greenblatt

I decided to run a concentrated portfolio. As Joel Greenblatt pointed out, holding eight stocks eliminates 81 percent of the risk in owning just one stock, and holding thirty-two stocks eliminates 96 percent of the risk. This insight struck me as incredibly important.
 —David Einhorn

Great ideas are rare . . .

The idea that it is hard to find good investments, so concentrate in a few, seems to me to be an obviously good idea. But ninety-eight percent of the investment world doesn't think this way.

—Charlie Munger

In the field of common stocks, a little bit of a great many can never be more than a poor substitute for a few of the outstanding.

—Phil Fisher

so focus, and concentrate in your best ideas.

Phil Fisher believed in concentrating in about ten good investments and was happy with a limited number. That is very much in our playbook. And he believed in knowing a lot about the things he did invest in. And that's in our playbook, too. And the reason why it's in our playbook is that to some extent we learned it from him.

—Charlie Munger

We believe that a policy of portfolio concentration may well decrease risk if it raises, as it should, both the intensity with which an investor thinks about a business and the comfort-level he must feel with its economic characteristics before buying into it.

—Warren Buffett

Avoid excessive diversification . . .

For individuals, any holding of over twenty different stocks is a sign of financial incompetence.

—Phil Fisher

because risk lies in not knowing what you are doing.

As time goes on, I get more and more convinced that the right method in investment is to put fairly large sums into enterprises which one thinks one knows something about and in the management of which one thoroughly believes. It is a mistake to think that one limits one's risk by spreading too much between enterprises about which one knows little and has no reason for special confidence.

—John Maynard Keynes

The desire to spread stock picking risks over a number of different securities must be balanced against the negative impacts of spreading research resources so thin that an intimate understanding of a company or industry is lost. In such cases, diversification can become "di-worse-ification."
  —Lee Ainslie

Avoid extreme concentration like Buffett and Munger, unless you have very high expertise . . .

If you can identify six wonderful businesses, that is all the diversification you need. And you will make a lot of money. And I can guarantee that going into a seventh one instead of putting more money into your first one is gotta be a terrible mistake. Very few people have gotten rich on their seventh best idea.
  —Warren Buffett

A well-diversified portfolio needs just four stocks.
  —Charlie Munger

instead, practice sufficient diversification . . .

For an individual investor you want to own at least ten and probably fifteen and as many as twenty different securities. Many people would consider that to be a relatively highly concentrated portfolio. In our view you want to own the best ten or fifteen businesses you can find, and if you invest in low leverage/high-quality companies, that's a comfortable degree of diversification.
  —Bill Ackman

and structure a concentrated yet diverse portfolio in terms of risk exposures.

Most investors think diversification consists of holding many different things, few understand that diversification is effective only if portfolio holdings can be counted on to respond differently to a given development in the environment.
  —Howard Marks

If each of our holdings turned out to involve similar bets (inflation hedges, interest rate sensitive, single market or asset type, etc.), we would be exposed to dramatic and sudden reversals in our entire portfolio were investor perceptions of the macro environment to change. Since we are not able to predict the future, we cannot risk such concentrations.
  —Seth Klarman

In May 1938, John Maynard Keynes outlined his investment policy in a memo distributed to the Estates Committee of King's College, Cambridge:

1. a careful selection of a few investments (or a few types of investment) having regard to their cheapness in relation to their probable actual and potential intrinsic value over a period of years ahead and in relation to alternative investments at the time;
2. a steadfast holding of these in fairly large units through thick and thin, perhaps for several years, until either they have fulfilled their promise or it is evident that they were purchased on a mistake; and
3. a balanced investment position, i.e., a variety of risks in spite of individual holdings being large, and if possible, opposed risks.[2]

In September 2006, Howard Marks wrote a memo entitled "Dare to Be Great," in which he praised a quote from the book *Pioneering Portfolio Management*, by David Swensen, Yale University's longtime chief investment officer: "Establishing and maintaining an unconventional investment profile requires acceptance of uncomfortably idiosyncratic portfolios, which frequently appear downright imprudent in the eyes of conventional wisdom."[3] (Warren Buffett's treatise on portfolio management in his January 1966 partnership letter is a tour de force on the subject.)

The Babe Ruth Effect

According to the late management guru Peter Drucker, "Efficiency is doing things right; effectiveness is doing the right things." In investing, the latter refers to picking the right stock and the former refers to appropriate allocation. Anyone can identify a winning stock, but the great investors differentiate themselves through superior individual position sizing. Given that the average success rate of an investment idea is less than 50 percent, even for the best investors, it really does matter that when you win, you make it count. When you find a great idea, buy enough of it to make a meaningful difference to your life. Successful investing is not only about being right per se—far from it. Success in investing boils down to how the great ideas are executed, that is, initial allocation and subsequent pyramiding. It is not the frequency of winning that matters, but the frequency times the magnitude of the payoff. Michael Mauboussin calls this the "Babe Ruth effect." It is what George Soros was referring to when he said, "It's not whether you're right or wrong that's important, but how much money you make when you're right and how much you lose when you're wrong."[4]

How can we inculcate this "expected value" way of thinking in our investment decision-making?

Take the probability of loss times the amount of possible loss from the probability of gain times the amount of possible gain. That is what we're trying to do. It's imperfect, but that's what it's all about.

—Warren Buffett

The stock market is a pari-mutuel system. Participants place their bets and the odds change based on these bets. Therefore, the only way to consistently outperform the market is to evaluate, better than other investors, the probabilities that market participants assign to potential outcomes.

The key to successful investing is to explicitly distinguish between fundamentals (i.e., the intrinsic value of the company based on expected future results) and market expectations (i.e., the stock price and the future results it currently is factoring in). Investing is all about expectations, and the outcomes are driven by revisions in expectations, which trigger changes in the stock price. Therefore, the ability to properly read market expectations and anticipate revisions of those expectations is the springboard for superior returns. To do this successfully, an investor needs to have "variant perception," that is, one must hold a well-founded view that is meaningfully different from the market consensus. (One of the most satisfying moments in investing is when the world looks at a business the same way you did three or four years earlier.)

Charlie Munger drew an analogy between investing and a pari-mutuel betting system in his 2003 University of California, Santa Barbara lecture: "To us, investing is the equivalent of going out and betting against the pari-mutuel system. We look for a horse with one chance in two of winning and which pays you three to one. You're looking for a mispriced gamble. That's what investing is. And you have to know enough to know whether the gamble is mispriced. That's value investing."[5]

The key investing lesson from the pari-mutuel system is to make a few large bets infrequently. Investors should adhere to Munger's simple but profound advice: "Look at lots of deals. Don't do almost all of them."[6]

In a 1994 lecture titled "A Lesson on Elementary, Worldly Wisdom as It Relates to Investment Management and Business," Munger said:

It's not given to human beings to have such talent that they can just know everything about everything all the time. But it is given to human beings who work hard at it—who look and sift the world for a mispriced bet—that they can occasionally find one.

And the wise ones bet heavily when the world offers them that opportunity. They bet big when they have the odds. And the rest of the time, they don't [emphasis added]. It's just that simple.[7]

But how can investors determine the optimal size of the individual bet? The Kelly criterion gives us the answer.

The Kelly Criterion

Formulated by John L. Kelly and popularized by the practical success of Ed Thorp, the Kelly criterion is a formula used to determine the optimal bet size for a given set of probabilities and payoffs. Although the formula can be stated in several ways, the following expanded version appeared in Thorp's interview in the book *Hedge Fund Market Wizards*:

$$F = P_W - (P_L/[\$W / \$L]),$$

where:
F = Kelly criterion fraction of capital to bet,
P_W = probability of winning the bet,
P_L = probability of losing the bet,
$\$W$ = dollars won if bet is won, and
$\$L$ = dollars lost if bet is lost.[8]

If an individual knows the odds and payouts of a given bet with precision, the Kelly criterion bet size will maximize capital over the long run. A key difficulty, however, is that people don't get precise odds, and only in the rare special situation or arbitrage do they obtain a reasonable picture of the payout. Another hurdle is that, when utilizing Kelly, the long run is based on the number of events, not on a time frame. An investor who bets infrequently will have trouble making enough investments to get the full long-term benefits of applying Kelly.

Another key limitation is that people tend to underestimate the role of infrequent, high-impact events, or Taleb's black swans. The probability and downside magnitude of negative black swans may not be given the necessary consideration when investors look to apply the Kelly criterion, and thus the formula, when applied by the human mind, may tend to overestimate F. And continual overestimation leads to ruin. Anything above the optimal bet size will lead to total loss sooner or later.

Despite the practical difficulties and impediments in its application to real-world investing, the underlying logic behind the Kelly criterion is highly beneficial as a way to think about whether to establish a position in a given situation and, if one is to be established, what proportion of capital should be invested in that position.

I size individual allocations in my portfolio according to my evaluation of potential risk, with the largest holdings having the lowest likelihood of permanent capital loss coupled with above-average return potential. I initiate new positions with a minimum weighting of 5 percent and subsequently average upward if the management executes above my expectations. Individual position sizing is important not only for its impact on overall portfolio performance but also for mental peace of mind. I sell down to my "sleeping point" if an individual position becomes a discomfortingly large percentage of my portfolio value. Always have bigger weights in businesses with high longevity, solid growth prospects, and disciplined capital allocators. As Mae West said, "Too much of a good thing can be wonderful."

Our constant focus as investors should be on increasing the intrinsic value of our portfolio and letting the market give us gains according to its own schedule. If we are patient, we eventually will get rewarded, because financial markets ultimately take money away from mediocre and stagnant businesses and redirect it toward growing, profitable ones. Money never sleeps. Every crisis brings an opportunity. We have a better way to look at the world and to think deeply about our investments. This is the glass-half-full approach, and it comes from a basic understanding of how capitalism functions. Every bust in one area of the market establishes the foundations for a boom in another. Every company's rising cost is another company's rising revenue; every company's declining revenue is another company's declining cost. The best part is that the stock market usually does an excellent job of recognizing the beneficiaries in each situation by sending their stocks to the fifty-two-week-high list. Money has a metaphysical-like attraction to places of its best possible use. This is one of the powerful correcting forces of capitalism. Take advantage of it.

We should not aim for the highest possible returns in the shortest period of time but rather we should seek above-average returns over a long period of time with the lowest possible risk. Risk management should take a higher precedence in the investment process, and risk-adjusted returns are a far superior indicator of performance than absolute returns. This is especially true during bull markets, when aggressive risk taking often is mistaken for intelligence. What's important is the underlying process used by the fund manager or investment advisory firm and the amount of risk taken on in client portfolios to achieve those high returns. That process is the key to long-term sustainability. High absolute returns in isolation carry little significance for assessing performance.

A bull market hides many mistakes. As Humphrey Neill said, "Don't confuse brains with a bull market." (For example, during a bull market year like 2017, if I made money on faulty picks like Lasa Supergenerics and White Organic, does that mean that I was smart? No. Making money on a stock is not the same as being right.) A bull market inculcates many bad habits in investors. The hard lessons are learned in the subsequent bear market. For instance, the perceived importance of being in the hands of good management diminishes in a bull market and increases manifold in a bearish market during the flight to quality. When a sector or a stock is in high demand, few investors care about the management's integrity—for which such individuals eventually pay the price when market conditions deteriorate. A bear market typically culminates with a plethora of frauds and scams (which, at times, are discovered to have been committed even by some erstwhile blue-chip names).

In a bull market, no price is too high, and investors seem to get a kick out of buying stocks at inflated prices. But in an uncertain market, they fuss about return ratios, cash flows, balance sheet quality, management integrity, and business models. Few earn alpha in bear markets, whereas all earn beta in bull markets. When profits pile up in a bull market, it's easy to assume that our analytical skills are responsible. The wise investor, however, knows the danger of hubris and graciously gives the bull market most of the credit for this performance. I humbly acknowledge that my personal portfolio benefited greatly from the strong performance of the Indian equity markets from 2014 to 2017.

If we continue to earn above-average returns over long periods of time and avoid permanent loss of capital in bear markets, the magic of long-term compounding ultimately will take care of the outcome.

Develop a Sound Process and Remain Faithful to Your Personal Philosophy

The best long-term performers in any probabilistic field, including investing, always emphasize process over outcome. An investment process is a set of guidelines that governs the behavior of investors in a way that allows them to remain faithful to the tenets of their personal philosophy. An intellectually sound and well-defined investment process helps investors stay the course during periods of underperformance or self-doubt and improves their chances of making prudent decisions with greater consistency across a full market cycle.

Deserved success comes when a sound process results in a favorable outcome. Poetic justice is served when a bad process is accompanied by an unfavorable outcome. Luck is a major contributor in the short term. To sustain high returns requires more than luck, however, and, over the long term, skill becomes the dominant factor. According to Michael Mauboussin,

> The key is this idea called the paradox of skill. As people become better at an activity, the difference between the best and the average and the best and the worst becomes much narrower. As people become more skillful, luck becomes more important. That's precisely what happens in the world of investing.
>
> The reason that luck is so important isn't that investing skill isn't relevant. It's that skill is very high and consistent. That said, over longer periods, skill has a much better chance of shining through.
>
> In the short term you may experience good or bad luck [and that can overwhelm skill], but in the long-term luck tends to even out and skill determines results.[9]

The investment industry is obsessed with outcomes in the short term over which one has no direct control. A sound process can occasionally generate poor results (bad luck), just as a bad process can occasionally generate superior results (dumb luck). During periods of poor performance, the pressure always builds to alter one's investment philosophy. An investment philosophy, however, is something that is gradually built over time. We cannot control the movement of the markets any more than we can control the returns. We can, however, always derive a great deal of intellectual satisfaction from following a sound process and staying true to our personal investment philosophy. To make money, we need luck. To create wealth, we need consistency. Any investment strategy, however sound, will have periodic phases of underperformance. The solution is not to keep changing the strategy but rather to stick to it, with the understanding that discipline is the price to be paid for long-term outperformance. Compounding is a lifelong journey, and an individual's impatience with his or her investment process could lead to a fatal decision and bring the journey to an abrupt end. Stay the course and remain faithful to your personal investment philosophy and your individual process. Focus is the key to success. Successful investors identify their niches and stick to them, gradually evolving over time as they learn and adapt. As Munger says, "All intelligent investing is value investing." And value investors do not equate risk with random fluctuations of stock prices, nor do they equate high risk with high return. Instead, they always think in terms of the positive relationship between intelligent effort and return. As Graham espoused in *The Intelligent Investor*,

> It has been an old and sound principle that those who cannot afford to take risks should be content with a relatively low return on their invested funds. From this there has developed the general notion that the rate of return which the investor should aim for is more or less proportionate to the degree of risk he is ready to run. Our view is different. *The rate of return sought should be dependent, rather, on the amount of intelligent effort the investor is willing and able to bring to bear on his task* [emphasis added].[10]

CHAPTER 25

TO FINISH FIRST, YOU MUST FIRST FINISH

If we can't tolerate a possible consequence, remote though it may be, we steer clear of planting its seeds.

—Warren Buffett

The worst case is far more consequential than the forecast itself. This is particularly true if the bad scenario is not acceptable. Yet the current phraseology makes no allowance for that. None.

—Nassim Nicholas Taleb

All I want to know is where I'm going to die, so I'll never go there.

—Charlie Munger

There are old investors, and there are bold investors, but there are no old bold investors.

—Howard Marks

The following is an excerpt from the "Life and Debt" section of Warren Buffett's 2010 letter, wherein he talks about the significance of liquidity and the perils of leverage:

The fundamental principle of auto racing is that *to finish first, you must first finish*. That dictum is equally applicable to business and guides our every action at Berkshire.

Unquestionably, some people have become very rich through the use of borrowed money. *However, that's also been a way to get very poor.* When leverage works, it magnifies your gains. Your spouse thinks you're clever, and your neighbors get envious. But leverage is addictive. Once having profited from its wonders, very few people retreat to more conservative practices. And as we all learned in third grade—and some relearned in 2008—*any series of positive numbers, however impressive the numbers may be, evaporates when multiplied by a single zero. History tells us that leverage all too often produces zeroes, even when it is employed by very smart people.*

Leverage, of course, can be lethal to businesses as well. Companies with large debts often assume that these obligations can be refinanced as they mature. That assumption is usually valid. Occasionally, though, either because of company-specific problems or a worldwide shortage of credit, maturities must actually be met by payment. For that, only cash will do the job.

Borrowers then learn that *credit is like oxygen. When either is abundant, its presence goes unnoticed. When either is missing, that's all that is noticed. Even a short absence of credit can bring a company to its knees* . . . [emphasis added].

. . . Moreover, during the episodes of financial chaos that occasionally erupt in our economy, we will be equipped both financially and emotionally to play offense while others scramble for survival. That's what allowed us to invest $15.6 billion in 25 days of panic following the Lehman bankruptcy in 2008.[1]

Cash is a call option on opportunity. Having ample liquid cash puts a valuable optionality in the hands of investors, to make bargain purchases when opportunities arise, and it also makes them antifragile. Cash is a much-underappreciated asset. It's one of the only price-stable assets that is simultaneously highly value-elastic: cash increases in value as other asset prices drop. The more they drop, the more valuable cash becomes.

Conversely, if you are forced to sell assets in a market with a small number of buyers, you may end up taking large haircuts. This is especially true in markets for illiquid stocks, luxury items, and other esoteric assets (such as art, wine, and so on).

So, how do you prevent this from happening to you? Have ample liquidity (cash reserves) so that you aren't forced to sell assets during periods of market turbulence and sharp drawdowns. Create an emergency fund equal to two years of living expenses and gradually increase it to five years as you increase your exposure to equities over time. If you need to spend money and you can't, that is risk. Nothing is worse for an investor than selling an asset at rock-bottom prices to get cash for essential purchases. This is the key differentiator between those who grow rich and those who don't—the rich invest in assets that generate recurring cash flow for them.

To get a more holistic understanding of what risk really means, we need to add the elements of time and expected future liabilities to the traditional definition of risk (the chance of losing money).

> Risk and time are opposite sides of the same coin, for if there were no tomorrow there would be no risk. *Time transforms risk, and the nature of risk is shaped by the time horizon* [emphasis added]: the future is the playing field.
> —Peter Bernstein

Any definition of risk must include a time horizon or it is incomplete. The time horizon changes how you perceive and experience risk. The more time you have, the less risk you bear. For example, the S&P 500 is typically more volatile over a one-year period than any long-term U.S. Treasury bond, but over any historical thirty-year period, the S&P 500 is far less risky. For all thirty-year periods for which we have data, the S&P 500 has outperformed U.S. ten-year Treasury bonds.

In his blog, Nick Maggiulli talks about an equation for how we should think about our ability to take risk:

$$\text{Ability to Take Risk} = \text{Assets} - \text{Liabilities} + \text{Time}$$

> . . . *Having more assets, fewer future liabilities, and more time all increase your ability to take risk* [emphasis added]. You can't control the amount of time you have; however, time provides the opportunity to recoup losses, so more is better.[2]

In a similar vein, Morgan Housel writes: "The most important question to ask when thinking about risk isn't how much volatility or upside you're looking for, *but how much time your emotions and goals need for that volatility to play out* [emphasis added]."[3]

If you borrow money to buy stocks, or if you run an open-ended fund with a daily or weekly redemption option, or if your personal temperament is not suited to long-term thinking, then, for you, volatility is equal to risk.

Focus on Consequences, Not Just Raw Probabilities

> *Whenever a really bright person who has a lot of money goes broke, it's because of leverage.*

> —Warren Buffett

When making critical decisions, we should focus on both the frequency and the magnitude of the consequences. (Because we tend not to do so, rare and implausible events frequently are grossly mispriced.) Prudent individuals define risk management as a process of dealing with the potential consequences of being wrong. In 2007, Buffett gave a talk to a group of MBA students at the University of Florida, wherein he shared his thoughts on the collapse of the hedge fund Long-Term Capital Management (LTCM):

> *To make money they didn't have and didn't need, they risked what they did have and did need,* and that's foolish. That is just plain foolish. Doesn't make any difference what your IQ is. If you risk something that is important to you for something that is unimportant to you, it just does not make any sense. I don't care whether the odds are 100 to one that you succeed or 1,000 to one that you succeed. If you hand me a gun with a thousand chambers—a million chambers in it—and there's a bullet in one chamber, and you said, "Put it up to your temple, how much do you want to be paid to pull it once?" I'm not going to pull it. *You can name any sum you want but it doesn't do anything for me on the upside and I think the downside is fairly clear.* [Laughter.] So I'm not interested in that kind of a game. *And yet people do it financially without thinking about it very much* [emphasis added].[4]

Life, business, and investing are games of probabilities, and almost all probabilities are less than 100 percent. So you are going to be wrong and lose sometimes, even when the odds are in your favor. As Peter Bernstein says, "You just have to be prepared to be wrong and understand that your ego had better not depend on being proven right. Being wrong is part of the process. Survival is the only road to riches."[5]

Always be aware of the potential downside. If the consequence of an action is not acceptable to us, then, no matter how low the probability, we must avoid that action. If bankruptcy, death, or loss of reputation are one of the potential downside risks, then it doesn't really matter what the various upside possibilities are because they become totally irrelevant. Certain bets in life, regardless of how asymmetric they may appear, should be avoided by any prudent individual. The key to long-term survival is planning your life to prepare for the odds of bad luck, which in turn requires a strategic focus on diversification, room for error, and avoiding single points of failure, particularly big, noninsurable risks. It is fine to trust our intuition on the small decisions, but we should always carefully think through the big decisions in our lives to avoid potentially fatal mistakes. This is why Buffett says, "We don't have to be smarter than the rest. We have to be more disciplined than the rest."[6]

A peaceful night's sleep and assured survival is much more important than higher relative returns for one's overall well-being.

Charlie and I believe in operating with many redundant layers of liquidity, and we avoid any sort of obligation that could drain our cash in a material way. That reduces our returns in 99 years out of 100. *But we will survive in the 100th while many others fail* [emphasis added]. And we will sleep well in all 100.

—Warren Buffett

As an investor, how can you be best prepared to survive the inevitable periodic, severe corrections and bear markets during your lifetime? Ensure that you have tennis balls (high-quality businesses) in your portfolio and not eggs (bad quality junk stocks) that will splatter after hitting the floor. In a market crash, both quality and junk fall. Quality eventually rises again and junk never recovers. Many individuals make large paper fortunes in bull markets but lose all of it when the bear market eventually arrives. How much you are able to retain after the recovery from a bear market is far more important than how much paper profit you make during a bull market. And quality of business matters the most in retaining long-term wealth.

A market always exists for the best of anything because people who appreciate quality always seem to have money. (This is as true of stocks and bonds as it is of real estate and antiques.) Once you have achieved financial independence, it is important to realign your portfolio to have the majority weight in high-quality businesses. After reaching a state of financial prosperity in life, ensure that you take all necessary steps to avoid being thrown back to the starting position. Achieving success and then losing everything has a far greater emotional impact than failing before ever having achieved success. Owners of outstanding businesses sleep better at night. Quality of the business and integrity of the management matter the most in creating and, much more important, in retaining the hard-earned long-term wealth. This is precisely why the handful of high-quality secular growth businesses in any stock market deservedly enjoy a scarcity premium and tend to trade at rich valuations for long periods of time.

I limit second-line stocks to less than 20 percent of my portfolio. Having been around in the markets for more than a decade, I have seen plenty of rising stars vanish without a trace. The returns from tried-and-tested front-line stocks may not be spectacular, but over longer periods of time, they tend to be more consistent and reliable. The key to a lifetime of investment success is not to make brilliant or complex decisions but to avoid doing foolish things.

People are trying to be smart—all I am trying to do is not to be idiotic, *but it's harder than most people think* [emphasis added].

—Charlie Munger

You Only Have to Get Rich Once

Having a large amount of leverage is like driving a car with a dagger on the steering wheel pointed at your heart. If you do that, you will be a better driver. There will be fewer accidents but when they happen, they will be fatal *[emphasis added].*

—Warren Buffett

During his LTCM speech at the University of Florida, Buffett highlighted how reliance on only the "documented" past leads to blind spots and neglect of "total exposure":

It's produced by an over-reliance . . . on things . . . those guys would tell me . . . a six sigma event wouldn't touch us . . . but they were wrong . . . history does not tell you the probabilities of future financial things happening. . . . The same thing in a different way could happen to any of us . . . where we really have a blind spot about something that's crucial because we know a whole lot about something else. . . . Henry Kaufman had once said . . . "the people who are going broke in this situation are of two types: the ones who knew nothing, and the ones that knew everything."[7]

At the 2006 Berkshire annual meeting, when asked about Berkshire's next chief investment officer, Buffett said:

I mentioned in the annual report that in looking for an investment manager to succeed me, we're looking for someone who doesn't only learn from things that have happened, but can also envision things *that have never happened.* This is our job in insurance and investments. *Many people are very smart, but are not wired to think about things that haven't happened before* . . . [emphasis added].
. . . Anything times zero is zero and I don't care how good the record is in every other year if one year there's a zero. We're looking for someone who is wired in such a way as to see risks that haven't occurred and be cognizant of risks that have occurred. Charlie and I have seen guys go broke or close to it because 99 of 100 of their decisions were good, but the 100th did them in.[8]

Daily decisions fall into one of the following three categories:

1. **Outcomes are known.** In this case, the range of outcomes is known and the individual outcome is also known. This is the easiest way to make decisions.
2. **Outcomes are unknown, but probabilities are known.** In this case, the range of outcomes is known but the individual outcome is unknown. This is risk. Think of this as gambling in Vegas, where all of the outcomes at the table are known, as are the probabilities of each.

3. **Outcomes are unknown and probabilities are unknown.** In this case, the distribution of outcomes is unknown and so are the individual outcomes. This is uncertainty. This is where black swans reside.

We behave in accordance with our embedded belief that we are making decisions in option number 2. We are prepared for a world much like number 2—a world with known outcomes and probabilities that can be estimated. Yet we live in a world that starkly resembles option number 3.

Welcome to the World of Extremistan

Extreme events are where ruin is found. It's also true that these extreme changes in securities prices may be much greater than you would expect from the Gaussian or normal statistics commonly used.

—Edward Thorp

The devil is in the residuals, as all of us have discovered to our sorrow.

—Howard Marks

According to Nassim Nicholas Taleb, the world could be divided into the safe and comfortable Mediocristan and the unsafe and seemingly improbable Extremistan. In Mediocristan, nothing is scalable; everything is constrained by boundary conditions, time, the limits of biological variation, and the limits of hourly compensation. Because of such constraints and the limits of our knowledge, random variation of attributes exists in Mediocristan and can be usefully described by Gaussian probability models (i.e., the bell curve or other distributions having a family resemblance to it).

In Extremistan, variation within distributions is far less constrained than in Mediocristan. It is the land of scalability and power laws. Generators of events produce distributions with large or small extreme values, frequently. Those extreme values affect the sum of attribute values in a sample distribution, and the mean value of such distributions. The probability of occurrence of extreme values varies greatly from Gaussian models. In fact, many attribute value distributions in Extremistan do not fit any known models well. Examples include everything from sales distributions for books per author to wealth and income distributions for individuals and businesses.

According to Sebastian Mallaby,

In the early 1960s, a maverick mathematician named Benoit Mandelbrot argued that the tails of the distribution might be fatter than the normal bell curve assumed; and Eugene Fama, the father of efficient-market theory, who got to know Mandelbrot at the time, conducted tests on stock-price changes that confirmed Mandelbrot's assertion. If price changes had been normally distributed, jumps greater than five standard deviations should have shown up in a daily price data about once every seven thousand years. *Instead, they cropped up about once every three to four years* [emphasis added].[9]

Benoit Mandelbrot was a Polish-born mathematician and polymath who developed a new branch of mathematics known as fractal geometry, which recognizes the hidden order in the seemingly disordered, the plan in the unplanned, the regular pattern in the irregularity of nature. Mandelbrot found that the underlying power law that was evident in random patterns in nature also applies to the positive and negative price movements of many financial instruments. The movement of stock prices followed a power law rather than a Gaussian or normal distribution.

In his book *The (Mis)Behavior of Markets*, written with Richard Hudson, Mandelbrot invoked the important concept of "clustering":

> *Market turbulence tends to cluster.* This is no surprise to an experienced trader. . . . They also know that is in those wildest moments—the rare but recurring crisis of the financial world—where the biggest fortunes of Wall Street are made and lost.
> . . . *Periods of big price changes groups together*, interspersed by intervals of more sedate variation—the tell-tale marks of long memory and persistence. It shows scaling.
> . . . Large price changes tend to be followed by more large price changes, positive or negative. Small changes tend to be followed by more small changes. *Volatility clusters* [emphasis added]. [10]

Clustering as a concept resembles the Pareto principle, which states that, for many events, 80 percent of the effects come from 20 percent of the causes. The clustering phenomenon has important implications for investors.

Market returns are largely clustered, followed by long periods of a ranged move. Volatility is often the greatest at turning points, diminishing as a new trend becomes established. Patience is extremely important. Beyond a certain point on a larger portfolio size, compounding becomes powerful. Long-term survival ensures a high probability of making money.

Within our portfolio, returns are clustered. A few stocks account for the bulk of the returns. Appropriate allocation is the key to generating better returns.

While studying an investment idea, our research efforts are clustered. A small fraction of the information and analysis determines the action on an idea.

Valuation clusters. We spend large amounts of time either in overvaluation or in undervaluation. We only briefly experience extreme undervaluation or extreme overvaluation, and rarely experience fair valuation. Good news tends to cluster and so, too, does bad news.

Watch for any sharp move, whether in margins, insider ownership, trading volumes for a stock, capital work in progress figure on the balance sheet, or other related areas. Such clustering raises many interesting ideas. Companies coming out of prolonged periods of trouble could experience clusters of improving performance. Similarly, companies with prolonged periods of strong performance could experience clusters of deteriorating performance. The inaugural edition of *Security Analysis* had as a frontispiece a quote from Horace's *Ars Poetica* that best sums up the essence of market cycles and sector leaders and laggards in bull and bear markets: "Many shall be restored that now are fallen, and many shall fall that now are in honor."[11]

Risk is what's left over after you've thought of everything possible, plausible, and probable. The human mind's tendency to completely discount six sigma and other rare events from the realm of possibility is what Taleb warns about in his book *The Black Swan*. We need to avoid clamoring for precise single-point predictions and instead stress-test our portfolio under a wider and darker range of "what-if" scenarios and outcomes. When we humbly accept that it's difficult to make predictions, especially about the future, we will be more inclined to build an investment strategy that is robust to a wide range of outcomes. Forewarned is forearmed. The world we live in is simply too complex. In other words, we simply have too many unknown unknowns. No one is alone in this world. No act is without consequences. According to chaos theory, in dynamical systems, the outcome of any process is sensitive to its starting point—or, in the famous cliché, the flap of a butterfly's wings in the Amazon can cause a tornado in Texas. In such a world, events in the distant past continue to echo in the present (path dependence). Or, as Taleb would say, we live primarily in an Extremistan world, one that is full of feedback loops, is filled with interdependence, and thus is black swan–ridden. Taleb's black swan theory refers to unexpected events of large magnitude and consequences and their dominant role in history. These events are the very reason for Vladimir Lenin's saying: "There are decades where nothing happens; and there are weeks where decades happen."

Here is my exhaustive list of black swan risks for the coming year:

1.

2.

3.

This list will always be empty because you can't predict a black swan event. A black swan is something that comes as a complete surprise to everyone. It's a risk that is unforeseen; therefore, by definition, it cannot be predicted.

Such events, considered extreme outliers, collectively play vastly larger roles than regular occurrences. We all contemplate and understand the things that happen within three standard deviations, but everything important in financial history takes place outside those three standard deviations. Still, many smart people do not consider these kinds of rare events to be even remotely plausible. In addition, complex mathematical models that can purportedly manage fat-tail risks create the illusion of control. Consequently, these people express this overconfidence in their beliefs by betting the entire house on their preferred bet and piling up tons of leverage. Ultimately, this blind reliance on only the documented past leads to ruin. Failure often comes from a failure to imagine failure.

> History teaches us that a crisis often causes problems to correlate in a manner undreamed of in more tranquil times. . . . *Linkage, when it suddenly surfaces, can trigger serious systemic problems* [emphasis added].
> —Warren Buffett

Never bet your entire capital on a single stock or sector. Even if you hold stocks from different industries, diversify thoughtfully to ensure that they are not vulnerable to a cascading impact from any one single event or common factor, such as all of them having operations in a common city or state or any other common-risk concentration factors. Statistically, any investment opportunity can appear to be attractive, but statistics, by definition, apply to a group. The bigger the sample size, the higher the statistical significance of the pattern observed. By putting all our money on an "almost" sure-shot bet, we could end up making a fatal financial mistake. Howard Marks shared a story about a gambler who bet everything on a race with only one horse in it. How could he lose? "Halfway around the track, the horse jumped over the fence and ran away. Invariably things can get worse than people expect. Maybe 'worst case' means 'the worst we've seen in the past.' But that doesn't mean things can't be worse in the future."[12]

This story has a valuable lesson for investors. Never bet the farm on a single investment, no matter how certain you are of the outcome. You never know when luck will hand you the equivalent of a crazy horse. Risk often originates from sources you can't imagine. Avoid going crazy with concentration. Instead, diversify prudently. As Buffett puts it,

> If significant risk exists in a single transaction, overall risk should be reduced by making that purchase one of many mutually independent commitments. Thus, you may consciously purchase a risky investment—one that indeed has a significant possibility of causing loss or injury—if you believe that your gain, weighted for probabilities, considerably exceeds your loss, compara-

bly weighted, and if you can commit to a number of similar, but unrelated opportunities. Most venture capitalists employ this strategy. Should you choose to pursue this course, you should adopt the outlook of the casino that owns a roulette wheel, which will want to see lots of action because it is favored by probabilities, but will refuse to accept a single, huge bet.[13]

The biggest risks are those that aren't in the news. People don't prepare for them because they're not being reported. Risk is always present, but we tend to become blind to it in bull markets. People forget that risk in the markets is never eliminated; it is only transferred from one person to another or converted from one form to another. In turbulent times, it pays to be a student of human behavior during similar chaotic situations in history.

> History is mostly the study of unprecedented events, ironically used as a map of the future. Stuff evolves, tastes change, paradigms shift. So what worked in the past may not work today or tomorrow. *The most valuable part of history is studying how people behaved when something unprecedented happened. It's the most consistent thing over time* [emphasis added].
> —Morgan Housel

Recency bias is all-pervasive. We tend to extrapolate recent trends into infinity as we assume them to reflect the new normal. Until it isn't normal in a cyclical world (figures 25.1a and 25.1b).

If a quantitative trading strategy works consistently for an initial period, it tends to become widespread. In 1998, it was convergence arbitrage. LTCM assumed that historical patterns in the relationship of certain assets would persist forever and leveraged its positions by more than 25 to 1. When those patterns changed for just a brief period, LTCM blew up.

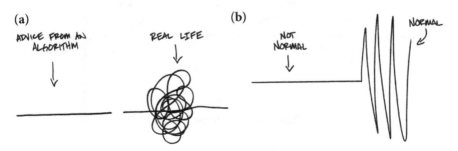

FIGURE 25.1 (a) Abrupt volatility is the norm in life and (b) financial markets.

Source: Behavior Gap.

In 2017, the S&P 500 did not have a 5 percent drawdown even once, and volatility was nearly nonexistent. But, as economist Hyman Minsky said, in the financial markets, "stability often breeds instability." Tranquil environments tend to lull us into a state of utter complacency and set us up for some nasty surprises.

On February 5, 2018, volatility, measured by the CBOE VIX (also known as the "Fear Index" on Wall Street), suddenly exploded a record 118 percent in a single day to the highest levels since the Lehman Brothers crisis. This event was accompanied by an intraday fall of nearly 1,600 points, the largest in the history of the Dow Jones Industrial Average. The most notable casualty of this episode was Credit Suisse's VelocityShares Daily Inverse VIX Short-Term exchange-traded note (ETN), or XIV for short.

The product, managed by Credit Suisse (which owned 32 percent of the note), shorted volatility by betting on calm market conditions, and it had increased in popularity over the past year as volatility in the markets reached historic lows. As the VIX shot through the roof, the XIV plunged 92 percent in a single day. It took six years for XIV to go from $11 to $144 and just one day for it to implode to nearly zero—six years of picking up pennies in front of a bulldozer, wiped away in a single session. XIV had been marketed exclusively to "professional investors" and it stayed true to the promise made on page 197 of its prospectus: "The long term expected value of your ETNs is *zero*. If you hold your ETNs as a long-term investment, it is likely you will lose all or a substantial portion of your investment."[14]

The ensuing negative feedback loop of selling is believed to have exacerbated the market turmoil on that particular day. These kinds of devastating events can occur in the market at any time, and they will happen again without any warning. You should expect the unexpected in this business; expect the extreme. Don't think in terms of boundaries that limit what the market might do. One of the single biggest realizations I have experienced in this business is that the unexpected and seemingly impossible continue to happen. This is why reading history and studying human behavior during past episodes of panic is valuable for an investor. The events of the week of February 5 to February 9, 2018, were eerily similar to those described in the chapter titled "Market Fluctuations" in John Brooks's classic *Business Adventures*. As Mark Twain rightly said, "History doesn't repeat itself but it often rhymes."

Never Depend on the Kindness of Strangers

In his 2008 letter, Buffett said, "We never want to count on the kindness of strangers in order to meet tomorrow's obligations."[15]

Certain businesses are inherently vulnerable because of their constant dependence on the "kindness of strangers" for their ongoing survival. Examples include lending businesses with low intrinsic return on equity, which need to tap the capital markets frequently to raise the money that is their raw material, as well as highly capital-intensive, negative-free-cash-flow companies, which require constant external funding. Levered institutions that depend on capital and trust are always susceptible to speculation and self-fulfilling prophecies. (In 1948, famed sociologist Robert K. Merton coined the term self-fulfilling prophecy: "The self-fulfilling prophecy is, in the beginning, a false definition of the situation evoking a new behavior which makes the original false conception come true." In other words, saying it can make it so. A public pronouncement might lead others to act in a way that will lead that pronouncement to be true, even if there's no basis in fact. In financial markets, that is often the case.)

Investors need to consider these aspects when evaluating the appropriate valuation for individual businesses. For example, unlike banks, which generally have a sticky deposit base, microfinance companies always depend on funds from the credit markets, which turn hostile as soon as an adverse business event could affect collections from borrowers. Add to this the ever-present political risks to which they are subject and the unsecured nature of their lending and it is clear why microfinance businesses should be accorded a lower valuation than banks with comparable return ratios and asset quality. A similar principle applies to businesses that depend on the kindness of one or two primary clients. The pricing power goes away if customers know that they are critical to the company's survival. Businesses with excessive customer concentration generally do not get a high valuation multiple. (Investors should study what happened to RS Software India, which used to get about 85 percent of its revenues from Visa.)

Many of life's most important lessons are learned the hard way. One lesson is about the lure of greed in a bull market and the subsequent perils of leverage. Raymond DeVoe Jr. has rightly said: "More money has been lost reaching for yield than at the point of a gun."[16]

Buffett has often said that if you are smart you don't need leverage and if you are dumb you have no business using it. In his 2017 letter, he made a strong argument against using borrowed money to buy stocks:

> There is simply no telling how far stocks can fall in a short period. Even if your borrowings are small and your positions aren't immediately threatened by the plunging market, your mind may well become rattled by scary headlines and breathless commentary. And an unsettled mind will not make good decisions.[17]

Cultivate Staying Power to Mitigate the Risk of Ruin

Time is the best test of fragility—it encompasses high doses of disorder—and nature is the only system that has been stamped "robust" by time. . . . Time is an eraser rather than a builder, and a good one at breaking the fragile— whether buildings or ideas.

—Nassim Nicholas Taleb

In his 2014 letter, Buffett shared the characteristics of companies with staying power:

> Financial staying power requires a company to maintain three strengths under all circumstances: (1) a large and reliable stream of earnings; (2) massive liquid assets and (3) no significant near-term cash requirements. Ignoring that last necessity is what usually leads companies to experience unexpected problems: Too often, CEOs of profitable companies feel they will always be able to refund maturing obligations, however large these are. In 2008–2009, many managements learned how perilous that mindset can be.[18]

Businesses with staying power have stable product characteristics, a strong competitive advantage, a fragmented customer and supplier base, prudent capital allocation, a growth mind-set with a razor-sharp focus on long-term profitability and sustainability, a corporate culture of intelligent and measured risk taking, a cash-rich promoter family or parent company that can infuse capital during periods of high stress, a highly liquid balance sheet, and both the willingness and the capacity to suffer by investing for the long term at the expense of short-term earnings. These companies thus have higher longevity, higher duration of cash flows, and thus higher intrinsic value.

From an investor's point of view, staying power comes from a strong passion for the investing discipline; a constant learning mind-set; a long remaining investing life span; low or no personal debt; frugality; discipline; a sound understanding of human behavior, market history, and cognitive biases; a patient, long-term mind-set; and a supportive family whose importance is appreciated in a big way during the periodic rough times in the market.

It seems fitting to end this chapter with Buffett's profound words on avoiding the risk of ruin: "It takes twenty years to build a reputation and five minutes to ruin it. If you think about that, you'll do things differently."[19]

SECTION V

DECISION-MAKING

CHAPTER 26

READ MORE HISTORY AND FEWER FORECASTS

If I have noticed anything over these 60 years on Wall Street, it is that people do not succeed in forecasting what's going to happen to the stock market.

—Benjamin Graham

We believe that short-term forecasts of stock or bond prices are useless. The forecasts may tell you a great deal about the forecaster; they tell you nothing about the future.

—Warren Buffett

Nobody can predict interest rates, the future direction of the economy, or the stock market. Dismiss all such forecasts and concentrate on what's actually happening to the companies in which you have invested.

—Peter Lynch

Be a business analyst, not a market, macroeconomics, or security analyst.

—Charlie Munger

We have two classes of forecasters: Those who don't know, and those who don't know they don't know.

—John Kenneth Galbraith

Warren Buffett has said, "Market forecasters will fill your ear but will never fill your wallet."[1] Just think about the damage to your wallet since 2009 if you had listened to so-called market experts from highly acclaimed sources in business media (figure 26.1).

The supremely confident-looking authority figures in the media are not afflicted by the faintest of doubts, despite being wrong most of the time. Have you ever wondered why the anchors and market experts on television make so many predictions day in and day out? And why they are so happy to make these predictions?

Jason Zweig explains the constant human urge to predict, in his book *Your Money and Your Brain*: "Just as nature abhors a vacuum, people hate randomness. The human compulsion to make predictions about the unpredictable originates in the dopamine centers of the reflexive brain. I call this human tendency *'the prediction addiction'* [emphasis added]."[2]

This tendency is driven by a pleasurable chemical in our brain called dopamine, the release of which gives us a natural high to make the next prediction, and the next one, and the next one, and so on.

The prediction addiction, as Zweig explains, is the compulsive desire to try to make sense out of just about everything in the world, including things that are impossible to predict, like future stock prices. (When the legendary J. P. Morgan was asked what the market would do, he said, "It will fluctuate.") None of us can predict even our future. Still, we fall prey to the illusion of control and try to predict macros, markets, currencies, and commodity prices.

FIGURE 26.1 S&P 500, 2009–2017.

Source: Morgan Housel (@morganhousel), "Easy money," Twitter, August 28, 2018, https://twitter.com/morganhousel/status/1034447231967887360.

Investment writer Dan Solin wrote about the prediction addiction in an article for the *Huffington Post*: "This addiction is a particularly bad one. Not only are our brains hard-wired to believe we can predict the future and make sense out of random acts, it rewards us for doing so. The brain of someone engaged in this activity experiences the same kind of pleasure that drug addicts get from cocaine or gamblers experience when they enter a casino."[3]

Prediction addicts are to the investor what the drug dealer is to the addict or the casino is to the gambler.

Try this fun exercise: check the Google results for past predictions by any market expert on any macro topic over any randomly chosen period of a few years. You'll not take any of those people seriously ever again. Predictions just grab eyeballs and achieve nothing else.

It is often said that bull markets climb a wall of worry. Since March 2009, numerous worrisome headlines have driven many investors to sell out of fear and exit the market completely.

> The fact that *bad news is disseminated ten times as fast as positive news* is one of the biggest reasons why it's so difficult to just capture market returns. You would think it's as simple as buying the total market index fund and leaving it alone. And it is that simple, but it certainly isn't that easy, *because bad news smashes your face against an amplifier, while good news just plays quietly in the background* [emphasis added].
> —Michael Batnick

> Progress happens too slowly to notice; setbacks happen too quickly to ignore.
> —Morgan Housel

> Whatever methods you use to pick stocks, your success will depend on your ability to ignore the worries of the world long enough to allow your stocks to succeed. No matter how intelligent you are, it isn't the head but the stomach that will determine your fate.
> —Peter Lynch

With rare exceptions, most of the miracles of humankind are long-term, constructed events. Progress comes bit by bit. The silent miracle of humanity's march is this: step by step, year by year, the world is improving. Not on every single measure, every single year, but as a rule. Although the world faces huge challenges, we have made tremendous progress. This is a fact-based worldview. We've cut the number of people living in extreme poverty worldwide by half over the past twenty years, but "Poverty Rates Drop Incrementally" has never dominated news headlines. When a trend is gradually improving over time, with periodic sharp dips, people are more likely to pay attention to the dips than to the overall improvement. The news media tends to focus on vivid events—the dramatic, the tragic—rather than on the daily improvements and routine goodness in the world. News channels compete to capture our attention with vivid stories and dramatic narratives. They tend to focus on the unusual rather than the common, and on the new or temporary rather than slowly changing patterns. Fundamental improvements that are world-changing events but too slow, too fragmented, or too small rarely qualify as news. The stories that circulate fastest have an element of fear or anger and instill a sense of helplessness. Open any news channel or go on social media. You likely will hear or read about political instability, market turbulence, natural disasters, murders, suicides, disease outbreaks, geopolitical tensions, and an endless list of bad news. People frequently label the current times "the worst ever," but these individuals have obviously never read a history book. The combination of negative dispositions and availability bias results in pervasive pessimism about the world. In reality, however, we are living in one of the most promising times in the history of humankind. The world has experienced an incredible amount of progress on many important parameters over almost any long-term time horizon you look at. It's just that bad news is an event or headline whereas good news is a process or statistic. And bad news, as opposed to statistics, makes for a more vivid and attention-grabbing story.

> I have observed that not the man who hopes when others despair, but the man who despairs when others hope, is admired by a large class of persons as a sage.
> —John Stuart Mill

Remember, the pessimist sounds smart, but it is the optimist who makes money. Commerce is the fundamental backbone of civilization. When we invest in stocks, we participate in commerce and support its constant progress. Those who focus on this big picture prosper in the long run. Others who focus only on crisis get jittery at the worst possible time and lose out on promising wealth-creation opportunities.

Investors should learn from Buffett's thoughts on the critical importance of focusing on individual businesses and ignoring all of the noise around interest rate hikes, sharp spikes in inflation, stock market crashes, oil shocks, toppling of government regimes, recessions, depressions, and even full-blown wars.

In his 1994 annual letter to shareholders, he wrote:

> We will continue to ignore political and economic forecasts, which are *an expensive distraction* for many investors and businessmen. Thirty years ago, no one could have foreseen the huge expansion of the Vietnam War, wage and price controls, two oil shocks, the resignation of a president, the dissolution

of the Soviet Union, a one-day drop in the Dow of 508 points, or Treasury bill yields fluctuating between 2.8 percent and 17.4 percent.

But, surprise—none of these blockbuster events made the slightest dent in Ben Graham's investment principles. *Nor did they render unsound the negotiated purchases of fine businesses at sensible prices.* Imagine the cost to us, then, if we had let a fear of unknowns cause us to defer or alter the deployment of capital. Indeed, *we have usually made our best purchases when apprehensions about some macro event were at a peak* [emphasis added]. Fear is the foe of the faddist, but the friend of the fundamentalist.

A different set of major shocks is sure to occur in the next 30 years. We will neither try to predict these nor try to profit from them. If we can identify businesses similar to those we have purchased in the past, external surprises will have little effect on our long-term results.[4]

And in his 2012 letter he stated:

A thought for my fellow CEOs: Of course, the immediate future is uncertain; America has faced the unknown since 1776. It's just that sometimes people focus on the myriad of uncertainties that always exist while at other times they ignore them (usually because the recent past has been uneventful).

American business will do fine over time. And stocks will do well just as certainly, since their fate is tied to *business performance*. Periodic setbacks will occur, yes, but investors and managers are in a game *that is heavily stacked in their favor*. (The Dow Jones Industrials advanced from 66 to 11,497 in the 20th Century, a staggering 17,320 percent increase that materialized despite four costly wars, a Great Depression and many recessions. And don't forget that shareholders received substantial dividends throughout the century as well.)

Since the basic game is so favorable, Charlie and I believe it's a terrible mistake to try to dance in and out of it based upon the turn of tarot cards, the predictions of "experts," or the ebb and flow of business activity. *The risks of being out of the game are huge compared to the risks of being in it* [emphasis added].[5]

Why does Buffett constantly emphasize that investors are in a game that is "heavily stacked in their favor"? Look at figure 26.2. If more than two centuries of data cannot convince you that what Buffett says is true, then probably nothing will.

Looking at figure 26.2, we can clearly understand why Buffett has warned against treating cash-equivalent holdings and currency-denominated instruments as risk-free assets, because holding them over long periods is actually quite risky. Buffett views risk as loss of purchasing power. And bonds, widely touted as offering risk-free returns, are today priced to deliver return-free risk.

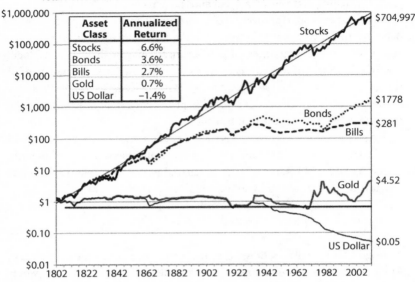

Total Real Returns on U.S. Stocks, Bonds, Bills, Gold, and the Dollar, 1802–2012

Asset Class	Annualized Return
Stocks	6.6%
Bonds	3.6%
Bills	2.7%
Gold	0.7%
US Dollar	−1.4%

FIGURE 26.2 Total real returns on U.S. stocks, bonds, bills, gold, and the dollar, 1802–2012.

Source: Jeremy Siegel, *Stocks for the Long Run* (New York: McGraw-Hill, 2014).

> Fear has a greater grasp on human action than does the impressive weight of historical evidence.
>
> —Jeremy Siegel

Whenever I am confronted with doubt, despair, or fear in the media about the current big picture, I try to concentrate on the even bigger picture, which is the one that's worth knowing about, if you expect to be able to maintain a firm conviction in equities for the long term.

The even bigger picture tells us that, for more than two centuries, in spite of all of the major and minor calamities and all of the hundreds and thousands of reasons continuously given for why the world might be coming to an end, equities have rewarded their owners with real gains of more than 6.5 percent a year, on average—far higher than Treasury bills, bonds, gold, and the world's reserve currency. History clearly shows that equities deliver the highest long-term real returns. Their predominance over the other classes of assets is completely overwhelming. Acting on this bit of information will be far more lucrative in the long run than reacting to the opinions and suggestions of commentators and advisory services that keep predicting the coming depression.

More money has been lost trying to anticipate and protect from corrections than actually in them.

—Peter Lynch

Howard Marks wrote, in his memo to Oaktree clients in February 1993: "The average annual return on equities from 1926 to 1987 was 9.44 percent. But if you had gone to cash and missed the best 50 of those 744 months, you would have missed *all* of the return. *This tells me that attempts at market timing are a source of risk, not protection* [emphasis added]."[6]

In response to a sharp correction, market experts usually say something like this: "The near-term outlook is not clear. . . . There is a lot of global uncertainty. . . . Stock prices may fall even further, so wait for some time until more clarity emerges. . . . Wait until the liquidity situation improves. . . . Wait until the elections are over. . . . There is currently a lot of political uncertainty."

In other words, "wait and watch." This particular advice almost always turns out to be expensive for those investors who want to enjoy the ecstasy of rising stock prices in a bull market while avoiding the pain of falling prices in a bear market. Superior stock market returns do not accrue in a uniform manner. Rather, they can be traced to a few periods of sudden bursts of strength. Moreover, the timing and the duration of these periods cannot be predicted accurately by anyone. A significant percentage of the total gain from a bull market tends to occur during the initial market recovery phase. If an investor is out of the market at that point in time, he or she is likely to miss a substantial portion of the gains.

According to a study done by SageOne Investment Advisors, even though the market index in India (Sensex) went up 251 times between 1979 and 2017 (15.5 percent annualized returns), if you missed 7 percent of the best months or 1 percent of the best days, your returns would have been zero.[7] Investors need to bear the periodic bouts of downside volatility as the price to be paid for earning superior returns from equities. Time in the market matters, not timing the market. The ability to keep investing at regular intervals, to stay the course through thick and thin, ups and downs, and bull markets and bear markets, and to not worry where the markets are going tomorrow, or next week, or next month is what matters. Simple.

It's simple but not easy.

Emotions cannot be back-tested; that's why all previous bear markets and the accompanying cheap stock valuations prevailing at those times look like cinch opportunities only in hindsight. From the time of its IPO in 1980 through 2012, Apple was a 225-bagger. A $10,000 investment in it turned into $2.25 million. But an investor would have had to suffer through two declines of more than 80 percent and several drops of more than 40 percent along the way. Even a quality business like Fairfax Financial (which, as of September 2019, has delivered returns of 18 percent compounded annual growth rate for thirty-three years) saw its stock price fall almost 80 percent between 1999 and 2002, delivering negative returns in each of those four years. How many investors do you think would have managed to hold on through a four-year, 80 percent drop? People have different tolerance levels for downside volatility—when they think about big market falls and when the market falls actually happen. (All investors should study Morgan Housel's *Motley Fool* article titled "The Agony of High Returns.")[8] The stock market is the only market in which things go on a fire sale and people run out of the store. Ignore the scary predictions and constant urging from the gurus and experts for you to cash out during times of fear and panic in the market, especially when you are sitting on sizeable unrealized gains (that is when your temptation to book your profits and cash out will be at its peak).

Jargon is the financial community's preferred method to sound more intelligent. For instance, there's an adage on Wall Street, "don't fight the Fed" (i.e., if the Fed is on a tightening course, don't be long—and if the Fed is lowering rates, don't be short). Sounds intuitive and logical, right? Now see the following:

1. January 3, 2001: The Fed cut rates 50 bps and the S&P 500 closed at 1,347. It declined 43 percent from that point to its October 2002 low while the Fed cut the whole way down.
2. September 18, 2007: The Fed cut rates 50 bps and the S&P 500 closed at 1,519. It declined 56 percent from that point to its March 2009 low while the Fed cut the whole way down.
3. June 30, 2004: The Fed hiked rates 25 bps and the S&P 500 closed at 1,140. It advanced 33 percent from that point to September 2007 rate cut while the Fed hiked 16 more times.
4. December 16, 2015: The Fed hiked rates 25 bps and the S&P 500 closed at 2,073. It advanced 45 percent from that point to July 2019 rate cut while the Fed hiked 8 more times.

Now consider these commonly heard comments in the business media:

1. "The market is turning weak because of rising interest rates."
2. "Historically, stocks do well during periods of rising rates."

You can choose your preferred narrative (which probably will be biased by your personal experiences). The majority of the intelligent-sounding voices in the media will most likely choose the first option during periods of sharp market declines when preceded by a rise in interest rates. Until the market does not react at all and remains sideways, the rising interest rates won't appear in screaming headlines. In fact, during those times, some experts may show historical charts or tables that illustrate periods of past bull markets during rising interest rate environments to justify the second option. The market moves first. The accompanying sense-making narrative follows later. Always.

The hard reality is that the stock market will do what it wants when it wants. Investors should not obsess over high-frequency macro indicators. Simply focus on individual businesses and their industry developments. That's the best one can do. Nothing more. Always remain humble and be intellectually honest.

Investors tend to replay their most recent traumatic market moments in their minds, over and over again, and those memories end up defining how those investors behave in the future. The examples shared in this chapter clearly illustrate why having a solid grounding in history is vital to develop the nerves of steel required during the periodic dislocations that occur in financial markets.

> I met Charlie Munger in my USC graduate school investment class and had the opportunity to ask him this important question, "If I could do one thing to make myself a better investment professional, what would it be?" He answered, "Read history! Read history! Read history!" This was among the best pieces of advice I ever received.
> —Bob Rodriguez

The study of history aims, above all, to make us aware of certain possibilities that we otherwise would not have considered. Quite often, we are surprised by something that hasn't happened yet in our lifetime, even though the so-called unprecedented event may have taken place many times before in history. Instead of engaging in futile attempts to predict the future, we should try to diligently learn as much as possible from the past. Study history and obtain relevant base rates, that is, historical data on relevant statistical groups over longer time horizons. This practice helps avoid recency and vividness bias in a world characterized by extreme brevity of financial memory despite the ubiquity of cycles.

The (Ir)relevance of Politics for Long-Term Investors

> If you do not know history, you think short term. If you know history, you think medium and long term.
>
> —Lee Kuan Yew

In 1901, Theodore Roosevelt (a Republican) was sworn into office after the assassination of President William McKinley. Fast-forward a few decades to Franklin D. Roosevelt (a Democrat). The period from the beginning of the

Republican Roosevelt's term to the end of the Democrat Roosevelt's time in office included a variety of economic adversities, including eight economic recessions, the Great Depression, the financial panic of 1907, and two long, brutal world wars. Despite these massive headwinds, however, America's gross domestic product (GDP) grew from $21 billion in 1901, when the first Roosevelt took office, to around $228 billion by the time the second Roosevelt died in office in 1945—a stunning eleven-fold increase in forty-four years. During this time, from the turn of the twentieth century through the end of World War II, Republicans held the White House for twenty-four years, Democrats for the other twenty. America continued to forge ahead, whether it was being led by the "red" or by the "blue."

The postwar era has seen a similar balance, as the political pendulum continues to swing back and forth. But, all the while, America marches on. From 1945 through the end of 2016—a seventy-two-year period—Republicans and Democrats have held the presidency for thirty-six years each. Through seventy-two years of Republicans and Democrats, America's nominal GDP has grown from $0.2 trillion to $18.6 trillion, a ninety-three-fold increase and a 6.4 percent compound annual growth rate. A better measure would involve adjusting these numbers for inflation, which produces numbers that are even more remarkable. Real GDP per capita was around $13,000 (in today's dollars) in the mid-1940s. The real GDP per capita today is around $56,000—more than a fourfold increase in purchasing power and standard of living in just two and a half generations. (Note that the average middle-class American today has access to daily life amenities and conveniences far superior to those enjoyed by America's richest man, John D. Rockefeller, a mere one hundred years ago.)

A big part of America's success has come by combining the benefits of its abundant natural resources with a system of government that has allowed its citizens the freedom to work hard, pursue innovative ideas, and risk capital in pursuit of financial gain. Adam Smith's "invisible hand" has played a significant role in unleashing the market forces of capitalism. Immigrants and capital are always attracted to countries with rule of law. Where there is rule of law, there is also more trust in business relations.

America will continue to attract the best talent from around the world and to create some of the world's best companies that provide innovative products and services to customers. This, in turn, will lead to greater profits and earning power for such companies, and, as part owners, investors will concurrently benefit from the growing prosperity of those firms.

The inherent checks and balances in America's system of government transcend the power of whoever sits in the White House. The fabric of this nation and the foundation of its system are much stronger than any one man or woman or any particular body of lawmakers. America's economic progress will continue while Republicans hold control in Washington, just as it will while

TABLE 26.1 India and its markets continue to march ahead regardless of the political regime

Lok Sabha term	Ministers of parliament of the ruling party or largest party in alliance	Form of government	Sensex compound annual growth rate during the term	Prime minister
1984–1989	414	Majority	21.8%	Rajiv Gandhi
1989–1991	143	Minority	48.6%	V.P. Singh, Chandra Shekhar
1991–1996	244	Minority	24.7%	P.V. Narasimha Rao
1996–1998	46	Minority	−5.3%	H.D. Deve Gowda, I.K. Gujral
1998–1999	182	Minority	24.3%	A.B. Vajpayee
1999–2004	182	Majority	4.0%	A.B. Vajpayee
2004–2009	143	Minority	19.0%	Manmohan Singh
2009–2014	206	Majority	10.0%	Manmohan Singh
2014–2019	282	Majority	11.5%	Narendra Modi

Democrats do. Owning a piece of this great system through a collection of quality businesses for the long term is a winner's game.

In India, a lot of noise and apprehension often surround government formation during election years and constant fear among investors of the market falling apart if a coalition government comes to power. But conventional beliefs are frequently shattered by hard data and statistics (table 26.1).

As the saying goes, "No force on earth can stop an idea whose time has come." And India's time has arrived. It took India nearly sixty years to reach its first trillion dollars in GDP but only seven years to reach its second trillion. The next consecutive trillions are expected to be reached in faster succession. Even if market cap to GDP remains around parity in the long run, one can envision the kind of wealth creation that lies in store for investors in great Indian businesses. Trillions of dollars. This, in turn, will have a positive multiplier effect on the prosperity of the nation.

Investors tend to get jitters whenever they experience sharp and sudden spikes in downside volatility. Regardless of the political regime, periodic downside volatility in both bull and bear markets is as predictable as night following day. Look at the following charts, which show the maximum drawdowns under different political regimes in the Indian equity markets (Nifty) since 1991 (figure 26.3) and in the American equity markets (S&P 500) since the late 1920s (table 26.2).

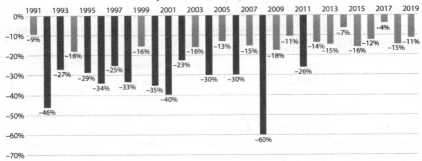

Nifty 50 Maximum Intrayear Drawdown

FIGURE 26.3 Largest drawdowns in the Indian equity markets (Nifty), 1991–2019.

Source: Arun Kumar, *The Eighty Twenty Investor* (blog), October 11, 2019, used by permission of the author.

TABLE 26.2 Largest drawdowns in the U.S. equity markets (S&P 500), 1929–present

President	Inauguration Date	End of Term	Worst Stock Market Drawdown
Herbert Hoover	March 4, 1929	March 3, 1933	−86.19%
Franklin Roosevelt	March 4, 1933	January 19, 1937	−33.93%
	January 20, 1937	January 19, 1941	−54.47%
	January 20, 1941	April 11, 1945	−28.79%
Harry Truman	April 12, 1945	January 19, 1949	−28.47%
	January 20, 1949	January 19, 1953	−14.02%
Dwight Eisenhower	January 20, 1953	January 20, 1957	−14.43%
	January 21, 1957	January 19, 1961	−20.66%
John F. Kennedy*	January 20, 1961	January 19, 1965	−27.97%
Lyndon Johnson	January 20, 1965	January 19, 1969	−22.18%
Richard Nixon**	January 20, 1969	January 19, 1973	−34.73%
	January 20, 1973	January 19, 1977	−47.32%
Jimmy Carter	January 20, 1977	January 19, 1981	−17.07%
Ronald Reagan	January 20, 1981	January 20, 1985	−25.30%
	January 21, 1985	January 19, 1989	−33.51%
George Bush	January 20, 1989	January 19, 1993	−19.92%
Bill Clinton	January 20, 1993	January 19, 1997	−8.94%
	January 20, 1997	January 19, 2001	−19.34%
George W. Bush	January 20, 2001	January 19, 2005	−43.46%
	January 20, 2005	January 19, 2009	−51.93%
Barack Obama	January 20, 2009	January 19, 2013	−22.60%
	January 21, 2013	January 19, 2017	−14.16%
Donald Trump	January 20, 2017	???	???

*Lyndon Johnson sworn in November 22, 1963.

**Gerald Ford sworn in August 9, 1974.

Did all this interim stock price volatility make even a slight dent in the long-term business performance of any of the many big wealth creators? No.

During the usual periodic sharp corrections and the occasional recessions, keep Paul Harvey's words in mind: "In times like these, it helps to recall that there have always been times like these."

Be a Keen Student of Financial History

There is nothing new in the world except the history you do not know.

—Harry Truman

Those who cannot remember the past are condemned to repeat it.

—George Santayana

A study of past manias and crashes should be part of every investor's body of historical knowledge. It informs and educates us, as almost no other subject can, about the psychology of people, governments, and nations. More important, it is yet another demonstration that hardly any events in the markets are unprecedented. The only thing that's new in finance is the history we haven't read. Our imagination is limited only by our knowledge of history. So, knowing the fullest possible range of what has gone wrong before makes us better prepared for what might go wrong again in the future.

French polymath Gustave Le Bon wrote one of the most influential works on social psychology, *The Crowd*, as a rant on French politics, but his observations also describe how stock market manias take place. The book, widely considered to be the definitive work on mass psychology, despite its 1895 publishing date, explains how a crowd goes from controlled logic to uncontrolled emotion, resulting in conscious personalities vanishing into a collective mind. Under the influence of crowds, individuals act bizarrely, in ways they never would alone. The key finding in Le Bon's work is that crowds are mentally unified at the lowest, most barbaric common denominator of their collective unconsciousness—instincts, passions, and feelings—not at the level of facts or reason. Crowds are impressed by spectacle, images, and myths. Misinformation and exaggeration become contagious. Prestige attaches to true believers who reaffirm shared beliefs. Under these conditions, crowds chase a delusion until it is finally destroyed by experience.

Jesse Livermore is quoted as saying:

There is profit in studying the human factors—the ease with which human beings believe what it pleases them to believe; and how they allow themselves—indeed, urge themselves—to be influenced by their cupidity or by the dollar-cost of the average man's carelessness. *Fear and hope remain the same; therefore the study of the psychology of speculators is as valuable as it ever was.*

. . . *Nowhere does history indulge in repetitions so often or so uniformly as in Wall Street* [emphasis added]. When you read contemporary accounts of booms or panics the one thing that strikes you most forcibly is how little either stock speculation or stock speculators today differ from yesterday. The game does not change and neither does human nature.[9]

Human nature has not changed in centuries, and the perennial emotions of greed and fear ensure that speculative follies keep playing out, leading to endless cycles of booms and busts. Prominent historical events include the Dutch tulip mania; the South Sea Bubble (during which a mythical company was chartered "for carrying on an undertaking of great advantage but no one to know what it is"); the Roaring Twenties (including the Florida land bubble), followed by the Great Crash of 1929; the "tronics boom" in the 1960s; and the Nifty Fifty in the 1970s. More recent events include the U.S. biotech bubble and Japan's asset bubble in the 1980s, the tech bubble in the 1990s, the housing bubble in the 2000s, and the cryptocurrency bubble of 2017. In many of these cases, investors believed they were taking part in an adventure that would reinvent the world. (When it comes to investments, the romantic appeal of being a party to a technological revolution or an entirely new industry or invention often dominates profit considerations in investors' minds.)

A bubble typically is characterized by some major technological revolution, cheap liquidity, financial innovation that disguises higher leverage (in John Kenneth Galbraith's words, "The world of finance hails the invention of the wheel over and over again, often in a slightly more unstable version"), amnesia about the last bubble, and abandonment of time-honored methods of security valuation. The fuel is borrowed cash and margin purchases.

When these conditions are present, always remember John Templeton's warning: "The four most dangerous words in investing are 'This time, it's different.'" Every bubble in financial history has eventually popped, but the timing has always been a surprise for everyone. You may get zero ideas in a year during periods of market frenzy, but it is better to be patient than poor. There are times to make money—and times to avoid losing money. The market is a great leveler. A sudden crash puts everything in perspective, cuts your ego in half, and makes you realize your shortcomings and blind spots. Most important, the fundamental lessons on durability of individual business models, quality of earnings, prudent diversification, and management integrity are reinstated. Bear markets bring the fundamental truths of investing to the fore. To be able to view them and imbibe them for our remaining investing life, we need to embrace humility and be willing to accept our mistakes.

Always be humble and remember that the ten years following the global financial crisis have been kind to investing track records and professional careers. If you got your start at any point during this period, be thankful—and do not skimp on reading history.

It seems fitting to end this chapter on the futility of forecasting with the following deep-meaning words from Peter Lynch: "There are 60,000 economists in the U.S., many of them employed full-time trying to forecast recessions and interest rates, and if they could do it successfully twice in a row, they'd all be millionaires by now. . . . But as far as I know, most of them are still gainfully employed, which ought to tell us something."[10]

I have nothing to add.

CHAPTER 27

UPDATING OUR BELIEFS IN LIGHT OF NEW EVIDENCE

If anyone can refute me—show me I'm making a mistake or looking at things from the wrong perspective—I'll gladly change. It's the truth I'm after and the truth never harmed anyone. What harms us is to persist in self-deceit and ignorance.

—Marcus Aurelius

The illiterate of the 21st century will not be those who cannot read and write, but those who cannot learn, unlearn, and relearn.

—Alvin Toffler

It is not the strongest of the species that survive, nor the most intelligent, but the one most responsive to change.

—Charles Darwin

When the facts change, I change my mind. What do you do, sir?

—John Maynard Keynes

To others, being wrong is a source of shame; to me, recognizing my mistakes is a source of pride. Once we realize that imperfect understanding is the human condition, there is no shame in being wrong, only in failing to correct our mistakes.

—George Soros

Charlie and I believe that when you find information that contradicts your existing beliefs, you've got a special obligation to look at it—and quickly.

—Warren Buffett

People tend to accumulate large mental holdings of fixed conclusions and attitudes that are not often re-examined or changed, even though there is plenty of good evidence that they are wrong.

—Charlie Munger

If you do not change direction, you may end up where you are heading.

—Lao Tzu

Faced with the choice between changing one's mind and proving that there is no need to do so, almost everyone gets busy on the proof.

—John Kenneth Galbraith

Confirmation bias—believing what you want to believe and discounting contrary information—it has destroyed countless portfolios and businesses alike.

—Scott Fearon

If we only look to confirm our beliefs, we will never discover if we're wrong. Be self-critical and unlearn your best-loved ideas. Search for evidence that disconfirms ideas and assumptions. Consider alternative outcomes, viewpoints and answers.

—Peter Bevelin

Anatomically modern humans—our human species, *Homo sapiens,* "man the wise"—first appeared in the fossil record in Ethiopia approximately 200,000 years ago. For tens of thousands of years,

Homo sapiens coexisted on the planet with other types of humans, including the famous Neanderthals, as well as other varieties less well known to science, now extinct. It is only in the past two hundred years that we have improved our standard of living. Michael Rothschild, in his book *Bionomics: Economy as Business Ecosystem*, shares a startling comparison. If we collapse these 200,000 years down to a twenty-four-hour day, in the first twenty-three hours or so, we were just hunters and gatherers. Then from 11:00 p.m. to 11:58 p.m., people survived by subsistence, farming, and crafts. As Rothschild puts it, all of modern industrial life has unfolded in the last ninety seconds of humanity's existence. We are new to change, and change is new to us.[1]

> Uber, the world's largest taxi company, owns no vehicles. Facebook, the world's most popular media owner, creates no content. Alibaba, the most valuable retailer, has no inventory. And Airbnb, the world's largest accommodation provider, owns no real estate. Something interesting is happening.
> —Tom Goodwin

"We are living in an ever-changing world" is both a cliché and an understatement. Regulations change all the time, new technologies emerge, unique business models evolve, and disruptive innovations take shape across all walks of life. It is an exciting time to be alive. Rockets are landing themselves, cars are driving themselves, and money is governing itself. In addition, the ongoing switch from "ownership that you purchase" to "access that you subscribe to" overruns many conventions. The five largest companies in the U.S. market (Apple, Google, Microsoft, Amazon, and Facebook) require virtually no capital to grow. All of these businesses scaled up much more quickly than Carnegie's steel plants or Rockefeller's oil refineries. It took decades of toil and sweat, and significant sums of capital, to go around the country and cobble together a network of refineries in the late-nineteenth and early twentieth centuries. It took Mark Zuckerberg just eight years to build Facebook from nothing to a business with $100 billion in valuation—and just four more years to reach $300 billion.

> The big picture is that software is eating the world—that is, many of the products and services developed over the past 150 years are transforming into, or being disrupted by software. . . . The implications are enormous; *software is infinitely replicable and, through the internet, can be delivered at zero marginal cost. When a major input to business—distribution cost—goes to zero, entire industries get disrupted* [emphasis added]. When one can build a business model from the ground up with entirely new assumptions, one can attack incumbents in a way that is very difficult to defend.
> —Marcelo Lima

Outdated and rigid models and methodologies to assess investments are being disrupted, and continued reliance on these old techniques may identify value traps as value investments. Value investing is not dead (as is often stated in the media), but rather how we measure value. For most of the past century, book value was the most relevant tool of valuation for most companies. Book value means little at companies like Google, Amazon, or Facebook. As innovation S-curves get steeper, adoption cycles also have gotten much faster. Today, new business models make money and they are here to stay. Although the adoption cycle for social media is different than it was for the radio or electricity, many investors project the past onto the future and end up missing great opportunities. The journey from tangibles to intangibles is the true essence of the journey of investing.

The great companies of a century ago were confined primarily to their industries. Rockefeller was an oilman. He wouldn't have even thought about getting into retail, banking, or any other industry. But companies like Amazon start in retail and then use their foundations and user bases to expand into multiple new lines of businesses.

In such a scenario, one of the key skills required to be successful in today's day and age is flexible thinking. In psychology, this is referred to as cognitive flexibility. Psychologists consider this flexibility to be one of the key mental skills required to succeed along with other skills, such as creativity, critical thinking, and problem solving. Henry Singleton, who, according to Warren Buffett, had the best operating and capital deployment record in American business in his time, said in an interview with *Business Week*, "My only plan is to keep coming to work. . . . I like to steer the boat each day rather than plan ahead way into the future." Singleton eschewed detailed strategic plans, preferring to remain flexible: "I know a lot of people have very strong and definite plans that they've worked out on all kinds of things, but we're subject to a tremendous number of outside influences and the vast majority of them cannot be predicted. So my idea is to stay flexible."[2] In a similar vein, Charlie Munger has said that, at Berkshire, "there has never been a master plan. Anyone who wanted to do it, we fired because it takes on a life of its own and doesn't cover new reality. *We want people taking into account new information* [emphasis added]."[3]

Flexible thinking is the ability to keep an open mind upon encountering new facts or situations and to be adaptive to changing a viewpoint from previously held thoughts or beliefs, however strongly held. Most of what has been written about the market tells you the way it ought to be, but successful investors do not rigidly hold on to the way it ought to be; they simply go with what is. Good investors read a lot and practice the learnings obtained from books, but the best investors make a calculated, reasoned, and conscious effort to adapt themselves to the actual ground realities of the individual local markets in which they operate.

In his book *Dead Companies Walking*, Scott Fearon writes, "Failure terrifies people. They'll do whatever they have to do to downplay it, wish it away, and just plain pretend it doesn't exist. Most of the time, they'll go on living in denial long after the truth of their predicament becomes obvious."[4]

Fearon is referring to what is known as "head-in-the-sand syndrome." Ostriches bury their heads in the sand when they are scared or threatened. They think they are safe if they can't see the danger. According to psychologists, this syndrome—ignoring information that can help us—arises from the need to avoid the negative feelings associated with accepting uncomfortable facts. This syndrome describes a common human fallibility to engage in psychological denial and refuse to acknowledge reality. Munger has talked about this human tendency: "I think that one should recognize reality even when one doesn't like it; indeed, *especially when one doesn't like it* [emphasis added]."

He has also said,

> Life, in part, is like a poker game, wherein you have to learn to quit, sometimes when holding a much-loved hand—you must learn to handle mistakes and new facts that change the odds.
>
> We all are learning, modifying, or destroying ideas all the time. Rapid destruction of your ideas when the time is right is one of the most valuable qualities you can acquire. You must force yourself to consider arguments on the other side.
>
> There's no way that you can live an adequate life without many mistakes. In fact, one trick in life is to get so you can handle mistakes. Failure to handle psychological denial is a common way for people to go broke.[5]

Businesspeople and investors tend to ignore these words and never give up on their pet projects and favorite stocks, even when it makes no sense to continue. They keep throwing good money after bad, or they keep averaging on the way down in bad businesses. They follow the same approach until they go broke. One of the surest ways to go broke is to keep getting an increasing share of a shrinking market. This is a slow but sure death. It is gradual, then sudden.

Unpleasant facts do not cease to exist just because they are ignored. We should learn from Munger's comments, during the 2000 Berkshire annual meeting, about gracefully accepting changing realities in the right spirit: "I think it's in the nature of things for some businesses to die. It's also in the nature of things that in some cases, you shouldn't fight it. There's no logical answer in some cases except to wring the money out and go elsewhere."[6]

These words remind me of a quote from Daniel Kahneman that is worth thinking about frequently:

> When I work I have no sunk costs. I like changing my mind. Some people really don't like it but for me changing my mind is a thrill. It's an indication that I'm

learning something. So I have no sunk costs in the sense that I can walk away from an idea that I've worked on for a year if I can see a better idea. It's a good attitude for a researcher. The main track that young researchers fall into is sunk costs. They get to work on a project that doesn't work and that is not promising but they keep at it. I think too much persistence can be bad for you in the intellectual world.[7]

Good investing is a peculiar balance between the conviction to follow your ideas and the flexibility to recognize when you have made a mistake. You need to believe in something but, at the same time, you need to recognize that you will be wrong a considerable number of times over the course of your investing career. This fact holds true for all investors, regardless of their stature. The balance between confidence and humility is best learned through extensive experience and mistakes. Always respect the person on the other side of the trade and ask yourself, Why does he or she want to buy or sell? What does he or she know that I don't? You must be intellectually honest with yourself at all times. The great investors are active seekers of truth. (All businesspeople and investors should study Buffett's 1985 letter, in which he explains his decision to shut down the textile operations of Berkshire. It is a remarkable case study in rationality and objectivity.)

In his 1994 lecture at the University of Southern California, Marshall School of Business, Munger shared his thoughts on Buffett's decision:

> The great lesson in microeconomics is to discriminate between when technology is going to help you and when it's going to kill you. *And most people do not get this straight in their heads.* But a fellow like Buffett does. . . .
>
> . . . He knew that the *huge productivity increases* that would come from a better machine introduced into the production of *a commodity product* would *all* go to the benefit of the *buyers* of the textiles. *Nothing* was going to stick to *our* ribs as *owners.*
>
> That's such an obvious concept—that there are all kinds of wonderful new inventions that give you nothing as owners *except the opportunity to spend a lot more money in a business that's still going to be lousy.* The money still *won't* come to *you. All of the advantages from great improvements* are going to flow through to the *customers.*
>
> Conversely, if you own the only newspaper in Oshkosh and they were to invent more efficient ways of composing the whole newspaper, then when you got rid of the old technology and got new fancy computers and so forth, all of the savings would come right through to the bottom line.
>
> In all cases, the people who *sell* the machinery—and, by and large, even the internal bureaucrats *urging you* to buy the equipment—show you *projections* with the amount you'll *save* at current prices with the new technology.

However, they don't do the second step of the analysis which is to determine how much is going to stay home and how much is just going to flow through to the customer. I've never seen a single projection incorporating that second step in my life [emphasis added].[8]

Conducting a discounted cash flow or net present value exercise without carrying out the necessary "second step of the analysis" leads to overlooking expected competitor actions (game theory) and results in a distorted view of reality that eventually leads to losses for investors and companies. When we experience a favorable policy change or an industry tailwind, competitive pressures may mean that all or most of the benefits are captured by customers. (A sustainably high return on invested capital, which indicates the presence of some form of competitive advantage, is the best sign that a company can beat this challenge.)

For many years, Buffett called himself an "aeroholic" and expressed serious reservations about investing in airline stocks. Then, in 2016, Berkshire Hathaway revealed holdings in not one but four airline stocks. Observe the remarkable flexibility in Buffett's thinking. When the industry dynamics of the airline sector changed, Buffett promptly changed his mind, after an objective and dispassionate consideration of the new facts.

If you are dispassionate, you'll win—that's my greatest learning from the *Bhagavad Gita*.
    —Ajay Piramal

New evidence should modify our prior beliefs and convert them into our posterior beliefs. The stronger the prior belief, the more difficult it will be to change it. (Buddhism has a concept called beginner's mind, which is an active openness to try new things and study new ideas, unburdened by past preconceptions.) If, however, we have no prior knowledge about a given situation at hand, then we will depend completely on the available evidence specific to the case. For this reason, a basic minimum understanding of the big ideas from the key disciplines is essential to form an initial hypothesis.

In one of his blog posts on 25iq.com, Tren Griffin describes the essence of Ray Dalio's decision-making process:

Dalio starts with a rational analysis of the information he has and from that he forms a hypothesis. He then exposes that hypothesis to thoughtful people with alternative points of view and methods of analysis who may disagree with him and then he wants a radically transparent "back and forth" discussion. As part of that process he wants to deeply understand the reasoning of any thoughtful opposing views. Only after he has understood these alternative points of view does Dalio believe he is in a position to reject or accept the alternative ideas and make a decision.[9]

We always need a devil's advocate to challenge our assumptions.

Professor Mihir Desai highlighted the importance of consciously seeking out diversity in viewpoints in his book *The Wisdom of Finance*:

> The relationships that are most enriching are ones that broaden our perspective beyond our usual experience—those relationships are, in finance terms, "imperfectly correlated assets," precisely the types of assets that most enhance the portfolios of our lives. . . . Homophily, or the desire to surround ourselves with like-minded people, is a common social instinct—and one that finance warns against. *Yes, it's easier to be around like-minded types, but finance recommends the hard work of exposing yourself to differences, not shielding yourself from them* [emphasis added].[10]

You can't really learn anything new if you're always surrounded by people who agree with you. As investors, we often have our personal group of intellectual peers with whom we discuss our ideas. But we should be careful that our sounding board does not turn into an echo chamber, for that would be harmful for our decision-making process. Amay Hattangadi and Swanand Kelkar wrote about this issue in a December 2016 report for Morgan Stanley titled "Connecting the Dots": "We tend to be surrounded by people who are like us and share our world view. Social media accentuates this by tailoring our news and opinion feeds to match our pre-set views. To avoid falling into this homogeneity trap, one needs to seek out and dispassionately engage with people whose views differ from your own and that's true not just for current affairs but your favorite stocks as well."[11]

The Internet, which provides the promise of access to a great diversity of viewpoints, in fact speeds our retreat into a confirmatory bubble. In an early article for Livemint newspaper, Hattangadi and Kelkar write:

> "Social media" will systematically find ways to ensure that we are fed with more of what we find appealing. . . . Our Facebook feed is filtered based on previous history of "likes." Amazon suggests books to buy based on our pattern of previous purchases. Twitter suggests whose tweets we should "follow" based on those we are already following. . . . The online world has magnified the decibel level of the reverberations in an echo chamber manifold.[12]

During our investing journey, we may come across certain special businesses that make us feel excited and, at the same time, challenge our prior beliefs and preconceived notions because these businesses may belong to difficult industries or less favored geographic locations. How can we overcome our personal prejudices against these businesses in such situations? How can we better calibrate our prior views in light of new evidence? The answer lies in an elementary mathematical concept all of us learned in school.

Conditional Probability

Conditional probability, also known as Bayes's rule, measures the probability of an event, given that another event has occurred. In his book *Thinking, Fast and Slow*, Daniel Kahneman has simplified the formula for us: "The simplest form of Bayes's rule is in odds form, posterior odds = prior odds × likelihood ratio, where the posterior odds are the odds (the ratio of probabilities) for two competing hypotheses."[13] According to this equation, one's prior beliefs (prior odds) are subject to revision with the help of the likelihood ratio. The higher that ratio, the higher should be the change in one's view of a given situation.

Although prior beliefs can come from many sources, an excellent source is base rates, which represent historical statistical information.

The likelihood ratio represents new information about a specific case that changes the odds. The higher the likelihood ratio, the higher the posterior odds. Sometimes the information and characteristics specific to the situation being examined are so vivid and persuasive that it leads us to overlook the base rates or the average historical experience. In those cases, Munger's warning usually comes true: "When you mix raisins with turds, you've still got turds."[14]

Bayes's Rule as a Way of Thinking

If you don't get this elementary, but mildly unnatural, mathematics of elementary probability into your repertoire, then you go through a long life like a one-legged man in an ass-kicking contest. You're giving a huge advantage to everybody else.

—Charlie Munger

Philip Tetlock, a prominent political science writer, has produced extensive research over the years debunking experts who have little predictive abilities. His extensive research also highlighted the characteristics of "superforecasters" who have built exceptional track records. Interestingly, although all of them practice Bayesian thinking as a way of life, they do not always engage in rigorous number crunching or complex math. In their book *Superforecasting*, Philip Tetlock and Dan Gardner write:

Do forecasters really have to understand, memorize, and use an algebraic formula? I have good news: No, they don't. The superforecasters are a numerate bunch: many know about Bayes' theorem and could deploy it if they felt it was worth the trouble. But they rarely crunch the numbers so explicitly. What matters far more to the superforecasters than Bayes' theorem is Bayes' core insight of *gradually getting closer to the truth by constantly updating in proportion to the weight of the evidence* [emphasis added].[15]

In his October 2015 white paper titled "Worldly Wisdom in an Equation," Professor Sanjay Bakshi shared six core insights from Bayesian thinking to keep in mind:

1. **Translate vague language into numeric probabilities.** Bayesians are careful about the language they use when they think in terms of probabilities. Tetlock writes,

> Strive to distinguish as many degrees of doubt as the problem permits but no more. Few things are either certain or impossible. And 'maybe' isn't all that informative. So your uncertainty dial needs more than three settings. Nuance matters. The more degrees of uncertainty you can distinguish, the better a forecaster you are likely to be. As in poker, you have an advantage if you are better than your competitors at separating 60/40 bets from 40/60—or 55/45 from 45/55. Translating vague-verbiage hunches into numeric probabilities feels unnatural at first but it can be done. It just requires patience and practice.[16]

The Central Intelligence Agency's publication "Words of Estimative Probability" offers a useful framework for translating Bayesian language (table 27.1).[17]

TABLE 27.1 **Translating Bayesian language**

100% Certainty		
The General Area of Possibility		
93%	Give or take about 6%	Almost certain
75%	Give or take about 12%	Probable
50%	Give or take about 10%	Chances about even
30%	Give or take about 10%	Probably not
7%	Give or take about 5%	Almost certainly not
0% Impossibility		

Source: "Words of Estimative Probability," Central Intelligence Agency, March 19, 2007, https://www.cia.gov/library/center-for-the-study-of-intelligence/csi-publications/books-and-monographs/sherman-kent-and-the-board-of-national-estimates-collected-essays/6words.html.

2. **Always keep base rates in mind.** Phil Fisher has referred to this in the past: "It seems logical that even before thinking of buying any common stock, the first step is to see how money has been most successfully made in the past." Investors are prone to overlook base rates, however, when they come across a vivid or enticing description of a specific case. Base rates are a boring piece of statistics. Stories, on the other hand, are seductive. In his book *What Works on Wall Street*, James O'Shaughnessy writes:

> Human nature makes it virtually impossible to forgo the specific information of an individual case (likelihood ratio) in favor of the results of a great number of cases (prior odds or base rates). *We're interested in this stock and this company, not with this class of stocks or this class of companies. Large numbers mean nothing to us.* As Stalin chillingly said: "One death is a tragedy; a million, a statistic." *When making an investment, we almost always do so on a stock-by-stock basis, rarely thinking about an overall strategy. If a story about one stock is compelling enough, we're willing to ignore what the base rate tells us about an entire class of stocks* [emphasis added].[18]

Before paying an exorbitantly high price-to-earnings (P/E) multiple for a business, one should study the historical averaged-out experience of paying such prices. Similarly, before committing money to highly expensive initial public offerings, one should look at the historical averaged-out experience. Before investing in a highly leveraged business, or a business in which the management has a track record of poor governance or capital allocation, one should look at the historical long-term outcomes of making investments in such situations.

Taking base rates into account helps check one's initial overenthusiasm after hearing an exciting story about a stock. When Buffett avoids investing in turnaround situations, it is because he relies on base rates. According to him, "Turnarounds seldom turn."[19] (This is why the best time to buy a turnaround is when evidence of a turnaround is already in place. You won't get in at the bottom, but you will have eliminated a lot of risk and uncertainty.) When Buffett avoids investing in fast-changing high-technology businesses and justifies that by stating that "severe change and exceptional returns usually don't mix,"[20] he is relying on base rates.

An effective way to think about base rates is to think in terms of the "outside view" and the "inside view," used by Daniel Kahneman. Tetlock writes:

> Daniel Kahneman has a much more evocative visual term for [base rates]. He calls it the "outside view"—in contrast to the "inside view," which is the specifics of the particular case. . . .
> *It's natural to be drawn to the inside view. It's usually concrete and filled with engaging detail we can use to craft a story about what's going on. The outside*

view is typically abstract, bare, and doesn't lend itself so readily to storytelling. So even smart, accomplished people routinely fail to consider the outside view [emphasis added].[21]

3. **All too-good-to-be-true-sounding stories are not necessarily bad.** A genuinely good story improves the likelihood ratio, which then translates into higher posterior odds. This is an important point for fundamental investors because they are bottom-up investors in individual businesses and are not investing in broad strategies. For a Graham and Dodd–style investor who believes in mean reversion and wants to invest in statistical bargains, base rates are extremely important, and specific stock stories are less important. For a qualitative investor who follows Fisher or Munger, however, learning as much as possible about the specific business is critically important. Of course, such an investor must never lose sight of the underlying base rate. But he or she should also be able to identify diamonds in the rough. In those cases, a compelling story usually makes the business unique, and it stands out from the rest of the industry. Usually, that story is about an extraordinary individual who has demonstrated capabilities of creating value even in businesses and industries in which it is difficult to do so. Munger calls such individuals "intelligent fanatics." Harvey Firestone describes such individuals in his book *Men and Rubber*: "The test of a business man is not whether he can make money in one or two boom years, or can make money through the luck of getting into the field first, but whether in a highly competitive field, without having any initial advantage over his competitors, he can outdistance them in a perfectly honorable way and keep the respect of himself and of his community."[22]

Intelligent fanatics let their execution and not their charisma do the talking. Judge them based on their execution track record and do not get influenced by the use of superlatives and adjectives by other people (which is usually more of a persuasion technique than anything else).

4. **Distinguish between the signal and the noise.** The signal is the truth. The noise is what distracts us from seeing it. In his book *The Signal and the Noise*, Nate Silver writes, "There isn't any more truth in the world than there was before the Internet or the printing press. Most of the data is just noise, as most of the universe is filled with empty space."[23] If we want to increase the signal-to-noise ratio, we need to first cut out the cacophony of all the noise surrounding us. As James Gleick says, "When information is cheap, attention becomes expensive."[24]

More data do not result in more insights. Often, they just lead to bad judgment. The scarcest resource for successful investors is not money but attention—how to manage the trade-off between time and rationality to best effect. Investment skill lies not in knowing everything but in judicious neglect:

making wise choices about what to overlook. To ferret out the valuable signal from the noisy news flow, first quiet the mind and then look for the slow, gradual changes that are taking place. The way to do that is to focus on long-term changes (and not quarterly, monthly, or daily changes). These could be changes in the quality of the balance sheet, the income statement, or the cash flow statement. Those changes should be related to a solid qualitative analysis of the reasons. And it is this kind of calm, measured, and thoughtful qualitative analysis that eventually leads to what noted value investor Paul Lountzis calls "differential insights."[25] The conventions of analyst research mean that long-term value is often underappreciated. For example, most research focuses on a one- or two-year forecast horizon, so companies with a large part of their value beyond this horizon may be undervalued.

5.   **Follow Darwin's golden rule of thinking.** Counterintuition was Darwin's specialty. He was so good at this way of thinking because he had a simple but highly unnatural habit of thought. He paid special attention to collecting facts that did not agree with his prior conceptions. Darwin called this the golden rule:

> I had, also, during many years followed a golden rule, namely, that whenever a published fact, a new observation or thought came across me, which was opposed to my general results, to make a memorandum of it without fail and at once; for I had found by experience that such facts and thoughts were far more apt to escape from memory than favorable ones. Owing to this habit, very few objections were raised against my views which I had not at least noticed and attempted to answer.[26]

Darwin's great success was driven by his ability to see, note, and learn from objections to his cherished thoughts. The *Origin of Species* has stood up in the face of 159 years of subsequent biological research because Darwin was so careful to make sure the theory was nearly impossible to refute. Later scientists would find the book slightly "incomplete" but not incorrect.

Darwin probably influenced Munger's prescription on the work required to hold an opinion: you must understand the opposite side of the argument better than the person holding that side does. Your opinion is more credible when you also can clearly articulate the contrary view. This way of thinking is quite unnatural in the face of our genetic makeup, wherein the more typical response is to look for as much confirming evidence as possible. When practiced in the right spirit, however, it is a powerful way to beat our shortcomings in becoming objective and unbiased.

Darwin's habits of completeness, diligence, accuracy, and habitual objectivity ultimately led him to make his greatest breakthroughs. His process was extremely tedious. No spark of divine insight gave him his edge. He just started with the right basic ideas and then worked for a long time and with extreme focus and objectivity, always keeping his eye on reality. A useful supplement to Darwin's golden rule of thinking is a basic pros and cons list, which Benjamin Franklin, in a 1772 letter to Joseph Priestley, referred to as "Moral or Prudential Algebra."

6.   **View the stock market as a pari-mutuel betting system.** In a pari-mutuel system, such as the stock market, one is betting against other investors. And in such a system, the behavior of other investors changes the odds. Bakshi writes:

> When, for example, an exceptionally well-managed niche business hiding inside a commodity industry is valued by the market as a commodity business, it represents an opportunity. While the thoughtful Bayesian investor takes care not to lose sight of the fact that business belongs to a commodity industry (low prior odds), he also factors in the key evidence specific to the business which makes it exceptional, resulting in a high likelihood ratio.

Therefore, for this investor, the posterior odds are far better than those implied by the stock market's assessment of the business. And that is an exploitable prejudice.[27]

Bayesian thinking helps us overcome our biases and personal prejudices. Many investors in the Indian markets have a prejudice against Hyderabad-based companies, microcap stocks, turnaround situations, conglomerates, highly leveraged companies, commodity stocks, and holding companies. That prejudice (baseline information) is reflected in the cheaper valuations. "At the same time, however," writes Bakshi, "you should recognize the possibility that this particular business which you are evaluating could be *different* from the statistical class to which it belongs." (For instance, I usually begin studying select leveraged distress situations after the borrowers have entered into a formal debt-restructuring arrangement.)

When the Facts Change, Change Your Mind

We are capable of changing our minds if the facts change. We've done this several times, but I must say, it is hard.

—Charlie Munger

In his book *Winning on Wall Street*, Martin Zweig talks about how bearish he was during a sell-off in February and March 1980: "I was sitting there looking at conditions and being as bearish as I could be—but the market had reversed. Things began to change as the Fed reduced interest rates and eased credit controls. *Even though I had preconceived ideas* that we were heading toward some type of calamity, *I responded to changing conditions* [emphasis added]." He concludes, "The problem with most people who play the market is that they are not flexible. . . . To succeed in the market you must have discipline, flexibility, and patience."[28]

Long-term investors buy stocks with the idea of holding them for many years. Even then, an investor needs to continually verify the validity of his or her original investment thesis. Whenever a trend reversal occurs, either up or down, it takes a while for people to recognize it. But when you have been invested in a stock for some time, you gradually develop a good understanding of the evolving business and industry dynamics, and you just know when the sustainable growth rate has permanently slowed down for good or when cracks begin to appear in your original investment thesis. This helps you exit in time, ahead of the subsequent P/E derating period, which is particularly painful to experience (and perplexing for many new investors), when the company's earnings continue to grow but at a slower pace than originally discounted in the steep valuations. The art of timely selling is gradually developed through real-life experience in the markets and increasing familiarity with the finer nuances of various industries and their evolving valuation dynamics over time.

One should not hurriedly sell a great business if it becomes temporarily overvalued (and if the stock in question is a bull market sector leader, then one should have the courage to hold on to it for the entire length of the bull run). In great businesses, one tends to get frequent positive surprises, and they tend to end up delivering much better performance than we initially envisaged (as was the case, for instance, with Bajaj Finance). When you find the goose that lays golden eggs, don't sell the goose. One big lesson I have learned over the years is to be reluctant to sell a great business that is trading at expensive valuations, especially when cash is the alternative. A better approach is to wait to sell until a far superior opportunity comes along, or until the stock has become absurdly overvalued. When we perceive great companies to be fairly valued on an immediate, short-term basis, they often are significantly undervalued on a long-term basis. As Fisher wrote in his book *Common Stocks and Uncommon Profits*:

> How can anyone say with even moderate precision just what is overpriced for an outstanding company with an unusually rapid growth rate? Suppose that instead of selling at twenty-five times earnings, as usually happens, the stock is now at thirty-five times earnings. Perhaps there are new products in the immediate future, the real economic importance of which the financial community has not yet grasped. Perhaps there are not any such products. *If the growth rate is so good that in another ten years the company might well have quadrupled, is*

it really of such great concern whether at the moment the stock might or might not be 35 percent overpriced? That which really matters is not to disturb a position that is going to be worth a great deal more later.

. . . If the job has been correctly done when a common stock is purchased, the time to sell it is—almost never [emphasis added].[29]

Over the long term, stocks should outperform most other asset classes and should almost certainly earn higher returns than cash. Cash will always prove to be valuable on occasion, but over a period of twenty to thirty years, the drag on portfolio performance from holding cash will be much more significant than the few occasional benefits one would get from taking advantage of any periodic downturn with "dry powder." John Templeton's quote on the subject of "when to invest" is one of my favorites: "The best time to invest is when you have money. This is because history suggests it is not timing which matters, but time."[30]

The key to wealth creation is to buy high-quality, growing businesses at reasonable valuations and then just sit on them for a very long time. If you take any random sample of a hundred successful investors who have compounded their capital at a good rate for a long time, you will invariably observe that almost all of them would have bought some great businesses and then just sat tight on them. As Munger says, "The big money is not in the buying and selling, but in the waiting."[31]

For most people, doing nothing is just unbearable. They want action, and fear losing their mark-to-market profits. As a result, they keep jumping from one stock to another, and in the process, drastically increase the potential for unforced errors. Blaise Pascal rightly said, "All men's miseries derive from not being able to sit in a quiet room alone."

As investors, we are continuously processing myriad incoming information. Assessing material facts with an open mind and changing one's mind when those facts change (for better or worse) is a valuable skill that increases the odds of investing success. Sometimes, it may happen that one of our long-term secular growth holdings (not the shorter-term commodity-cyclical-special situation holding, for which the primary focus is on mispricing and mean reversion rather than quality of business and management) begins to make our stomach churn. We are no longer comfortable holding it for certain corporate governance reasons or management integrity issues that we may have discovered after our initial purchase. Even though I may expect that company to report high earnings growth for the next few years and its stock may well go up a lot in the interim period, in those cases, I usually exit my position. I do not want to trade a peaceful night's sleep for a few extra percentage points of return. As Walter Schloss used to say, "Investing should be fun and challenging, not stressful and worrying." In an interview, Schloss's son Edwin said that his father's longevity and investing philosophy were probably related: "A lot of money managers today worry about quarterly comparisons in earnings. They're up biting their fingernails until five in the morning. My dad never worried about quarterly comparisons. He slept well."[32]

Quality of life is a better way to measure winning and losing. It is a well-documented fact that stress is a killer. Investors often talk about risk-adjusted returns but rarely about stress-adjusted returns. In my view, the latter matters more. Sleeping well is more important than eating well. Avoid shorting stocks. Avoid taking on personal debt to buy stocks. Avoid entering into long-term partnerships with management teams that make your stomach churn. (As Benjamin Graham says, "You cannot make a quantitative deduction to allow for an unscrupulous management; the only way to deal with such situations is to avoid them."[33])

An investor should be flexible in his or her thinking and make difficult decisions like selling a stock even if it means incurring a loss (big or small) on it. Be emotionally detached from the outcomes and make decisions based on a dispassionate analysis of factual data. Treat losses with equanimity and note the lessons learned. Optimism is a good thing, but self-delusion is not. As Peter Lynch says, "There's no shame in losing money on a stock. Everybody does it. What is shameful is to hold on to a stock, or worse, to buy more of it when the fundamentals are deteriorating."[34] Do not hold on to a stock with worsening fundamentals in the mere hope that things will somehow get better. Always acknowledge and embrace reality for what it is and don't engage in what Munger calls "thumb-sucking." If you are unsure about a stock even after your best efforts to resolve your doubts, just exit and get out. Otherwise, you will end up selling in panic, at a much lower price, during the next sharp market correction. You need to materially adapt when losing and remain faithful when winning. If you have the discipline to do just these two things, you will succeed as an investor.

Use Bayesian reasoning and update probabilities as new evidence arises that affects your expected returns. Some evidence points to look for: excessive valuations, corporate governance concerns, a sharp slowdown in growth rates, loss of competitiveness as reflected in declining market share and falling margins, and loss of bargaining power with customers or suppliers as reflected in deterioration of the working capital situation. It is perfectly okay to be wrong, but it is not okay to remain wrong. One of the great lessons I have learned over the course of my life and investing career is this: if you want to win better than the rest, you must learn how to lose better than the rest. I am happy to have learned Confucius's teaching well: "A man who has committed a mistake and doesn't correct it is committing another mistake."

CHAPTER 28

LIFE IS A SERIES OF OPPORTUNITY COSTS

If you take the best text in economics by Mankiw, he says intelligent people make decisions based on opportunity costs—in other words, it's your alternatives that matter. That's how we make all of our decisions.

—Charlie Munger

As investors, we are in the business of intelligently allocating capital. With limited capital at our disposal and several alternatives, the critical concept of opportunity cost arises. An opportunity cost is defined as the value of the second-best opportunity, which we forgo when we make a choice. In a world in which alternatives are mutually exclusive and we must choose A over B, or B over A, our opportunity cost would be the potential gain of B if we choose A, and vice versa.

Charlie Munger has said:

When someone presented a company in an emerging market to Warren Buffett, Warren said, "I don't feel more comfortable [buying this] than I feel about adding to our position in Wells Fargo." He thinks highly of the company and the managers and the position they were in. He was using this as his opportunity cost. He was saying, "Don't talk about anything unless it's better than buying more Wells Fargo." It doesn't matter to Warren where the opportunity is.

He has no preconceived ideas about whether Berkshire's money ought to be in this or that. He's scanning the world trying to get his opportunity cost as high as he can so his individual decisions would be better.[1]

Munger's words have significant implications for investors. If you expect to achieve a much higher level of returns from one stock that you do not expect to achieve in the others, then why should you continue to allocate capital to the rest of them? Wouldn't it make more sense to remain fully invested until a much better return opportunity appears? All too often, investors succumb to the "do something" syndrome and relax their standards for incoming investments instead of firmly maintaining a high hurdle rate at all times. Be unreasonable.

> It's a funny thing about life; if you refuse to accept anything but the best, you very often get it.
> —W. Somerset Maugham

Capital is finite and always carries an opportunity cost, which is what you can do with the next best alternative. If your next best alternative is 1 percent, your opportunity cost is 1 percent, and if it is 10 percent, the cost is 10 percent, no matter what some formula created in academia might say. Always remember: the highest and best use of capital should always be measured by the next best possible use.

> If I know I have something that yields 8 percent for sure, and something else came along at 7 percent, I'd reject it instantly. Everything is a function of opportunity cost.
> —Warren Buffett

If a business doesn't earn a return that investors could earn elsewhere, then from an investor's standpoint, for all practical purposes that business destroys value. Said another way, if the return on capital isn't equal to or better than the cost of capital (what investors could earn elsewhere), then the business is, in effect, destroying value for shareholders.

Acknowledging and Accounting for Mistakes of Omission

Mistakes of omission are situations in which we have identified a promising business to invest in but fail to pull the trigger. Because we act penny wise and pound foolish, our inaction results in a huge opportunity cost. In the long run, opportunity costs can really matter a lot and sometimes are far more significant than errors of commission. Mistakes of commission are capped at 100 percent, but mistakes of omission have no such ceiling. When people think about costs, they don't think in terms of opportunity costs. For most people, the explicit out-of-pocket costs carry more meaning than opportunity costs, and because forgone opportunities are not out-of-pocket costs, people underweigh them. For long-term investors, hesitancy in paying up for high-quality businesses often carries a big opportunity cost. These costs do not show up in profit-and-loss (P&L) statements because a P&L does not reflect what they could have done but did not do.

Investors need to regularly review their estimate of the expected long-term return from a stock based on the current market price. If it falls below the return available on existing passive income instruments, then it is time to replace that stock with a superior one. Many investors fall in love with their existing holdings (especially if they have identified it after a lot of hard work) and subsequently engage in lazy thinking and do not conduct a rigorous opportunity cost analysis on a regular basis. Every single dollar spends the same, and investors should strive to achieve the biggest bang for their buck from every single dollar invested. Use a high hurdle rate when assessing any potential investment opportunity. Be unreasonable.

You often hear investors making irrational statements like "I am happy to hold this stock because I bought it at a lower price," even if the long-term appreciation potential from the current price is poor. Anchoring bias is powerful, and it occurs automatically, at a subconscious level. An effective way to counter this bias is to mentally liquidate your portfolio before the start of every trading day and ask yourself a simple question: "Given all the current and updated information I now have about this business, would I buy it at the current price?" If you conclude that you would not buy the shares today but find that you cannot push the sell button, be aware that this is because of endowment bias and not because of a logical hold thesis. Sell. Clinging to stocks with unsatisfactory expected future returns from their current price is a costly mistake that negatively affects an investor's long-term net worth.

The opportunity cost mental model should be used in conjunction with the circle of competence principle. Things that you are incapable of understanding should not form part of the opportunity set from which you determine your opportunity cost.

If I come across a superlative investment opportunity within my circle of competence, then I do not mind immediately selling the weak holdings, if any, in my portfolio, even at a loss, if required, without any hesitation. At any time, we always hold one or two stocks in our portfolio that are our "least favorites." They are not always bad stocks per se. We just are subconsciously aware that they are weaker than the other stocks in our portfolio (but we still tend to hold on to them!) and that we would not mind selling them at a future date, if required. When you come across what you strongly believe is a great investment idea, conduct a rigorous analysis to actively search for disconfirming evidence within all your existing holdings. In most cases, you will find that your smallest-weight holdings will be the ones that get sold, because you had less conviction in them to start with (as indicated by their low weights).

It is always better to go with certainty when uncertainty is not expected to yield a whole lot greater expected return. As an investor, I have a simple rule when looking at new ideas. If I am going to add a new position to my portfolio, it needs to be "significantly better" than what I already own. When we are truly disciplined and highly demanding in the required hurdle rate for incoming ideas, then the best stock to buy at any given time is usually among the ones we already own in our portfolio. Don't diversify just for the sake of it. Avoid adding anything to your life, your investment portfolio, or your business unless it makes them better.

Opportunity Costs Are Applicable in All Aspects of Our Lives

Opportunity costs are all about the most basic of economic concepts: trade-offs. If you make a choice, you forgo all the other options (at least for the time being). Sometimes the option you didn't choose turns out to have been the wiser choice, which is why opportunity cost is best measured in hindsight. Opportunity costs can be best understood by looking at what would have been given up if certain path-breaking individuals had chosen to do something else.

What if Sam Walton had not decided to start Walmart stores at forty-four years of age?

What if Thomas Edison had stopped working on the light bulb when he failed the first few thousand times?

What if Steve Jobs had never returned to Apple to lead its resurgence, fundamentally reshaping the future of consumer technology?

We are no different from these renowned individuals. We make decisions every day about how we spend our time, money, brainpower, and energy, and for every decision we make, there is an alternative that we didn't choose. And it is the choice not taken that represents our opportunity cost. All rejected alternatives are paths to possible futures in which things could be better or worse than the path we chose. Every decision commits us to some course of action that, by definition, eliminates acting on other alternatives. We always have an opportunity cost when we make choices.

What if you had learned a new skill that got you a promotion instead of binge-watching *Game of Thrones*?

What if you had worked during college instead of taking out a big student loan?

What if you had become a fitness enthusiast instead of a junk foodie?

In essence, you make your choices, and then your choices make you. Every decision, no matter how slight, alters the trajectory of your life. Every choice's compound effect is in action all the time. Your life today is a result of your past choices. Hard choices, easy life. Easy choices, hard life.

Most people fail to appreciate the deep meaning in Benjamin Franklin's words "Beware of little expenses; a small leak will sink a great ship." Let's say you pick up your daily morning cup of coffee at Starbucks for $4. Every single time, in exchange for a beverage you could make at home for a few cents, you spend $4. If you buy fifty coffees this year (about one per week) for $200, you are giving up $23,500 in future wealth fifty years from now (assuming you invested the money in a low-cost index fund at an expected annual return of 10 percent). Investing is nothing but deferring gratification today to consume more at a future date, and opportunity costs lie at the heart of investing.

The point is not to give up everything you love but rather to emphasize the opportunity cost of the daily decisions you make. A more positive approach is to increase your earning power, because it is easier to figure out how to make an extra thousand dollars than it is to skip a latte for 365 days straight. Reducing your expenses shortens the time it takes to reach financial freedom. Although there are limits on how low your expenses can go, there are no limits on how much you can earn. The best investment you can make is an investment in yourself.

Fine-Tuning Our Thinking Process to Incorporate Opportunity Costs

Our brain sees only what is right in front of us. This is known as availability bias. We are blind to other opportunities, and in most cases, we ignore them. Daniel Kahneman defines this problem with the abbreviation WYSIATI—what you see is all there is. To overcome this challenge, maintain a checklist and add opportunity cost as an item. Before making any major decision in life, refer to the checklist. This will ensure that you always consider other alternatives.

Is there a way we can overcome availability bias when faced with a complex problem?

Turns out, there is indeed a simple way to do it.

It's simple but not easy.

It requires us to train our minds to think in a certain manner. According to Sanjay Bakshi:

Well, Charlie already taught us how to do that; we just follow what he says. We try to look at a problem from multiple perspectives. That's, I think, the correct way of doing it. When you are trying to evaluate something, you are trying to ask the question *Why?* Why did this happen? And when you reflect upon it, you find that the answer sometimes comes from multiple disciplines, and you get down to that and try to figure it out. It is very enjoyable to do it in that way. The process for me has always been to ask the question *Why?* and wait. Because the mind will tend to jump to a certain answer, *and that's not the only answer.*

So the way I think about it is, wherever there is a complex question I am trying to answer, I always start with the words *"Part of the reason is this"—which means there must be other parts too.* I'd like to think about what those parts might be. There don't have to be twenty of them—even if there are three or four of them, that's better than one. So it helps me to ask the question *Why?* and then look for answers [emphasis added].[2]

When something is at the forefront of our thoughts, we assume it to be correct. Sometimes this works. Sometimes it doesn't, and usually that involves second- or third-level consequences. Ray Dalio has written about this in his book *Principles.* Similarly, Howard Marks has often advocated the adoption of second-level thinking. Second-level (and beyond) thinking is to ask, "And then what?" at each stage of the decision-making process, while humbly acknowledging "Part of the reason is this." Looking at things through the "And then what?" lens can help you avoid making hurried decisions in life based on emotions. Whether you are looking to invest in a business or in a new relationship or career, never forget to ask, "And then what?"

It may well turn out to be a lifesaver.

CHAPTER 29

PATTERN RECOGNITION

Charlie and I have seen—we're not remotely perfect at this—but we've seen patterns. Pattern recognition gets very important in evaluating humans and businesses. And the pattern recognition isn't 100 percent and none of the patterns exactly repeat themselves, but there are certain things in business and securities markets we've seen over and over.

—Warren Buffett

Untapped Pricing Power

Within the growth stock model, there's a sub-position: There are actually businesses that you will find a few times in a lifetime where any manager could raise the return enormously just by raising prices—and yet they haven't done it. So they have huge untapped pricing power that they're not using. That is the ultimate no-brainer.

—Charlie Munger

Although nominal pricing power is generally considered to be the best hedge against inflation, it is only a necessary but not sufficient condition for identifying great businesses. The dream scenario for a business owner is the ability to raise the price of his or her product or service in excess of inflation without affecting market share or unit volume. This real pricing power can create significant value for investors as part owners of the business. Look at how See's Candies effortlessly raises prices every year on December 26. This is a rare and attractive business to own. A business that can increase prices at a rate that only offsets inflation is good, but it is not exceptional. And although it is good to identify a business that has consistently raised its prices, it actually might be better to find a business that has not raised its prices in a long time, for one reason or another, thus causing its product or service to become underpriced and undervalued to customers. This situation creates a sort of pent-up pricing power that can be released in the form of future real price increases for a certain period of time.

Real pricing power indicates an inefficiently priced product or service. This undervaluation is a source of great potential value as the business begins to price its product or service more efficiently, that is, to raise prices in real terms. For example, Hester Biosciences plans to sell its *Peste des Petits Ruminants* (PPR) vaccines at around three cents per dose, compared with its global competitors, who plan to sell at around ten cents per dose. Hester's net profit margins are already approaching 25 percent, even despite its Nepal plant (which will be manufacturing Hester's PPR vaccines) running at a loss because sales of PPR vaccines had not commenced as of October 2019. Margins and earnings could get a significant boost if and when Hester decides to increase the selling price of its PPR vaccines even modestly in the future, after its Nepal plant gradually ramps up capacity utilization. No wonder low-cost producers are a perennial favorite of Buffett. In most cases, they are also prosocial businesses and engage in a positive-sum game for all stakeholders involved. Such firms tend to follow the GARP principle: growth at reasonable profitability.

Just as we search for undervalued or mispriced stocks, we also should look out for undervalued or mispriced products and services that have untapped pricing power, as both situations eventually tend to correct themselves. Significant value can be unlocked over time for the owners in such situations, especially when the business is currently operating at low margins, because in those cases the percentage gain in profitability is quite high. In investing, always focus on delta, that is, on the rate of change in earnings growth and its underlying quality.

Aspirational Yet Affordable Brands with Dominant Share of Mind

Just as animals flourish in niches, people who specialize in some narrow niche can do very well.

—Charlie Munger

Sector leaders in a niche area are promising investments, especially if they are identified at a small market-cap stage. Their products usually enjoy premium pricing and the brand tends to become synonymous with the product category. Think Eicher Motors in leisure motorbikes, Symphony in air coolers, or Page Industries (Jockey India) in underwear. The best competitive advantage is to have no competitors in customers' minds. The brand recall should be so strong that it should be difficult to recall the next-closest competitor. These businesses tend to have strong bargaining power with customers and suppliers and operate on negative working capital, that is, with other people's money. The wording "advances from customers" in an annual report is a good cue to start digging. This type of advance is essentially a form of float, which is an unencumbered source of value resulting from the absence of covenants like collateral, repayment dates, or interest.

People Calculate Too Much and Think Too Little

In certain instances, stock price movements, quantitative screeners, and reported valuation ratios can lead to inaccurate conclusions. Computers and artificial intelligence cannot capture certain softer attributes in investing. Let me share a few examples.

1. As of October 2019, Hester Biosciences was yet to begin generating meaningful revenues from its international PPR vaccine business, which means that the entire growth from this highly promising segment has potential for the next many years. Yet many investors avoid this stock, terming it expensive based on trailing valuations while ignoring the fact that Hester's high trailing price-to-earnings (P/E) ratio is not representative of its true earning power, as international orders have not yet started. Multi Commodity Exchange of India charges fees based on the value of a transaction rather than on volume. A few years back, many investors were citing its high P/E ratio as the reason for avoiding this stock. But this ratio was based on depressed commodity prices prevailing at the time. Investors should always evaluate their long-term ideas based on normalized earning power. Similar opportunities emerge when the current earnings of a company are depressed because of ongoing expansion expenses, which result in an optically high P/E ratio. Investors who primarily rely on screening tools to generate ideas end up missing such opportunities.

2. Receiving voluntary praise from a competitor is always a positive sign for a firm. But these softer aspects cannot be captured by quants, Excel spreadsheets, or screeners.

3. The stock of Avanti Feeds abruptly fell 10 percent on the day before the release of its first quarter FY2018 results, in the absence of any public news. During that same day, however, its peer Waterbase was going up after releasing

its results, and another peer, IFB Agro, was also up in trade. This indicated that no negative news pertaining to the industry at large had been reported. (Generally, when the sector leader falls sharply, the secondary players suffer from fear by association and fall in sympathy.) Avanti reported strong earnings the next day, in line with my expectations, and the stock appreciated significantly after that. Develop a feel for the market. (For example, if the leading stocks of a sector are falling sharply even after reporting strong earnings or are going up even after bad earnings, the market is trying to tell you something important.)

4. How a stock closes in trade after an earnings release (or any seemingly important event that is reported overnight) is much more important than how it initially reacts or opens in trade.

5. Many investors feel more confident investing in consumer businesses because of familiarity with their products. But consumer preferences can change rapidly and unpredictably. Many business-to-business companies (though not all) face much slower changes in customer preferences, making financial modeling easier.

6. Sometimes analyst reports mindlessly "annualize" the quarterly or semi-annual numbers without accounting for seasonality in the business operations. (Always take seasonality into consideration when looking at the quarter-on-quarter growth of a business following its latest quarterly results announcement.) For example, in February 2018, some initial public offering reports on HG Infra Engineering were quoting valuation estimates based on annualized numbers for the first half of FY2018, even though road construction companies derive about 65 percent to 70 percent of their annual earnings in the second half of the fiscal year (October to March).

7. It often is not the consolidated quarterly results that stock prices react to. Rather, market participants are primarily interested in only the performance of one or two specific business segments, and it is only the operating results of those segments that drive the stock price.

8. Seemingly expensive trailing valuations can quickly become cheap when raw materials prices fall sharply. Optically inexpensive trailing valuations can quickly become expensive when the price of raw materials rises sharply.

9. Be careful about drawing conclusions from high operating margins alone. Efficiency in the business is a good reason for such margins to occur. Greed, cutting corners in dealings with stakeholders, and penalizing long-term value creation to prop up short-term earnings and the stock price are bad reasons for these margins.

10. Look for anomalies in plain sight. Many parallels exist between the work of a good detective and that of a good investor. One of the most popular Sherlock Holmes short stories, "Silver Blaze," featured the famous incident of the dog that did not bark:

TABLE 29.1 Sum of the parts valuation

Business segment	Price/share (Rs)	Valuation method
Existing power business	956	1× FY2019 book value
Chandrapur power plant	61	15% discount on invested equity
Haldia power plant	86	On equity invested
CESC property	19	On equity invested
Spencer's and others	**(58)**	**Discount for loss-making retail business**

Gregory (Scotland Yard detective): Is there any point to which you would wish to draw my attention?
Holmes: To the curious incident of the dog in the night-time.
Gregory: The dog did nothing in the night-time.
Holmes: That was the curious incident.[1]

Let's observe the curious incident in early 2018 pertaining to the demerger of Calcutta Electric Supply Corporation (CESC). Just look at the completely illogical sum-of-the-parts valuation exercise in which some analysts were engaging for CESC at the time (table 29.1). (Analysts who do a sum-of-the-parts analysis for a conglomerate should understand that if the cash produced from one business is funding another business, then the sum-of-the-parts analysis has no meaning. If management wants to continue doing this cross-funding of their different businesses, they would not do a demerger in the first place.) Spencers, as a separately listed entity following the demerger, obviously could not have a negative market value. No wonder Charlie Munger has said, "People calculate too much and think too little."

11. The reported earnings in financial statements are becoming less useful for analytical purposes in the modern digital world. In his second quarter 2018 letter to Heller House fund clients, Marcelo Lima wrote:

"Cheap" is a poor proxy for value: the new business models . . . —SaaS [software as a service] in particular—are not well suited to traditional GAAP [generally accepted accounting principles] accounting. Here's why: if distribution costs are zero, the optimal strategy is to gain as many customers for your software product, as quickly as possible. In digital businesses, there are increasing advantages to scale, and many of these companies operate in winner-take-all or winner-take-most markets. The name of the game is thus to build, grow, then monetize. Frequently, this means spending a lot of money in sales and marketing, which depresses reported earnings.

Thus, SaaS companies spend to acquire customers upfront, and recognize revenue from those customers over many years. This mismatch burdens the income statement. Some of the most successful—and highest performing stocks—in the SaaS world have spent many years growing despite producing no meaningful accounting profits. They are very profitable in terms of unit economics, and once they stop reinvesting every dollar generated into further growth. The traditional method of screening for low P/E stocks doesn't work in this scenario.[2]

For these SaaS companies, study the incremental unit economics—that is, how much it costs to acquire each customer and how much value they deliver over a span of time—and then analyze what the business margins and cash flows look like at a steady state once the investment phase slows down. Then discount those cash flows back to the present.

In a February 2018 *Harvard Business Review* article, three professors from the Columbia and Dartmouth business schools, Vijay Govindarajan, Shivaram Rajgopal, and Anup Srivastava, summarized their work on accounting for intangible investments. Their key finding, which builds on Baruch Lev and Feng Gu's analysis in their book *The End of Accounting*, is that "accounting earnings are practically irrelevant for digital companies." Likewise, Govindarajan, Rajgopal, and Srivastava found that reported earnings mean less for younger companies than for older companies because of the different nature of younger companies' expenditures. In fact, they found that "earnings explain only 2.4 percent of variation in stock returns for a 21st century company—which means that almost 98 percent of the variation in companies' annual stock returns are not explained by their annual earnings."[3] These claims correlate nicely with those published in Lev and Gu's book (figure 29.1). The authors found that variations in financial metrics, like earnings and book value, explain 90 percent of the variations in stock prices for companies that went public between 1950 and 1959, compared with explaining only about 20 percent of the variation for companies that have gone public since 2000.

Younger companies tend to be less tangible-capital intensive and more intangible-capital intensive than older firms. This tendency creates a big problem for financial analysts because accounting rules explicitly treat tangible and intangible capital investments differently. When a firm engages in research and development, advertising, software development, or employee training, it must account for those long-term value-creating expenditures in the same way that it accounts for a routine general expense like office space rents. That is, all those productive investments (the upward sloping line in figure 29.1) are treated as expenses and are charged against current period earnings, which significantly depresses reported profits for highly innovative companies. The same mechanism distorts the balance sheet by making assets look artificially low, because if something is expensed, it never makes its way to the balance sheet as an asset.

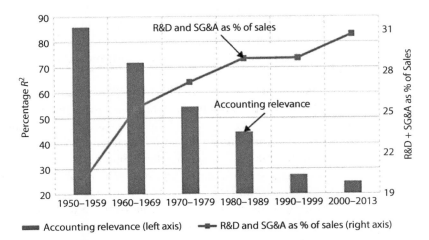

FIGURE 29.1 R^2s of market values regressed on earnings and book values of companies entering the public market in successive decades, 1950–2013.

Source: Baruch Lev and Feng Gu, *The End of Accounting* (New York: Wiley, 2016).

Govindarajan, Rajgopal, and Srivastava found that "intangible investments have surpassed property, plant, and equipment as the main avenue of capital creation for U.S. companies."[4] Yet all these intangible assets are absent from the balance sheet, and thus analysts cannot form accurate opinions about firms' earning potential. Lev identified this lack of information many years ago as the source of a market anomaly that causes highly innovative companies to systematically outperform their less innovative peers. This anomaly can be termed the "knowledge factor."

Sidecar Investing

From John Templeton making a fortune by buying a basket of penny stocks on the eve of World War II to Warren Buffett selling super-cat insurance, successful investors have earned extraordinary returns through the unknown and the unknowable, and they have done so on a reasoned, calculated basis. "Unknown and unknowable" refers to the situation in which both the possible future states of the world and their probabilities are unknown and unknowable.

"Sidecar investing" is a term introduced by Richard Zeckhauser in his famous essay, "Investing in the Unknown and Unknowable."[5] In this brilliant essay (a must-read for all investors), Zeckhauser shares many important insights.

First, most investors fail to distinguish between risk and uncertainty. When they encounter uncertainty, they equate it with risk and shun the stock in question. This creates great buying opportunities for value investors who shun risk (permanent loss of capital) but seek uncertainty on highly favorable terms (a large margin of safety).

Second, some types of unknowable situations have been associated with highly profitable outcomes, and we can think about these situations systematically. People overwhelmingly prefer to take on (measurable and quantifiable) risk in situations in which they know specific odds rather than an alternative risk scenario in which the odds are completely ambiguous. They tend to choose a known probability of winning over an unknown probability of winning, even if the known probability is low and the unknown probability could be a guarantee of winning. (This paradox in decision theory in which people's choices violate the postulates of subjective expected utility is known as the Ellsberg paradox.) Fear of the unknown is one of the most potent kinds of fear, and the natural reaction is to get as far away as possible from what is feared. Unknown unknowns make most of us withdraw from the game. These, however, are also the circumstances in which extraordinary returns are possible. (Readers should study the case study of the most successful investment ever in the history of mankind—Masayoshi Son's investment in Alibaba in 1999 which delivered a 6,500× return.) Fortune favors the brave, and market prices and valuations tend to reflect our innate tendency to avoid uncertainty. One way to think about unknowable situations is to recognize the hugely asymmetric payoffs they offer. If you have a chance to multiply your money ten to twenty times, and that chance is offset by the possibility that you could lose all of it in that particular commitment, then it is a good bet to be exercised, provided you are sufficiently diversified. This is how to bet in asymmetric payoffs. This is the Babe Ruth effect in action. Provide for low-probability outcomes. Play for high-probability outcomes. This applies to both value investors and corporate capital allocators.

Third, big money can be made by those who possess complementary skills. These people bring something to the table that we cannot. They get deals that we cannot. Individuals who lack such skills can still make it big by partnering with people who do possess complementary skills. Think of buying shares in Berkshire Hathaway in the 1980s, riding along with Warren Buffett and paying nothing to him for the privilege. An example that comes to mind is the deal Buffett got from Goldman Sachs when he bought the investment bank's preferred stock on favorable terms during the financial crisis of 2008: a $5 billion investment in Goldman's preferred stock and common stock warrants, with a 10 percent dividend yield on the preferred and an attractive conversion privilege on the warrants.

Zeckhauser says that some people can get amazing deals and have the ability to source these transactions. They have certain attributes that attract such deals to them. Perhaps they have capital, contacts, reputation, or something innate that a general public markets investor does not have. This is akin to an investor riding along in a sidecar pulled by a powerful motorcycle driven by an individual who has complementary skills. The more the investor is distinctively positioned to have confidence in the driver's integrity and his motorcycle's capabilities, says Zeckhauser, the more attractive is the investment. Zeckhauser advises that when the opportunity arises to make a sidecar investment on favorable terms alongside such individuals, we should not miss it.

An opportunity for making a sidecar investment may occur when a founder demonstrates complete detachment and objectivity and sells a legacy business (which has been an integral part of his or her life) in the best interests of the minority shareholders, and then begins a fresh entrepreneurial journey through a new entity that is listed on the stock exchange. A related pattern is found when the key professional from a promoter group company with a proven track record of strong execution incubates a new business in a previously dormant listed group entity and infuses personal funds into it through a preferential allotment.

Yet another opportunity for making a sidecar investment with an individual who has highly complementary skills occurs when such an individual joins an ordinarily run listed company and picks up a majority or a significant minority stake in it. This ensures skin in the game.

Investing in Businesses with a Sector Tailwind

There's a model that I call "surfing"—when a surfer gets up and catches the wave and just stays there, he can go a long, long time.

—Charlie Munger

One of the lessons your management has learned—and, unfortunately, sometimes re-learned—is the importance of being in businesses where tailwinds prevail rather than headwinds.

—Warren Buffett

Newton's first law of motion states that an object in motion stays in motion. Things in motion possess inertia. The stock market is characterized by an analogous property; a trend in force tends to remain in force until something occurs to change it. In other words, the trend is your friend.

Recognizing the big picture matters as much as correctly identifying the prospects of an individual business. According to Adam Parker, former U.S. equity strategist at Morgan Stanley, the impact of sector-specific factors on a typical stock's annual return accounts for more than half of a stock's performance. Based on my personal investing experiences over the years, I have found that it is better to buy a good company in a great sector than a great company in a bad sector. In both careers and in investments, it helps enormously to pick the right train, that is, to choose a field with long-term secular growth. In his 2005 talk with students at Tuck School of Business, Buffett said, "We come to my second recommendation, which is to get on the right train; that is, moving in the right direction. There's no course in business school called 'Getting on the Right Train,' but it's really important. You can be an average passenger but if you get on the right train it will carry you a long way."[6]

No awards for bravery are given in investing. Don't fight the trends, especially the long-term, inevitable ones. Psychological denial of reality leads people to go broke. In other words, invest in companies with tailwinds, not headwinds. Let me illustrate this important investing principle through my portfolio holdings:

1. Secular growth of housing finance, microfinance, and private banking industry in India: Aavas Financiers, CreditAccess Grameen, Bandhan Bank, AU Small Finance Bank, and Ujjivan Small Finance Bank.
2. Gradual shift of chemicals manufacturing away from China and toward India: Vinati Organics.
3. Structural long-term trend of urbanization and increasing financialization of savings in India: PSP Projects, HDFC Life, and HDFC Asset Management Company.
4. Planned spending of $7.6 billion on eradication of PPR disease over a span of fifteen years by the Food and Agriculture Organization of the United Nations: Hester Biosciences.
5. Secular growth of aspirational India's discretionary consumption: Bajaj Finance, Dixon Technologies, SBI Cards.

Along the way, we have the strong tailwind of capitalism at our backs, which makes the stock market a positive-sum game over the long run as corporations retain earnings and further earn on those retained earnings. People obsess about the problems in the world and underestimate the most persistent and bullish long-term phenomenon: the constant, inherent desire in the human race to improve its current state of being.

Perhaps the greatest advantage of all in buying high-quality businesses without visible ceilings on their growth is that, when we do so, we give ourselves the chance to profit from the unforeseeable and the incalculable. Year after year, humankind achieves the impossible but persists in underrating what it can and will accomplish in the future.

Investing in Businesses That Are About to Complete a Large Expansion

Be unreasonable in situations in which an expansion is in the offing. Don't settle merely for businesses that are about to complete small brownfield expansions. Instead, look for businesses undergoing a large greenfield capital expenditure program (no business does a large capacity expansion without strong conviction in the future demand for its product), and then buy them three to six months ahead of the scheduled completion date. Use screening tools to short-list companies with a large recent increase in capital work in progress on their balance sheet.

A big idea I took away from Bruce Greenwald's book *Competition Demystified* was the concept of "local economies of scale," which he demonstrated through the case study of Nebraska Furniture Mart. I often use the criterion of a large single-location facility when selecting an investment in manufacturing businesses. For example, Hester Biosciences operates Asia's largest single-location animal biological manufacturing facility. Having the entire manufacturing setup in a single location minimizes the cost of logistics. When a business with a primarily fixed-cost structure scales up its operations, the per-unit cost becomes smaller, operating leverage takes over, and net profit grows exponentially. The fixed cost per unit becomes low compared with small-scale competitors, and it becomes almost impossible for a new entrant to compete on price with the lowest-cost incumbent without bleeding losses for a long time.

A lending business that has just raised a large amount of growth capital should be viewed in the same way as a manufacturing business that has just completed a big capacity expansion. In fact, equity dilution is not really bad in the case of richly valued and well-managed financiers with a high return on equity. This is because they are valued on a price-to-book basis. As a result, their intrinsic value actually increases along with book value after a rights issue, a follow-on offering, or a qualified institutional placement. This presents a good opportunity to average upward in such lending businesses, especially those with good or improving asset quality. (Lending businesses with declining non-performing assets, rising return on equity, and improving provision coverage ratio tend to undergo a valuation rerating. An expanding price-to-book ratio leads to a virtuous cycle for such businesses, which then can raise capital in the future with a lower equity dilution.)

In a lending business, growth is never an issue; many people want to borrow from you. What really matters in such a highly leveraged business is the risk management practices and asset quality. When assessing asset quality, investors should pay careful attention to loss given default (LGD), which is a more comprehensive and appropriate risk measure than nonperforming assets (NPAs). All things considered, I'd rather invest in a lending institution that has survived a past down-cycle than in one that has never been tested in challenging times. As the saying goes, "What doesn't kill you makes you stronger."

In his 1990 letter, Buffett articulated his rationale for investing in Wells Fargo:

> The banking business is no favorite of ours. When assets are twenty times equity—a common ratio in this industry—mistakes that involve only a small portion of assets can destroy a major portion of equity. And mistakes have been the rule rather than the exception at many major banks. . . .
>
> Because leverage of 20:1 magnifies the effects of managerial strengths and weaknesses, we have no interest in purchasing shares of a poorly-managed bank at a "cheap" price. Instead, *our only interest is in buying into well-managed banks at fair prices* [emphasis added].[7]

Carefully note Buffett's words: "leverage . . . magnifies the effects of managerial strengths and weaknesses." This implies that whenever leverage is high, the management factor is critically important.

Pay Careful Attention to Slow, Gradual Changes

Cognition, misled by tiny changes involving low contrast, will often miss a trend that is destiny.

—Charlie Munger

Human beings are wired to react to sudden changes in the environment, not to slow, gradual ones. But slow changes, both improvements and deteriorations, are magnified over time, even though they are barely noticeable over short periods. This is particularly true in the field of technological disruption, which eventually leads to significant upheavals at the macro level.

Lately, scientists and the popular press have been talking about the possibility of Moore's law petering out in the medium term. The physics of putting ever-greater numbers of transistors on silicon chips eventually will meet physical limitations. At some point, scientists believe, it will be extremely difficult and prohibitively expensive for conventional chip technology to sustain the pace dictated by Moore's law. Some analysts believe that the death of Moore's law will signal the end of exponential growth in computing, but Ray Kurzweil believes that the evolution of technology will start a new computing paradigm that will continue or accelerate this trend. In his deeply profound book *The Singularity Is Near*, Kurzweil writes: "Most long-range forecasts of what is technically feasible in future time periods dramatically underestimate the power of future developments because they are based on what I call the 'intuitive linear' view of history rather than the 'historical exponential' view."[8]

In a nonlinear world, we all think linearly. Promoters. Managements. Investors. Analysts.

But Munger looks for lollapalooza effects. George Soros seeks to profit from reflexivity. Nassim Taleb emphasizes the presence of fat tails. Peter Thiel talks about power laws. All of them are looking to arbitrage between the linear environment in which we evolved and the nonlinear environment that we have created.

> A business should be viewed as an unfolding movie, not as a still photograph.
> —Warren Buffett

> The financial community is usually slow to recognize a fundamentally changed condition, unless a big name or a colorful single event is publicly associated with that change.
> —Philip Fisher

Along with the slow and gradual macro changes, investors should also be alert to tiny changes at the micro level. Be alert to tiny changes like the declaration of a maiden dividend; receipt of a large order or a landmark contract; appointment of a Big Four auditor; increased or first-time disclosures or discussion about business prospects and future plans in annual reports, presentations, or press releases; a chair or chief executive of a listed company sharing business commentary for the first time; a highly promising but illiquid micro-cap or small-cap stock, which to date was stuck in the yearly price limits imposed by the stock exchange, suddenly becoming available for purchase during a sharp corrective phase in the market; a company holding an analyst or investor conference call for the first time or after a long time; an upgrade of a company's debt instruments by the ratings agencies (always read credit reports); a sudden increase in the market value of a company's bonds (bonds are more sensitive than stocks to changes in the economic fortunes of a company); or notable improvements or deteriorations in the working capital cycle (always monitor the "direction" of the quality of earnings).

Such an elaborate and exhaustive exercise requires total dedication on the part of the investor, but it is highly rewarding. A personal example from my

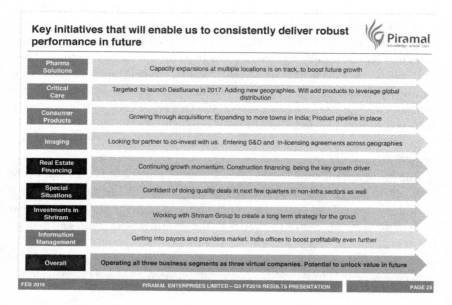

FIGURE 29.2 Piramal Enterprises reference to potential demerger.

Source: Piramal Enterprises third quarter FY2016 results presentation, February 2016.

investing journey illustrates this fact. In February 2016, for the first time ever, Piramal Enterprises made a subtle reference (on one of the slides in its third quarter FY2016 results presentation) to a potential demerger of its various businesses in the future (figure 29.2).

I had been closely following Piramal for many months, but it was this tiny bit of information in one of its filings that was the catalyst for my investment at the attractive prevailing price. I subsequently realized a handsome profit.

Louis Pasteur rightly said, "Chance favors the prepared mind." There is no alternative to hard work.

CHAPTER 30

ACKNOWLEDGING THE ROLE OF LUCK, CHANCE, SERENDIPITY, AND RANDOMNESS

We are quick to forget that just being alive is an extraordinary piece of good luck, a remote event, a chance of occurrence of monstrous proportions. Imagine a speck of dust next to a planet a billion times the size of earth. The speck of dust represents the odds in favor of your being born; the huge planet would be the odds against it. So stop sweating the small stuff. . . . Remember you are a Black Swan.

—Nassim Nicholas Taleb

Each of us has what I call an ensemble of stochastic life paths—the choices we make. You make each choice in life based on your understanding of the possibility that it will take you where you want to be. But you don't determine the outcome, only the probabilities. Each path leads to more choices: a cascade to echo all the other cascades that rule our lives. Choosing the path is the extent of your control—beyond that, it's out of your hands. You choose, and then life rolls the dice.

—Arthur De Vany

The greatest superpower is luck.

—Stan Lee

Luck (n.): Success or failure apparently brought by chance rather than through one's own actions.

What does it take to succeed? What are the secrets of the most successful people? Judging by the popularity of magazines, such as *Success, Forbes*, and *Entrepreneur*, interest in these questions is significant. We assume that we can learn from successful people because they have certain personal characteristics—such as talent, skill, hard work, tenacity, optimism, growth mind-set, and emotional intelligence—that got them where they are today.

But is this assumption correct?

Luck's role is hidden because outstanding success is spotlighted; failure is all around but unpublicized and unseen. Jennifer Aniston and Sandra Bullock worked as waitresses before they became movie stars. The remaining thousands of waiters and waitresses in Los Angeles probably never got a casting call. For every Mark Zuckerberg, thousands of tech entrepreneurs and employees have little to show for decades of effort.

In his book *How to Get Lucky*, Max Gunther writes a tour de force on luck, chance, serendipity, and randomness:

It isn't enough just to be good. You've got to be lucky, too. . . .

. . . Good luck is the essential basic component of success, no matter what your personal definition of "success" may be. . . .

Luck. It blunders in and out of our lives, unbidden, unexpected, sometimes welcome and sometimes not. It plays a role in *all* our affairs, *often the commanding role*. No matter how carefully you design your life, you cannot know how that design will be changed by the working of random events. You can only know the events will occur. You can only wait for them and hope they are in your favor.

Luck is the supreme insult to human reason. *You can't ignore it, yet you can't plan for it.* Man's grandest and most meticulous designs will fail if they are hit with bad luck, but the silliest ventures will succeed with good luck. . . .

Such events—good luck and bad luck—are the main shaping forces of human life. *If you believe you are in perfect control of your life, you are kidding yourself.* . . .

Why do people deny the role of luck? For one thing, we hate to think we are at the mercy of random happenings. *We prefer to stay snugly wrapped in the illusion that we control our own destinies.*

Life seems safer when I can say to myself, "The future will happen as I plan it." It won't, of course. Deep inside, we all know it won't. But the truth is too scary to contemplate without an illusion to snuggle up against. . . .

We are culturally conditioned to deny the role of luck. . . .

. . . Luck isn't "meaningful" enough. We yearn for life to have meaning. Acknowledging luck's role takes half the meaning out of it.

If I do wrong and come to a bad end as a direct result of my own wickedness or weakness, the episode is supposed to teach some kind of lesson to me and others. But if I'm peacefully walking along the street and get run over by a truck, nobody learns anything.

Life is like that much of the time: completely random and meaningless. Not only college English professors but all the rest of us are uncomfortable with that fact. But it is a fact you must look square in the eye if you want to do something about your luck.

The first step toward improving your luck is to *acknowledge* that it exists [emphasis added].[1]

Figures 30.1 and 30.2 illustrate humility's role in sustaining success.

Let me do my bit and acknowledge the significant role of luck in my investing journey. Luck was responsible for my multiple big winners during the 2014 bull market in India. At the time, I had hardly any investing expertise to speak of, but still, within my portfolio, Avanti Feeds went from INR 500 to INR 2,410 (~382 percent), Gati went from INR 60 to INR 275 (~359 percent), Symphony went from INR 700 to INR 1,200 (~71 percent), VST Tillers went from INR 800 to INR 1,740 (~118 percent), Ajanta Pharma went from INR 650 to INR 1,350 (~108 percent), Mayur Uniquoters went from INR 230 to INR 440 (~91 percent), Astral Poly Technik went from INR 250 to INR 400 (60 percent), and Atul Auto went from INR 350 to INR 600 (~71 percent).

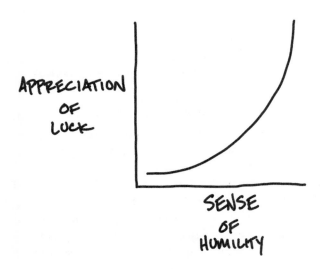

FIGURE 30.1 Improving luck requires the humility to acknowledge its presence.

Source: Behavior Gap

Jason Zweig ●
@jasonzweigwsj

(Follow) ∨

Whenever I meet anyone at the peak of success who insists luck isn't a huge factor, I make a mental note to check back on him* five years later.

Five years later, none of these people have still been at the peak.

*(yes, they've all been male, but that's another story)

> **Jon Ulin, CFP®** @JonUlin
> If you're so smart, why aren't you rich? Turns out it's just chance. - MIT Technology Review
> technologyreview.com/s/610395/if-yo...
> Show this thread

8:25 AM - 9 Mar 2018

FIGURE 30.2 Always remain humble.

Source: Jason Zweig (@jasonzweigwsj), "Whenever I meet anyone at the peak of success who insists luck isn't a huge factor," Twitter, March 9, 2018, https://twitter.com/jasonzweigwsj/status/972131380460163074.

With the exception of Gati, all these stocks had been purchased on borrowed conviction from some intelligent-sounding discussion on a prominent investing blog in India called ValuePickr. The primary reason for my purchase of all these stocks was my supposedly brilliant personal thought that because these stocks had delivered fabulous returns during the tough economic conditions of the preceding five years (I checked this in the Factset database), then these stocks logically should deliver even better returns during an economic recovery. As for Gati, I naively presumed that if e-commerce grew rapidly in India, then Gati's courier business would do quite well. I did not even check the quality of the company's earnings.

Just as I had no personal conviction or good understanding of my choices when buying these stocks, I did not have any better insight when selling them. Yes, this is true. This was my pitiful state as an investor at the time, even after being present in the markets since 2007. I had initiated my self-education on value investing in 2013, and the power of compounding knowledge had not yet kicked in.

Many of my friends, seniors, and peers bought these stocks at far lower prices and obtained big multibagger returns. Although all of them had deserved success, I was merely a big beneficiary of dumb luck in a bull market. Even during the subsequent three years, a significant portion of my portfolio returns was primarily driven by the valuation rerating of many small-cap and mid-cap stocks in India. Only luck was responsible for me deploying a meaningful amount of capital in stocks in late 2013, which was exactly when the present multiyear bull market in India began. Before that time, I had invested insignificant sums.

Be Passionately Curious

The best way to approach learning is with childlike curiosity. All of us came into this world with abundant curiosity. As children, we were inherently curious and constantly engaging in joyful discoveries. Exploration preceded explanation. As we grew up, however, a fear of looking stupid dampened this curiosity. Snap out of it. Adopt the motto "ABC: Always Be Curious." (As Charlie Munger often says, if we want to become smarter, the question we need to keep asking is "Why, why, why?") A questioning mentality is more valuable than a knowing mentality. Questions are more productive and useful than commands for shaping ideas and solutions. Although you can't force your brain to come up with creative ideas on demand, you can program it to launch the imaginative process simply by asking questions. It is exciting to be curious, because it means you are always discovering something interesting. Inspiration often comes from completely unexpected sources, which is why a curious mind is so beneficial. Albert Einstein once wrote to a friend, "I have no special talents. I am only passionately curious." Even Leonardo da Vinci's distinguishing and most inspiring trait was his intense curiosity.

Things are constantly happening within the framework of our self-narrating story, which subjectively unfolds alongside an expanding universe that we have yet to fully comprehend.

Don't think about why you question, simply don't stop questioning. Don't worry about what you can't answer, and don't try to explain what you can't know. Curiosity is its own reason. Aren't you in awe when you contemplate the mysteries of eternity, of life, of the marvelous structure behind reality? And this is the miracle of the human mind—to use its constructions, concepts, and formulas as tools to explain what man sees, feels and touches. Try to comprehend a little more each day. Have holy curiosity.

—Albert Einstein

As a passionately inquisitive individual since childhood, I have always engaged in constant inquiry about the world around me. This very trait has allowed serendipity to constantly open doors to newer opportunities for me. Serendipity led me to discover Eicher Motors through a random reading of a UBS report in November 2013. Serendipity drove me to watch Udayan Mukherjee on CNBC one morning in 2015, when he was speaking about the business recovery in SKS Microfinance (now known as Bharat Financial). Later, in March 2017, I also came to understand the long-term growth potential of insurance and asset management industries in India thanks to Mukherjee. I randomly viewed a YouTube video in which he was speaking about the long-term secular trend of financialization of savings in the country. In a similar vein, I accidently discovered many multibaggers during the course of my investing journey, discoveries that were fully driven by chance events or random discussions during the course of my daily life. I could go so far as to say that luck, chance, serendipity, and randomness have played a big role, in some form or another, in all my stock investments to date and likely will continue to do so forever.

In fact, luck is the sole reason that I am alive today and able to share my story. I have survived three potentially fatal accidents in my personal life—once, I fell down the stairs of my building during my childhood years and underwent a surgery; once, I toppled over while riding an all-terrain vehicle in Thailand and miraculously incurred only minor bruises; and, on a third occasion, I was badly injured in a bike accident during my MBA college days in Ahmedabad, India. As a survivor, I remain ever grateful for the smallest of things in my life. Every new day is God's gift to me. I am truly blessed.

Improving Luck Requires the Humility to Acknowledge Its Presence

Successful investors appreciate the role of luck. They are intellectually honest and conscious of alternative histories, that is, the silent events in their lives. These are the events that could have happened but didn't. Let me share a personal example to illustrate this important but hugely underappreciated aspect of our lives.

On March 28, 2016, the Bombay Stock Exchange announced suspension of trading in shares of Cupid Ltd., effective March 31, 2016. I had almost 20 percent of my portfolio value in shares of Cupid at the time, but the very next day, before I had the chance to exit, the stock was immediately locked in a lower circuit and continued to hit lower circuits until March 31, after which it was indefinitely suspended from trading. What followed over the subsequent few weeks was an extremely tense and uncertain period for Cupid's shareholders. Eventually, the company got a clean chit, trading in its shares resumed on April 20, and I was able to exit the stock at close to my original cost price.

But what if I had not been given the opportunity to exit?

Warren Buffett credits a large part of his success to his winning the "ovarian lottery" by being born in America, where his skill of allocating capital earned him billions of dollars. Similarly, I consider myself lucky to have been born and brought up in India, a vibrant democracy with a rich, diverse culture and a plethora of high-growth investment opportunities in its stock market, where trillions of dollars of wealth is expected to be created in the future.

Is there a way to improve our luck, once we acknowledge its presence? Indeed, there is, as Gunther explains:

> It turns out that lucky people characteristically organize their lives in such a way that they are in position to experience good luck and to avoid bad luck. . . .
>
> The lucky approach is to say to yourself, "Okay I'm going to get into this risky situation—this roulette game, this mutual fund investment. But I am not operating under the delusion that planning will make it turn out my way. I see luck looming large in it, so I will be careful not to let myself grow too confident and relaxed. I will expect rapid change. I won't make large, irrevocable commitments. I'll stay poised to bail out the minute I see a change I don't like." . . .
>
> To be lucky in this game you must discard bad hands when you get them. . . .
>
> You would recognize, in the first place, that things usually are as bad as they seem. In fact, often they're worse. You would say to yourself, "I'm willing to be optimistic, but I've got to be shown some reason why." And then you would study the situation. Is there some likelihood that the problems will go away? Or do you have some realistic hope of fixing them? If so, stay aboard. If not, get out and go looking for better luck elsewhere. . . .
>
> Much more often what starts to go wrong stays wrong—or goes wronger. In a souring situation, with no compelling reason to think things will get better, you are always right to cut your loss and go. You are right even when, in retrospect, you turn out to have been wrong.[2]

Gunther's concluding words remind me of what Buffett has said about his experiences with difficult businesses: "There's never just one cockroach in the kitchen."[3]

You can increase your surface area for good luck by taking appropriate action. Many people think that successful people are simply born lucky. Gunther shows us how some people get luckier than others by arranging their lives in certain characteristic patterns. They tend to position themselves in the path of onrushing luck. They tend to go where events are moving fastest and where they can find their lucky break. They try their hand at multiple ventures with low-risk and high-payoff characteristics. They surround themselves with smarter and wiser people. When pursuing their goals, they always leave some room for serendipity. They do not ignore the importance of accidental discoveries (e.g., events, parties, meetings, conferences, and chance happenings), and they keep an open mind to all possibilities. They take calculated risks. They stick with their initial convictions, but not when all hope is lost. They believe in the dictum "Strong beliefs, loosely held." In short, they move with life, not against it. As a result, lucky people are able to take advantage of life's good breaks, while minimizing the effects of bad breaks.

> Obvious responses to opportunities and circumstances, rather than studied decisions, have put me on the particular roads I have followed.
> —Herbert Simon

All of us have the opportunity to be "lucky," because beyond having the basics of health and sustenance, luck simply comes down to a series of choices. If you live in a free society, you are lucky. Luck surrounds you every day; you constantly have lucky things happen to you, whether or not you recognize it.

Lucky people are those who acknowledge just how fortunate they are and feel grateful for what they have. If you want to feel rich, just count all the gifts you have that money can't buy. In my view, this self-realization is the most important step toward being lucky. You may not be doing well at your job or with your investments, but if you have a loving family and good health, it's worth being grateful for already having some of the most precious things in life. As Nick Maggiulli writes:

> Think about the story you tell yourself about yourself. In all the lives you could be living, in all of the worlds you could simulate, how much did luck play a role in this one? Have you gotten more than your fair share? Have you had to deal with more struggles than most? I ask you this question because *accepting luck as a primary determinant in your life is one of the most freeing ways to view the world. Why? Because when you realize the magnitude of happenstance and serendipity in your life, you can stop judging yourself on your outcomes and start focusing on your efforts. It's the only thing you can control* [emphasis added].[4]

Fooled by Randomness

> *What you should learn when you make a mistake because you did not anticipate something is that the world is difficult to anticipate. That's the correct lesson to learn from surprises—that the world is surprising.*

> —Daniel Kahneman

Because logic thrives on cause and effect, analytic thinkers often confuse coincidence with causality and correlation with causation. A typical by-product of the analyzer's need for causality can be seen when the talking heads, pundits, and experts review the day's market action.

In reality, the market is moving up or down on any given day because of a multitude of interrelated factors that are too complex, diffuse, and intangible to be identified.

In his book *The Zurich Axioms*, Max Gunther masterfully demonstrates how a complex adaptive system like the stock market is characterized by complete randomness, because human behavior is utterly unpredictable:

> *The fact is, nobody has the faintest idea of what is going to happen next year, next week, or even tomorrow.* . . . It is of the utmost importance that you never take economists, market advisers, or other financial oracles seriously.
>
> Of course, they are right sometimes, *and that is what makes them dangerous.* Each of them, after being in the prophecy business for a few years, can point proudly to a few guesses that turned out right. "Amazing!" everybody says. *What never appears in the prophet's publicity is a reminder of all the times when he or she was wrong.*
>
> "It's easy to be a prophet," the noted economist Dr. Theodore Levitt once told *Business Week*. "You make twenty-five predictions *and the ones that come true are the ones you talk about.*" Not many seers are that frank, but all would privately agree with Dr. Levitt's formula for success. Economists, market advisers, political oracles, and clairvoyants all know the basic rule by heart: *If you can't forecast right, forecast often.* . . .
>
> Not all oracles have been able to organize the annual forecast-revising dance of the economists, but all are followers of the basic rule. *They all forecast often and hope nobody scrutinizes the results too carefully.* . . .
>
> It is easy to get dazzled by a successful prophet, *for there is a hypnotic allure in the supposed ability to look into the future. This is especially true in the world of money. A seer who enjoys a few years of frequently right guesses will attract an enormous following.* . . .
>
> One of the traps money-world prophets fall into is that they forget they are dealing with *human behavior.* They talk as though things like the inflation rate or the ups and downs of the Dow are physical events of some kind. *Looking at such a phenomenon as a physical event, an oracle can understandably succumb to the illusion that it will be amenable to forecasting. The fact is, of course, that all money phenomena are manifestations of human behavior.* . . .
>
> . . . An oracle can always cry "unforeseeable events" in explanation of a forecast that turns out wrong. *But that is just the trouble. Every forecast has the possibility of unforeseeable events ahead of it. No forecast about human behavior can ever be compounded of 100 percent foreseeable events. Every prediction is chancy. None can ever be trusted.* . . .

. . . Disregard all prognostications. In the world of money, which is a world shaped by human behavior, nobody has the foggiest notion of what will happen in the future. Mark that word. Nobody. . . .

. . . Money seems cool, rational, amenable to reasoned analysis and manipulation. If you want to get rich, it would seem that you need only find a sound rational approach. A Formula.

Everybody is looking for this Formula. *Unfortunately, there isn't one.*

The truth is that the world of money is a world of patternless disorder, utter chaos. Patterns seem to appear in it from time to time, as do patterns in a cloudy sky or in the froth at the edge of the ocean. But they are ephemeral. They are not a sound basis on which to base one's plans. . . .

. . . It is surprising how many smart people allow themselves to be fooled by the Gambler's Fallacy. . . . Toss a coin enough times, and sooner or later you are going to have a long run of heads. But there is nothing orderly about this run. You *cannot* know *in advance* when it will start. And when it has started, you cannot know *how long* it will continue. And so it is with roulette, the horses, the art market, or any other game in which you put money at risk. If you play long enough, you will enjoy winning streaks—perhaps some memorable ones. . . . *But there is no orderly way in which you can cash in on these streaks.* You can't see them coming, and you can't predict their duration. They are merely one more part of the chaos. . . .

. . . Countless speculators and gamblers have been bankrupted by failing to quit while they were ahead. The Gambler's Fallacy tends to encourage that failure, for it engenders the feeling that one is temporarily invincible. *That is a dangerous feeling to have.* Nobody is invincible, not even for half a second. . . . It might be hard, indeed, to remain perfectly rational after an experience like that [emphasis added].[5]

This is exactly what Buffett was referring to in his 2000 letter when he wrote, "The line separating investment and speculation, which is never bright and clear, becomes blurred still further when most market participants have recently enjoyed triumphs. Nothing sedates rationality like large doses of effortless money."[6]

Investors succumb to such folly because they fail to recognize one of the most powerful forces in the world of finance.

Reversion to the Mean

Reversion to the mean says that an event that is not average will be followed by an event that is closer to the average. This principle is significant in those activities or situations in which some element of randomness is involved. The intensity with which mean reversion affects an activity is directly proportional to the element of luck controlling the outcome in that activity. Individual sports and games like running, swimming, or chess are activities in which luck plays a relatively small role. They are dominated by skill, resulting in consistent and predictable outcomes.

Stock market investing is an activity in which luck plays a significant role. Consider the typical process that many retail investors follow. They look at a fund manager's most recent few years of performance and invest their money in his or her mutual fund if it has been a recent outperformer. And then their chosen fund starts underperforming the benchmark for the next few years. Frustrated, these investors pull out the money and find another fund manager based on the same criteria—the manager with the most recent few years' outperformance. A similar episode is repeated. The investors are completely baffled as to why their chosen fund's performance deteriorates immediately after they put their money into it.

Mean reversion, my friend.

> Most fund buyers look at past performance first, then at the manager's reputation, then at the riskiness of the fund, and finally (if ever) at the fund's expenses. The intelligent investor looks at those same things—but in the opposite order.
> —Jason Zweig

In the stock market, periods of above-average returns usually are followed by periods of below-average returns and vice versa. Investors tend to let their emotions get the better of them and chase the latest investment fad or sell when they should be buying. As per behavioral research firm Dalbar, the S&P 500 returned 5.6 percent per year in the 20-year period ending in 2018 while the average investor return in all U.S. equity funds was just 1.9 percent per year—a significant underperformance of 3.7 percent per annum for 20 years caused entirely due to the investors' own harmful behaviors and their poor attempts at market timing (also known as the "behavior gap").[7]

Buffett is referring to nothing but mean reversion when he says, "Be fearful when others are greedy and greedy when others are fearful."[8] This is exactly why one should not be swayed by outcomes, that is, by a few recent years of high return performance by any money manager or investment advisor.

If that is the case, then how can we separate luck, chance, and randomness from true skill when evaluating investment track records? Lord Krishna provides us with the answer.

The Big Investing Lesson from the *Bhagavad Gita*

> *Karmanye vadhikaraste, ma phaleshou kada chana.*
> *Ma karma phala hetur bhurmatey sangostva akarmani.*
> —Bhagavad Gita

In this verse from the *Bhagavad Gita*, Lord Krishna explains to Arjuna that he must perform his duties, as the latter was unwilling to fight the Mahabharata war. Translated, it reads:

> You have the right to perform your actions, but you are not entitled to the fruits of the actions.
> Do not let the fruit be the purpose of your actions, and therefore you won't be attached to not doing your duty.

Krishna asks Arjuna to continue performing his duties without being attached to the result of his actions. His teaching is encapsulated in the idea of karma yoga, or the "discipline of action." The word "karma" is derived from the Sanskrit root *kri*, meaning "to do."

This is the big lesson for all investors. Focus on the "karma"—the process and action—and not on the outcome.

Numerous research studies have identified a common trait among successful professionals in fields of probabilistic activity: they all emphasize process over outcome.

> Whatever the future holds, we will stick to our process. We are not guaranteed of getting what we want all the time—far from it—but we believe it is the best foundation for getting what we want over time.
> —Chuck Akre

Although the returns (outcome) may be evident for everyone to see, investors rarely ask whether that outcome was the result of skill (a sound investment process) or plain randomness. If you focus only on the outcome, you are less likely to achieve it. Instead, if you focus on adhering to a sound process, the outcome will take care of itself in the long term, although the short-term results almost always will be driven by luck. Over the long run, a sound process can be counted on to deliver desirable results in a sustained manner and produce more reliable outcomes.

Robert Rubin, the former U.S. Treasury secretary, said it best: "Any individual decision can be badly thought through, and yet be successful, or exceedingly well thought through, but be unsuccessful, because the recognized possibility of failure in fact occurs. But over time, more thoughtful decision-making will lead to better overall results, and more thoughtful decision-making can be encouraged by evaluating decisions on how well they were made rather than on outcome."[9]

CHAPTER 31

THE EDUCATION OF A VALUE INVESTOR

I like people admitting they were complete stupid horses' asses. I know I'll perform better if I rub my nose in my mistakes. This is a wonderful trick to learn.

—Charlie Munger

The chief difference between a fool and a wise man is that the wise man learns from his mistakes, while the fool never does.

—Phil Fisher

Bias from Overinfluence of Authority

Copy-pasting is often respectably known as imitating, or cloning, or coat-tailing. Some people also call it "inspired action." Of course, it's always good to get inspired by others. But the problem occurs when we allow others to think on our behalf, and when we blindly copy/clone/coat-tail what others have done/are doing or said/are saying. It's a natural human bias to act this way, especially when we are working under the influence of an authority or someone who has had success in the past.

—Vishal Khandelwal

During 2016, I bought a stock solely on the basis of the rationale of a peer who I admired and looked up to for his investing skills. A few weeks later, the stock fell sharply, post weak quarterly earnings, and I exited my position at a 14 percent loss because I lacked the personal conviction to hold. To rub salt into the wounds, the stock then doubled in less than ten months. Ouch.

You can borrow someone's idea, but you will never be able to borrow their conviction. Hard work has no alternative. I often have had people strongly recommend a stock to me as a great long-term buy—and then they have sold it the very next week or month. I have no right to blame them if I lose money on their recommendations. We are personally responsible for our decisions. Learn from everyone's best qualities, but never blame them for your losses. As Jim Rohn aptly put it, "The day you graduate from childhood to adulthood is the day you take full responsibility for your life." It is fine to be aware of the investment choices of investors we admire and respect, but we should always do the necessary study at our end and pull the buy trigger only if the concerned business falls within our circle of competence and offers a good margin of safety.

Personally speaking, the real joy and thrill of investing comes from the underlying research and discovery process. When you blindly clone someone else's stock picks without doing any due diligence, you forgo the very aspect that makes value investing such an intellectually satisfying activity. As Vishal Khandelwal puts it:

> You will make mistakes even when you invest in original ideas, but at least those mistakes would be your own and maybe leave you with worthwhile lessons. But when you make mistakes just because the thesis of the one you cloned was wrong, whom do you lay the blame on? *And what lessons do you learn?* . . .
>
> . . . Over time, you become a 20 percent clone each of the five people you associate with the most. This is a good way to live, but only when you choose the right people to associate with.
>
> This is also true in investing. *Choose the right people, then clone their behavior, thinking, process, and orientation—and never blindly their ideas—and you will become like them over time* [emphasis added].[1]

All of us have obeyed an authority figure at some point in our life—parents, teachers, policemen, and so on. Obeying authority has several advantages in situations in which we require guidance. But blindly following authority can result in serious problems (best exemplified by one of the most famous psychological studies of obedience: the Milgram experiment).

During 2013, I bought shares of Subex solely on the basis of a renowned market expert's recommendation on business television. The stock promptly crashed by more than 50 percent within a few months of my purchase, and

I exited it at a significant realized loss. I wish I had, before this, read Benjamin Franklin's words: "It is the first duty of every citizen to question authority."

In hindsight, this was a valuable experience, as I never again invested on the basis of recommendations by experts. The people we read about and see in financial media create authority bias and a halo effect. They are well dressed, speak fluent English, and use complex jargon—all ingredients of drama. Drama always sells. Many of these experts do not have any credible long-term track record. Yet, they never hesitate to tout their "sure-shot" recommendations. In other words, they engage in what Charlie Munger calls "twaddle tendency" and possess superficial "chauffeur knowledge." This leads to serious problems for the audience, as the so-called expert or authority figure often turns out to be grossly wrong. At times, conflicts of interest are involved and the expert willfully acts in an unethical manner.

Questioning authority is an effective antidote to this problem, as shown by Robert Cialdini in his book *Influence*. When confronted with a situation in which you agree with an expert, pause and ask two important questions:

1. Is this authority truly an expert? This question helps verify the credibility of the expert.
2. How truthful can we expect this expert to be? This question should help us understand the expert's incentives and any potential conflicts of interest before we give any credence to the advice.

Although it is good to learn from the best in the business, never blindly follow the recommendation of anyone without adequate inquiry, reasoning, and due diligence—no matter how renowned the expert is. Thankfully, markets are efficient enough to make expert commentary look dumb in the morning and dumber by the afternoon.

Bias from Anchoring

As soon as our intuition gets fixated with a number—and that can be any number—it sticks with us. Most of our decision-making errors result from mental shortcuts that are a normal part of the way we think. The brain uses mental shortcuts to simplify the very complex tasks of information processing and decision-making. Anchoring is the psychologist's term for one shortcut the brain uses. The brain approaches complex problems by selecting an initial reference point (the anchor) and making small changes as additional information is received and processed.

—Vishal Khandelwal

During 2013, I bought the stocks of CORE Education and Wockhardt only because their stock prices had sharply fallen by more than 50 percent in a very short time span. In the case of Wockhardt, the fall had taken less than three months, whereas in the case of CORE Education, the fall had happened in a single day. I excitedly bought the stocks of both these companies without having any idea about their underlying value. Both of them promptly crashed by another 50 percent after my purchase, and I exited both at near the bottom for that year. I was the living example of Phil Fisher's dictum that the stock market is filled with individuals "who know the price of everything and the value of nothing."[2] I should have noted that a stock that is down 95 percent first falls 90 percent and then goes down 50 percent more. (One of the worst ways to identify undervalued stocks is using the distance from the fifty-two-week high price. But it is also one of the easiest and, hence, most frequently used methods among investors.)

Investors often anchor themselves not only to the stock price but also to the past actions of the promoter, even if the promoter has since been reformed and has taken corrective steps like closing down a bad division, improving investor communications, or professionalizing the board. Learn to develop empathy for the promoter. As Oscar Wilde said, "Every saint has a past, every sinner has a future." Sometimes, even if the underlying business model has undergone a significant positive transformation, investors tend to anchor to the past history of the business.

Until 2016, Manappuram Finance was historically a volatile gold loan business, but the management changed the company's business model to giving short-term gold loans, which significantly reduced the underlying business volatility. Many investors overlooked this important change and bought the stock only after it had discounted most of the new positive changes in the company's business model.

We live in a world in process, and it changes continuously, every single minute. Nothing stays the same. Thomas Russo likes to give the analogy of a seven-hundred-year-old temple in Japan. The temple is made of wood, and none of the wood is seven hundred years old, as the pieces have been replaced numerous times over the years. But we still talk about the temple as if it is seven hundred years old. In the stock markets, we see the effect of change in similar ways. Consider the S&P 500, one of the most frequently cited market indexes. On average, over the past fifty years, more than twenty companies are swapped out each year. Yet investors cite and treat the S&P 500 as if it were a monolithic, unchanging object. It clearly isn't. The constituents of the S&P 500 of 2020 are completely different from the S&P 500 of 2000, even though our language infers otherwise when we say things like, "The S&P 500 is trading at a premium/discount to its ten-year average."

If the first time we are introduced to an investment idea we look at its long-term price chart and see that it has consistently declined for the past ten years, we are likely to subconsciously label it as a "dog stock." Thereafter, this taints our view of the business even when the underlying facts might have changed profoundly for the better. So perfectly good companies can be shunned for no good reason. Whenever you study a fallen angel from the past, mentally date it, and you will observe interesting results. Many investors scoffed at the idea of investing in Manappuram$_{2016}$ because they couldn't get Manappuram$_{2013}$ out of their heads. Mentally date each business you study and acknowledge reality for what it is—a mere point-in-time observation.

Investors hold an irrational bias of always trying to buy shares in "round numbers" (those round numbers become the anchor) even though some cash may be left over after such a transaction. Never ignore the opportunity cost of that small amount of idle cash. When compounded over decades, it can amount to a significant sum.

Another common and highly irrational anchoring bias among investors occurs when they aim to buy a stock, which they expect to go up "hundreds of percentage points" over time, only at an arbitrarily fixed desired purchase price that is a bit lower than the current market price. These investors act penny wise and pound foolish and end up incurring huge opportunity costs in many cases (similar to those who defer a justified sale of a stock solely to make it a long-term holding and save some short-term capital gains tax).

> For the great majority of transactions, being stubborn about a tiny fractional difference in the price can prove extremely costly.
> —Philip Fisher

A common anchor is the original cost price of a stock, which makes investors hang on to loser investments in the hope of exiting once they break even. These investors overlook Phil Fisher's warning on the huge costs of this bias:

> More money has probably been lost by investors holding a stock they really did not want until they could "at least come out even" than from any other single reason. If to these actual losses are added the profits that might have been made through the proper reinvestment of these funds if such reinvestment had been made when the mistake was first realized, the cost of self-indulgence becomes truly tremendous.[3]

Most investors wait to recover what's gone rather than retaining what's left. They don't realize that loss recovery does not necessarily have to be made from the same stock on which the loss was made. If the story has gone wrong, simply book your losses and move on to a better opportunity. Continuity of compounding is the key to success in this long-term game. After buying a stock, forget what you paid, or this knowledge will forever affect your judgment.

Another faulty anchor is the past price of a stock—that is, the point at which an investor originally contemplated buying it but failed to pull the trigger, after which point the stock has appreciated significantly. Missing out on an early opportunity creates regret. That regret often is unwarranted because, for a truly outstanding business, multiple opportunities to buy the stock exist. By definition, a hundred-bagger is a ten-bagger twice over. Even if someone bought it after it became 10×, it still went up another 10×. This shows the importance of actively keeping up with a company's story even after you have exited it. Think of investments not as disconnected events but as continuing sagas that need to be reevaluated periodically for new twists and turns in the plot. Unless a company goes bankrupt, the story is never over.

One of the most counterintuitive ideas in investing is averaging upward, or adding to a winning position (also known as pyramiding). If we are invested in a great business that will be worth several times its current market cap (over time, an investor's mind evolves into thinking in terms of market cap rather than stock price) in the medium to long term, then we must not hesitate to add more shares at a higher (sometimes much higher) price than our original cost basis. Our focus as investors should always be on expected returns based on the current price.

This applies to selling as well. Selling a big winner from our portfolio is never easy, because we tend to get emotionally attached to it over the years. After all, it has been responsible for our wealth creation. But a stock does not know that we own it. Just as we cling to outdated beliefs, we hang on to these stocks because we remain fixated on meaningless anchors like our lower original cost price. But the investor of today does not benefit from yesterday's growth.

Anchoring bias afflicts analysts as well. In the investment world, anchoring explains why an earnings surprise typically follows prior surprises. Analysts tend to slowly adjust earnings numbers for a company in their valuation models. No one likes to acknowledge that they were wrong, especially if the change requires making a complete about-face. As a result, change tends to be a slow process of gradual adjustment. Surprise after surprise.

Envy and Ego

It's not greed that drives the world, but envy.

—Warren Buffett

Once you get something that works fine in your life, the idea of caring terribly that somebody else is making money faster strikes me as insane.

—Charlie Munger

There is a complicating factor that makes the handling of investment mistakes more difficult. This is the ego in each of us.

—Phil Fisher

Failure to ignore and avoid the temptation that comes from watching other people get rich thanks to a sharp rise in the prices of their stock holdings may lead to the destruction of your wealth, if you fall prey to the fear of missing out. Even the legendary Isaac Newton succumbed to this bias during the South Sea Bubble of 1720 (figure 31.1). He had invested in South Sea stock before its euphoric rise and had exited with a handsome profit of more than 100 percent in a few months. Lured by social proof—his friends continued to make even bigger returns on the stock after his exit—he caved and bought the stock again near its peak. I'll bet you can guess what happened next.

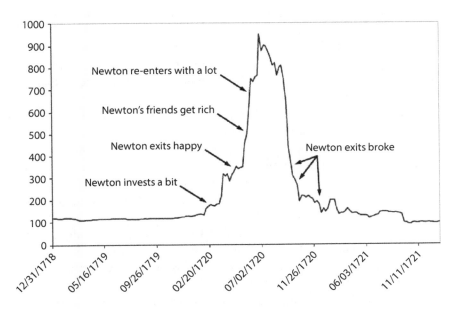

FIGURE 31.1 South Sea Stock, December 1718–December 1721.

Source: "Isaac Newton's Nightmare During the South Sea Stock Bubble (Dec 1718 – Dec 1721)," Bamboo Innovator (blog), https://bambooinnovator.com/2013/04/04/isaac-newtons-nightmare-during-the-south -sea-stock-bubble-dec-1718-dec-1721/.

I wish I had known this story earlier. In late 2015, I bought shares of Capital Trust only because a close friend recently had made more than 150 percent on it in less than a year. As Charles Kindleberger says, "There is nothing so disturbing to one's well-being and judgment as to see a friend get rich."[4] I did not want to get left behind in this competitive race with my close friend, so I bought the stock of Capital Trust even though I did not properly understand its underlying business. Within two months of my purchase, the stock price corrected by almost 30 percent, and I exited it in panic. To add insult to injury, the stock then tripled in less than eight months. Ouch.

Envy is the only one of the seven deadly sins that offers no upside. Envious people are always miserable, because envy has only downside risks and envy offers no upside reward. We are unnecessarily influenced even when others are playing a different game than we are. Do not compare yourself with others. The only person you need to be better than today is the person you were yesterday. Competing with others makes you bitter. Competing with yourself makes you better. Great wisdom can be found in Ernest Hemingway's words: "There is nothing noble in being superior to your fellow man; true nobility is being superior to your former self."

Sometimes, our ego makes us bypass a stock simply because an investing peer bought it many years ago at next to the stock's lowest price or at its lowest price in the past year or even the past month. We stupidly anchor ourselves to this peer's low purchase price and refuse to assess the prospects for the stock at the current market price. Also, during an ego tussle with a peer investor, for any random personal reason, we tend to ignore his or her publicly available solid stock recommendations because of envy, intellectual ego, and sometimes even anger and hatred.

This is mighty foolish behavior. The stock does not know who owns it. Avoid imposing personal emotions and opinions about others onto an investment decision. This will only lead to forgone profits and lost opportunities and significantly erode your long-term net worth. I have committed all these asininities at some point of time in the past and have suffered both financially and emotionally. You should not. As Munger says, "You don't have to pee on an electric fence to learn not to do it."[5]

Successful investing is investing that lets you sleep peacefully at night. Success is not about who makes the highest returns or who makes the most money. It is about achieving our financial goals in a timely manner with the lowest possible risk.

When practiced in a truly honest and sincere manner, value investing not only leads to great wealth but also makes us better human beings. With the passage of time, we learn to recognize that value investing is not merely about stocks and business fundamentals.

It is a life discipline.

Liking and Disliking Tendency

When we have a negative opinion about the person delivering the message, we close our minds to what they are saying and miss a lot of learning opportunities because of it. Likewise, when we have a positive opinion of the messenger, we tend to accept the message without much vetting. Both are bad.

—Annie Duke

In *Influence*, Cialdini talks about a subtle but highly insidious bias: liking tendency. We tend to like those who are physically attractive, popular, or cooperative, or people we have positive associations with, and those who are similar to us in background, opinion, lifestyle, interest, attitude, looks, values, or beliefs. We like and trust anything familiar. Most of us prefer to say yes to the requests made by someone we know and like. It is natural to ignore the faults of those we find likeable and to do the opposite with people we don't like.

According to Munger, "Liking/Loving Tendency . . . acts as a conditioning device that makes the liker or lover tend:

1. to ignore the faults of, and comply with wishes of, the object of his affection;
2. to favor people, products, and actions merely associated with the object of his affection . . .; and
3. to distort other facts to facilitate love."[6]

In contrast, in the case of disliking bias, we tend to ignore the virtues of the concerned subject and to distort facts to maintain our negative view.

In investing, always consciously separate the stock from the personality of the individual at the helm of the company. Concentrate on the merits and economics of the underlying business. Look at the facts and assess the situation objectively. This will save you from making many costly mistakes. I wish I had read Cialdini's book before I made my investment in Virat Crane Industries in 2016. I felt emotionally attached to its founder, Grandhi Subba Rao, after I read about his life story of hardship, struggle, and perseverance. My strong liking bias for the promoter in turn drove confirmation bias, and I began to justify my entry into the stock by considering only the positive points and completely sidelining various negative aspects, such as low margins and related-party transactions, even though I was aware of them.

Conversely, I once displayed disliking bias by delaying my decision to buy the stock in a great business just because I did not like the rude verbal tone of its promoter on television. This was completely irrational behavior. The business had good economics and the promoter had a clean corporate governance track record.

A highly capable CEO may be arrogant, loud, flamboyant, and smoke cigars, whereas another CEO might be humble, introverted, and a self-disciplined individual of high moral character. We tend to be biased toward people who display qualities we admire or who are similar to us, but the people we like are not necessarily the people who have the capabilities to execute and deliver results. Emotions and expenses are two of the biggest enemies of an investor, and in several instances in my investing career, I paid the price for getting overly emotional about the individual at the helm of a company and acting on my subjective opinion. In all of those cases, I did not make any money from the stock and incurred a big opportunity cost while holding it. I willfully ignored the various headwinds each of those businesses were facing, and I consciously turned a blind eye to their problems when I should have been objective and unbiased in my evaluation. Always strive to disentangle the facts of a situation from the elements of human psychology.

Stress-Influence Tendency and Cognitive Dissonance

Stress (n.): a state of mental or emotional strain or tension resulting from adverse or very demanding circumstances.

In the fast-paced world of the stock market, adrenaline tends to produce faster and more extreme reactions. Some stress can improve performance, but heavy stress often leads to dysfunction in our cognitive apparatus.

One form of stress is cognitive dissonance. We experience this type of stress when we simultaneously hold onto two contradictory thoughts, beliefs, opinions, or attitudes. This dissonance often leads to illogical and irrational actions. A personal example from my investing journey illustrates this experience.

In November 2016, I sold my entire holding in SKS Microfinance (now known as Bharat Financial) because I believed that its microfinance business (which depended heavily on cash collections) would be adversely affected by the Indian government's demonetization announcement and that it would result in a spike in SKS's nonperforming assets. I was experiencing severe mental stress at the time, as SKS's stock price was rapidly falling off a cliff. But what I did immediately after my sale of SKS's stock exemplified cognitive dissonance at its finest. I deployed the sale proceeds into buying shares of Manappuram Finance because I had been closely following it over the past few months and had been enthused by the prospects of its fast-growing microfinance subsidiary. Fortunately, I realized my folly quickly and exited the stock at a minor loss.

A remedy to stress-influence tendency is to delay making decisions until the time at which you feel less stressed. Give yourself a cooling-off period and take stock of the situation when you are feeling calm and relaxed. And then, peacefully think over your decision. Ensure that you refer to your checklist if it is a critical decision.

Loss Aversion

During a previous instance, I had put in a stop-loss order for Goa Carbon on the morning of its results day. I wanted to preserve my quick profits of more than 50 percent, which I had earned within just a few months of my purchase. The stock market is an auction-driven mechanism, and stock prices often fluctuate sharply on either side, many times just plain randomly. My stop loss was triggered for no apparent reason, within minutes of my placing the order. Goa Carbon reported stellar results an hour after that, and the stock shot up in the latter half of the trading session and then went on to rise more than 100 percent within just a few months of that date. Ouch.

The reason for the stop-loss order on HEG (discussed earlier in the book) was valid, because I was uncertain about the impact of the potential imposition of the export duty on it. But in the case of Goa Carbon, my actions were completely irrational. Just a week before my sale, I had become aware of the company's improved prospects (figure 31.2).

It does not make sense to put stop-loss orders on our long-term secular growth stocks, but nothing is wrong with using them for short-term commodity holdings during periods of uncertainty with regard to their prospects, especially if we are sitting on big profits. In both cases, however, the same fundamental principle applies. Future prospects always drive stock prices, not past reported earnings. Because I was aware of the improved prospects for Goa Carbon in the coming quarters, as a result of the recent surge in its calcined petroleum coke product prices, it was completely contradictory behavior to

 **Darshan Mehta**
@darshanvmehta1   Follow   ∨

Rain Industries in focus as CPC prices are up 3000₹ in last 10 days as per dealers

9:00 PM - 8 Oct 2017

FIGURE 31.2 Goa Carbon's prospects had improved as a result of an increase in its product prices.

Source: Darshan Mehta (@darshanvmehta1), "Rain industries in focus on CPC prices are up 3000," Twitter, October 8, 2017, https://twitter.com/darshanvmehta1/status/917238376863895552.

even think about placing a stop-loss order just ahead of the company's results announcement for the previous quarter.

What drove this irrational behavior? What drove my desire to "preserve" my existing profits on a holding by placing a stop-loss order? The answer lies in an attribute intrinsic to all humans and the overarching theory that forms the bedrock for most biases in behavioral finance.

Loss aversion.

Human beings are more motivated by the thought of losing something than by the thought of gaining something of equal value. This is especially true under conditions of uncertainty. The threat of potential loss plays a significant role in our decision-making, and we have a natural tendency to be loss averse.

Or, in Munger's words, "The quantity of a man's pleasure from a ten-dollar gain does not exactly match the quantity of his displeasure from a ten-dollar loss."[7] This is the foundational principle of Daniel Kahneman and Amos Tversky's prospect theory (figure 31.3).

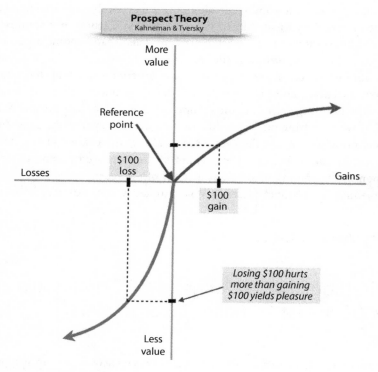

FIGURE 31.3 Prospect theory.

Source: Dave Rothschild, "How People Think About Buying New Products," JTBD.info, August 21, 2015, https://jtbd.info/getting-consumers-to-switch-to-your-solution-fa292bb29cea.

When reframing the problem from a "gain frame" to a "loss frame," we shift from a sure-shot (conservative) option toward the riskier option— gambling. Loss aversion converts us into risk-seeking people. People tend to avoid risk when a positive frame is presented but to seek risks when a negative frame is presented. How a message is communicated affects the way it is received; therefore, framing has important implications when it comes to behavior. We find "99 percent fat-free" food products appealing, but if the same message said "Contains 1 percent fat," it would trigger a different response in us. Similarly, consider an example of winning $1,000 and then losing $900 of it, versus losing $1,000 and winning $900 back—we are likely to be happier that we "only" lost $100, versus the outcome in which we "only" won $100.

Framing is an outcome of our aversion to losses. Evolution has pro-grammed our brain to seek loss minimization instead of gain maximization. In investing, narrow framing, a variant of the framing effect, is our inability to zoom out in a given situation. We like winning more than losing, and we keep an internal score for each stock in our portfolio. We maintain a separate mental account for each of our stocks, and we want to close every future sale transaction only with a gain. Instead of looking at overall portfo-lio performance, we try to gain from every single stock. This narrow framing is known as the disposition effect, and it results in selling winners and hold-ing on to losers. As Peter Lynch puts it, this is the equivalent of "cutting the flowers and watering the weeds."

Richard Thaler and Cass Sunstein take the idea of aversion to loss one step further.[8] They explain that investors also suffer from myopic loss aversion; the more often we evaluate our portfolios, the more likely we are to see losses. And the more often we see losses, the more often we experience loss aversion, which then becomes a vicious cycle. (Financial losses are processed in the same area of the brain that responds to mortal danger.)

Investors should learn the big lesson from Buffett's insurance underwrit-ing practices: always think in terms of expected value. Be risk averse but do not be loss averse, that is, do not be afraid to take calculated risks. Investing is not a business in which every investment is profitable. Most investors find this to be decisively true but difficult to accept. If you are obsessed with individual wins and losses, then you will end up being miserable even if your overall portfolio performs well. Occasional losses are part of the game, so diversify prudently to ensure that no single loss has a major adverse impact on your portfolio in percentage terms and the risk of ruin is not possible. Always zoom out—think in terms of percentage changes in your overall wealth rather than absolute value changes in your individual stocks. Remember, you may look at your portfolio in horror on some days, but not decades.

Greed and Fear

October. This is one of the peculiarly dangerous months to speculate in stocks. The others are July, January, September, April, November, May, March, June, December, August, and February.

—Mark Twain

The degree of one's emotion varies inversely with one's knowledge of the facts—the less you know, the hotter you get.

—Bertrand Russell

The vividness of an event acts as an impediment in our logical reasoning, because of our tendency to overweigh the importance of a vivid event and to underweigh the more important but no-so-vivid gradual changes taking place on a daily basis. (For example, most people would be highly surprised to know that, in 2016, mosquitos killed more people per day, on average, than sharks killed cumulatively over the preceding one hundred years.)[9] If the said event is recent and more easily available to recall, it can potentially lead to some hasty and rash decisions. These events tend to take place during times of excessive or overblown coverage of a dramatic media event, when investors bypass their checklists because they experience an adrenaline rush and end up making hurried decisions.

In June 2016, immediately after the Brexit verdict, I sold 5 percent of my existing holdings in Eicher Motors to buy a put option on Yes Bank, which had near-term plans to raise $1 billion through a share sale. I thought the global markets would crash, as Brexit was being termed by many experts on television, "the biggest political event since World War II." (If something is too much in the news, it is already discounted in the price.) This made me nervous, but I decided to capitalize on the widespread fear to make a quick buck. I thought that once my put options on Yes Bank surged in value, I would sell them and buy back even more shares of Eicher Motors than I had temporarily sold. I had it all figured out in a logical manner. How could I lose?

The very next week, stock markets globally had their biggest rally in many years. All those fear-mongering experts were now completely conspicuous by their absence in the media and conveniently replaced by hypercharged bulls on business television. The stock of Eicher Motors surged in price and the value of my put option on Yes Bank promptly crashed to nearly zero. Ouch.

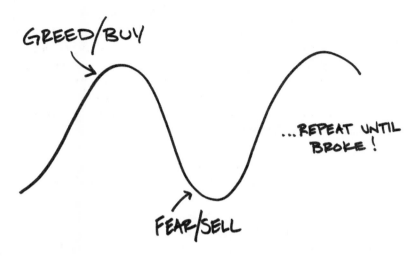

FIGURE 31.4 Greed and fear.

Source: Behavior Gap.

I know what these emotions (figure 31.4) feel like, because I committed many atrocities in my initial investing years:

1. Trying to make some "quick money" by taking a loan from the broker to buy shares in a "hot" initial public offering (IPO), with the sole objective of "flipping" it on listing day.

2. Taking margin exposure in a stock by paying interest to the broker, with the sole objective of selling the stock at a small but "quick profit" immediately after its expected (by me) strong results, scheduled for release the next day or next week.

3. Buying a stock solely based on a multibagger recommendation from a widely followed blog, intending to sell it after a small but quick rise.

4. Buying a stock in the secondary market in the hope of making a quick profit driven solely by valuation rerating ahead of the near-term, highly anticipated IPO of a leading company from the same sector.

5. Getting lured into buying a rapidly rising small-cap stock in a hot sector out of greed and the fear of missing out, and bypassing the necessary initial research work, like studying its annual reports, past track record, financials, and management quality.

6. Buying a company's stock based on vivid stories about a glamorous and highly publicized joint venture or partnership with a global giant in its industry,

without bothering to look at the economics of the arrangement. In the hands of a good storyteller, almost every stock looks like a winner. (To safeguard yourself, always assume you're not being told the whole story.) Great story-tellers can lower their cost of capital because they can raise investors' expectations and these investors end up overlooking the cautionary words of both Benjamin Graham ("Operations for profit should be based not on optimism but on arithmetic") and Louis Brandeis ("Remember, O Stranger, arithmetic is the first of the sciences, and the mother of safety").[10]

Dopamine rushes are expensive indeed. Brokers make their money off our activity. We should embrace inactivity and avoid disturbing the process of compounding (figure 31.5).

In a paper titled "Why Do Investors Trade Too Much?" finance professors Brad Barber and Terrance Odean looked at nearly 100,000 stock trades made by retail investors at a major discount brokerage firm from 1987 through 1993. They found, on average, that the stocks these investors bought underperformed the market by 2.7 percentage points over the subsequent year, whereas the stocks they sold outperformed the market by 0.5 points in the subsequent year.[11] Similarly, in a paper published by the Brookings Institution, economists Josef Lakonishok, Andrei Shleifer, and Robert Vishny showed that the stock trades made by pension fund managers subtracted 0.78 percent from the returns they would have earned by keeping their portfolios constant.[12]

When we trade excessively, the only people who become rich are the intermediaries and brokers. Consider a startling calculation to open your eyes to this fact. Assume that both you and the intermediary can earn 8 percent per year, but you incur frictional costs amounting to 4 percent of your portfolio each year. Meanwhile, the intermediaries invest their commissions at 8 percent. After seventeen years, they would have accumulated more money than you;

ACTIVITY   RESULTS

FIGURE 31.5 Activity versus results.

Source: Behavior Gap.

after twenty-eight years, they would have twice as much as you—even though they initially started with zero capital. They became rich off your tiny expenses.

Albert Einstein had said, "Compound interest is the eighth wonder of the world. He who understands it, earns it. He who doesn't, pays it." I have paid my fair share in the past. With time and experience, I have come to appreciate the deep wisdom in Graham's words: "The investor's chief problem—and even his worst enemy—is likely to be himself."[13]

> There is nothing like losing all you have in the world for teaching you what not to do. *And when you know what not to do in order not to lose money, you begin to learn what to do in order to win* [emphasis added].
>
> —Jesse Livermore

I shared the mistakes from my investing journey because I consider them to be my greatest teachers, and the lessons learned helped me improve significantly over the years. I have a deep appreciation for the valuable experience and wisdom that each loss has brought me. There are no mistakes in life, only lessons. When you adopt a positive mind-set, you never lose. You either win or you learn. Good judgment comes from experience, and experience comes from bad judgment. (I have had a great deal of experience.)

Investing isn't a game of perfection. It's a game of continuous improvement. Making quick money through a lucky trade early on is the worst way to win. The bad habit that it reinforces often leads to a lifetime of losses. Beginner's luck often turns out to be beginner's curse in the field of investing. An early (and manageable) failure is a blessing. Get most of your investing mistakes out of the way while you're young and have a significant amount of human capital but little in the way of financial capital.

According to Otto Von Bismarck, "Only a fool learns from his own mistakes. The wise man learns from the mistakes of others." Munger agrees: "The more hard lessons you can learn vicariously, instead of from your own terrible experiences, the better off you will be."[14]

I hope the vicarious learning from my mistakes benefits my readers in their lives and investing careers.

CONCLUSION: UNDERSTANDING THE TRUE ESSENCE OF COMPOUNDING

Life is like a snowball. The important thing is finding wet snow and a really long hill.

—Warren Buffett

Understanding both the power of compound interest and the difficulty of getting it is the heart and soul of understanding a lot of things.

—Charlie Munger

I have come to realize that the best things to learn from Warren Buffett have nothing to do with investing. Read, reread, and reflect on these words from him:

You only get one mind and one body. And it's got to last a lifetime. Now, it's very easy to let them ride for many years. But if you don't take care of that mind and that body, they'll be a wreck forty years later. . . .

It's what you do right now, today, that determines how your mind and body will operate ten, twenty, and thirty years from now.[1]

These are great words to live by. I have yet to come across a better example of long-term thinking with respect to the daily decisions that eventually have an enormous impact on one's life. Now that you have read this, I want you to think for a moment.

Are you creating habits and taking actions that will support your body and mind for the rest of your life? Are you putting systems in place so you can spend more time on the things that really matter to you in your life?

Many of us aspire to become successful but lack the blueprint to do so. Being successful doesn't mean only making truckloads of money. Money without health is pointless. Money with no good relationships will leave you lonely. We spend a lot of time focusing on compounding our financial capital, but we overlook the fact that social and intellectual capital also compound. Investing in yourself, in your relationships, and in your understanding of the world pays massive dividends over time. Understand what is truly important to you and pursue your dreams with full dedication in a principled manner. Everything you are looking for is closer than you think, but sometimes you have to go on a journey to find it. And in your journey, the power of compounding will help you achieve what you are striving for: becoming happier, healthier, better, wealthier, smarter, and more honorable.

Compounding Positive Thoughts

Whatever the mind of man can conceive and believe, it can achieve. Thoughts are things! And powerful things at that, when mixed with definiteness of purpose, and burning desire, can be translated into riches.

—Napoleon Hill

Positive thoughts generate the consistent energy we need to reach our long-term goals. Our mind automatically generates thoughts related to the information we consume. Even if we're adept at avoiding negativity and have trained ourselves to be relentlessly positive, when it comes to sensationalism, our basic nature can't resist. Media masters understand that. They know your nature in many ways better than you. The media has always used shocking and sensational headlines to draw attention. Your mind is like an empty glass; it'll hold anything you put into it. You put in sensational news, negative headlines, talk-show rants, and you're pouring dirty water into your glass. If you've got dark, dismal, worrisome water in your glass, everything you create in your mind will be filtered through that muddy mess, because that's what you'll be thinking about. Be conscious of your information diet.

Acknowledging the good that you already have in your life is the foundation for all abundance.
—Eckhart Tolle

Kaizen is as much a life philosophy and belief system as it is a strategy for success in changing or enhancing behavior. Kaizen encourages us to be grateful for our health. For our moments with family and friends. For our next breath. The world looks, acts, and responds to you differently when you have an orientation of gratitude for that which you already have. When you appreciate, optimize, and leverage what you do have instead of ruminating over what you don't have, you have the power to change your circumstances. Inhale blessings. Exhale gratitude. Gratitude is the most effective path to find contentment. If you need to wake up early as a parent, you should feel grateful for having children to love. If you need to clean or repair your home, you should feel grateful for having a place to live. If you have laundry chores to take care of, you should feel grateful for having clothes to wear. If you have dishes to clean, you should feel grateful for having food to eat. If you feel tired in bed, you should feel grateful for being alive in this beautiful world. When famous American songwriter Warren Zevon was suffering from terminal cancer, David Letterman asked him what wisdom he had drawn from his illness. Zevon's answer was pure kaizen: "Enjoy every sandwich."

> The mind is everything. What you think, you become.
> —Gautama Buddha

Our attitude determines our altitude. Honest mistakes are perfectly acceptable. As Charlie Munger would put it, "It seemed like a good idea at the time." But failing to learn from our mistakes is not acceptable. The difference between winners and losers is that winners take ownership of their mistakes and, as a result, they learn from them and progress in life. The key to learning from mistakes is to acknowledge them without excuses and to make the necessary changes to improve going forward. If you can't admit your mistakes, you won't grow. When negative emotions come into play, your mind is telling you that something is wrong on your current path and that you need to change direction. Most people tend to ignore this warning.

You are not a product of your circumstances. You are a product of what you think. Happiness is all about the quality of thoughts you put in your head, so ensure that you entertain the right ones. Your thoughts influence your words and actions. If you want to be a better person, you need to discipline your mind. When you begin to change yourself internally, the world around you responds. When your consciousness or mental attitude shifts in the right direction, remarkable things begin to happen. Try to read or watch something productive or inspirational before going to sleep. The mind continues to process the last information consumed before bedtime, so you want to focus your attention on something constructive and helpful in making progress with your goals and ambitions. This ensures that you finish strong every day.

The first thing you have to know is yourself. People who are self-aware can step outside and observe their reactions. Self-awareness allows you to experience life twice—first with a detached point of view and second with the usual set of sensorial reactions embedded in thoughts and emotions. Two versions of your experiences are living together in the shadows of your consciousness. One version gives you a fulfilling life, and the other version creates a life of regrets. The version to which you give your attention will grow, so choose wisely.

The underlying nature of the universe is insecure, impermanent, and ultimately fleeting. Therefore, don't seek security, permanence, or prolongation. Instead, make peace with your place in the greater process. The universe is in a constant state of regeneration. To evolve, the new replaces the old. The same applies at the cellular level in the human body. This is a lesson in letting go and detachment. Our body is made up of approximately 37 trillion cells, and each day our body and mind go through countless permutations and transformations. Yet, if we really pay attention, we are bound to discover a single, clear, and authentic voice. This is our true self, and is the source of all meaning. The Zen concept of calmness and deep concentration through meditation helps develop this ability. I can't emphasize this enough: learn to meditate. When you train your mind to focus on something as simple as the breath, it also gives you the discipline to focus on much bigger things and to tell the difference between what's really important and everything else.

> Many of life's failures are people who did not realize how close they were to success when they gave up.
> —Thomas Edison

Success lies on the same road as failure; success is just a little farther down that road. Keep plugging away; you never know when your next action is going to hit it big. Never give up after putting in hard work and effort, because compounding bestows its benefits on you only after a long time, after testing your patience and conviction to the fullest. This is true not only in business and investing but also in life and relationships.

Most people develop interests in life, but few make a real commitment. The difference between interest and commitment is the will to not give up. When you truly commit to something, you have no alternative but success. Getting interested will get you started, but commitment gets you to the finish line.

When you've prepared, practiced, worked hard, and consistently put in the required effort, sooner or later you'll be presented with your moment of truth in life. In that moment, you will define who you are and who you are becoming. It's not getting to the wall that counts; it's what you do after you hit it. These are the defining moments of success and progress. Growth and improvement live in those very moments—when we either step forward or shrink back.

Instead of quitting every time you hit a mental or physical wall, recognize that your competitors are facing the same challenges. At this moment, if you persist and keep going, you will end up miles ahead. This "little longer" results in a massive expansion of your limits. This is compounding in action, and because its power is back-loaded, you end up exponentially multiplying the results of that little extra in your efforts.

> Nothing in the world can take the place of persistence. Talent will not; nothing is more common than unsuccessful men with talent. Genius will not; unre-warded genius is almost a proverb. Education will not; the world is full of edu-cated derelicts. Persistence and determination alone are omnipotent.
> —Calvin Coolidge

Persistence is more important than knowledge. You must persevere if you wish to succeed. Knowledge and skill can be acquired through study and prac-tice, but nothing great comes to those who quit. Rudyard Kipling described triumph and disaster as two imposters. Treat them just the same, and you will be fine, come what may. Every success is an opportunity to demonstrate humility. Every setback is an opportunity to demonstrate resilience and build character.

Munger believes that adversity causes some people to transform themselves into a victim:

> Whenever you think that some situation or some person is ruining your life, it's actually you who are ruining your life. It's such a simple idea. Feeling like a vic-tim is a perfectly disastrous way to go through life. If you just take the attitude that however bad it is in any way, it's always your fault and you just fix it as best you can—the so-called iron prescription—I think that really works.[2]

In his blog, Joshua Kennon wrote about Munger's excruciatingly painful experiences with multiple adversities during his lifetime:

> In 1953, Charlie was 29 years old when he and his wife divorced. He had been married since he was 21. Charlie lost everything in the divorce, his wife keeping the family home in South Pasadena. Munger moved into "dreadful" conditions at the University Club and drove a terrible yellow Pontiac. . . .
>
> Shortly after the divorce, Charlie learned that his son, Teddy, had leukemia. In those days, there was no health insurance, you just paid everything out of pocket and the death rate was near 100 percent since there was nothing doctors could do. Rick Guerin, Charlie's friend, said Munger would go into the hospital, hold his young son, and then walk the streets of Pasadena crying.
>
> One year after the diagnosis, in 1955, Teddy Munger died. Charlie was 31 years old, divorced, broke, and burying his 9-year-old son. Later in life,

he faced a horrific operation that left him blind in one eye with pain so terrible that he eventually had his eye removed.

It's a fair bet that your present troubles pale in comparison. Whatever it is, get over it. Start over. He did it. You can, too.[3]

My eyes went moist with emotion the first time I read this. I immediately recalled a hard-hitting moment from the preface of Kenneth Marshall's book *Good Stocks Cheap*: "Those who discover value investing tend to do so via one of two routes: trauma or exposure. Trauma, alas, is far more common."[4]

Through reflection, we learn that adversity is a natural part of life. The purpose of reflecting on adversity is to understand that it is inevitable, indiscriminate, and arbitrary. Bad things can and do happen to good people. But we all have a hidden reserve of great strength inside that emerges when life puts us to the test. You never know how strong you are until being strong is the only choice you have.

In the end, we are defined by how we respond to failures and setbacks in our lives. Indifference toward the things outside our control is the essence of the stoic discipline—and it is one of the most liberating realizations in life.

God, grant me the serenity to accept the things I cannot change, courage to change the things I can, and the wisdom to know the difference.
—"Serenity Prayer"

All of us can find peace by cultivating indifference to things outside our control. Acceptance is pragmatic. We cannot change what has already happened, but we can choose our reaction. In his memoir *Man's Search for Meaning*, Viktor Frankl wrote about this intrinsic virtue in all of us: "Everything can be taken from a man but one thing: the last of the human freedoms—*to choose one's attitude in any given set of circumstances, to choose one's own way* [emphasis added]."[5] Montaigne, the great French philosopher, adopted these seventeen words as the motto of his life: "A man is not hurt so much by what happens, as by his opinion of what happens." And our opinion of what happens is entirely up to us. Whatever happens in our lives, our capacity to choose our response is eternal and cannot be taken from us. From this capacity, we can draw great strength. Even in the confines of a concentration camp, Frankl witnessed the inherent ability to choose one's own way in the prisoners who comforted others, some even giving away their last piece of bread. Our view of the world can be completely transformed when we embrace the belief that people are inherently good.

When we see the human side of everyone, we learn to accept each other. When we see the good in everyone, we start to develop compassion and understanding and, in so doing, we begin treating others the way we would want to be treated: with honor, dignity, respect, empathy, and humanity. When we learn to see the smallest of positive attributes in everyone, we begin to respect and care for each person we encounter. And that love, friendship, and trust, in turn, brings out the best virtue in each one of us. When we treat people like we wanted to be treated, everyone becomes happier and better, and positivity spreads across our civilization.

This is compounding positive thoughts in action.

> Our life is what our thoughts make it.
> —Marcus Aurelius

When you change the way you look at things, the things you look at change. If you form a habit of looking for the good, you will find it in the smallest of things around you and your mind will fill with happiness. And happiness, being one of the purest forms of strength, is the key to success. Once you've successfully achieved some goals, you start believing you can achieve any other goal, that is, positive thoughts start *compounding* in your mind. That's why every success drives more successes.

These words of Charles Fillmore, from his book *Prosperity*, go right to the heart of what gives us our single greatest power as human beings:

> You can do anything with the thoughts of your mind. They are yours and under your control. You can direct them, coerce them, hush them, or crush them. You can dissolve one thought and put another in its stead. There is no other place in the universe where you are the absolute master. The dominion given you as your divine right is over your own thoughts only. When you fully apprehend this and begin to exercise your God-given dominion, you begin to find the way to God, the only door to God, the door of mind and thought.[6]

Compounding Good Health

> *To keep the body in good health is a duty, otherwise we shall not be able to keep our mind strong and clear.*
>
> —Gautama Buddha

> *Take care of your body. It's the only place you have to live.*
>
> —Jim Rohn

It's not dying you should worry about; it's chronic disease. What you can expect from not making the right health decisions isn't an early death—in fact, that's the least of your worries. Instead, you should be concerned about years, possibly decades, of suffering from chronic disease in your old age. As the pendulum has swung away from deaths caused by acute illness, it has gravitated toward chronic illness. Today, a great number of working professionals die from heart problems, strokes, diabetes, and lung disease. Our cars, Internet connections, and lives have become faster, but our physical activities have become slower.

The primary goal of exercise is to bring about muscular contraction. Research has shown that sitting, or plain inactivity, characterized by lack of muscular contraction, is an independent risk factor in developing lifestyle diseases. Sitting is the new smoking. Chronic diseases and their effects can last years or even decades. That's why they are called chronic—they go on and on, resulting in a slow but painful death.

The motivating factor for taking care of your health should not be how long you live but how you are going to live in your old age. For example, an American who reaches age sixty is expected to live, on average, at least another twenty years. You need to be concerned with the quality of your life during that time. You need to change your lifestyle early in life, not to live longer but to live better in your seventies, eighties, and beyond. You should take care of your body as if it needs to serve you for a hundred years. What you do when you're young will catch up with you when you get old. As James Clear aptly puts it, "The costs of your good habits are in the present. The costs of your bad habits are in the future." When you are young, take care of your body, get full medical checkups done periodically (even when you're feeling well), and keep yourself in good health. Chronic diseases are largely preventable. The World Health Organization makes it clear that chronic disease is primarily caused by common, modifiable risk factors, with the big three being unhealthy diet, physical inactivity, and tobacco use.

The food you eat can be either the most powerful form of medicine or the slowest form of poison. When it comes to food, always think nutrients, not calories. Vitamins, minerals, protein, carbohydrates, and fat all require adequate representation in your diet. When it comes to fruits, eat, don't drink, them. Exposure to the air oxidizes the fruit's nutrients and robs you of vitamins and minerals. Vitamin and mineral supplements are no match for a healthy diet, regular exercise, and, most important, a positive attitude. Stress is the biggest enemy of an efficient digestive system and the fat-burning process, because stress leads to secretion of cortisol in our body. The function of cortisol is to lower our metabolic rate, to prevent fat burning, and to convert food to fat. The body has learned this response as a means to cope with scarcity brought about by drought, famine, floods, and other environmental hazards. (It also led to the evolution and survival of the human species from caveman mode to what we are today.) We can reduce cortisol production through a disciplined lifestyle, regular exercise, and positive thinking. In fact, studies have shown that exercise is much more effective than antidepressants as a form of therapy (with you looking better as the only side effect).

Your energy levels are low only when you fail to reinvest into it the means of a stronger foundation. Slowly deconstruct (through workouts, weight training, and meditation) and reconstruct (through sleep, water, and nutrition) the only receptacle your self will ever have. Your body dictates the nature of your thoughts. If you are in a good physical shape, the thoughts popping into your head during a workout session won't be "Damn that's hard. I wanna give up," but rather "I can do more. Yes, I definitely can."

That's why it's critical to break out of the vicious cycle of being unfit. Poor health triggers negative feelings, thoughts, and emotions, which hinder your performance and prevent you from reaching your potential. If you don't approach your limits (which is a prerequisite for deliberate practice), you won't improve. With enough dedication and discipline, what was once your stretch goal will become your warm-up routine. Those who have undergone major healthy changes realize how the state of their body correlates with the clarity of their mind and the stability of their emotions. These, in turn, influence the quality of social interactions.

High performance often hides behind boring solutions and underused basic insights. The fundamentals aren't cool or sexy. They just work. One of the best health habits is to exercise for one hour three to four times every week and to avoid prolonged sedentary periods. The second habit is to get eight hours of sleep every night. The third is to drink more water and consume less sugar and junk food. All three are obvious, but they are often overlooked. They have a more meaningful and immediate impact on the quality of your mental and physical health than 99 percent of all productivity tips. Systems are better than goals because once you reach a goal (e.g., to lose twenty pounds), you tend to stop doing the very thing that made achieving that goal possible, and you revert back to your old ways.

Avoid going on extreme diets. When you crash diet, you lose weight because your lean body weight (the weight of everything except fat) goes down while your fat body weight remains the same (and sometimes actually increases). The higher the amount of lean body weight you carry, the greater your fat-burning capacity. Your total weight or overall body mass index measurements are not useful as an indicator of your health or fitness level, your fat percentage is. Ideally, this percentage should be under 20 percent for men and under 25 percent for women.

Eat right and at the right time during the day. The key to good health lies in three words: moderation, consistency, and sustainability. Inculcate these as a part of your daily life and you will experience compounding good health in action.

Compounding Good Habits

What you are is what you have been. What you'll be is what you do now.

—Gautama Buddha

The compound effect is always in action, and it doesn't apply to money only. Intellectual and physical aptitudes behave similarly. A person who puts in continuous effort for ten years may achieve more in one week than someone who, having started six months ago, will achieve in an entire year.

Keeping a goal in mind and using it to direct our actions requires constant willpower. In his seminal book on habit formation, *The Power of Habit*, Charles Duhigg writes, "Willpower isn't just a skill. It's a muscle, like the muscles in your arms or legs, and it gets tired as it works harder, so there's less power left over for other things."[7] During times when other parts of our lives deplete our supply of willpower, we may end up neglecting our goals.

Goals rely on extrinsic motivation. But habits, once formed, operate automatically. Habits put our brains on autopilot. Once we develop a habit, our brains actually transform to make a required behavior easier to complete. By switching our focus from achieving specific goals to creating positive long-term habits, we can make continuous improvement a way of life. This is evident from the documented habits of many successful people. For example, Buffett and Munger have a habit of reading for hours every day. According to Duhigg's research, habits make up 40 percent of our waking hours. These actions add up and make us who we are. And the effects of these actions compound. Every single manifestation of our thoughts and emotions is a direct consequence of a succession of habits that have been compounding through the years. As the saying goes, "First we make our habits, then our habits make us."

When you suddenly drop or change a bad habit, it can feel excruciating, or at least quite uncomfortable, for a short while. But just as the body adjusts to a changing environment through a process called homeostasis, we have a similar homeostatic ability to adjust to unfamiliar behavior. We usually can regulate ourselves physiologically and psychologically, adjusting to the new circumstances quite quickly. For some of your long-standing and deep-rooted habits, it may be more effective to take small steps to ease into unwinding them. You may have spent decades repeating, cementing, and fortifying those habits, so it is good to give yourself some time to unravel them, one step at a time.

Whenever you're having trouble sticking to a new habit, try a smaller version until it becomes automatic. Do less than you're capable of, but do it consistently. That is the key to compounding. You have to build a program that you can do for decades, not weeks or months. It's far easier and requires a lot less energy to take off once and maintain a regular speed (even if it is slower than everyone else) all along the way. Start with the easiest things so you gain momentum and confidence to tackle the more difficult things later. Pursue small, incremental victories. A small, concrete win creates momentum and affirms our faith in our further success. Confidence is like a muscle. The more you use it, the stronger it gets.

The best way to change is by doing mental exercises. Enlist the help of Duhigg's three-step "habit loop" to connect the rewards to the actions, rewiring your brain to love learning and beneficial change. The first step is a cue, some "trigger that tells your brain to go into automatic mode and which habit to use," according to Duhigg. Step two is the routine, "which can be physical or mental or emotional." Finally, there is the reward, which helps your brain figure out whether the particular loop in question is "worth remembering for the future." (This anticipation and craving is the key to operant conditioning.) Repetition reinforces this loop until, over time, it becomes automatic. The best way to deal with a habit is to respect the habit loop. Duhigg says, "To change a habit, you must keep the old cue, and deliver the old reward, but insert a new routine."[8]

We can work to change the stimulus that releases dopamine in our brain. Our brain is built to seek positive self-image updates. We can work on fine-tuning the routine of what gives us the good feeling in our narrative. We can work to get the reward of feeling good about ourselves from being a genuine credit giver, a candid mistake admitter, an honest finder of mistakes even in good outcomes, and a keen learner.

Habits form the foundation of productivity. The more you do automatically, the more you are subsequently freed to do. This effect compounds. Focus on your environment (virtual and physical), because it nudges your subconscious and affects your habits. It is more effective to design an environment in which you don't need willpower than to rely on willpower to conquer your surroundings. Set up an environment that plays to your strengths and minimizes your weaknesses. Remember, acknowledging your weaknesses is not the same as surrendering to them. Acknowledgement is the first positive step toward overcoming weaknesses.

We likely have good reasons for our bad habits. Our experiences to date have set us in stone to a certain extent, and the older we are, the more likely that is to be true. Buffett often says, "The chains of habit are too light to be felt until they are too heavy to be broken."[9] We all are slaves of habits. Once a habit becomes ingrained, it can last for life, so inculcate good habits. Most bad habits creep in slowly. Be careful of making small compromises. The adverse (although subtle) effect of such actions compound over time. A single poor habit, which doesn't look like much in the moment, ultimately can land you miles off course from the direction of your goals and the life you desire.

The real question isn't "Who am I?" The real question is "Who am I becoming?" We are constantly evolving, but the person you will be in the next five to ten years is feeding on the habits and decisions you make today.

Our decisions determine our trajectory, but our habits determine how far we travel along that path. To paraphrase James Clear, "Our outcomes are a lagging measure of our habits. Our net worth is a lagging measure of our financial habits. Our knowledge is a lagging measure of our learning habits. Our health is a lagging measure of our eating habits. Our energy is a lagging measure of our sleep habits. Our fitness is a lagging measure of our exercise habits." We get what we repeat, so our current trajectory matters more than our current results. Success is earned—one day at a time.

The seeds of greatness are planted in the daily grind. In his book *Good to Great*, Jim Collins explains that in the transition from good to great, the flywheel starts slowly, and through consistent, small actions, momentum builds. Most people end up in this cycle: hard, hard, hard, hurt. I'd rather go: slow, slow, slow, never stop. Slow but consistent gains add up much faster than you can imagine. Small, positive changes add up to massive improvements over time (figure 32.1). If we can get 5 percent better every year, then we will be about twice as good in less than fifteen years. In less than thirty years, our growth will be 4×. This is how

FIGURE 32.1 This is compounding good habits in action.

Source: Behavior Gap.

people with average intellect surpass far more intelligent people. It is also why Peter Kaufman says, "The most powerful force that could be potentially harnessed is dogged incremental constant progress over a very long time frame."[10]

Compounded efforts in the right direction within the various important areas of our lives lead to increasingly higher lows and lower volatility. Little things can quickly add up. Do not underestimate what you can achieve in the long term. For example, if you don't trust your social skills, start going out once a week and meet one new individual. After two years, that adds up to more than one hundred new connections. Social self-confidence is built on habits.

Time is the greatest ally of compounding and confers exponential powers upon those who think and act long term. This is because n is the only element in the compound interest equation that exists in the exponent and is the numeric that the entire expression is raised to the power of. Maintain a steadfast consistency in your efforts over a long period of time and you will surpass all expectations. Whether at the scale of the universe, civilization, or individual lives, time is a translating machine constantly processing the input of efforts. An "overnight success" is the result of many compounded efforts over a long period of time that lacked the key to connect it all together. No magic bullet exists for success in life—only compounding efforts in the right direction and some good luck.

In my view, Buffett's greatness does not stem from his superlative investment track record or even his highly generous philanthropic contributions. His greatest gift to humanity is a well-documented life in which he has led by example in demonstrating to all of us how integrity, honesty, ethics, hard work, independent thinking, following one's passion, and embracing lifelong learning can lead to immense success. These are great habits and virtues to adopt.

> When you improve a little each day, eventually big things occur. When you improve conditioning a little each day, eventually you have a big improvement in conditioning. Not tomorrow, not the next day, but eventually a big gain is made. Don't look for the big, quick improvement. Seek the small improvement one day at a time. That's the only way it happens—and when it happens, it lasts.
> —John Wooden

Compounding Wealth

> *Good investing isn't necessarily about earning the highest returns, because the highest returns tend to be one-off hits that kill your confidence when they end. It's about earning pretty good returns that you can stick with for a long period of time [emphasis added]. That's when compounding runs wild.*

> —Morgan Housel

The first thing to realize is that it takes a long time. I started when I was eleven. Accumulating money is a little like having a snowball going downhill; it's important to have a very long hill. I've had a fifty-six-year hill. It's important to work in sticky snow and you need a little snowball to start with, which I got from delivering the Post *actually. It's better if you're not in too much of a hurry and keep doing sound things [emphasis added].*

—Warren Buffett

Buffett has always considered the long-term game to be the best game. This circles back to his love for compound interest, which was so strong that when his wife, Susie, wanted to give to charity, years ago, Buffett insisted on waiting, so that eventually the giveaway could be far greater. Buffett is a man who thinks really long term—in ten-year or even twenty-year increments. He doesn't waste a dollar today because he knows how compound interest will make that dollar worth more in the future. A lot more. The human mind is not naturally wired to think in exponential terms and thus fails to intuitively appreciate the incredible power of compounding.

The greatest shortcoming of the human race is our inability to understand the exponential function.
—Al Bartlett

According to the rule of seventy-two, we double our capital every three years by compounding at 26 percent, ten times in ten years, and one hundred times in twenty years. The day I understood the dynamics of reinvested profit and compound interest, I immediately knew that I was going to become wealthy in my lifetime. I just needed to get started. I began looking forward to every day as a new opportunity to learn and improve. The goals of investment should be happiness, joy, growth, intellectual satisfaction, and eventually, peace, and serenity. Wealth and financial prosperity are natural by-products of lifelong learning.

You will often notice a common trait among many value investors: the day we finally realize the power of compound interest is a transformational moment for us, and we embrace frugality and simple living as a way of life. (Frugality isn't about avoiding spending money, it's about spending money only on things that add value to your life.) The key to wealth creation in investing is time, and the opportunity costs of not inculcating a good saving habit early in life can be huge. Let us look at an example of two individuals who make all the same choices except one—their use of time.

Paul is eighteen years old. He gets an after-school job and opens a Roth IRA. He saves $5,000 per year in it and continues doing this until he turns seventy years old. He is a know-nothing investor, invests in cheap, low-cost index funds, dollar-cost averages, reinvests his dividends, and earns the same nominal return the market has for the past century (around 10 percent). As a result, he ends up with a little more than $7 million in wealth.

Peter is also eighteen years old. He also gets an after-school job, but he doesn't save anything as he wants to engage in instant gratification and conspicuous consumption during his "fun" years. He waits until he is thirty years old, at which point, he opens a retirement account, saves $5,000 per year in it, and then does all the same things as Paul. Peter is only $60,000 in total contributions behind Paul, and he still has forty years to go before he turns seventy, so he figures it isn't too bad. When he reaches retirement, though, he has only $2.2 million.

A mere $60,000 difference between Paul and Peter in cumulative investment turned into a $4.8 million difference in net worth. This example shows, as John Bogle would call it, "the relentless rules of humble arithmetic."[11]

Time is power in investing. This is best illustrated by the timeless tale of Benjamin Franklin's experiment with compound interest, which was driven by the strong optimism he had for his newly formed country at the time:

> When Franklin died in 1790, he left a gift of $5,000 to each of his two favorite cities, Boston and Philadelphia. He stipulated that the money was to be invested and could be paid out at two specific dates, the first 100 years and the second 200 years after the date of the gift. After 100 years, each city was allowed to withdraw $500,000 for public works projects. After 200 years, in 1991, they received the balance—*which had compounded to approximately $20 million for each city*. Franklin's example teaches all of us, in a dramatic way, the power of compounding. As Franklin himself liked to describe the benefits of compounding, "*Money makes money. And the money that money makes, makes money* [emphasis added]."[12]

If you remain unconvinced about the all-powerful role of time in compounding wealth, consider this: If Warren Buffett had begun investing at age thirty, he would be worth "only" about $2 billion today. Instead, he started in third grade, accumulated $1 million by the age of thirty, and has around $81 billion today—an extra $79 billion. And more than 99 percent of Buffett's net worth was created after his fiftieth birthday. The key takeaway is this: the power of compounding is back-loaded. Rule number 1: Never lose money. Rule number 2: Live a long and healthy life.

Here is the mathematical equation for successfully compounding wealth:

+ Add to your savings every month;
− Eliminate biases, greed, and wasteful expenses;
× Multiply your time horizon;
÷ Divide across asset classes as appropriate for your stage in life and your personal circumstances;
∧ Achieve the exponential power of compounding.

The "wasteful expenses" in this equation include excessive taxes on capital gains because of frequent churning, and frictional costs, including brokerage commissions, and statutory charges.

> Tax-paying investors will realize a far, far greater sum from a single investment that compounds internally at a given rate than from a succession of investments compounding at the same rate.
> —Warren Buffett

In his 1989 letter, Buffett illustrated the importance of not churning one's portfolio too frequently:

> Imagine that Berkshire had only $1, which we put in a security that doubled by yearend and was then sold. Imagine further that we used the after-tax proceeds to repeat this process in each of the next 19 years, scoring a double each time. At the end of the 20 years, the 34 percent capital gains tax that we would have paid on the profits from each sale would have delivered about $13,000 to the government and we would be left with about $25,250. Not bad. If, however, we made a single fantastic investment that itself doubled 20 times during the 20 years, our dollar would grow to $1,048,576. Were we then to cash out, we would pay a 34 percent tax of roughly $356,500 and be left with about $692,000.
>
> The sole reason for this staggering difference in results would be the timing of tax payments. Interestingly, the government would gain from Scenario 2 in exactly the same 27:1 ratio as we—taking in taxes of $356,500 vs. $13,000— though, admittedly, it would have to wait for its money.[13]

In both cases, the investment doubles annually, but in the end, we have a staggering twenty-seven times difference. No wonder Munger says, "The first rule of compounding: Never interrupt it unnecessarily."[14] The way to wealth is to buy right and hold on. By doing so, an investor minimizes paperwork, transaction costs, and capital gains taxes. To reap genuine riches, one needs to invest in long-term winners and hold on for compounded, tax-free growth. No more effective tax haven exists than unrealized appreciation in a long-lived, soundly growing company. Compounding, combined with patience, is an incredible force over time.

In addition to the greater tax outgo, be mindful of the huge impact that tiny frictional costs can have on your net worth in the long run. A small leak can sink a great ship.

In the course of our daily lives, we treat a 2 percent charge as a small amount. In the world of investing, however, 2 percent is a huge deal. It has the potential to change your life completely. A tiny difference in incremental returns over a long period of time results in a massive difference in accumulated wealth. The effects of compounding are too small to be noticed until they are too large to be ignored.

To illustrate the impact a tiny 2 percent of savings in frictional costs can make in the long run, let's assume that you invest $30,000 today in three fixed income instruments yielding 7 percent, 9 percent, and 11 percent, respectively. Figure 32.2 shows what this investment will look like after forty years.

Now it is the turn of equities—the greatest long-term wealth-creating asset class. Figure 32.3 shows what happens if you invest the same sum of money in

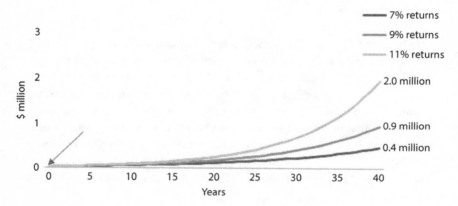

FIGURE 32.2 The 2 percent difference.

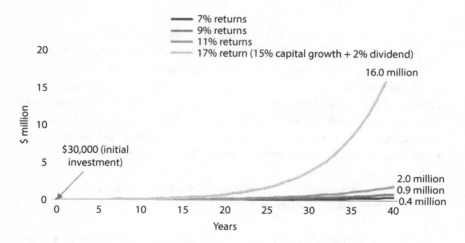

FIGURE 32.3 This is compounding wealth in action.

a portfolio of high-quality stocks with an average annual earnings growth of 15 percent and a 2 percent dividend, for a total of 17 percent return.

Instead of treating dividends as "free money" and engaging in mental accounting, investors should resist instant gratification and always immediately reinvest their dividends. Reinvesting your dividends through a dividend reinvestment plan (DRIP) is a great way to take maximum advantage of the power of long-term compounding. A DRIP automatically uses your dividends to buy more shares of the holdings in your portfolio. You can enroll all your stocks in a DRIP through your brokerage firm. They do not charge commissions or have minimum investment requirements and you gain the added benefit of dollar-cost averaging. After enough years go by, the benefits accrue in the form of higher dividends that may be a multiple of the original investment.

This is the power of compound interest. In addition to earning returns on the money you invest, you also earn returns on those returns over time. This compound growth is what causes your wealth to snowball over time.

When we reinvest dividends, we enjoy the power of double compounding, or "compound interest on steroids."

This shows you the incredible wealth-creation potential of equities in the long term. And our example assumed that you did not make even a single additional contribution throughout your earning years. Just imagine how your compounding engine will skyrocket once you make regular contributions, too. The final figure then becomes truly astonishing.

Compounding Knowledge

When we bought See's Candy, we didn't know the power of a good brand. Over time, we just discovered that we could raise prices 10 percent a year and no one cared. Learning that changed Berkshire. It was really important. You have to be a lifelong learner to appreciate this stuff. We think of it as a moral duty. Increasing rationality and improving as much as you can no matter your age or experience is a moral duty *[emphasis added].*

—Charlie Munger

Buffett articulated his zeal for constant learning in his 1991 lecture at the University of Notre Dame:

I read all kinds of business publications. I read a lot of industry publications. . . . I'll grab whatever comes in the morning. *American Banker* comes every day, so I'll read that. I'll read the *Wall Street Journal*. Obviously. I'll read *Editor and Publisher*, I'll read *Broadcasting*, I'll read *Property Casualty Review*, I'll read Jeffrey Meyer's *Beverage Digest*. I'll read everything. And I own 100 shares of almost every stock I can think of just so I know I'll get all the reports. And I carry around prospectuses and proxy material.[15]

In a similar vein, during the 2001 Berkshire annual meeting, Buffett remarked, "When I started, I went through the pages of the manuals page by page. I mean, I probably went through 20,000 pages in the Moody's industrial, transportation, banks, and finance manuals. And I did it twice. And I actually, you know, looked at every business. I didn't look very hard at some."[16]

Munger sees his knowledge accumulation as an acquired, rather than natural, genius. And he gives all the credit to studying: "Neither Warren nor I is smart enough to make the decisions with no time to think. We make actual decisions very rapidly, but that's because we've spent so much time preparing ourselves by quietly sitting and reading and thinking."[17]

One of my favorite Buffett stories on the virtues of building up one's mental database over time comes from a 1993 interview of Buffett with George Goodman, popularly known by the pen name of "Adam Smith":

Adam Smith: If a younger Warren Buffett were coming into the investment field today, what areas would you tell him to point himself in?

Warren Buffett: Well, if he were doing—if he were coming in and working with small sums of capital I'd tell him to do exactly what I did forty-odd years ago, *which is to learn about every company in the United States that has publicly traded securities, and that bank of knowledge will do him or her terrific good over time.*

Smith: But there's 27,000 public companies.

Buffett: Well, *start with the A's* [emphasis added].[18]

Buffett acquired many of his mental models by reading hundreds of annual reports every year and by running business operations for decades. He applied these models to analyzing more businesses and used the accumulated knowledge to make further investments. In his 1997 speech at the California Institute of Technology, Buffett highlighted this very point:

Owning See's Candies, which we bought in 1972, really taught me a lot about the value of brands and what could be done with them, so I understood Coca-Cola better when it came along in 1988 than if I had never been in See's. We've got a profit of close to $10 billion dollars in Coke. Now a significant part of that is attributable to the fact that we bought See's Candy for $25 million dollars in 1972.

The nice thing about investments is that knowledge accumulates on you
[emphasis added] *and if you understand a business or industry once you are
going to understand it for the next fifty years.*[19]

Indeed, great benefits accrue from gradually building up a large mental
database of businesses and industries, because knowledge builds on previous
foundations and grows over time, just like compound interest.

And this, in turn, leads to pattern recognition.

Learning about the concept of local economies of scale from Bruce
Greenwald's book *Competition Demystified* helped me identify Hester
Biosciences. Learning about the capital cycle theory from Edward Chancellor's
book *Capital Returns* helped me identify HEG. Learning about the banking
industry from Tamal Bandyopadhyay's book on HDFC Bank helped me
identify Bandhan Bank, AU Small Finance Bank, and Ujjivan Small Finance
Bank. Learning about the importance of project execution capabilities from
Dilip Buildcon helped me identify PSP Projects. Learning about the housing
finance industry from Can Fin Homes helped me identify Aavas Financiers.
Learning about the microfinance industry from Bharat Financial helped me
identify CreditAccess Grameen.

This is compounding knowledge in action.

When we compound knowledge, we advance not only ourselves but also
the world at large. It takes a small individual action to kick-start a learning
revolution.

This is what Confucius wrote in "Higher Education":

When things are investigated, knowledge is extended.
When knowledge is extended, the will becomes sincere.
When the will is sincere, the heart is set right.
When the heart is right, the personal life is cultivated.
When personal lives are cultivated,
families become harmonious.
When families are harmonious,
government becomes orderly.
And when government is orderly,
there will be peace in the world.[20]

And this is what Li Lu told the students at the Guanghua School of Management
in China in October 2015:

When two people exchange knowledge, they learn more than just what the
other is thinking; their meeting will also create the sparks of new ideas.
The sharing of knowledge requires no exchange like trading corn for milk.

But when you combine knowledge you begin to see growth happen in large increments thanks to the benefits of compounding. Only when each exchange can produce such large incremental benefits will society be able to speedily create wealth.

This kind of continuous inter-personal exchange multiplied billions of times created the modern free market economy. And this is Civilization 3.0. Continuous, sustainable economic growth is only possible with this kind of exchange. This kind of economic system is the only way to fully release mankind's energy and true motivations. This system is probably the greatest innovation in the history of mankind [emphasis added].[21]

Confucius and Li Lu make us aware of our impact on the world when we engage in constant learning. But in my view, compounding knowledge is so powerful that its impact is not limited to our world.

The reverberations are felt across the entire universe.

Ray Dalio explains this in his book *Principles*:

It is a reality that each one of us is only one of about seven billion of our species alive today and that our species is only one of about ten million species on our planet. Earth is just one of about 100 billion planets in our galaxy, which is just one of about two trillion galaxies in the universe. And our lifetimes are only about 1/3,000 of humanity's existence, which itself is only 1/20,000 of the Earth's existence. In other words, we are unbelievably tiny and short-lived and no matter what we accomplish, our impact will be insignificant. At the same time, we instinctually want to matter and to evolve, and we can matter a tiny bit—*and it's all those tiny bits that add up to drive the evolution of the universe* [emphasis added].[22]

Profound.

Compounding Goodwill

Let no one ever come to you without leaving better and happier.

—Mother Teresa

In March 2015, Mohnish Pabrai and Guy Spier gave a talk at the Stanford Graduate School of Business. The core theme of the talk was the concept of giving without expecting anything in return: of being a giver, not a taker. Guy talked about the extraordinary power of compounding goodwill when we

FIGURE 32.4 Goodwill over time.

Source: Jana Vembunarayanan (blog), https://janav.wordpress.com/2015/07/18/think-long-term/.

are a giver. In the initial years, we won't see much happening to our goodwill account. But, as years progress, goodwill snowballs and starts to grow exponentially (figure 32.4). Buffett's goodwill account is at its peak and is poised to grow at a scintillating pace well beyond his lifetime.

> When you get to my age, you'll really measure your success in life by how many of the people you want to have love you actually do love you. . . . The more you give love away, the more you get.
> —Warren Buffett

Giving makes us richer than getting. The selfless act of helping others unconditionally is such a great virtue that I would like to illustrate it with an example from my life that is close to my heart.

During my initial years as an investor, when I was really struggling, I looked to Ian Cassel of MicroCapClub for constant inspiration, because he regularly posted motivational content on his blog. As a mark of my gratitude for his positive influence, I began sharing content that I thought would be helpful for him through LinkedIn. As is always the case with compounding, for a long time, nothing seemed to happen.

And then this happened (figure 32.5).

Ian Cassel ✔
@iancassel

It's great to finally see @Gautam__Baid on twitter. He's been sending me great information, articles, for a long time.

3:29 AM - 14 Dec 2016

Ian Cassel ✔
@iancassel

It was great to finally talk to @Gautam__Baid today. An amazing story of perseverance and he is only getting started.

11:52 AM - 8 Mar 2017

Ian Cassel ✔
@iancassel

A great interview with @Gautam__Baid
gurufocus.com/news/495551/19...

Strong brands with share of mind—which confer pricing power, network effects, high switching costs, patents, favorable access to a strategic raw material resource or proprietary technology and government regulation which prevents easy entry – these can confer a strong competitive advantage which in turn enables high returns on invested capital for long periods of time (also known as the competitive advantage period or CAP). Growing firms with longer CAPs are more valuable in terms of net present value. One of the most highly underappreciated sources of a sustainable and difficult to replicate competitive advantage is "culture," best epitomized by Berkshire Hathaway. To illustrate the critical importance of culture just consider this: Between 1957 to 1969, Buffett did not mention the word "culture" even once in his annual letters. From 1970 to 2016, he has mentioned the word 30 times! Some of my favorite books on competitive advantage are "The Little Book

7:53 PM - 28 Mar 2017

Ian Cassel ✔
@iancassel

Great dinner with @BrentBeshore @morganhousel @farnamstreet @iddings_sean @Gautam__Baid @MikeDDKing @jtkoster

8:25 PM - 20 Sep 2017

FIGURE 32.5 This is compounding goodwill in action.

Source: https://twitter.com/iancassel/status/808982314449600512; https://twitter.com/iancassel/status /839549332609241090; https://twitter.com/iancassel/status/846903205439037440; https://twitter.com /iancassel/status/910691321031077888.

Spend time building new relationships. Too many stop building relationships after school, or after marriage, and then you find yourself in a rut and your only relationships represent who you used to be & not where you want to go.

—Ian Cassel

Making connections by e-mail or phone is nothing like meeting in person. You need to really make a genuine effort to create strong bonds with people who are on the same path as you. If you do this with utmost sincerity, your network of compounded relationships will open many unexpected, joyful doors for you in the future. Just take that first small step. You will be mighty surprised at how far you end up reaching with regard to building your relationships. Never underestimate the power of a heartfelt handwritten note. It can potentially open the door for serendipity to enter your life. Be humble with everyone you meet irrespective of who they are and be fully present and genuine. In addition to this, give due credit generously to those who deserve it, and connect people who would benefit from knowing each other.

The takeaway from connecting the philosophies described in this chapter is to think and act long term—really long term. The other key insights are as follows:

- It takes a long time to create anything that is valuable.
- Work hard every day, even without seeing any results in the short term.
- Keep doing it consistently for a long time without giving up.
- Enjoy the process and live life according to the inner scorecard.
- Do not compare yourself to others. Instead, always endeavor to become a better version of yourself compared to what you were the previous day.

Anybody who is doing all of these things is most likely going to succeed in his or her pursuit in life. This is exactly what Buffett meant when he said, "Games are won by players who focus on the field, not the ones looking at the scoreboard."[23]

Mahatma Gandhi described compounding in all its glory when he said these words: "Your beliefs become your thoughts. Your thoughts become your words. Your words become your actions. Your actions become your habits. Your habits become your values. Your values become your destiny."

It all starts with one small belief, one small thought, one small word, one small action, one small habit, one small value.

And that makes one big destiny.

A happy, healthy, and successful life follows the same route. One small step at a time.

Take care, and keep learning.

APPENDIX A

SLOW DANCE

DAVID L. WEATHERFORD

Have you ever watched kids on a merry-go-round,
or listened to rain slapping the ground?
Ever followed a butterfly's erratic flight,
or gazed at the sun fading into the night?

You better slow down, don't dance so fast,
time is short, the music won't last.

Do you run through each day on the fly,
when you ask "How are you?" do you hear the reply?
When the day is done, do you lie in your bed,
with the next hundred chores running through your head?

You better slow down, don't dance so fast,
time is short, the music won't last.

Ever told your child, we'll do it tomorrow,
and in your haste, not see his sorrow?
Ever lost touch, let a friendship die,
'cause you never had time to call and say hi?

You better slow down, don't dance so fast,
time is short, the music won't last.

When you run so fast to get somewhere,
you miss half the fun of getting there.
When you worry and hurry through your day,
It's like an unopened gift thrown away.

Life isn't a race, so take it slower,
hear the music before your song is over.[1]

APPENDIX B

IF—

RUDYARD KIPLING

If you can keep your head when all about you
Are losing theirs and blaming it on you,
If you can trust yourself when all men doubt you,
But make allowance for their doubting too;
If you can wait and not be tired by waiting,
Or being lied about, don't deal in lies,
Or being hated, don't give way to hating,
And yet don't look too good, nor talk too wise:

If you can dream—and not make dreams your master;
If you can think—and not make thoughts your aim;
If you can meet with Triumph and Disaster
And treat those two impostors just the same;
If you can bear to hear the truth you've spoken
Twisted by knaves to make a trap for fools,
Or watch the things you gave your life to, broken,
And stoop and build 'em up with worn-out tools:

If you can make one heap of all your winnings
And risk it on one turn of pitch-and-toss,
And lose, and start again at your beginnings
And never breathe a word about your loss;
If you can force your heart and nerve and sinew
To serve your turn long after they are gone,
And so hold on when there is nothing in you
Except the Will which says to them: "Hold on!"

If you can talk with crowds and keep your virtue,
Or walk with Kings—nor lose the common touch,
If neither foes nor loving friends can hurt you,
If all men count with you, but none too much;
If you can fill the unforgiving minute
With sixty seconds' worth of distance run,
Yours is the Earth and everything that's in it,
And—which is more—you'll be a Man, my son.[1]

ACKNOWLEDGMENTS

The best thing I did was to choose the right heroes.

—Warren Buffett

Our personal philosophies are largely a product of what we practice and who we follow as our role models and teachers. I have been fortunate to have learned from some truly great ones.

Warren Buffett and Adam Smith enlightened me on the virtues of living life according to the inner scorecard.

Charlie Munger inspired me to embark on a path of lifelong learning and made me aware of the power of incentives in any given situation.

Benjamin Graham taught me the importance of having the right temperament in investing, looking at stocks as a part ownership stake in a business, profiting from Mr. Market's follies, and emphasizing the margin of safety at all times.

Benjamin Franklin taught me the virtues of good personhood and focusing on daily rituals with complete integrity.

Napoleon Hill, David Schwartz, and Ian Cassel taught me that the right mind-set is the starting point for all riches.

Geoff Colvin, Daniel Coyle, Cal Newport, and Anders Ericsson educated me on the science behind skill development.

Charles Duhigg and James Clear educated me on the science behind positive habit formation.

Robert Maurer and Darren Hardy enlightened me on the incredible power of compounding small, consistent, positive actions over a long period of time.

Gillian Zoe Segal and Scott Adams showed me how one can fail repeatedly and still win big.

Guy Spier, Vishal Khandelwal, and Morgan Housel inspired me to become a better human being.

Robert Kiyosaki taught me how to make money work for me by building assets to generate regular passive income.

George Clason taught me the fundamental first rule of building wealth: pay yourself first.

Thomas Stanley, William Danko, David Bach, and Harv Eker taught me the virtues of frugality.

Shane Parrish and Professor Sanjay Bakshi taught me how goodwill compounds when we generously share knowledge with others.

Mohnish Pabrai taught me the importance of being unreasonable in investing by keeping a very high hurdle rate for incoming investments.

Basant Maheshwari inspired me to dream big in the stock market.

Nassim Nicholas Taleb, Max Gunther, and Leonard Mlodinow helped me appreciate the role of luck, chance, serendipity, and randomness in life.

Taleb also highlighted the presence of high-impact, unexpected events in our world. Kenneth Posner shared a pragmatic approach for being better prepared to cope with their adverse effects.

Sun Tzu, Michael Porter, W. Chan Kim, Youngme Moon, and Bruce Greenwald educated me on competitive strategy.

Peter Bernstein, Howard Marks, and Seth Klarman gave me the wisdom to appreciate the role of risk and risk management.

Peter Thiel taught me the significance of monopolies, power laws, and highly innovative companies.

Clayton Christensen made me aware of the constant threats posed by disruptive innovation.

Peter Bevelin gave me some of the finest pieces of work on multidisciplinary thinking and inversion.

Thornton Oglove, Howard Schilit, and Charles Mulford educated me on how to assess the quality of reported earnings.

Stephen Penman and Baruch Lev taught me the finer nuances of interpreting accounting information from the vantage point of a business analyst and a value investor.

Daniel Kahneman, Amos Tversky, Richard Thaler, Dan Ariely, and James Montier educated me on the various cognitive biases. Herbert Simon enlightened me on bounded rationality, that is, the cognitive limitations of our minds.

Fred Schwed made me aware of the inherent conflicts of interest in the investment industry.

Robert Cialdini made me aware of the various psychological tactics used by compliance practitioners.

Nate Silver and Philip Tetlock educated me on the follies of forecasting and how we can improve our skills at making estimates through probabilistic thinking, Bayesian belief updating, and the use of relevant base rates.

John Allen Paulos, Barbara Oakley, and Jana Vembunarayanan taught me how to engage in intelligent mathematical thinking.

Darrell Huff and Charles Wheelan taught me how to interpret statistics more analytically.

Atul Gawande and Michael Shearns educated me on the vital role of checklists in improved decision making.

Phil Rosenzweig, Elliot Aronson, and Duncan Watts made me aware of the widespread prevalence of hindsight bias.

Michael Mauboussin and Annie Duke taught me how to distinguish luck from skill. Mauboussin also educated me on how to distinguish between knowledge of a company's fundamentals and the current market expectations implied by the stock price.

Jason Zweig and Gary Belsky taught me how an understanding of neuroeconomics helps avoid money mistakes.

John Burr Williams, Alfred Rappaport, Bharat Shah, and Utpal Sheth taught me the fundamental principles of value creation.

Charles Mackay, Charles Kindleberger, John Galbraith, John Brooks, Edward Chancellor, Robert Shiller, and Maggie Mahar educated me on the history of market cycles, speculative manias, and the subsequent busts.

Peter Senge and Donella Meadows educated me on systems thinking and a more interconnected view of the world.

George Soros, Benoit Mandelbrot, and Richard Bookstaber made me aware of the intricate and highly dynamic feedback loops present in markets and social systems.

John Maynard Keynes enlightened me on the significance of prevailing sentiments in markets and economies, and the critical role of timely government intervention.

Burton Malkiel, Charles Ellis, and John Bogle taught me the importance of minimizing costs and staying the course.

Phil Fisher, Peter Lynch, Ralph Wanger, Pat Dorsey, Tom Gayner, Terry Smith, Chuck Akre, Peter Cundill, William O'Neil, Jesse Stine, and Nicolas Darvas taught me how to pick a stock.

Jesse Livermore taught me how to hold on to a stock and to respect the market's collective wisdom above all else.

Thomas Phelps and Thomas Russo taught me the virtues of patience in investing.

Anurag Sharma taught me how to actively look for disconfirming evidence.

Gustave Le Bon educated me on the social dynamics of crowd psychology.

Professor Aswath Damodaran taught me how to distinguish between the possible, the plausible, and the probable in investing.

Sam Zell educated me on the deep significance of the fundamental economic principles of demand and supply.

Maurice Schiller, Joel Greenblatt, and Martin Whitman taught me how to analyze special situations in investing.

Laura Rittenhouse taught me the importance of candor in reporting to stakeholders.

Roger von Oech taught me how to engage in creative thinking.

Richard Feynman taught me the difference between knowing the name of something and knowing something.

Seneca, Aurelius, Epictetus, and Ryan Holiday enlightened me on the virtues of stoicism and of being in control of our personal reaction to any event in our lives.

Will Durant, Ariel Durant, and Yuval Noah Harari educated me on the history of human civilization.

Steven Pinker and Hans Rosling instilled great optimism in me about the constant, ongoing improvements in our world on a daily basis.

My life truly epitomizes Isaac Newton's saying: "If I have seen further, it is by standing upon the shoulders of giants."

The Joys of Compounding is my heartfelt tribute to all of my teachers who helped me achieve financial independence, become a better and wiser person, and embark on the path to a fulfilling and meaningful life. Over the years, I have learned vicariously through the writings and speeches of others. Readers have observed the influence of the many great minds whose wisdom has been shared throughout the book. They are duly referenced where appropriate. Any omissions are not intentional. Mistakes are mine alone.

Being a value investor, I always had a quiet dream of working with Columbia University Press on a book someday. It has been my privilege to work with the remarkable Myles Thompson and his all-star team.

I appreciate John Mihaljevic, Vishal Khandelwal, John Huber, and Sean Iddings for taking the time to review the manuscript and sharing thoughtful input and feedback.

I further appreciate Craig Pierce of Harriman House for giving me his kind approval to share detailed extracts from Max Gunther's works in this book.

A very special note of thanks to Guy Spier for penning the foreword.

Without Warren Buffett's permission to quote generously from his shareholder letters, this book would not have been possible. My gratitude to him and to Debbie Bosanek, his assistant, is immeasurable.

Thanks to my family and friends for their love, motivation, and support over the years.

Last but not least, obvious and immediate gratitude is due to you and all the readers.

Thank you all.

NOTES

1. The Best Investment You Can Make Is an Investment in Yourself

1. Charlie Munger, USC School of Law commencement speech, University of Southern California Gould School of Law, May 13, 2007, Los Angeles, CA, https://genius.com/Charlie-munger-usc-law-commencement-speech-annotated.
2. John Nieuwenberg, "Warren Buffett Just Sits and Reads All Day," W5 Coaching, accessed December 5, 2019, https://w5coaching.com/warren-buffett-just-sits-reads-day/.
3. Charlie Munger, *Berkshire Hathaway 2014 Annual Letter to Shareholders*, February 27, 2015, http://www.berkshirehathaway.com/letters/2014ltr.pdf.
4. Morgan Housel, "The Peculiar Habits of Successful People," *USA Today*, August 24, 2014, https://www.usatoday.com/story/money/personalfinance/2014/08/24/peculiar-habits-of-successful-people/14447531.
5. Steve Jordon, "Investors Earn Handsome Paychecks by Handling Buffett's Business," *Omaha World-Herald*, April 28, 2013, https://www.omaha.com/money/investors-earn-handsome-paychecks-by-handling-buffett-s-business/article_bb1fc40f-e6f9-549d-be2f-be1ef4c0da03.html.
6. Arthur Conan Doyle, *The Memoirs of Sherlock Holmes: The Reigate Puzzle* (CreateSpace Independent Publishing Platform, 2016).
7. Michael D. Eisner and Aaron R. Cohen, *Working Together: Why Great Partnerships Succeed* (New York: Harper Business, 2012).
8. Patricia Sellers, "Warren Buffett and Charlie Munger's Best Advice," *Fortune*, October 31, 2013, http://fortune.com/2013/10/31/warren-buffett-and-charlie-mungers-best-advice.
9. Aaron Task, "Money 101: Q&A with Warren Buffett," *Yahoo Finance*, April 8, 2013, https://finance.yahoo.com/news/money-101--q-a-with-warren-buffett-140409456.html.
10. Alice Schroeder, *The Snowball: Warren Buffett and the Business of Life* (New York: Bantam, 2009).

2. Becoming a Learning Machine

1. Whitney Tilson, "Notes from the 2003 Wesco Annual Meeting," Whitney Tilson's Value Investing Website, http://www.tilsonfunds.com/motley_berkshire_wscmtg03notes.php.
2. Charlie Munger, See's Candy Seventy-Fifth Anniversary Lunch, March 1998, Los Angeles, CA.
3. Morgan Housel, "Ideas That Changed My Life," *Collaborative Fund* (blog), March 7, 2018, http://www.collaborativefund.com/blog/ideas-that-changed-my-life.
4. Andrew McVagh, "Charlie Munger's System of Mental Models: How to Think Your Way to Success," My Mental Models (blog), August 7, 2018, https://www.mymentalmodels.info/charlie-munger-mental-models/.
5. Shane Parrish, "Why You Shouldn't Slog Through Books," *Farnam Street* (blog), September 2017, https://www.fs.blog/2017/09/shouldnt-slog-books.
6. Morgan Housel, "How to Read Financial News," *Collaborative Fund* (blog), December 6, 2017, http://www.collaborativefund.com/blog/how-to-read-financial-news.
7. Nassim Nicholas Taleb, *Fooled by Randomness: The Hidden Role of Chance in Life and in the Markets* (New York: Random House, 2005).
8. Goodreads.com, https://www.goodreads.com/quotes/9122-the-smallest-bookstore-still-contains-more-ideas-of-worth-than.
9. Nassim Nicholas Taleb, *Antifragile: Things That Gain from Disorder* (New York: Random House, 2014).
10. "No. 18 Naval Ravikant—Angel Philosopher," The Knowledge Project with Shane Parrish, February 27, 2017, audio, https://theknowledgeproject.libsyn.com/2017/02.
11. James Clear, "First Principles: Elon Musk on the Power of Thinking for Yourself," The Mission, February 2, 2018, https://medium.com/the-mission/first-principles-elon-musk-on-the-power-of-thinking-for-yourself-8b0f275af361.
12. Elon Musk, "I Am Elon Musk, CEO/CTO of a Rocket Company, AMA!" Reddit, 2015, https://www.reddit.com/r/IAmA/comments/2rgsan/i_am_elon_musk_ceocto_of_a_rocket_company_ama/?st=jg8ec825&sh=4307fa36.
13. Richard Feynman, "Atoms in Motion," California Institute of Technology, The Feynman Lectures on Physics, http://www.feynmanlectures.caltech.edu/I_01.html.

3. Obtaining Worldly Wisdom Through a Latticework of Mental Models

1. Shane Parrish, "Mental Models: The Best Way to Make Intelligent Decisions (109 Models Explained)," *Farnam Street* (blog), https://www.fs.blog/mental-models.
2. Herbert A. Simon, *Models of My Life* (Cambridge, MA: MIT Press, 1996).
3. Tren Griffin, *Charlie Munger: The Complete Investor* (New York: Columbia University Press, 2015).
4. Richard Lewis, "Charlie Munger: Full Transcript of Daily Journal Annual Meeting 2017," Latticework Investing, February 17, 2017, http://latticeworkinvesting.com/2017/02/17/charlie-munger-full-transcript-of-daily-journal-annual-meeting-2017.
5. Charlie Munger, "The Psychology of Human Misjudgment by Charles T. Munger," Harrison Barnes, January 17, 2015, https://www.hb.org/the-psychology-of-human-misjudgment-by-charles-t-munger/#07.
6. Peter Kaufman, quoted in Christopher M. Begg, "2014 3rd Quarter Letter," East Coast Asset Management, November 10, 2014, http://www.eastcoastasset.com/wp-content/uploads/ecam_2014_3q_letter.pdf.

7. Charlie Munger, "A Lesson on Elementary, Worldly Wisdom as It Relates to Investment Management and Business," 1994, *Farnam Street* (blog), https://fs.blog/a-lesson-on-worldly-wisdom/.

8. Charlie Munger, "Wesco Financial's Charlie Munger," CS Investing, May 5, 1995, http://csinvesting.org/wp-content/uploads/2014/05/Worldly-Wisdom-by-Munger.pdf.

9. Farnam Street (blog), "Charlie Munger on Getting Rich, Wisdom, Focus, Fake Knowledge and More," accessed December 5, 2019, https://fs.blog/2017/02/charlie-munger-wisdom/.

10. Farnam Street (blog), "Charlie Munger and the Pursuit of Worldly Wisdom," accessed December 5, 2019, https://fs.blog/2015/09/munger-worldly-wisdom/.

11. Griffin, *Charlie Munger*.

12. William Deresiewicz, "Solitude and Leadership," *American Scholar*, March 1, 2010, https://theamericanscholar.org/solitude-and-leadership/#.Wt-DKUxFydI.

13. Edward Burger and Michael Starbird, *The 5 Elements of Effective Thinking* (Princeton, NJ: Princeton University Press, 2012).

14. Charlie Munger, "Outstanding Investor Digest," speech at Stanford Law School Class of William Lazier, March 13, 1998, Stanford, CA.

4. Harnessing the Power of Passion and Focus Through Deliberate Practice

1. See Michael E. Bernard, *Rationality and the Pursuit of Happiness: The Legacy of Albert Ellis* (Hoboken, NJ: Wiley-Blackwell, 2010).

2. Alice Schroeder, *The Snowball: Warren Buffett and the Business of Life* (New York: Bantam, 2009).

3. Warren Buffett, *Berkshire Hathaway 1998 Annual Letter to Shareholders*, March 1, 1999, http://www.berkshirehathaway.com/letters/1998pdf.pdf.

4. "Warren Buffett's Career Advice," *CNN Money*, November 16, 2012, http://money.cnn.com/video/magazines/fortune/2012/11/16/f-buffett-career-advice.fortune/index.html?iid=HP_LN.

5. Christopher Tkaczyk and Scott Olster, "Best Advice from CEOs: 40 Execs' Secrets to Success," *Fortune*, October 29, 2014, http://fortune.com/2014/10/29/ceo-best-advice.

6. Steve Jobs, "'You've Got to Find What You Love,' Jobs Says" (prepared text of commencement address, June 12, 2005), *Stanford News*, June 14, 2005, https://news.stanford.edu/2005/06/14/jobs-061505.

7. Anne Dunnewold, "Life's Prizes," Anne Dunnewold, Ph.D., *Mind Life Balance* (blog), March 15, 2010, http://anndunnewold.com/lifes-prizes/.

8. Steve Jobs, "'You've Got to Find What You Love,' Jobs Says," *Stanford News*, https://news.stanford.edu/2005/06/14/jobs-061505.

9. Brian Christian and Tom Griffiths, *Algorithms to Live By: The Computer Science of Human Decisions* (New York: Henry Holt, 2016).

10. Malcolm Gladwell, *Outliers: The Story of Success* (New York: Back Bay, 2011).

11. James Clear, Twitter, January 31, 2018, https://twitter.com/james_clear/status/958824949367615489?lang=en.

12. Geoff Colvin, *Talent Is Overrated: What Really Separates World-Class Performers from Everybody Else* (London: Nicholas Brealey, 2019).

13. Daniel Coyle, *The Little Book of Talent: 52 Tips for Improving Your Skills* (New York: Bantam, 2012).

14. Frank Herron, "It's a MUCH More Effective Quotation to Attribute It to Aristotle, Rather Than to Will Durant," *The Art of Quotesmanship and Misquotesmanship* (blog),

May 8, 2012, http://blogs.umb.edu/quoteunquote/2012/05/08/its-a-much-more-effective
-quotation-to-attribute-it-to-aristotle-rather-than-to-will-durant/.

5. The Importance of Choosing the Right Role Models, Teachers, and Associates in Life

1. Guy Spier, *The Education of a Value Investor: My Transformative Quest for Wealth, Wisdom, and Enlightenment* (New York: St. Martin's, 2014).
2. "Exclusive Interview with Arnold Van Den Berg," *Manual of Ideas* 7, no. 9 (September 2014), https://www.manualofideas.com/wp-content/uploads/2014/09/the-manual-of-ideas
-arnold-van-den-berg-201409.pdf.
3. Warren Buffett, *Berkshire Hathaway 2002 Annual Letter to Shareholders*, February 21, 2003, http://www.berkshirehathaway.com/letters/2002pdf.pdf.
4. Jack Welch quote from goodreads.com, https://www.goodreads.com/author/quotes
/3770.Jack_Welch?page=3.
5. Laurence Endersen, *Pebbles of Perception: How a Few Good Choices Make All the Difference* (CreateSpace Independent Publishing Platform, 2014).

6. Humility Is the Gateway to Attaining Wisdom

1. Morgan Housel, "We're All Innocently Out of Touch," *Collaborative Fund* (blog), November 17, 2017, http://www.collaborativefund.com/blog/were-all-out-of-touch.
2. Morgan Housel, "Getting Rich vs. Staying Rich," *Collaborative Fund* (blog), February 16, 2017, http://www.collaborativefund.com/blog/getting-rich-vs-staying-rich.
3. Jason Zweig, *The Devil's Financial Dictionary* (New York: PublicAffairs, 2015).
4. Richard P. Feynman, *The Pleasure of Finding Things Out: The Best Short Works of Richard P. Feynman* (New York: Basic Books, 2005). Subsequent Feynman quotes are to this text unless otherwise indicated.
5. *Becoming Warren Buffett* (HBO Documentary Films, January 30, 2017), https://www
.youtube.com/watch?v=PB5krSvFAPY.
6. Warren Buffett, *Berkshire Hathaway 1996 Annual Letter to Shareholders*, February 28, 1997, http://www.berkshirehathaway.com/letters/1996.html.
7. Alice Schroeder, *The Snowball: Warren Buffett and the Business of Life* (New York: Bantam, 2009).
8. Chuck Carnevale, "How to Use the Correct Discount Rate," *ValueWalk*, September 27, 2013, https://www.valuewalk.com/2013/09/use-correct-discount-rate.
9. "Go Ask Alice," Motley Fool, board comment by Elias Fardo, March 18, 2003, http://
boards.fool.com/you-might-want-to-discount-the-float-growth-at-a-18762436.aspx.
10. "Links," Value Investing World, April 5, 2018, http://www.valueinvestingworld.com
/2018/04/links_5.html.
11. "Q&A with Warren Buffett (Tuck School of Business)," October 24, 2005, http://
valueinvestorindia.blogspot.com/2005/10/qa-with-warren-buffett-tuck-school-of
.html.
12. Charlie Munger, "A Lesson on Elementary, Worldly Wisdom as It Relates to Investment Management and Business," *Farnam Street* (blog), 1994, https://fs.blog/a-lesson-on
-worldly-wisdom/.

7. The Virtues of Philanthropy and Good Karma

1. Charles W. Collier, *Wealth in Families* (Cambridge, MA: Harvard University, 2006).
2. Ian Wilhelm, "Warren Buffett Shares His Philanthropic Philosophy," *Chronicle of Philanthropy*, March 8, 2010, https://www.philanthropy.com/article/Warren-Buffett-Shares-His/225907.
3. Andrew Carnegie, "Wealth," *North American Review* no. 391 (June 1889), https://www.swarthmore.edu/SocSci/rbannis1/AIH19th/Carnegie.html.
4. Alice Schroeder, *The Snowball: Warren Buffett and the Business of Life* (New York: Bantam, 2009).

8. Simplicity Is the Ultimate Sophistication

1. Brainyquote, accessed December 6, 2019, https://www.brainyquote.com/quotes/warren_buffett_149683.
2. "Warren Buffett Remarks on European Debt Crisis, the 'Buffett Rule' and the American Worker: Interview by Business Wire CEO Cathy Baron Tamraz," *Business Wire*, November 15, 2011, https://www.businesswire.com/news/home/20111115006090/en/Warren-Buffett-Remarks-European-Debt-Crisis-.
3. John Maynard Keynes, *The General Theory of Employment, Interest, and Money* (San Diego, CA: Harcourt, Brace & World, 1965).
4. Mohnish Pabrai, *The Dhandho Investor: The Low-Risk Value Method to High Returns* (Hoboken, NJ: Wiley, 2007).
5. Buffett FAQ, *2008 Berkshire Hathaway Annual Meeting*, https://www.businessinsider.com/charlie-munger-quotes-investing-things-2016-1.
6. Warren Buffett, *Berkshire Hathaway 2004 Annual Letter to Shareholders*, February 28, 2005, http://www.berkshirehathaway.com/letters/2004ltr.pdf.
7. "Special Situation Videos: Lecture 1 and 2," September 25, 2012, Greenblatt Columbia Lecture 2005, CS Investing, http://csinvesting.org/2012/09/25/special-situation-video-lecture-1.
8. Cited by Thomas Oppong, "The Only Mental Model You Need to Simplify Your Life," Medium, accessed December 6, 2019, https://medium.com/personal-growth/the-only-mental-model-you-need-to-simplify-your-life-b734f5c6200f.
9. Warren Buffett, *Berkshire Hathaway 1992 Annual Letter to Shareholders*, March 1, 1993, http://www.berkshirehathaway.com/letters/1992.html.
10. Whitney Tilson, "Notes from the 2002 Wesco Annual Meeting," Whitney Tilson's ValueInvesting Website, https://www.tilsonfunds.com/motley_berkshire_brkmtg02notes.php.
11. Chuck Saletta, "4 Steps to Getting Rich from Warren Buffett's Right-Hand Man," *Business Insider*, May 31, 2013, http://www.businessinsider.com/charlie-mungers-secrets-to-getting-rich-2013-5.
12. Erika Andersen, "23 Quotes from Warren Buffett on Life and Generosity," *Forbes*, December 2, 2013, https://www.forbes.com/sites/erikaandersen/2013/12/02/23-quotes-from-warren-buffett-on-life-and-generosity/#5f2270aaf891.
13. Michael Mauboussin and Dan Callahan, "What Does a Price-Earnings Multiple Mean? An Analytical Bridge between P/Es and Solid Economics," January 29, 2014, https://www.valuewalk.com/wp-content/uploads/2014/02/document-805915460.pdf; Epoch Investment Partners, "The P/E Ratio: A User's Manual," June 17, 2019, http://www.eipny.com/white-papers/the_p-e_ratio_a-users_manual/.

14. Berkshire Hathaway, press conference, May 2001.
15. John Szramiak, "This Story About Warren Buffett and His Long-Time Pilot Is an Important Lesson About What Separates Extraordinarily Successful People from Everyone Else," *Business Insider*, December 4, 2017, http://businessinsider.com/warren -buffetts-not-to-do-list-2016-10?r=US&IR=T.
16. "Our National Predicament: Excerpts from Seth Klarman's 2010 Letter," Mungerisms, March 2, 2011, http://myinvestingnotebook.blogspot.com/2011/03/our-national -predicament-excerpts-from.html.

9. Achieving Financial Independence

1. Charles Dickens, *David Copperfield* (London: Penguin Classics, 2004).
2. Peter Lynch, *Learn to Earn: A Beginner's Guide to the Basics of Investing and Business* (New York: Simon and Schuster, 1996).
3. Brian Portnoy, *The Geometry of Wealth: How to Shape a Life of Money and Meaning* (Hampshire, UK: Harriman House, 2018).
4. Paraphrased from Jonathan Ping, "Charlie Munger's Life as a Financial Independence Blueprint," *My Money* (blog), January 18, 2018, http://www.mymoneyblog.com/charlie -munger-financial-independence-blueprint.html.
5. Michael J. Mauboussin, *The Success Equation: Untangling Skill and Luck in Business, Sports, and Investing* (Boston: Harvard Business Press, 2012).
6. Dave Ramsey, *The Total Money Makeover: A Proven Plan for Financial Fitness* (Nashville, TN: Nelson, 2003).
7. Charles Ellis and James Vertin, *Classics: An Investor's Anthology* (New York: Business One Irwin, 1988).
8. Seneca, *Letters from a Stoic* (London: Penguin, 1969).
9. Morgan Housel, "Saving Money and Running Backwards," *Collaborative Fund* (blog), September 27, 2017, http://www.collaborativefund.com/blog/saving-money-and -running-backwards.

10. Living Life According to the Inner Scorecard

1. Goodreads, accessed December 6, 2019, https://www.goodreads.com/quotes/831517-in -the-short-run-the-market-is-a-voting-machine.
2. Warren Buffett, Buffett Partnership letter, January 25, 1967, in *Buffett Partnership Letters 1957 to 1970*, 100, CS Investing, http://csinvesting.org/wp-content/uploads/2012/05 /complete_buffett_partnership_letters-1957-70_in-sections.pdf.
3. Warren Buffett, Buffett Partnership letter, October 9, 1967, in *Buffett Partnership Letters 1957 to 1970*, 111, CS Investing, http://csinvesting.org/wp-content/uploads/2012/05/complete _buffett_partnership_letters-1957-70_in-sections.pdf.
4. Warren Buffett, Buffett Partnership letter, January 22, 1969, in *Buffett Partnership Letters 1957 to 1970*, 123, CS Investing, http://csinvesting.org/wp-content/uploads/2012/05 /complete_buffett_partnership_letters-1957-70_in-sections.pdf.
5. Warren Buffett, Buffett Partnership letter, October 9, 1969, in *Buffett Partnership Letters 1957 to 1970*, 132, CS Investing, http://csinvesting.org/wp-content/uploads/2012/05 /complete_buffett_partnership_letters-1957-70_in-sections.pdf.

6. Warren Buffett, *Berkshire Hathaway 2001 Annual Letter to Shareholders*, February 28, 2002, https://www.berkshirehathaway.com/2001ar/2001letter.html.

7. Li Lu, "The Prospects for Value Investing in China," trans. Graham F. Rhodes, October 28, 2015, https://brianlangis.files.wordpress.com/2018/03/li-lu-the-prospects-for-value-investing-in-china.pdf.

8. The Conservative Income Investor, "Raise A Glass to Rose Blumkin," November 23, 2018, https://theconservativeincomeinvestor.com/rose-blumkin/.

9. Benjamin Graham and Jason Zweig, *The Intelligent Investor: The Definitive Book on Value Investing*, rev. ed. (New York: Harper Business, 2006).

10. Janet Lowe, *Damn Right! Behind the Scenes with Berkshire Hathaway Billionaire Charlie Munger* (Hoboken, NJ: Wiley, 2003), 154.

11. Steve Fishman, "Bernie Madoff, Free at Last," *New York*, June 6, 2010, http://nymag.com/news/crimelaw/66468.

12. "Warren Buffett: The Inner Scorecard," *Farnam Street* (blog), August 2016, https://www.fs.blog/2016/08/the-inner-scorecard.

13. Charlie Munger, USC School of Law commencement speech, University of Southern California Gould School of Law, May 13, 2007, Los Angeles, CA, https://genius.com/Charlie-munger-usc-law-commencement-speech-annotated.

14. Charlie Munger, "The Psychology of Human Misjudgment by Charles T. Munger," Harrison Barnes, January 17, 2015, https://www.hb.org/the-psychology-of-human-misjudgment-by-charles-t-munger/#07.

15. Whitney Tilson, "2004 Wesco Meeting Notes," May 5, 2004, in *The Best of Charlie Munger: 1994–2011*, 193, http://www.valueplays.net/wp-content/uploads/The-Best-of-Charlie-Munger-1994-2011.pdf.

16. Seneca, *Letters from a Stoic* (London: Penguin, 1969).

11. The Key to Success in Life Is Delayed Gratification

1. Peter D. Kaufman, ed., *Poor Charlie's Almanack* (Marceline, MO: Walsworth, 2005).

2. Elle Kaplan, "Why Warren Buffett's '20-Slot Rule' Will Make You Insanely Successful and Wealthy," *Inc.*, July 22, 2016, https://www.inc.com/elle-kaplan/why-warren-buffett-s-20-slot-rule-will-make-you-insanely-wealthy-and-successful.html.

3. Adi Ignatius, "Jeff Bezos on Leading for the Long-Term at Amazon," *Harvard Business Review*, January 2013, https://hbr.org/2013/01/jeff-bezos-on-leading-for-the.

4. Jeff Bezos, *Amazon 2014 Letter to Shareholders*, https://ir.aboutamazon.com/static-files/a9bd5c6a-c11c-4b38-9532-ae2f73d8bd10.

5. Ignatius, "Jeff Bezos on Leading."

6. James B. Stewart, "Amazon Says Long Term and Means It," *New York Times*, December 16, 2011, https://www.nytimes.com/2011/12/17/business/at-amazon-jeff-bezos-talks-long-term-and-means-it.html.

7. Jeff Bezos, *Amazon 1997 Letter to Shareholders*, http://media.corporate-ir.net/media_files/irol/97/97664/reports/Shareholderletter97.pdf.

8. Warren Buffett, *Berkshire Hathaway 1998 Annual Letter to Shareholders*, March 1, 1999, http://www.berkshirehathaway.com/letters/1998pdf.pdf.

9. Warren Buffett, *Berkshire Hathaway 2010 Annual Letter to Shareholders*, February 26, 2011, http://www.berkshirehathaway.com/letters/2010ltr.pdf.

10. Warren Buffett, *An Owner's Manual*, Berkshire Hathaway, June 1996, http://www.berkshirehathaway.com/ownman.pdf.

11. Tim Koller, Marc Goedhard, and David Wessels, *Valuation: Measuring and Managing the Value of Companies*, 6th ed. (Hoboken, NJ: Wiley, 2015).

12. Anshul Khare, "Investing and the Art of Metaphorical Thinking," Safal Niveshak, November 21, 2016, https://www.safalniveshak.com/investing-art-metaphorical-thinking.

13. Dean LeBaron and Romesh Vaitilingam, *Dean LeBaron's Treasury of Investment Wisdom: 30 Great Investing Minds* (Hoboken, NJ: Wiley, 2001).

14. Steven Levy, "Jeff Bezos Owns the Web in More Ways Than You Think," *Wired*, November 13, 2011, https://www.wired.com/2011/11/ff_bezos/.

15. Aye M. Soe, Berlinda Liu, and Hamish Preston, *SPIVA U.S. Scorecard*, S&P Dow Jones Indices, Year-End 2018, https://www.spindices.com/documents/spiva/spiva-us-year-end-2018.pdf.

16 Boyar's Intrinsic Value Research, "Thoughts About the Stock Market and the Economy," October 31, 2019, http://boyarvaluegroup.com/bvg-pdf/BoyarResearch_3Q2019.pdf.

17. John Maynard Keynes, *The General Theory of Employment, Interest, and Money* (San Diego, CA: Harcourt, Brace and World, 1965).

18. Peter Bevelin, *Seeking Wisdom: From Darwin to Munger*, 3rd ed. (Malmö, Sweden: PCA Publications, 2007).

19. Sanjay Bakshi, *What Happens When You Don't Buy Quality? And What Happens When You Do?* OctoberQuest 2013, October 11, 2013, https://www.dropbox.com/s/haqe3psl29u1scx/October_Quest_2013.pdf?dl=0.

20. Jason Zweig, "The Secrets of Berkshire's Success: An Interview with Charlie Munger," *Wall Street Journal*, September 12, 2014, https://www.wsj.com/articles/the-secrets-of-berkshires-success-an-interview-with-charlie-munger-1410543815.

21. Yuval Noah Harari, *Sapiens: A Brief History of Humankind* (New York: Harper, 2015).

12. Building Earning Power Through a Business Ownership Mind-Set

1. Warren Buffett, *Berkshire Hathaway 1977 Annual Letter to Shareholders*, March 14, 1978, http://www.berkshirehathaway.com/letters/1977.html.

2. Warren Buffett, "Buffett: How Inflation Swindles the Equity Investor (Fortune Classics, 1977)," *Fortune*, June 12, 2011, http://fortune.com/2011/06/12/buffett-how-inflation-swindles-the-equity-investor-fortune-classics-1977.

3. Warren Buffett, *Berkshire Hathaway 1993 Annual Letter to Shareholders*, March 1, 1994, http://www.berkshirehathaway.com/letters/1993.html.

13. Investing Between the Lines

1. Laura J. Rittenhouse, *Investing Between the Lines: How to Make Smarter Decisions by Decoding CEO Communications* (New York: McGraw-Hill Education, 2013). Subsequent citations are to this edition unless otherwise noted.

2. Warren Buffett, *An Owner's Manual*, Berkshire Hathaway, June 1996, http://www.berkshirehathaway.com/ownman.pdf.

3. Warren Buffett, *Berkshire Hathaway 2014 Annual Letter to Shareholders*, February 27, 2015, http://www.berkshirehathaway.com/letters/2014ltr.pdf.

4. Rittenhouse, *Investing Between the Lines.*

14. The Significant Role of Checklists in Decision-Making

1. Sheeraz Raza, "Great Interview with Alice Schroeder via Simoleon Sense," ValueWalk, November 6, 2010, https://www.valuewalk.com/2010/11/great-interview-alice-schroeder-simoleon-sense.
2. Goodreads.com, accessed December 9, 2019, https://www.goodreads.com/quotes/8956691-what-the-human-being-is-best-at-doing-is-interpreting.
3. Quoted in Atul Gawande, *The Checklist Manifesto* (Gurgaon, India: Penguin Random House, 2014).
4. Charlie Munger, "Wesco 2002 Annual Meeting," Mungerisms, Pasadena, CA, 2002, http://mungerisms.blogspot.com/2009/08/wesco-2002-annual-meeting.html.
5. Peter Bevelin, *Seeking Wisdom: From Darwin to Munger*, 3rd ed. (Malmö, Sweden: PCA Publications, 2007).

15. Journaling Is a Powerful Tool for Self-Reflection

1. Goodreads.com, accessed December 9, 2019, https://www.goodreads.com/quotes/8116811-man-is-not-a-rational-animal-he-is-a-rationalizing.
2. Benjamin Graham and Jason Zweig, *The Intelligent Investor: The Definitive Book on Value Investing*, rev. ed. (New York: Harper Business, 2006).
3. Stephen King, *On Writing: A Memoir of the Craft* (New York: Simon and Schuster, 2000).

16. Never Underestimate the Power of Incentives

1. Laurence Endersen, *Pebbles of Perception: How a Few Good Choices Make All the Difference* (CreateSpace Independent Publishing Platform, 2014). Subsequent references are to this edition unless otherwise noted.
2. William Ophuls, *Plato's Revenge: Politics in the Age of Ecology* (Cambridge, MA: MIT Press, 2011).
3. Charlie Munger, "The Psychology of Human Misjudgment by Charles T. Munger," Harrison Barnes, January 17, 2015, https://www.hb.org/the-psychology-of-human-misjudgment-by-charles-t-munger/#07.
4. Charlie Munger, "A Lesson on Elementary, Worldly Wisdom as it Relates to Investment Management and Business," *Farnam Street* (blog), 1994, https://fs.blog/a-lesson-on-worldly-wisdom/.
5. Peter D. Kaufman, ed., *Poor Charlie's Almanack* (Marceline, MO: Walsworth, 2005).
6. Warren Buffett, *Berkshire Hathaway 1996 Annual Letter to Shareholders*, February 28, 1997, http://www.berkshirehathaway.com/letters/1996.html.
7. Warren Buffett, *Berkshire Hathaway 1996 Annual Letter to Shareholders*.
8. Warren Buffett, *Berkshire Hathaway 1994 Annual Letter to Shareholders*, March 7, 1995, http://www.berkshirehathaway.com/letters/1994.html.
9. Nassim Nicholas Taleb and George A. Martin, "How to Prevent Other Financial Crises," *SAIS Review* 32, no. 1 (Winter–Spring 2012), http://www.fooledbyrandomness.com/sais.pdf.

10. Seth A. Klarman, *Margin of Safety: Risk-Averse Value Investing Strategies for the Thoughtful Investor* (New York: Harper Collins, 1991).

11. Sanjay Bakshi, "The Psychology of Human Misjudgment VI," LinkedIn SlideShare, December 16, 2012, https://www.slideshare.net/bakshi1/the-psychology-of-human-misjudgment-vi.

12. Warren Buffett, *Berkshire Hathaway 2005 Annual Letter to Shareholders*, February 28, 2006, http://www.berkshirehathaway.com/letters/2005ltr.pdf.

13. Alex Crippen, "Warren Buffett's 5-Minute Plan to Fix the Deficit," CNBC, July 11, 2011, https://www.cnbc.com/id/43670783.

17. Always Think About the Math, but Avoid Physics Envy

1. Berkshire Hathaway, 2000 Annual Meeting, *Outstanding Investor Digest*, December 18, 2000.

2. Charlie Munger, "Academic Economics: Strengths and Faults After Considering Interdisciplinary Needs," Herb Kay Undergraduate Lecture, University of California, Santa Barbara, Economics Department, October 3, 2003, Santa Barbara, CA, http://www.tilsonfunds.com/MungerUCSBspeech.pdf.

3. Peter D. Kaufman, ed., *Poor Charlie's Almanack* (Marceline, MO: Walsworth, 2005).

4. Quoted in Tim Sullivan, "Embracing Complexity," *Harvard Business Review*, September 2011, https://hbr.org/2011/09/embracing-complexity.

5. Benjamin Graham and Jason Zweig, *The Intelligent Investor: The Definitive Book on Value Investing*, rev. ed. (New York: Harper Business, 2006).

6. Goodreads.com, accessed December 9, 2019, https://www.brainyquote.com/quotes/warren_buffett_149692.

7. Warren Buffett, *An Owner's Manual*, Berkshire Hathaway, June 1996, http://www.berkshirehathaway.com/ownman.pdf.

8. Warren Buffett, *Berkshire Hathaway 2005 Annual Letter to Shareholders*, February 28, 2006, http://www.berkshirehathaway.com/letters/2005ltr.pdf; *Berkshire Hathaway 2000 Annual Letter to Shareholders*, February 28, 2001, http://www.berkshirehathaway.com/letters/2000pdf.pdf.

9. Tren Griffin, "A Dozen Things I've Learned from Charlie Munger About Inversion," *25iq* (blog), September 12, 2015, https://25iq.com/2015/09/12/a-dozen-things-ive-learned-from-charlie-munger-about-inversion-including-the-importance-of-being-consistently-not-stupid-2.

10. Berkshire Hathaway, 1990 Annual Meeting, *Outstanding Investor Digest*, May 31, 1990.

18. Intelligent Investing Is All About Understanding Intrinsic Value

1. Warren Buffett, *Berkshire Hathaway 1986 Annual Letter to Shareholders*, February 27, 1987, http://www.berkshirehathaway.com/letters/1986.html.

2. Warren Buffett, *Berkshire Hathaway 1992 Annual Letter to Shareholders*, March 1, 1993 http://www.berkshirehathaway.com/letters/1992.html.

3. "35 Quotes from Benjamin Graham," Caproasia Online, May 8, 2015, http://www.caproasia.com/2015/05/08/35-quotes-from-benjamin-graham.

4. Warren Buffett, *Berkshire Hathaway 1984 Annual Letter to Shareholders*, February 25, 1985, http://www.berkshirehathaway.com/letters/1984.html.

5. Warren Buffett, *Berkshire Hathaway 2014 Annual Letter to Shareholders*, February 27, 2015, http://www.berkshirehathaway.com/letters/2014ltr.pdf.

6. "Charlie Munger on 'Frozen Corporation,'" ValueWalk, July 16, 2015, https://www.valuewalk.com/2015/07/charlie-munger-on-frozen-corporation.

7. Warren Buffett, *Berkshire Hathaway 2000 Annual Letter to Shareholders*, https://www.berkshirehathaway.com/2000ar/2000letter.html.

8. Benjamin Graham and David Dodd, *Security Analysis*, 6th ed. (New York: McGraw-Hill Education, 2008).

9. Buffett FAQ, 2003 Berkshire Hathaway Annual Meeting, http://buffettfaq.com.

10. Quoted in Paul D. Sonkin and Paul Johnson, *Pitch the Perfect Investment: The Essential Guide to Winning on Wall Street* (Hoboken, NJ: Wiley, 2017).

11. Graham and Dodd, *Security Analysis*, 6th ed.

12. Benjamin Graham and David Dodd, *Security Analysis: The Classic 1934 Edition* (New York: McGraw-Hill Education, 1996).

13. Warren Buffett, *Berkshire Hathaway 1984 Annual Letter to Shareholders*, https://www.berkshirehathaway.com/letters/1984.html.

14. Thomas Phelps, *100 to 1 in the Stock Market: A Distinguished Security Analyst Tells How to Make More of Your Investment Opportunities* (Brattleboro, VT: Echo Point, 2015).

19. The Three Most Important Words in Investing

1. Jeremy Siegel, "Valuing Growth Stocks: Revisiting the Nifty Fifty," *American Association of Individual Investors Journal*, October 1998, https://www.aaii.com/journal/article/valuing-growth-stocks-revisiting-the-nifty-fifty.

2. Lawrence Hamtil, "Price Is What You Pay; Value Is What You Get—Nifty Fifty Edition," *Fortune Financial* (blog), May 24, 2018, http://www.fortunefinancialadvisors.com/blog/price-is-what-you-pay-value-is-what-you-get-nifty-fifty-edition.

3. Brent Beshore, "Going Pro: 2017 Year In Review," Adventures, https://www.adventur.es/2017-annual-letter-going-pro.

4. Charles D. Ellis, "The Loser's Game," *Financial Analysts Journal*, January–February 1975, https://www.cfapubs.org/doi/pdf/10.2469/faj.v51.n1.1865.

5. Benjamin Graham, *The Intelligent Investor*, 4th rev. ed. (New York: Harper and Row, 1973).

6. Credit Suisse, "Was Warren Buffet Right: Do Wonderful Companies Remain Wonderful?" *HOLT Wealth Creation Principles*, June 2013, https://research-doc.credit-suisse.com/mercurydoc?language=ENG&format=PDF&document_id=1019433381&serialid=*EMAIL_REMOVED*&auditid=1182867.

7. Phil DeMuth, "The Mysterious Factor 'P': Charlie Munger, Robert Novy-Marx and the Profitability Factor," *Forbes*, June 27, 2013.

8. Warren Buffett, *Berkshire Hathaway 1980 Annual Letter to Shareholders*, February 27, 1981, http://www.berkshirehathaway.com/letters/1980.html.

9. Warren Buffett, *Berkshire Hathaway 1983 Annual Letter to Shareholders*, March 14, 1984, http://www.berkshirehathaway.com/letters/1983.html.

10. Warren Buffett, *Berkshire Hathaway 1989 Annual Letter to Shareholders*, March 2, 1990, http://www.berkshirehathaway.com/letters/1989.html.

20. Investing in Commodity and Cyclical Stocks Is All About the Capital Cycle

1. Tobias E. Carlisle, *Deep Value: Why Activist Investors and Other Contrarians Battle for Control of Losing Corporations* (Hoboken, NJ: Wiley, 2014).
2. Edward Chancellor, *Capital Returns: Investing Through the Capital Cycle: A Money Manager's Reports 2002–15* (Basingstoke, UK: Palgrave Macmillan, 2016). Subsequent citations are to this edition unless otherwise noted.
3. Howard Marks, *The Most Important Thing Illuminated: Uncommon Sense for the Thoughtful Investor* (New York: Columbia University Press, 2013).
4. Malcolm Gladwell, *Blink: The Power of Thinking Without Thinking* (New York: Little, Brown, 2005).
5. Peter Lynch, *One Up on Wall Street: How to Use What You Already Know to Make Money in the Market* (New York: Simon and Schuster, 2000).
6. Charlie Munger, "Wesco Financial Corporation Letter to Shareholders," in *Charlie Munger's Wesco Financial Corporation Annual Letters 1983–2009*, 182, https://remembering theobvious.files.wordpress.com/2012/08/wesco-charlie-munger-letters-1983-2009 -collection.pdf.
7. Bhavin Shah, "My Best Pick 2018," *Outlook Business*, January 08, 2018, https://outlook business.com/specials/my-best-pick_2018/bhavin-shah-4052.

21. Within Special Situations, Carefully Study Spinoffs

1. Quoted in Cogitator Capital, "Special Situation Investing," ValueWalk, 2008, http:// www.valuewalk.com/wp-content/uploads/2010/09/37200720-33263413-Special -Situation-Investing-by-Ben-Graham.pdf.
2. Quoted in Cogitator Capital, "Special Situation Investing."
3. The Edge Consulting Group, *Global Spinoffs and the Hidden Value of Corporate Change*, vol. 2, *Executive Summary*, December 2014, https://www.hvst.com/attachments /1437/Exec_Summary_-_The_Edge_Deloitte_Global_Spinoff_Study_-_Dec_2014 .pdf.
4. "Spin-Offs—The Urge to Demerge," SBICAP Securities, June 19, 2017, https://drive .google.com/file/d/0B5meW_TNaEhNcFY4ME9ZeTBUNWM/view.
5. Seth A. Klarman, *Margin of Safety: Risk-Averse Value Investing Strategies for the Thoughtful Investor* (New York: Harper Collins, 1991).
6. Rich Howe, "What Klarman and Greenblatt Have to Say About Investing in Spinoffs— Part II," *ValueWalk*, March 15, 2018, https://www.valuewalk.com/2018/03/klarman -greenblatt-investing-spinoffs.
7. Joel Greenblatt, *You Can Be a Stock Market Genius: Uncover the Secret Hiding Places of Stock Market Profits* (New York: Touchstone, 1999). Subsequent citations are to this edition unless otherwise noted.
8. Peter Lynch, *One Up on Wall Street: How to Use What You Already Know to Make Money in the Market* (New York: Simon and Schuster, 2000).
9. Peter Lynch, *One Up on Wall Street*.
10. Peter Lynch, *One Up on Wall Street*.
11. "Look at All These Spinoffs Beating the Market," *Old School Value* (blog), July 6, 2011, https://www.oldschoolvalue.com/blog/special_situation/look-at-all-these-spinoffs -beating-the-market.

22. The Holy Grail of Long-Term Value Investing

1. Warren Buffett, *Berkshire Hathaway 1984 Annual Letter to Shareholders*, February 25, 1985, http://www.berkshirehathaway.com/letters/1984.html.
2. Charlie Munger, "A Lesson on Elementary, Worldly Wisdom as it Relates to Investment Management and Business," *Farnam Street* (blog), 1994, https://fs.blog/a-lesson-on -worldly-wisdom.
3. Carol Loomis, "Mr. Buffett on the Stock Market," *Fortune*, November 22, 1999, http:// archive.fortune.com/magazines/fortune/fortune_archive/1999/11/22/269071/index.htm.
4. Warren Buffett, *Berkshire Hathaway 2007 Annual Letter to Shareholders*, February 2008, http://www.berkshirehathaway.com/letters/2007ltr.pdf.
5. John Train, *The Money Masters* (New York: Harper Business, 1994).
6. "Financial Crisis Inquiry Commission Staff Audiotape of Interview with Warren Buffett, Berkshire Hathaway," *Santangel's Review*, May 26, 2010, http://dericbownds.net /uploaded_images/Buffett_FCIC_transcript.pdf.
7. Marian L. Tupy, "Corporations Are Not as Powerful as You Think," HumanProgress, November 1, 2017, https://humanprogress.org/article.php?p=785.
8. James K. Glassman and Kavin A. Hassett, "Dow 36,000," *The Atlantic*, September 1999, https://www.theatlantic.com/magazine/archive/1999/09/dow-36-000/306249.
9. Benjamin Graham and Jason Zweig, *The Intelligent Investor: The Definitive Book on Value Investing*, rev. ed. (New York: Harper Business, 2006).
10. Loomis, "Mr. Buffett on the Stock Market."
11. Buffett, *Berkshire Hathaway 2007 Annual Letter*.
12. John Maynard Keynes, quoted in "Warren Buffett on the Stock Market," *Fortune*, December 10, 2001, http://www.berkshirehathaway.com/2001ar/FortuneMagazine%20 DEC%2010%202001.pdf.
13. Warren Buffett, *Berkshire Hathaway 1987 Annual Letter to Shareholders*, February 29, 1988, https://www.berkshirehathaway.com/letters/1987.html.
14. Warren Buffett, *Berkshire Hathaway 1996 Annual Letter to Shareholders*, February 28, 1997, http://www.berkshirehathaway.com/letters/1996.html.
15. Ian Cassel, "A New Mental Model for Investing," MicroCapClub, February 1, 2018, https://microcapclub.com/2018/02/new-mental-model-investing.
16. Philip A. Fisher, *Common Stocks and Uncommon Profits and Other Writings*, 2nd ed. (Hoboken, NJ: Wiley, 2003).
17. Warren Buffett, *Berkshire Hathaway 1999 Annual Letter to Shareholders*, March 1, 2000, http://www.berkshirehathaway.com/letters/1999htm.html.
18. Warren Buffett, *Berkshire Hathaway 1982 Annual Letter to Shareholders*, March 3, 1983, http://www.berkshirehathaway.com/letters/1982.html.
19. William N. Thorndike, *The Outsiders: Eight Unconventional CEOs and Their Radically Rational Blueprint for Success* (Brighton, MA: Harvard Business Review Press, 2012).
20. Warren Buffett, Buffett Partnership letter, October 9, 1967, in *Buffett Partnership Letters 1957 to 1970*, 111, http://csinvesting.org/wp-content/uploads/2012/05/complete_buffett _partnership_letters-1957-70_in-sections.pdf.

23. The Market Is Efficient Most, but Not All, of the Time

1. Warren Buffett, *Berkshire Hathaway 1987 Annual Letter to Shareholders*, February 29, 1988, http://www.berkshirehathaway.com/letters/1987.html.

2. Benjamin Graham and Jason Zweig, *The Intelligent Investor: The Definitive Book on Value Investing*, rev. ed. (New York: Harper Business, 2006).
3. Quoted in Mohnish Pabrai, *The Dhandho Investor: The Low-Risk Value Method to High Returns* (Hoboken, NJ: Wiley, 2007).
4. Carol Loomis, "Warren Buffett on the Stock Market," *Fortune*, December 10, 2001, http://archive.fortune.com/magazines/fortune/fortune_archive/2001/12/10/314691/index.htm.
5. Carol Loomis, "Mr. Buffett on the Stock Market," *Fortune*, November 22, 1999, http://archive.fortune.com/magazines/fortune/fortune_archive/1999/11/22/269071/index.htm.
6. Carol J. Loomis, *Tap Dancing to Work: Warren Buffett on Practically Everything, 1966–2013* (New York: Portfolio, 2013)
7. Alex Barrow, "Stanley Druckenmiller on Liquidity, Macro, and Margins," Macro Ops, June 23, 2017, https://macro-ops.com/stanley-druckenmiller-on-liquidity-macro-margins.
8. Evan Sparks, "John Templeton," Philanthropy Roundtable, http://www.philanthropyroundtable.org/almanac/hall_of_fame/john_m._templeton.
9. Peter Lattman, "Bull and Bear Markets, According to Oaktree's Howard Marks," *Wall Street Journal*, March 20, 2008, https://blogs.wsj.com/deals/2008/03/20/bull-and-bear-markets-according-to-oaktrees-howard-marks.
10. "There Are 3 Stages in a Typical Bull Market," *Ivanhoff Capital* (blog), February 2, 2012, http://ivanhoff.com/2012/02/02/there-are-3-stages-in-a-typical-bull-market.
11. Jeremy Goldman, "13 Insightful Quotes from Intel Visionary Andy Grove," inc.com, accessed December 10, 2019, https://www.inc.com/jeremy-goldman/13-insightful-quotes-from-intel-visionary-andy-grove.html.
12. Charles MacKay, *Extraordinary Popular Delusions and the Madness of Crowds* (New York: Dover, 2003).
13. Howard Marks, "You Can't Predict. You Can Compare," memo to Oaktree clients, November 20, 2001, https://www.oaktreecapital.com/docs/default-source/memos/2001-11-20-you-cant-predict-you-can-prepare.pdf?sfvrsn=2.
14. Peter Lynch, *Beating the Street* (New York: Simon and Schuster, 1994).
15. Warren Buffett, *Berkshire Hathaway 1986 Annual Letter to Shareholders*, February 27, 1987, http://www.berkshirehathaway.com/letters/1986.html.
16. Daniel Kahneman, *Thinking, Fast and Slow* (New York: Farrar, Straus and Giroux, 2013).
17. Warren Buffett, *Berkshire Hathaway 2016 Annual Letter to Shareholders*, February 25, 2017, http://www.berkshirehathaway.com/letters/2016ltr.pdf.
18. Kahneman, *Thinking, Fast and Slow*.
19. G. E. Miller, "In the Short Run, the Market Is a Voting Machine, but in the Long Run, It Is a Weighing Machine," 20somethingfinance.com, May 8, 2019, https://20somethingfinance.com/in-the-short-run-the-market-is-a-voting-machine-but-in-the-long-run-it-is-a-weighing-machine/.
20. Sanjay Bakshi, "All I Care About Is Virginity," *Fundoo Professor* (blog), October 19, 2012, https://fundooprofessor.wordpress.com/2012/10/19/virginity.
21. Michael Maloney and J. Harold Mulherin, "The Complexity of Price Discovery in an Efficient Market: The Stock Market Reaction to the Challenger Crash," *Journal of Corporate Finance* 9, no. 4 (2003): 453–479, https://www.sciencedirect.com/science/article/pii/S092911990200055X.
22. Francis Galton, "Vox Populi," *Nature*, March 7, 1907, http://galton.org/essays/1900-1911/galton-1907-vox-populi.pdf.

24. The Dynamic Art of Portfolio Management and Individual Position Sizing

1. Unless stated otherwise, all quotes in this chapter are from various articles on the ValueWalk website, https://www.valuewalk.com.
2. Allen C. Benello, Michael van Biema, and Tobias E. Carlisle, *Concentrated Investing: Strategies of the World's Greatest Concentrated Value Investors* (Hoboken, NJ: Wiley, 2016).
3. Howard Marks, "Dare to Be Great," memo to Oaktree clients, September 7, 2006, https://www.oaktreecapital.com/docs/default-source/memos/2006-09-07-dare-to-be -great.pdf?sfvrsn=2.
4. Bryan Rich, "Do You Think Like George Soros?" *Forbes*, June 1, 2016, https://www.forbes. com/sites/bryanrich/2016/06/01/do-you-think-like-george-soros/#499e4c835f0d.
5. Charlie Munger, "Academic Economics: Strengths and Faults After Considering Interdisciplinary Needs," Herb Kay Undergraduate Lecture, University of California, Santa Barbara, Economics Department, October 3, 2003, Santa Barbara, CA, http:// www.tilsonfunds.com/MungerUCSBspeech.pdf.
6. Quoted by Morgan Housel, Twitter, June 15, 2017, https://twitter.com/morganhousel /status/875547615592665088.
7. Charlie Munger, "A Lesson on Elementary, Worldly Wisdom as It Relates to Investment Management and Business," *Farnam Street* (blog), 1994, https://fs.blog/a-lesson-on -worldly-wisdom/.
8. Jack Schwager, *Hedge Fund Market Wizards: How Winning Traders Win* (Hoboken, NJ: Wiley, 2012).
9. Quoted in Karen Damato, "Is Your Manager Skillful . . . or Just Lucky?" *Wall Street Journal*, November 2, 2012, https://www.wsj.com/articles/SB10000872396390444734804 578062890110146284.
10. Benjamin Graham and Jason Zweig, *The Intelligent Investor: The Definitive Book on Value Investing*, rev. ed. (New York: Harper Business, 2006).

25. To Finish First, You Must First Finish

1. Warren Buffett, *Berkshire Hathaway 2010 Annual Letter to Shareholders*, February 26, 2011, http://www.berkshirehathaway.com/letters/2010ltr.pdf.
2. Nick Maggiulli, "Against the Gods," *Of Dollars and Data* (blog), July 18, 2017, https:// ofdollarsanddata.com/against-the-gods-3729ed3bb192.
3. Morgan Housel, "Risk Is How Much Time You Need," *Collaborative Fund* (blog), March 30, 2017, http://www.collaborativefund.com/blog/risk.
4. Quoted in David Foulke, "Warren Buffett on LTCM, Blind Spots, Leverage, and Unnecessary Risk," Alpha Architect, September 8, 2015, https://alphaarchitect.com/2015/09/08 /warren-buffett-ltcm-blind-spots-leverage-taking-unnecessary-risks/.
5. Quoted in Morgan Housel, "What I Believe Most," *Collaborative Fund* (blog), July 5, 2017, http://www.collaborativefund.com/blog/what-i-believe-most.
6. Robert G. Hagstrom, *The Warren Buffett Way*, 2nd ed. (Hoboken, NJ: Wiley, 2005).
7. Quoted in Foulke, "Warren Buffett on LTCM."
8. Buffett FAQ, *2006 Berkshire Hathaway Annual Meeting*, http://buffettfaq.com.
9. Sebastian Mallaby, *More Money Than God: Hedge Funds and the Making of a New Elite* (London: Penguin, 2011).

10. Benoit Mandelbrot and Richard L. Hudson, *The (Mis)Behavior of Markets: A Fractal View of Financial Turbulence* (New York: Basic Books, 2006), 20, 217, 248.

11. Benjamin Graham and David Dodd, *Security Analysis: The Classic 1934 Edition* (New York: McGraw-Hill Education, 1996).

12. Howard Marks, *The Most Important Thing Illuminated: Uncommon Sense for the Thoughtful Investor* (New York: Columbia University Press, 2013).

13. Warren Buffett, *Berkshire Hathaway 1993 Annual Letter to Shareholders*, March 1, 1994, http://www.berkshirehathaway.com/letters/1993.html.

14. Natasha Turak, "Credit Suisse Defends Controversial Financial Product at the Center of the Market Turmoil," CNBC.com, Feb 7, 2018, https://www.cnbc.com/2018/02/07/credit-suisse-defends-controversial-xiv-etn-amid-market-turmoil.html.

15. Warren Buffett, *Berkshire Hathaway 2008 Annual Letter to Shareholders*, February 27, 2009, http://www.berkshirehathaway.com/letters/2008ltr.pdf.

16. Ben Carlson, "Don't Reach for Yield," A Wealth of Commonsense, April 5, 2013, https://awealthofcommonsense.com/2013/04/dont-reach-for-yile/.

17. Warren Buffett, *Berkshire Hathaway 2017 Annual Letter to Shareholders*, February 24, 2018, http://www.berkshirehathaway.com/letters/2017ltr.pdf.

18. Warren Buffett, *Berkshire Hathaway 2014 Annual Letter to Shareholders*, February 27, 2015, http://www.berkshirehathaway.com/letters/2014ltr.pdf.

19. James Berman, "The Three Essential Warren Buffett Quotes to Live By," *Forbes*, April 20, 2014, https://www.forbes.com/sites/jamesberman/2014/04/20/the-three-essential-warren-buffett-quotes-to-live-by/#a6a575a65439.

26. Read More History and Fewer Forecasts

1. Warren Buffett, *Berkshire Hathaway 2014 Annual Letter to Shareholders*, February 27, 2015, http://www.berkshirehathaway.com/letters/2014ltr.pdf.

2. Jason Zweig, *Your Money and Your Brain: How the New Science of Neuroeconomics Can Help Make You Rich* (New York: Simon and Schuster, 2008).

3. Dan Solin, "Do You Have 'Prediction Addiction?'" *Huffington Post*, May 25, 2011, https://www.huffingtonpost.com/dan-solin/do-you-have-prediction-ad_b_66570.html.

4. Warren Buffett, *Berkshire Hathaway 1994 Annual Letter to Shareholders*, March 7, 1995, http://www.berkshirehathaway.com/letters/1994.html.

5. Warren Buffett, *Berkshire Hathaway 2012 Annual Letter to Shareholders*, March 1, 2013, http://www.berkshirehathaway.com/letters/2012ltr.pdf.

6. Howard Marks, "The Value of Predictions, or Where'd All This Rain Come From?" memo to Oaktree clients, February 15, 1993, https://www.oaktreecapital.com/docs/default-source/memos/1993-02-15-the-value-of-predictions-or-where-39-d-all-this-rain-come-from.pdf?sfvrsn=2.

7. Samit S. Vartak, *SageOne Investment Advisors Letter*, August 10, 2017, http://sageoneinvestments.com/wp-content/uploads/2017/08/SageOne-Investor-Memo-Aug-2017.pdf.

8. Morgan Housel, "The Agony of High Returns," *Motley Fool*, February 9, 2016, https://www.fool.com/investing/general/2016/02/09/the-agony-of-high-returns.aspx.

9. Edwin Lefèvre, *Reminiscences of a Stock Operator* (Hoboken, NJ: Wiley, 2006).

10. Peter Lynch, *One Up on Wall Street: How to Use What You Already Know to Make Money in the Market* (New York: Simon and Schuster, 2000).

27. Updating Our Beliefs in Light of New Evidence

1. Michael Rothschild, *Bionomics: Economy as Business Ecosystem* (Beard Books, 1990).
2. Carter Johnson, "Dr. Henry Singleton and Teledyne," ValueWalk, April 27, 2018, https://www.valuewalk.com/2018/04/dr-henry-singleton-and-teledyne.
3. Whitney Tilson, "Notes from the 2004 Wesco Annual Meeting," Whitney Tilson's Value Investing Website, May 5, 2004, https://www.tilsonfunds.com/wscmtg04notes.doc.
4. Scott Fearon and Jesse Powell, *Dead Companies Walking: How a Hedge Fund Manager Finds Opportunity in Unexpected Places* (New York: St. Martin's, 2015).
5. "Charlie Munger on Getting Rich, Wisdom, Focus, Fake Knowledge and More," *Farnam Street* (blog), February 2017, https://fs.blog/2017/02/charlie-munger-wisdom.
6. Warren Buffett, "Morning Session—2000 Meeting," CNBC, Warren Buffett Archive, April 29, 2000, video, https://buffett.cnbc.com/video/2000/04/29/morning-session---2000-berkshire-hathaway-annual-meeting.html.
7. Morgan Housel, "A Chat with Daniel Kahneman," *Collaborative Fund* (blog), January 12, 2017, http://www.collaborativefund.com/blog/a-chat-with-daniel-kahneman.
8. Charlie Munger, "A Lesson on Elementary, Worldly Wisdom as It Relates to Investment Management and Business," *Farnam Street* (blog), 1994, https://fs.blog/a-lesson-on-worldly-wisdom/.
9. Tren Griffin, "How to Make Decisions Like Ray Dalio," *25iq* (blog), April 28, 2017, https://25iq.com/2017/04/28/how-to-make-decisions-like-ray-dalio.
10. Mihir Desai, *The Wisdom of Finance: Discovering Humanity in the World of Risk and Return* (Boston: Houghton Mifflin Harcourt, 2017).
11. Amay Hattangadi and Swanand Kelkar, "Connecting the Dots," Morgan Stanley, December 2016, http://capitalideasonline.com/wordpress/wp-content/uploads/2016/12/Article-1.pdf.
12. Amay Hattangadi and Swanand Kelkar, "Reverberations in an Echo Chamber," Livemint, November 15, 2015, https://www.livemint.com/Opinion/FbpaBdLvJ1cdx3p02wwe1M/Reverberations-in-an-echo-chamber.html.
13. Daniel Kahneman, *Thinking, Fast and Slow* (New York: Farrar, Straus and Giroux, 2011).
14. AZ quotes, accessed December 10, 2019, https://www.azquotes.com/quote/730268.
15. Philip E. Tetlock and Dan Gardner, *Superforecasting: The Art and Science of Prediction* (New York: Broadway, 2016).
16. Sanjay Bakshi, "Worldly Wisdom in an Equation," *Fundoo Professor* (blog), October 9, 2015, https://fundooprofessor.wordpress.com/2015/10/08/worldly-wisdom-in-an-equation/.
17. "Words of Estimative Probability," Central Intelligence Agency, March 19, 2007, https://www.cia.gov/library/center-for-the-study-of-intelligence/csi-publications/books-and-monographs/sherman-kent-and-the-board-of-national-estimates-collected-essays/6words.html.
18. James P. O'Shaughnessy, *What Works on Wall Street*, 4th ed. (New York: McGraw-Hill Education, 2011).
19. Warren Buffett, *Berkshire Hathaway 1979 Annual Letter to Shareholders*, March 3, 1980, http://www.berkshirehathaway.com/letters/1979.html.
20. Warren Buffett, *Berkshire Hathaway 1987 Annual Letter to Shareholders*, February 29, 1988, http://www.berkshirehathaway.com/letters/1987.html.
21. Tetlock and Gardner, *Superforecasting*.
22. Harvey S. Firestone, *Men and Rubber: The Story of Business* (Whitefish, MT: Kessinger, 2003).

23. Nate Silver, *The Signal and the Noise: Why So Many Predictions Fail—but Some Don't* (London: Penguin, 2015).
24. Goodreads.com, accessed December 10, 2019, https://www.goodreads.com/quotes /393102-when-information-is-cheap-attention-becomes-expensive.
25. Ian Cassel, "Paul Lountzis on Differential Insights," MicroCapClub, October 10, 2016, https://microcapclub.com/2016/10/paul-lountzis-differential-insights/.
26. Charles Darwin, *The Life and Letters of Charles Darwin, Volume 1*, Classic Literature Library, 36, https://charles-darwin.classic-literature.co.uk/the-life-and-letters-of-charles -darwin-volume-i/ebook-page-36.asp.
27. Bakshi, "Worldly Wisdom in an Equation."
28. Martin Zweig, *Martin Zweig's Winning on Wall Street*, rev. ed. (New York: Warner, 1997).
29. Philip A. Fisher, *Common Stocks and Uncommon Profits and Other Writings*, 2nd ed. (Hoboken, NJ: Wiley, 2003).
30. "13 Steps to Financial Freedom—Step 10: Invest Like the Masters," Motley Fool, https:// www.fool.ca/13-steps-to-financial-freedom/step-10-invest-like-the-masters.
31. Quotefancy.com, accessed December 10, 2019, https://quotefancy.com/quote/756828 /Charlie-Munger-The-big-money-is-not-in-the-buying-and-selling-but-in-the-waiting.
32. Laurence Arnold, "Walter Schloss, 'Superinvestor' Praised by Buffett, Dies at 95," Bloomberg, February 20, 2012, https://www.bloomberg.com/news/articles/2012-02-20 /walter-schloss-superinvestor-who-earned-buffett-s-praise-dies-at-95.
33. Benjamin Graham and David Dodd, *Security Analysis*, 6th ed. (New York: McGraw-Hill Education, 2008).
34. Peter Lynch, *Beating the Street* (New York: Simon and Schuster, 1994).

28. Life Is a Series of Opportunity Costs

1. Adam Parris, "Value Investors and Bear Markets," ValueWalk, September 9, 2017, https://www.valuewalk.com/2017/09/value-investors-bear-markets.
2. Shane Parrish, "Why Mental Models? My Interview with Professor and Value Investor Sanjay Bakshi," The Knowledge Project, Ep. #3, *Farnam Street* (blog), audio, https:// www.fs.blog/2015/09/sanjay-bakshireading-mental-models-worldly-wisdom.

29. Pattern Recognition

1. Arthur Conan Doyle, *Silver Blaze* (Ada, MI: Baker, 2016).
2. Marcelo P. Lima, *Q2 2018 Letter to Investors*, Heller House Opportunity Fund, L.P., August 28, 2018.
3. Vijay Govindarajan, Shivaram Rajgopal, and Anup Srivastava, "Why Financial Statements Don't Work for Digital Companies," *Harvard Business Review*, February 26, 2018, https://hbr.org/2018/02/why-financial-statements-dont-work-for-digital-companies.
4. Govindarajan, Rajgopal, and Srivastava, "Why Financial Statements Don't Work."
5. Richard Zeckhauser, "Investing in the Unknown and Unknowable," *Capitalism and Society* 1, no. 2, article 5 (2006), https://sites.hks.harvard.edu/fs/rzeckhau/Investingin UnknownandUnknowable.pdf.
6. "Visita a Warren Buffett," Think Finance, 2005, http://www.thinkfn.com/wikibolsa/Visita _a_Warren_Buffett.

7. Warren Buffett, *Berkshire Hathaway 1990 Annual Letter to Shareholders*, March 1, 1991, http://www.berkshirehathaway.com/letters/1990.html.

8. Ray Kurzweil, *The Singularity Is Near: When Humans Transcend Biology* (London: Penguin, 2006).

30. Acknowledging the Role of Luck, Chance, Serendipity, and Randomness

1. Max Gunther, *How to Get Lucky: 13 Techniques for Discovering and Taking Advantage of Life's Good Breaks* (London: Harriman House, 2010).

2. Gunther, *How to Get Lucky*.

3. William Watts, "Birthday Boy Warren Buffett Reaffirms His Love for Apple, but Sinks Mondelez," MarketWatch, August 30, 2017, https://www.marketwatch.com/story/birthday-boy-warren-buffett-reaffirms-his-love-for-apple-but-sends-mondelez-tumbling-2017-08-30.

4. Nick Maggiulli, "Why Winners Keep Winning," *Of Dollars and Data* (blog), May 8, 2018, https://ofdollarsanddata.com/why-winners-keep-winning.

5. Max Gunther, *The Zurich Axioms: The Rules of Risk and Reward Used by Generations of Swiss Bankers* (London: Harriman House, 2005).

6. Warren Buffett, *Berkshire Hathaway 2000 Annual Letter to Shareholders*, February 28, 2001, http://www.berkshirehathaway.com/2000ar/2000letter.html.

7. WBI Investments, "Investors Are Told to Buy and Hold, but Do They?" WBI Insights, June 4, 2019, https://wbiinsights.com/2019/06/04/investors-are-told-to-buy-and-hold-but-do-they/.

8. Goodreads.com, accessed December 10, 2019, https://www.goodreads.com/quotes/29255-be-fearful-when-others-are-greedy-and-greedy-when-others.

9. Robert Rubin, "Harvard Commencement Address," 2001.

31. The Education of a Value Investor

1. Vishal Khandelwal, "Investing and the Art of Cloning," Safal Niveshak, May 14, 2018, https://www.safalniveshak.com/investing-and-cloning.

2. Philip A. Fisher, *Common Stocks and Uncommon Profits and Other Writings*, 2nd ed. (Hoboken, NJ: Wiley, 2003).

3. Fisher, *Common Stocks and Uncommon Profits*.

4. Charles P. Kindleberger, *Manias, Panics, and Crashes: A History of Financial Crises* (Hoboken, NJ: Wiley, 2000).

5. Goodreads.com, accessed December 10, 2019, https://www.goodreads.com/quotes/7609885-you-don-t-have-to-pee-on-an-electric-fence-to.

6. Charlie Munger, "The Psychology of Human Misjudgment by Charles T. Munger," Harrison Barnes, January 17, 2015, https://www.hb.org/the-psychology-of-human-misjudgment-by-charles-t-munger/#07.

7. Thinkmentalmodels.com, "Deprival Syndrome—The Takeaway," accessed December 10, 2019, http://www.thinkmentalmodels.com/page66/page89/page89.html.

8. Richard H. Thaler and Cass R. Sunstein, *Nudge: Improving Decisions About Health, Wealth, and Happiness*, rev. ed. (New York: Penguin, 2009).

9. Bill Gates, "This Animal Kills More People in a Day Than Sharks Do in a Century," GatesNotes, April 23, 2018, https://www.gatesnotes.com/Health/Mosquito-Week-2018.

10. Benjamin Graham and Jason Zweig, *The Intelligent Investor: The Definitive Book on Value Investing*, rev. ed. (New York: Harper Business, 2006); Louis Brandeis, in C. C. Gaither and Alma E Cavazos-Gaither, *Mathematically Speaking: A Dictionary of Quotations* (Boca Raton, FL: CRC Press, 1998).

11. Brad M. Barber and Terrance Odean," Why Do Investors Trade Too Much?" (research summary, University of California Davis Graduate School of Management, Davis, CA, 2006), https://www.safalniveshak.com/wp-content/uploads/2012/07/Why-Do-Investors-Trade-Too-Much.pdf.

12. Josef Lakonishok, Andrei Shleifer, and Robert Vishny, "The Structure and Performance of the Money Management Industry," *Brookings Papers: Macroeconomics 1992*, https://scholar.harvard.edu/files/shleifer/files/structure_performance.pdf.

13. Graham and Zweig, *The Intelligent Investor*.

14. Sheeraz Raza, "Munger Quotes," ValueWalk, April 4, 2016, https://www.valuewalk.com/2016/04/charlie-munger-quotes-2.

32. Understanding the True Essence of Compounding

1. Alice Schroeder, *The Snowball: Warren Buffett and the Business of Life* (New York: Bantam, 2009).

2. Tren Griffin, "Charlie Munger AMA: How Does Charlie Munger Recommend Dealing with Adversity?" *25iq* (blog), November 14, 2015, https://25iq.com/2015/11/14/charlie-munger-ama-how-does-charlie-munger-recommend-dealing-with-adversity.

3. Joshua Kennon, "If Charlie Munger Didn't Quit When He Was Divorced, Broke, and Burying His 9-Year-Old Son, You Have No Excuse," April 12, 2011, https://www.joshuakennon.com/if-charlie-munger-didnt-quit-when-he-was-divorced-broke-and-burying-his-9-year-old-son-you-have-no-excuse.

4. Kenneth Jeffrey Marshall, *Good Stocks Cheap: Value Investing with Confidence for a Lifetime of Stock Market Outperformance* (New York: McGraw-Hill Education, 2017).

5. Viktor E. Frankl, *Man's Search for Meaning* (Boston: Beacon, 2006).

6. Charles Fillmore, *Prosperity* (Eastford, CT: Martino Fine Books, 2011).

7. Charles Duhigg, *The Power of Habit: Why We Do What We Do in Life and Business* (New York: Random House, 2014).

8. Duhigg, *The Power of Habit*.

9. Quotecatalog.com, accessed December 10, 2019, https://quotecatalog.com/quote/warren-buffett-the-chains-of-h-K7QObga/.

10. Richard Lewis, "Peter Kaufman on the Multidisciplinary Approach to Thinking: Transcript," Latticework Investing, April 6, 2018, http://latticeworkinvesting.com/2018/04/06/peter-kaufman-on-the-multidisciplinary-approach-to-thinking.

11. John Bogle, "The Relentless Rules of Humble Arithmetic," *Financial Analysts Journal* 61, no. 6 (2005): 22–35.

12. Burton G. Malkiel and Charles D. Ellis, *The Elements of Investing: Easy Lessons for Every Investor* (Hoboken, NJ: Wiley, 2013).

13. Warren Buffett, *Berkshire Hathaway 1989 Annual Letter to Shareholders*, March 2, 1990, http://www.berkshirehathaway.com/letters/1989.html.

14. Investment Masters Class, "Compounding," accessed December 10, 2019, http://mastersinvest.com/compounding.

15. Whitney Tilson, ed., "Three Lectures by Warren Buffett to Notre Dame Faculty, MBA Students and Undergraduate Students," Whitney Tilson's Value Investing Website, Spring 1991, http://www.tilsonfunds.com/BuffettNotreDame.pdf.

16. Warren Buffett, "Morning Session—2001 Meeting," CNBC, Warren Buffet Archive, April 28, 2001, video, https://buffett.cnbc.com/video/2001/04/28/morning-session---2001-berkshire-hathaway-annual-meeting.html.

17. Josh Funk, "Berkshire's No. 2 Man Helps from the Background," ABC News, https://abcnews.go.com/Business/story?id=4881678&page=1.

18. Andrew Kilpatrick, *Of Permanent Value: The Story of Warren Buffett* (Mountain Brook, AL: Andy Kilpatrick Publishing Empire, 2018).

19. Rich Rockwood (@rrockw), "Excerpts from 1997 Caltech Speech," Motley Fool, board comment, January 4, 2003, http://boards.fool.com/excerpts-from-1997-caltech-speech-18377397.aspx?sort=postdate.

20. Confucius, "Higher Education," in *Wisdom Bible*, trans. Sanderson Beck (World Peace Communications, 1996), http://www.san.beck.org/Tahsueh.html.

21. Li Lu, "The Prospects for Value Investing in China," trans. Graham F. Rhodes, October 28, 2015, https://brianlangis.files.wordpress.com/2018/03/li-lu-the-prospects-for-value-investing-in-china.pdf.

22. Ray Dalio, *Principles: Life and Work* (New York: Simon and Schuster, 2017).

23. Tyler Tervooren, "Advice from Warren Buffet [*sic*]: Games Are Won By Players Who Focus on the Field," Riskology, https://www.riskology.co/focus-on-the-field.

Appendix A

1. David L. Weatherford, "Slow Dance," http://www.davidlweatherford.com/slowdance.html.

Appendix B

1. Rudyard Kipling, "If—," in *Rewards and Fairies* (New York: Doubleday, 1910).

BIBLIOGRAPHY

"13 Steps to Financial Freedom—Step 10: Invest Like the Masters." Motley Fool. https://www.fool.ca/13-steps-to-financial-freedom/step-10-invest-like-the-masters.

"35 Quotes from Benjamin Graham." Caproasia Online, May 8, 2015. http://www.caproasia.com/2015/05/08/35-quotes-from-benjamin-graham.

"A Conversation with Charlie Munger: DuBridge Distinguished Visitor Lecture." Caltech, March 11, 2008. http://www.caltech.edu/content/conversation-charlie-munger-dubridge-distinguished-visitor-lecture.

Allison, Graham, Robert D. Blackwill, and Ali Wyne. *Lee Kuan Yew: The Grand Master's Insights on China, the United States, and the World.* Cambridge, MA: MIT Press, 2013.

Andersen, Erika. "23 Quotes from Warren Buffett on Life and Generosity." *Forbes,* December 2, 2013. https://www.forbes.com/sites/erikaandersen/2013/12/02/23-quotes-from-warren-buffett-on-life-and-generosity/#5f2270aaf891.

Arnold, Laurence. "Walter Schloss, 'Superinvestor' Praised by Buffett, Dies at 95." Bloomberg, February 20, 2012. https://www.bloomberg.com/news/articles/2012-02-20/walter-schloss-superinvestor-who-earned-buffett-s-praise-dies-at-95.

Baer, Drake. "Why Productive People Have Empty Schedules." *Fast Company,* May 10, 2013. https://www.fastcompany.com/3009536/why-productive-people-have-empty-schedules.

Bakshi, Sanjay. "All I Care About Is Virginity." *Fundoo Professor* (blog), October 19, 2012. https://fundooprofessor.wordpress.com/2012/10/19/virginity.

——. "The Psychology of Human Misjudgment VI." LinkedIn SlideShare, December 16, 2012. https://www.slideshare.net/bakshi1/the-psychology-of-human-misjudgment-vi.

——. *What Happens When You Don't Buy Quality? And What Happens When You Do?* OctoberQuest 2013, October 11, 2013. https://www.dropbox.com/s/haqe3psl29u1scx/October_Quest_2013.pdf.

——. "Worldly Wisdom in an Equation." *Fundoo Professor* (blog), October 9, 2015. https://fundooprofessor.wordpress.com/2015/10/08/worldly-wisdom-in-an-equation/.

Barber, Brad M., and Terrance Odean. *Why Do Investors Trade Too Much?* Research summary. University of California Davis Graduate School of Management, Davis, CA, 2006. https://www.safalniveshak.com/wp-content/uploads/2012/07/Why-Do-Investors-Trade-Too-Much.pdf.

Barrow, Alex. "Stanley Druckenmiller on Liquidity, Macro, and Margins." Macro Ops, June 23, 2017. https://macro-ops.com/stanley-druckenmiller-on-liquidity-macro-margins.

Bartlett, Al. "Arithmetic, Population and Energy: A Talk by Al Bartlett." Video. http://www.albartlett.org/presentations/arithmetic_population_energy_video1.html.

Batnick, Michael. "Gradual Improvements Go Unnoticed." Irrelevant Investor, March 20, 2017. http://theirrelevantinvestor.com/2017/03/20/gradual-improvements-go-unnoticed.

Becoming Warren Buffett. HBO Documentary Films, 2017. https://www.youtube.com/watch?v=PB5krSvFAPY.

Begg, Christopher M. "2014 3rd Quarter Letter." East Coast Asset Management, November 10, 2014. http://www.eastcoastasset.com/wp-content/uploads/ecam_2014_3q_letter.pdf.

Benello, Allen C., Michael van Biema, and Tobias E. Carlisle. *Concentrated Investing: Strategies of the World's Greatest Concentrated Value Investors.* Hoboken, NJ: Wiley, 2016.

Benoit, Andy. "The Case for the . . . Broncos." *Sports Illustrated*, January 13, 2014. https://www.si.com/vault/2014/01/13/106417354/the-case-for-the-broncos.

Berkshire Hathaway. "1990 Annual Meeting." *Outstanding Investor Digest*, May 31, 1990.

——. "2000 Annual Meeting." *Outstanding Investor Digest*, December 18, 2000.

——. "2005 Annual Meeting." *Outstanding Investor Digest*, March 9, 2006.

——. Press conference, May 2001.

Berman, James. "The Three Essential Warren Buffett Quotes to Live By." *Forbes*, April 20, 2014. https://www.forbes.com/sites/jamesberman/2014/04/20/the-three-essential-warren-buffett-quotes-to-live-by/#a6a575a65439.

Bernard, Michael E. *Rationality and the Pursuit of Happiness: The Legacy of Albert Ellis.* Hoboken, NJ: Wiley-Blackwell, 2010.

Bernstein, Peter L. *Against the Gods: The Remarkable Story of Risk.* Hoboken, NJ: Wiley, 1998.

Beshore, Brent. "Going Pro: 2017 Year In Review." Adventures. https://www.adventur.es/2017-annual-letter-going-pro.

"Best Moments from Buffett's Annual Berkshire Shareholder Meeting." *Forbes*, May 9, 2016. https://www.forbes.com/sites/gurufocus/2016/05/09/best-moments-from-buffetts-annual-berkshire-shareholder-meeting/#480b98082e55.

The Best of Charlie Munger: 1994–2011: A Collection of Speeches, Essays, and Wesco Annual Meeting Notes. Compiled by Yanan Ma Bledsoe. Value Plays. http://www.valueplays.net/wp-content/uploads/The-Best-of-Charlie-Munger-1994-2011.pdf.

Bevelin, Peter. *Seeking Wisdom: From Darwin to Munger*, 3rd ed. Malmö, Sweden: PCA Publications, 2007.

Bezos, Jeff. *Amazon 1997 Letter to Shareholders.* http://media.corporate-ir.net/media_files/irol/97/97664/reports/Shareholderletter97.pdf.

——. *Amazon 2014 Letter to Shareholders.* http://phx.corporate-ir.net/External.File?item=UGFyZW50SUQ9MjgxMzIwfENoaWxkSUQ9LTF8VHlwZToz&t=1.

Bloch, Robert L. *My Warren Buffett Bible: A Short and Simple Guide to Rational Investing.* New York: Skyhorse, 2015.

Bogle, John C. *The Little Book of Common Sense Investing: The Only Way to Guarantee Your Fair Share of Stock Market Returns.* Hoboken, NJ: Wiley, 2017.

Boodell, Peter et al. "Berkshire Hathaway Annual Meeting, Omaha, Nebraska." Tilson Funds, May 3, 2008. http://www.tilsonfunds.com/BRKnotes08.pdf.

Brooks, John. *Business Adventures: Twelve Classic Tales from the World of Wall Street.* New York: Open Road, 2014.

Buffett, Peter. *Life Is What You Make It: Find Your Own Path to Fulfillment.* New York: Three Rivers Press, 2011.

Buffett FAQ. *2003 Berkshire Hathaway Annual Meeting.* http://buffettfaq.com.

——. *2006 Berkshire Hathaway Annual Meeting.* http://buffettfaq.com.

——. *2008 Berkshire Hathaway Annual Meeting.* http://buffettfaq.com.

Buffett, Warren. *Berkshire Hathaway Inc. Shareholder Letters.* http://www.berkshirehathaway.com/letters/letters.html.

——. *Berkshire Hathaway 1977 Annual Letter to Shareholders.* March 14, 1978. http://www.berkshirehathaway.com/letters/1977.html.

——. *Berkshire Hathaway 1979 Annual Letter to Shareholders.* March 3, 1980. http://www.berkshirehathaway.com/letters/1979.html.

——. *Berkshire Hathaway 1980 Annual Letter to Shareholders.* February 27, 1981. http://www.berkshirehathaway.com/letters/1980.html.

——. *Berkshire Hathaway 1982 Annual Letter to Shareholders.* March 3, 1983. http://www.berkshirehathaway.com/letters/1982.html

——. *Berkshire Hathaway 1983 Annual Letter to Shareholders.* March 14, 1984. http://www.berkshirehathaway.com/letters/1983.html.

——. *Berkshire Hathaway 1984 Annual Letter to Shareholders.* February 25, 1985. http://www.berkshirehathaway.com/letters/1984.html.

——. *Berkshire Hathaway 1986 Annual Letter to Shareholders.* February 27, 1987. http://www.berkshirehathaway.com/letters/1986.html.

——. *Berkshire Hathaway 1987 Annual Letter to Shareholders.* February 29, 1988. https://www.berkshirehathaway.com/letters/1987.html.

——. *Berkshire Hathaway 1989 Annual Letter to Shareholders.* March 2, 1990. http://www.berkshirehathaway.com/letters/1989.html.

——. *Berkshire Hathaway 1990 Annual Letter to Shareholders.* March 1, 1991. http://www.berkshirehathaway.com/letters/1990.html.

——. *Berkshire Hathaway 1992 Annual Letter to Shareholders.* March 1, 1993. http://www.berkshirehathaway.com/letters/1992.html.

——. *Berkshire Hathaway 1993 Annual Letter to Shareholders.* March 1, 1994. http://www.berkshirehathaway.com/letters/1993.html.

——. *Berkshire Hathaway 1994 Annual Letter to Shareholders.* March 7, 1995. http://www.berkshirehathaway.com/letters/1994.html.

——. *Berkshire Hathaway 1996 Annual Letter to Shareholders.* February 28, 1997. http://www.berkshirehathaway.com/letters/1996.html.

——. *Berkshire Hathaway 1998 Annual Letter to Shareholders.* March 1, 1999. http://www.berkshirehathaway.com/letters/1998pdf.pdf.

——. *Berkshire Hathaway 1999 Annual Letter to Shareholders.* March 1, 2000. http://www.berkshirehathaway.com/letters/1999htm.html.

——. *Berkshire Hathaway 2000 Annual Letter to Shareholders.* February 28, 2001. http://www.berkshirehathaway.com/letters/2000pdf.pdf.

——. *Berkshire Hathaway 2001 Annual Letter to Shareholders.* February 28, 2002. https://www.berkshirehathaway.com/2001ar/2001letter.html.

——. *Berkshire Hathaway 2002 Annual Letter to Shareholders.* February 21, 2003. http://www.berkshirehathaway.com/letters/2002pdf.pdf

——. *Berkshire Hathaway 2004 Annual Letter to Shareholders.* February 28, 2005. http://www.berkshirehathaway.com/letters/2004ltr.pdf.

——. *Berkshire Hathaway 2005 Annual Letter to Shareholders.* February 28, 2006. http://www
.berkshirehathaway.com/letters/2005ltr.pdf.

——. *Berkshire Hathaway 2007 Annual Letter to Shareholders.* February 2008. http://www
.berkshirehathaway.com/letters/2007ltr.pdf.

——. *Berkshire Hathaway 2008 Annual Letter to Shareholders.* February 27, 2009. http://www
.berkshirehathaway.com/letters/2008ltr.pdf.

——. *Berkshire Hathaway 2010 Annual Letter to Shareholders.* February 26, 2011. http://www
.berkshirehathaway.com/letters/2010ltr.pdf

——. *Berkshire Hathaway 2012 Annual Letter to Shareholders.* March 1, 2013. http://www
.berkshirehathaway.com/letters/2012ltr.pdf.

——. *Berkshire Hathaway 2014 Annual Letter to Shareholders.* February 27, 2015. http://www
.berkshirehathaway.com/letters/2014ltr.pdf.

——. *Berkshire Hathaway 2016 Annual Letter to Shareholders.* February 25, 2017. http://www
.berkshirehathaway.com/letters/2016ltr.pdf.

——. *Berkshire Hathaway 2017 Annual Letter to Shareholders.* February 24, 2018. http://www
.berkshirehathaway.com/letters/2017ltr.pdf.

——. "Buffett: How Inflation Swindles the Equity Investor (Fortune Classics, 1977)." *Fortune*,
June 12, 2011. http://fortune.com/2011/06/12/buffett-how-inflation-swindles-the-equity
-investor-fortune-classics-1977.

——. "Buffett Partnership Letter, January 25, 1967." In *Buffett Partnership Letters 1957 to 1970*,
100. CS Investing. http://csinvesting.org/wp-content/uploads/2012/05/complete_buffett
_partnership_letters-1957-70_in-sections.pdf.

——. "Buffett Partnership Letter, October 9, 1967." In *Buffett Partnership Letters 1957 to 1970*,
111. CS Investing. http://csinvesting.org/wp-content/uploads/2012/05/complete_buffett
_partnership_letters-1957-70_in-sections.pdf.

——. "Buffett Partnership Letter, January 22, 1969." In *Buffett Partnership Letters 1957 to 1970*,
123. CS Investing. http://csinvesting.org/wp-content/uploads/2012/05/complete_buffett
_partnership_letters-1957-70_in-sections.pdf.

——. "Buffett Partnership Letter, October 9, 1969." In *Buffett Partnership Letters 1957 to 1970*,
132. CS Investing. http://csinvesting.org/wp-content/uploads/2012/05/complete_buffett
_partnership_letters-1957-70_in-sections.pdf.

——. "Morning Session—2000 Meeting." CNBC, Warren Buffett Archive, April 29, 2000.
Video. https://buffett.cnbc.com/video/2000/04/29/morning-session---2000-berkshire
-hathaway-annual-meeting.html.

——. "Morning Session—2001 Meeting." CNBC, Warren Buffet Archive, April 28, 2001.
Video. https://buffett.cnbc.com/video/2001/04/28/morning-session---2001-berkshire
-hathaway-annual-meeting.html.

——. *An Owner's Manual.* Berkshire Hathaway, June 1996. http://www.berkshirehathaway
.com/ownman.pdf.

Burger, Edward B., and Michael Starbird. *Five Elements of Effective Thinking.* Princeton, NJ:
Princeton University Press, 2012.

Butler, Hartman. "An Hour with Mr. Graham." Graham and Doddsville, March 6, 1976.
http://www.grahamanddoddsville.net/wordpress/Files/Gurus/Benjamin%20Graham
/an-hour-ben-graham.pdf.

Carlisle, Tobias E. *Deep Value: Why Activist Investors and Other Contrarians Battle for Control
of Losing Corporations.* Hoboken, NJ: Wiley, 2014.

Carlson, Ben. *A Wealth of Common Sense: Why Simplicity Trumps Complexity in Any
Investment Plan.* Hoboken, NJ: Bloomberg Press, 2015.

Carlson, Ben. "Peter Lynch on Stock Market Losses." A Wealth of Common Sense, August 2,
2014. http://awealthofcommonsense.com/2014/08/peter-lynch-stock-market-losses.

——. "Why Simple Beats Complex." A Wealth of Common Sense, July 9, 2017. http://awealthofcommonsense.com/2017/07/why-simple-beats-complex.

Carnegie, Andrew. "Wealth." North American Review no. 391 (June 1889). https://www.swarthmore.edu/SocSci/rbannis1/AIH19th/Carnegie.html.

Carnevale, Chuck. "How to Use the Correct Discount Rate." ValueWalk, September 27, 2013. https://www.valuewalk.com/2013/09/use-correct-discount-rate.

Carr, Nicholas. "Situational Overload and Ambient Overload." Rough Type, March 7, 2011. http://www.roughtype.com/?p=1464.

Cassel, Ian. "A New Mental Model for Investing." MicroCapClub, February 1, 2018. https://microcapclub.com/2018/02/new-mental-model-investing.

—— (@Ian Cassel). "Spend time building new relationships." Twitter, August 16, 2018. https://twitter.com/iancassel/status/1030069258305368065.

Chancellor, Edward. Capital Returns: Investing Through the Capital Cycle: A Money Manager's Reports 2002–15. Basingstoke, UK: Palgrave Macmillan, 2016.

"Charlie Munger on 'Frozen Corporation.'" ValueWalk, July 16, 2015. https://www.valuewalk.com/2015/07/charlie-munger-on-frozen-corporation.

"Charlie Munger on Getting Rich, Wisdom, Focus, Fake Knowledge and More." Farnam Street (blog), February 2017. https://fs.blog/2017/02/charlie-munger-wisdom.

"Charlie Munger on Mistakes." 25iq (blog), November 16, 2012. https://25iq.com/2012/11/16/charlie-munger-on-mistakes.

Christian, Brian, and Tom Griffiths. Algorithms to Live By: The Computer Science of Human Decisions. New York: Henry Holt, 2016.

"Chuck's 3 Legged Stool." Investment Masters Class, August 8, 2018. https://mastersinvest.com/newblog/2018/8/3/chucks-3-legged-stool.

Cialdini, Robert. Influence: Science and Practice. Essex, UK: Pearson, 2014.

Clear, James. "First Principles: Elon Musk on the Power of Thinking for Yourself." The Mission, February 2, 2018. https://medium.com/the-mission/first-principles-elon-musk-on-the-power-of-thinking-for-yourself-8bof275af361.

—— (@JamesClear). "Motion does not equal action." Twitter, January 31, 2018. https://twitter.com/james_clear/status/958824949367615489?lang=en.

Cogitator Capital. "Special Situation Investing." ValueWalk, 2008. http://www.valuewalk.com/wp-content/uploads/2010/09/37200720-33263413-Special-Situation-Investing-by-Ben-Graham.pdf.

Collier, Charles W. Wealth in Families. Cambridge, MA: Harvard University, 2006.

Collins, Jim. Good to Great: Why Some Companies Make the Leap—And Others Don't. New York: HarperCollins, 2011.

Colvin, Geoff. Talent Is Overrated: What Really Separates World-Class Performers from Everybody Else. London: Nicholas Brealey, 2019.

"Commitment–Confirmation–Consistency Bias." Investment Masters Class. http://mastersinvest.com/confirmationquotes.

Confucius. "Higher Education." In Wisdom Bible. Translated by Sanderson Beck. World Peace Communications, 1996. http://www.san.beck.org/Tahsueh.html.

Coyle, Daniel. The Little Book of Talent: 52 Tips for Improving Your Skills. New York: Bantam, 2012.

Credit Suisse. "Was Warren Buffet Right: Do Wonderful Companies Remain Wonderful?" HOLT Wealth Creation Principles, June 2013. https://research-doc.credit-suisse.com/mercurydoc?language=ENG&format=PDF&document_id=1019433381&serialid=*EMAIL_REMOVED*&auditid=1182867.

Crippen, Alex. "Warren Buffett's 5-Minute Plan to Fix the Deficit." CNBC, July 11, 2011. https://www.cnbc.com/id/43670783.

Dalio, Ray. *Principles: Life and Work*. New York: Simon and Schuster, 2017.

Damato, Karen. "Is Your Manager Skillful . . . or Just Lucky?" *Wall Street Journal*, November 2, 2012. https://www.wsj.com/articles/SB10000872396390444734804578062890110146284.

Darwin, Charles. *The Life and Letters of Charles Darwin*, Volume 1. Classic Literature Library. https://charles-darwin.classic-literature.co.uk/the-life-and-letters-of-charles-darwin -volume-i/ebook-page-36.asp.

Dawson, William James. *The Quest of the Simple Life*. Boston, MA: Qontro Classic, 2010.

Deresiewicz, William. "Solitude and Leadership." American Scholar, March 1, 2010. https:// theamericanscholar.org/solitude-and-leadership/#.Wt-DKUxFydI.

Desai, Mihir. *The Wisdom of Finance: Discovering Humanity in the World of Risk and Return*. Boston: Houghton Mifflin Harcourt, 2017.

DeMuth, Phil. "Charlie Munger's 2015 Daily Journal Annual Meeting—Part 1." *Forbes*, April 7, 2015. https://www.forbes.com/sites/phildemuth/2015/04/07/charlie-mungers-2015-daily -journal-annual-meeting-part-1/#2f3663b8f183.

——. "The Mysterious Factor 'P': Charlie Munger, Robert Novy-Marx and the Profitability Factor." *Forbes*, June 27, 2013.

De Vany, Arthur. *The New Evolution Diet: What Our Paleolithic Ancestors Can Teach Us About Weight Loss, Fitness, and Aging*. Emmaus, PA: Rodale, 2011.

Dickens, Charles. *David Copperfield*. London: Penguin Classics, 2004.

Dobelli, Rolf. *The Art of Thinking Clearly*. New York: HarperCollins, 2013.

Dorsey, Pat. *Competitive Advantage and Capital Allocation*. Dorsey Asset Management, March 2917. https://dorseyasset.com/wp-content/uploads/2016/07/mit-sloan-investment -conference_competitive-advantage-and-capital-allocation_dorsey-asset-management _march-2017.pdf.

Doyle, Arthur Conan. *The Memoirs of Sherlock Holmes: The Reigate Puzzle*. CreateSpace Independent Publishing Platform, 2016.

——. *Silver Blaze*. Ada, MI: Baker, 2016.

Duhigg, Charles. *The Power of Habit: Why We Do What We Do in Life and Business*. New York: Random House, 2014.

Duke, Annie. *Thinking in Bets: Making Smarter Decisions When You Don't Have All the Facts*. New York: Portfolio, 2018.

Durant, Will, and Ariel Durant. *The Lessons of History*. New York: Simon and Schuster, 2010.

The Edge Consulting Group. *Global Spinoffs and the Hidden Value of Corporate Change*, Vol. 2, *Executive Summary*, December 2014. https://www.hvst.com/attachments/1437/Exec _Summary_-_The_Edge_Deloitte_Global_Spinoff_Study_-_Dec_2014.pdf.

Eisner, Michael D., and Aaron R. Cohen. *Working Together: Why Great Partnerships Succeed*. New York: Harper Business, 2012.

EliasFardo. "Go Ask Alice." Motley Fool, board comment, March 18, 2003. http://boards.fool .com/you-might-want-to-discount-the-float-growth-at-a-18762436.aspx.

Ellis, Charles D. "The Loser's Game." *Financial Analysts Journal*, January–February 1995. https://www.cfapubs.org/doi/pdf/10.2469/faj.v51.n1.1865.

Ellis, Charles, and James Vertin. *Classics: An Investor's Anthology*. New York: Business One Irwin, 1988.

Endersen, Laurence. *Pebbles of Perception: How a Few Good Choices Make All the Difference*. CreateSpace Independent Publishing Platform, 2014.

Epoch Investment Partner. "The P/E Ratio: A User's Manual." Epoch, June 17, 2019. http:// www.eipny.com/white-papers/the_p-e_ratio_a-users_manual/.

"Exclusive Interview with Arnold Van Den Berg." *Manual of Ideas* 7, no. 9 (September 2014). https://www.manualofideas.com/wp-content/uploads/2014/09/the-manual-of-ideas -arnold-van-den-berg-201409.pdf.

Fearon, Scott, and Jesse Powell. *Dead Companies Walking: How a Hedge Fund Manager Finds Opportunity in Unexpected Places*. New York: St. Martin's, 2015.

Feynman, Richard P. "Atoms in Motion." California Institute of Technology, The Feynman Lectures on Physics. http://www.feynmanlectures.caltech.edu/I_01.html.

——. *Perfectly Reasonable Deviations (from the Beaten Track)*. New York: Basic, 2006.

——. *Perfectly Reasonable Deviations from the Beaten Track: The Letters of Richard P. Feynman*. New York: Basic, 2005.

——. *The Pleasure of Finding Things Out: The Best Short Works of Richard P. Feynman*. New York: Basic, 2005.

Fillmore, Charles. *Prosperity*. Eastford, CT: Martino, 2011.

"Financial Crisis Inquiry Commission Staff Audiotape of Interview with Warren Buffett, Berkshire Hathaway." *Santangel's Review*, May 26, 2010. Audio. http://dericbownds.net/uploaded_images/Buffett_FCIC_transcript.pdf.

Firestone, Harvey. *Men and Rubber: The Story of Business*. Whitefish, MT: Kessinger, 2003.

Fisher, Phil. *Common Stocks and Uncommon Profits and Other Writings*, 2nd ed. Hoboken, NJ: Wiley, 2003.

Fishman, Steve. "Bernie Madoff, Free at Last." *New York*, June 6, 2010. http://nymag.com/news/crimelaw/66468.

Flores, Brian. "Why Investors Must Always Consider Opportunity Costs." GuruFocus, February 18, 2016. https://www.gurufocus.com/news/393334/why-investors-must-always-consider-opportunity-costs.

Foulke, David. "Warren Buffett on LTCM, Blind Spots, Leverage, and Unnecessary Risk." Alpha Architect, September 8, 2015. https://alphaarchitect.com/2015/09/08/warren-buffett-ltcm-blind-spots-leverage-taking-unnecessary-risks/.

Frankl, Viktor E. *Man's Search for Meaning*. Boston: Beacon, 2006.

Fundsmith Equity Fund Owner's Manual. https://www.fundsmith.co.uk/docs/default-source/analysis---owners-manuals/owners-manual-pdf.pdf?sfvrsn=16.

Funk, Josh. "Berkshire's No. 2 Man Helps from the Background." ABC News. https://abcnews.go.com/Business/story?id=4881678&page=1.

Gaither, C. C., and Alma E Cavazos-Gaither. *Mathematically Speaking: A Dictionary of Quotations*. Boca Raton, FL: CRC Press, 1998.

Galbraith, John Kenneth. *Economics, Peace and Laughter*. New York: Signet, 1972.

Galton, Francis. "Vox Populi." *Nature*, March 7, 1907. http://galton.org/essays/1900-1911/galton-1907-vox-populi.pdf.

Gates, Bill. "This Animal Kills More People in a Day Than Sharks Do in a Century." GatesNotes, April 23, 2018. https://www.gatesnotes.com/Health/Mosquito-Week-2018.

Gawande, Atul. *The Checklist Manifesto*. Gurgaon, India: Penguin Random House, 2014.

Gayner, Tom. "Identifying Great Capital Allocators." Presentation at the 11th Annual Value Investor Conference, May 1 and 2, 2014. http://www.valueinvestorconference.com/2014presentations/VIC%2014%20Gayner%20Transcript.pdf.

Gladwell, Malcolm. *Blink: The Power of Thinking Without Thinking*. New York: Little, Brown, 2005.

——. *Outliers: The Story of Success*. New York: Back Bay, 2011.

Glassman, James K., and Kavin A. Hassett. "Dow 36,000." *The Atlantic*, September 1999. https://www.theatlantic.com/magazine/archive/1999/09/dow-36-000/306249.

Goodwin, Tom. "The Battle Is for the Customer Interface." TechCrunch, March 3, 2015. https://techcrunch.com/2015/03/03/in-the-age-of-disintermediation-the-battle-is-all-for-the-customer-interface/.

Govindarajan, Vijay, Shivaram Rajgopal, and Anup Srivastava. "Why Financial Statements Don't Work for Digital Companies." *Harvard Business Review*, February 26, 2018. https://hbr.org/2018/02/why-financial-statements-dont-work-for-digital-companies.

Graham, Benjamin. *The Intelligent Investor*, 4th rev. ed. New York: Harper and Row, 1973.

——. *Security Analysis: The Classic 1951 Edition*. New York: McGraw-Hill Education, 2004.

Graham, Benjamin, and David Dodd. *Security Analysis*, 6th ed. New York: McGraw-Hill Education, 2008.

——. *Security Analysis: The Classic 1934 Edition*. New York: McGraw-Hill Education, 1996.

Graham, Benjamin, and Jason Zweig. *The Intelligent Investor: The Definitive Book on Value Investing*, rev. ed. New York: Harper Business, 2006.

Greenblatt, Joel. *You Can Be a Stock Market Genius*. New York: Touchstone, 2010.

Greenwald, Bruce C. N. *Value Investing: From Graham to Buffett and Beyond*. Hoboken, NJ: Wiley, 2004.

Greenwald, Bruce, and Judd Kahn. *Competition Demystified: A Radically Simplified Approach to Business Strategy*. New York: Portfolio, 2014.

Griffin, Ten. "Charlie Munger." *25iq* (blog). https://25iq.com/quotations/charlie-munger.

——. "Charlie Munger AMA: How Does Charlie Munger Recommend Dealing with Adversity?" *25iq* (blog), November 14, 2015. https://25iq.com/2015/11/14/charlie-munger -ama-how-does-charlie-munger-recommend-dealing-with-adversity.

——. *Charlie Munger: The Complete Investor*. New York: Columbia University Press, 2015.

——. "A Dozen Things I've Learned from Charlie Munger About Capital Allocation." *25iq* (blog), October 3, 2015. https://25iq.com/2015/10/03/a-dozen-things-ive-learned-from -charlie-munger-about-capital-allocation.

——. "A Dozen Things I've Learned from Charlie Munger About Inversion." *25iq* (blog), September 12, 2015. https://25iq.com/2015/09/12/a-dozen-things-ive-learned-from-charlie -munger-about-inversion-including-the-importance-of-being-consistently-not-stupid-2.

——. "How to Make Decisions Like Ray Dalio." *25iq* (blog), April 28, 2017. https://25iq .com/2017/04/28/how-to-make-decisions-like-ray-dalio.

Gunther, Max. *How to Get Lucky: 13 Techniques for Discovering and Taking Advantage of Life's Good Breaks*. London: Harriman House, 2010.

——. *The Zurich Axioms: The Rules of Risk and Reward Used by Generations of Swiss Bankers*. London: Harriman House, 2005.

Hagstrom, Robert G. *The Warren Buffett Way*, 2nd ed. Hoboken, NJ: Wiley, 2005.

Hamtil, Lawrence. "Price Is What You Pay; Value Is What You Get—Nifty Fifty Edition." *Fortune Financial* (blog), May 24, 2018. http://www.fortunefinancialadvisors.com/blog /price-is-what-you-pay-value-is-what-you-get-nifty-fifty-edition.

Harari, Yuval Noah. *Sapiens: A Brief History of Humankind*. New York: Harper, 2015.

Hattangadi, Amay, and Swanand Kelkar. *Connecting the Dots*. Morgan Stanley, December 2016. http://capitalideasonline.com/wordpress/wp-content/uploads/2016/12/Article-1.pdf.

——. "Reverberations in an Echo Chamber." Livemint, November 15, 2015. https://www.livemint .com/Opinion/FbpaBdLvJ1cdx3p02wwe1M/Reverberations-in-an-echo-chamber.html.

Hill, Napoleon. *Think and Grow Rich*. 1937. Reprint, Shippensburg, PA: Sound Wisdom, 2016.

Holiday, Ryan. "How to Read More Books—A Lot More." Thrive Global, August 13, 2018. https://medium.com/thrive-global/how-to-read-more-books-a-lot-more-1b459ac498b3.

Housel, Morgan. "Charlie Munger's Thoughts on the World: Part 1." Motley Fool, July 2, 2011. https://www.fool.com/investing/general/2011/07/02/charlie-mungers-thoughts-on-the -world-part-1.aspx.

——. "A Chat with Daniel Kahneman." *Collaborative Fund* (blog), January 12, 2017. http:// www.collaborativefund.com/blog/a-chat-with-daniel-kahneman.

——. "How to Read Financial News." *Collaborative Fund* (blog), December 6, 2017. http:// www.collaborativefund.com/blog/how-to-read-financial-news.

——. "Ideas That Changed My Life." *Collaborative Fund* (blog), March 7, 2018. http://www .collaborativefund.com/blog/ideas-that-changed-my-life.

——. "Investing Is a Fascinating Business." Motley Fool, August 30, 2016. https://www.fool
.com/investing/2016/08/30/investing-is-a-fascinating-business.aspx.

——. "The Peculiar Habits of Successful People." *USA Today*, August 24, 2014. https://www
.usatoday.com/story/money/personalfinance/2014/08/24/peculiar-habits-of-successful
-people/14447531.

——. "The Psychology of Money." *Collaborative Fund* (blog), June 1, 2018. http://www
.collaborativefund.com/blog/the-psychology-of-money.

——. "Risk Is How Much Time You Need." *Collaborative Fund* (blog), March 30, 2017. http://
www.collaborativefund.com/blog/risk.

——. "Saving Money and Running Backwards." *Collaborative Fund* (blog), September 27, 2017.
http://www.collaborativefund.com/blog/saving-money-and-running-backwards.

—— (@morganhousel). "Charlie Munger investment strategy." Twitter, June 15, 2017. https://
twitter.com/morganhousel/status/875547615592665088.

——. "We're All Innocently Out of Touch." *Collaborative Fund* (blog), November 17, 2017.
http://www.collaborativefund.com/blog/were-all-out-of-touch.

——. "What I Believe Most." *Collaborative Fund* (blog), July 5, 2017. http://www.collaborative
fund.com/blog/what-i-believe-most.

Howe, Rich. "What Klarman and Greenblatt Have to Say About Investing in Spinoffs—Part II."
ValueWalk, March 15, 2018. https://www.valuewalk.com/2018/03/klarman-greenblatt
-investing-spinoffs.

Ignatius, Adi. "Jeff Bezos on Leading for the Long-Term at Amazon." *Harvard Business
Review*, January 2013. https://hbr.org/2013/01/jeff-bezos-on-leading-for-the.

"Investing Instinct." Investment Masters Class. http://mastersinvest.com/investinginstinct
quotes.

Jobs, Steve. "'You've Got to Find What You Love,' Jobs Says." *Stanford News*, June 14, 2005.
https://news.stanford.edu/2005/06/14/jobs-061505.

Johnson, Carter. "Dr. Henry Singleton and Teledyne." ValueWalk, April 27, 2018. https://www
.valuewalk.com/2018/04/dr-henry-singleton-and-teledyne.

Jordon, Steve. "Investors Earn Handsome Paychecks by Handling Buffett's Business." *Omaha
World-Herald*, April 28, 2013. https://www.omaha.com/money/investors-earn-handsome
-paychecks-by-handling-buffett-s-business/article_bb1fc40f-e6f9-549d-be2f
-be1ef4c0da03.html.

Kahneman, Daniel. *Thinking, Fast and Slow*. New York: Farrar, Straus and Giroux, 2013.

Kaplan, Elle. "Why Warren Buffett's '20-Slot Rule' Will Make You Insanely Successful and
Wealthy." *Inc.*, July 22, 2016. https://www.inc.com/elle-kaplan/why-warren-buffett-s-20
-slot-rule-will-make-you-insanely-wealthy-and-successful.html.

Kaufman, Peter D., ed. *Poor Charlie's Almanack*. Marceline, MO: Walsworth, 2005.

Keller, Gary, and Jay Papasan. *The ONE Thing: The Surprisingly Simple Truth Behind
Extraordinary Results*. San Francisco: Instaread, 2016.

Kennon, Joshua. "If Charlie Munger Didn't Quit When He Was Divorced, Broke, and Burying
His 9-Year-Old Son, You Have No Excuse." April 12, 2011. https://www.joshuakennon
.com/if-charlie-munger-didnt-quit-when-he-was-divorced-broke-and-burying-his-9
-year-old-son-you-have-no-excuse.

Keynes, John Maynard. *The General Theory of Employment, Interest, and Money*. San Diego,
CA: Harcourt, Brace & World, 1965.

Khandelwal, Vishal. "In Investing, Catch the Right Anchor to Avoid Sinking." Safal Niveshak,
September 21, 2011. https://www.safalniveshak.com/in-investing-catch-the-right-anchor
-to-avoid-sinking.

——. "Investing and the Art of Cloning." Safal Niveshak, May 14, 2018. https://www.safalniveshak
.com/investing-and-cloning.

Khare, Anshul. "Investing and the Art of Metaphorical Thinking." Safal Niveshak, November 21, 2016. https://www.safalniveshak.com/investing-art-metaphorical-thinking.

Kilpatrick, Andy. *Of Permanent Value: The Story of Warren Buffett.* Birmingham, AL: Andy Kilpatrick Publishing Empire, 2018.

Kindleberger, Charles P. *Manias, Panics, and Crashes: A History of Financial Crises.* Hoboken, NJ: Wiley, 2000.

King, Stephen. *On Writing: A Memoir of the Craft.* New York: Simon and Schuster, 2000.

Kiyosaki, Robert T. *Rich Dad's Who Took My Money? Why Slow Investors Lost and Fast Money Wins!* New York: Warner Business Books, 2004.

Klarman, Seth A. *Margin of Safety: Risk-Averse Value Investing Strategies for the Thoughtful Investor.* New York: Harper Collins, 1991.

Koller, Timothy. "Why Value Value?—Defending Against Crises." McKinsey & Company, April 2010. https://www.mckinsey.com/business-functions/strategy-and-corporate-finance/our-insights/why-value-value-and-defending-against-crises.

Koller, Tim, Marc Goedhard, and David Wessels. *Valuation: Measuring and Managing the Value of Companies,* 6th ed. Hoboken, NJ: Wiley, 2015.

Kurzweil, Ray. *The Singularity Is Near: When Humans Transcend Biology.* London: Penguin, 2006.

Lakonishok, Josef, Andrei Shleifer, and Robert Vishny. "The Structure and Performance of the Money Management Industry." *Brookings Papers: Macroeconomics 1992.* https://scholar.harvard.edu/files/shleifer/files/structure_performance.pdf.

Latimore, Ed (@EdLatimore). Twitter, April 15, 2018. https://twitter.com/EdLatimore/status/1156550021363486721.

Lattman, Peter. "Bull and Bear Markets, According to Oaktree's Howard Marks." *Wall Street Journal,* March 20, 2008. https://blogs.wsj.com/deals/2008/03/20/bull-and-bear-markets-according-to-oaktrees-howard-marks.

LeBaron, Dean, and Romesh Vaitilingam. *Dean LeBaron's Treasury of Investment Wisdom: 30 Great Investing Minds.* Hoboken, NJ: Wiley, 2001.

Le Bon, Gustave. *The Crowd: A Study of the Popular Mind.* Mineola, NY: Dover, 2002.

Lefèvre, Edwin. *Reminiscences of a Stock Operator.* Hoboken, NJ: Wiley, 2006.

Leo, Jacqueline. *Seven: The Number for Happiness, Love, and Success.* New York: Twelve, 2009.

Lev, Baruch, and Feng Gu. *The End of Accounting.* Hoboken, NJ: Wiley, 2016.

"Leverage." Investment Masters Class. http://mastersinvest.com/leveragequotes.

Levy, Steven. "Jeff Bezos Owns the Web in More Ways Than You Think." *Wired,* November 13, 2011. https://www.wired.com/2011/11/ff_bezos.

Lewis, Richard. "Charlie Munger: Full Transcript of Daily Journal Annual Meeting 2017." Latticework Investing, February 17, 2017. http://latticeworkinvesting.com/2017/02/17/charlie-munger-full-transcript-of-daily-journal-annual-meeting-2017.

——. "Peter Kaufman on the Multidisciplinary Approach to Thinking: Transcript." Latticework Investing, April 6, 2018. http://latticeworkinvesting.com/2018/04/06/peter-kaufman-on-the-multidisciplinary-approach-to-thinking.

"Li Lu—Know What You Don't Know." Graham & Doddsville, Columbia Business School investment newsletter, Spring 2013. https://www8.gsb.columbia.edu/valueinvesting/sites/valueinvesting/files/files/Graham%20%26%20Doddsville%20-%20Issue%2018%20-%20Spring%202013_0.pdf.

Lima, Marcelo P. *Q2 2018 Letter to Investors.* Heller House Opportunity Fund, L.P., August 28, 2018.

"Links." Value Investing World, April 5, 2018. http://www.valueinvestingworld.com/2018/04/links_5.html.

Loeb, Gerald. *The Battle for Investment Survival*. Radford, VA: Wilder, 2014.

"Look at All These Spinoffs Beating the Market." *Old School Value* (blog), July 6, 2011. https://www.oldschoolvalue.com/blog/special_situation/look-at-all-these-spinoffs-beating-the-market.

Loomis, Carol. "Mr. Buffett on the Stock Market." *Fortune*, November 22, 1999. http://archive.fortune.com/magazines/fortune/fortune_archive/1999/11/22/269071/index.htm.

——. *Tap Dancing to Work: Warren Buffett on Practically Everything, 1966–2013*. New York: Portfolio, 2013.

——. "Warren Buffett on the Stock Market." *Fortune*, December 10, 2001. http://archive.fortune.com/magazines/fortune/fortune_archive/2001/12/10/314691/index.htm.

Loop, Floyd D. "Management Lessons from the Cleveland Clinic." American Management Association, September 22, 2009. http://www.amanet.org/training/articles/printversion/management-lessons-from-the-cleveland-clinic.aspx.

Lowe, Janet. *Damn Right: Behind the Scenes with Berkshire Hathaway Billionaire Charlie Munger*. Hoboken, NJ: Wiley, 2003.

Lu, Li. "The Prospects for Value Investing in China." Translated by Graham F. Rhodes. Brian Langis, October 28, 2015. https://brianlangis.files.wordpress.com/2018/03/li-lu-the-prospects-for-value-investing-in-china.pdf.

Lynch, Peter. *Beating the Street*. New York: Simon and Schuster, 1994.

——. *Learn to Earn: A Beginner's Guide to the Basics of Investing and Business*. New York: Simon and Schuster, 1996.

——. *One Up on Wall Street: How to Use What You Already Know to Make Money in the Market*. New York: Simon and Schuster, 2000.

MacKay, Charles. *Extraordinary Popular Delusions and the Madness of Crowds*. New York: Dover, 2003.

Maggiulli, Nick. "Against the Gods." *Of Dollars and Data* (blog), July 18, 2017. https://ofdollarsanddata.com/against-the-gods-3729ed3bb192.

——. "Why Winners Keep Winning." *Of Dollars and Data* (blog), May 8, 2018. https://ofdollarsanddata.com/why-winners-keep-winning.

Mahalakshmi, N. "Secret Diary of an Entrepreneur." Outlook Business, March 16, 2018. http://www.piramal.com/assets/pdf/Outlook-Business-16th-March-Pg-21-42.pdf.

Mahapatra, Lisa. "8 Brilliant Lessons from the Investor That Taught Warren Buffett Everything He Knows." *Business Insider*, February 6, 2013. https://www.businessinsider.com/eight-lessons-from-benjamin-graham-2013-2.

Malkiel, Burton G., and Charles D. Ellis. *The Elements of Investing: Easy Lessons for Every Investor*. Hoboken, NJ: Wiley, 2013.

Mallaby, Sebastian. *More Money Than God: Hedge Funds and the Making of a New Elite*. London: Penguin, 2011.

Maloney, Michael, and H. Harold Mulherin. "The Complexity of Price Discovery in an Efficient Market: The Stock Market Reaction to the Challenger Crash." *Journal of Corporate Finance* 9, no. 4 (2003): 453–479. https://www.sciencedirect.com/science/article/pii/S092911990200055X.

Mandelbrot, Benoit, and Richard L. Hudson. *The (Mis)Behavior of Markets: A Fractal View of Financial Turbulence*. New York: Basic Books, 2006.

Marks, Howard. "Dare to Be Great." Memo to Oaktree clients. Oaktree, September 7, 2006. https://www.oaktreecapital.com/docs/default-source/memos/2006-09-07-dare-to-be-great.pdf.

——. "Howard Marks: Investing in an Unknowable Future." *Barron's*, June 8, 2015. https://www.barrons.com/articles/howard-marks-investing-in-an-unknowable-future-1433802168.

——. *The Most Important Thing Illuminated: Uncommon Sense for the Thoughtful Investor.* New York: Columbia University Press, 2013.

——. "The Value of Predictions, or Where'd All This Rain Come From?" Memo to Oaktree clients. Oaktree, February 15, 1993. https://www.oaktreecapital.com/docs/default-source /memos/1993-02-15-the-value-of-predictions-or-where-39-d-all-this-rain-come-from.pdf.

——. "You Can't Predict. You Can Compare." Memo to Oaktree clients. Oaktree, November 20, 2001. https://www.oaktreecapital.com/docs/default-source/memos/2001-11-20-you-cant -predict-you-can-prepare.pdf.

Marshall, Kenneth Jeffrey. *Good Stocks Cheap: Value Investing with Confidence for a Lifetime of Stock Market Outperformance.* New York: McGraw-Hill Education, 2017.

Mauboussin, Michael J. *The Success Equation: Untangling Skill and Luck in Business, Sports, and Investing.* Boston: Harvard Business Press, 2012.

——. "What Does a Price-Earnings Multiple Mean?" Credit Suisse, January 29, 2014. https:// www.valuewalk.com/wp-content/uploads/2014/02/document-805915460.pdf.

Maurer, Robert. *One Small Step Can Change Your Life: The Kaizen Way.* Bhopal, India: Manjul Publishing House, 2017.

"Mohnish Pabrai's Q&A Session at Dakshana Valley (Pune District), December 26, 2017." YouTube, February 15, 2018. Video. https://www.youtube.com/watch?v=KJpipU-JYxc.

Munger, Charlie. "Academic Economics: Strengths and Faults After Considering Interdisci-plinary Needs." Herb Kay Undergraduate Lecture, University of California, Santa Barbara, Economics Department, October 3, 2003, Santa Barbara, CA. http://www.tilsonfunds .com/MungerUCSBspeech.pdf.

——. *Berkshire Hathaway 2014 Annual Letter to Shareholders.* February 27, 2015, http://www .berkshirehathaway.com/letters/2014ltr.pdf.

——. "A Lesson on Elementary, Worldly Wisdom as It Relates to Investment Management and Business." *Farnam Street* (blog), 1994. https://fs.blog/a-lesson-on-worldly-wisdom/.

——. "Outstanding Investor Digest." Speech at Stanford Law School Class of William Lazier, March 13, 1998, Stanford, CA.

——. "The Psychology of Human Misjudgment by Charles T. Munger." Harrison Barnes, January 17, 2015. https://www.hb.org/the-psychology-of-human-misjudgment-by-charles -t-munger/#07.

——. See's Candy Seventy-Fifth Anniversary Lunch, March 1998, Los Angeles, CA.

——. USC School of Law commencement speech. University of Southern California Gould School of Law, May 13, 2007, Los Angeles, CA. https://genius.com/Charlie-munger -usc-law-commencement-speech-annotated.

——. "Wesco Financial Corporation Letter to Shareholders." In *Charlie Munger's Wesco Financial Corporation Annual Letters 1983–2009,* 182. https://rememberingtheobvious .files.wordpress.com/2012/08/wesco-charlie-munger-letters-1983-2009-collection.pdf.

——. "Wesco 2002 Annual Meeting." Mungerisms, 2002. http://mungerisms.blogspot.com /2009/08/wesco-2002-annual-meeting.html.

——. "Wesco Financial's Charlie Munger." CS Investing, May 5, 1995. http://csinvesting.org /wp-content/uploads/2014/05/Worldly-Wisdom-by-Munger.pdf.

Musk, Elon (u/ElonMuskOfficial). "I Am Elon Musk, CEO/CTO of a Rocket Company, AMA!" Reddit, 2015. https://www.reddit.com/r/IAmA/comments/2rgsan/i_am_elon_musk _ceocto_of_a_rocket_company_ama/?st=jg8ec825&sh=4307fa36.

Ophuls, William. *Plato's Revenge: Politics in the Age of Ecology.* Cambridge, MA: MIT Press, 2011.

Oppong, Thomas. "How to Be 1% Better Every Day (the Kaizan Approach to Self-Improvement)." *The Mission Daily,* December 8, 2016. https://medium.com/the-mission/get-1-better-every -day-the-kaizan-approach-to-self-improvement-b79c9e045678.

O'Shaughnessy, James. *What Works on Wall Street*, 4th ed. New York: McGraw-Hill Education, 2011.

"Our National Predicament: Excerpts from Seth Klarman's 2010 Letter." Mungerisms, March 2, 2011. http://myinvestingnotebook.blogspot.com/2011/03/our-national-predicament-excerpts -from.html.

Pabrai, Mohnish. *The Dhandho Investor: The Low-Risk Value Method to High Returns.* Hoboken, NJ: Wiley, 2007.

Parris, Adam. "Value Investors and Bear Markets." ValueWalk, September 9, 2017. https:// www.valuewalk.com/2017/09/value-investors-bear-markets.

Parrish, Shane. "Daniel Kahneman—What I Know." *Farnam Street* (blog), July 2012. https:// fs.blog/2012/07/daniel-kahneman-what-i-know/.

——. "Mental Models: The Best Way to Make Intelligent Decisions (109 Models Explained)." *Farnam Street* (blog). https://www.fs.blog/mental-models.

——. "No. 18 Naval Ravikant—Angel Philosopher." The Knowledge Project with Shane Parrish, February 27, 2017. Audio. https://theknowledgeproject.libsyn.com/2017/02.

—— (@ShaneAParrish). "People Who Arbitrage Time Will Almost Always Outperform." Twitter, February 19, 2018. https://twitter.com/farnamstreet/status/965594833422245889?lang=en.

——. "Warren Buffett: The Inner Scorecard." *Farnam Street* (blog), August 2016. https://www .fs.blog/2016/08/the-inner-scorecard.

——. "Why Mental Models? My Interview with Professor and Value Investor Sanjay Bakshi." The Knowledge Project, Ep. #3. *Farnam Street* (blog). Audio. https://www.fs.blog/2015/09 /sanjay-bakshireading-mental-models-worldly-wisdom.

——. "Why You Shouldn't Slog Through Books." *Farnam Street* (blog), September 2017. https://www.fs.blog/2017/09/shouldnt-slog-books.

"'Person to Person': Warren Buffett." CBS News, November 16, 2012. https://www.cbsnews .com/news/person-to-person-warren-buffett.

Phelps, Thomas William. *100 to 1 in the Stock Market: A Distinguished Security Analyst Tells How to Make More of Your Investment Opportunities.* Brattleboro, VT: Echo Point, 2015.

Ping, Jonathan. "Charlie Munger's Life as a Financial Independence Blueprint." *My Money* (blog), January 18, 2018. http://www.mymoneyblog.com/charlie-munger-financial-independence -blueprint.html.

Portnoy, Brian. *The Geometry of Wealth: How to Shape a Life of Money and Meaning.* Hampshire, UK: Harriman House, 2018.

"Q&A with Warren Buffett (Tuck School of Business)." http://mba.tuck.dartmouth.edu /pages/clubs/investment/WarrenBuffett.html.

Ramsey, Dave. *The Total Money Makeover: A Proven Plan for Financial Fitness.* Nashville, TN: Nelson, 2003.

Ravikant, Naval. "The Knowledge Project." Farnam Street Learning Community. *Farnam Street* (blog), February 2017. https://fs.blog/wp-content/uploads/2017/02/Naval-Ravikant-TKP.pdf.

—— (@naval). Medium, April 2, 2018. https://medium.com/@haseebinc/the-internet-is-the -best-school-ever-created-b8da4b327192.

Raza, Sheeraz. "Great Interview with Alice Schroeder via Simoleon Sense." ValueWalk, November 6, 2010. https://www.valuewalk.com/2010/11/great-interview-alice-schroeder -simoleon-sense.

——. "Munger Quotes." ValueWalk, April 4, 2016. https://www.valuewalk.com/2016/04 /charlie-munger-quotes-2.

Reed, John. *Succeeding.* Alamo, CA: John T. Reed, 2011.

Reiff, Nathan. "The Greatest Investors: Julian Robertson." Investopedia. https://www.investopedia .com/university/greatest/julianrobertson.asp.

Reklaitis, Victor. "5 Quotes That Tell You Everything You Need to Know About Forecasting." MarketWatch, March 8, 2017. https://www.marketwatch.com/story/5-quotes-that-tell-you-everything-you-need-to-know-about-forecasting-2017-01–11.

Rich, Bryan. "Do You Think Like George Soros?" *Forbes*, June 1, 2016. https://www.forbes.com/sites/bryanrich/2016/06/01/do-you-think-like-george-soros/#499e4c835fod.

Ritholtz, Barry. "MiB: Danny Kahneman on Heuristics, Biases & Cognition." *The Big Picture*, August 9, 2016. https://ritholtz.com/2016/08/mib-kahneman-heuristics-biases-cognition/.

Rittenhouse, Laura. *Investing Between the Lines: How to Make Smarter Decisions by Decoding CEO Communications*. New York: McGraw-Hill Education, 2013.

Rockwood, Rich (@rrockw). "Excerpts from 1997 Caltech Speech." Motley Fool, board comment, January 4, 2003. http://boards.fool.com/excerpts-from-1997-caltech-speech-18377397.aspx.

Rothschild, Michael. *Bionomics: Economy as Business Ecosystem*. Marysville, WA: Beard, 1990.

Saletta, Chuck. "4 Steps to Getting Rich from Warren Buffett's Right-Hand Man." *Business Insider*, May 31, 2013. http://www.businessinsider.com/charlie-mungers-secrets-to-getting-rich-2013-5.

Schroeder, Alice. *The Snowball: Warren Buffett and the Business of Life*. New York: Bantam, 2009.

Schwager, Jack. *Hedge Fund Market Wizards: How Winning Traders Win*. Hoboken, NJ: Wiley, 2012.

Sellers, Patricia. "Warren Buffett and Charlie Munger's Best Advice." *Fortune*, October 31, 2013. http://fortune.com/2013/10/31/warren-buffett-and-charlie-mungers-best-advice.

Seneca. *Letters from a Stoic*. London: Penguin, 1969.

——. *On the Shortness of Life*. Plano, TX: Vigeo, 2016.

"Seth Klarman—30 Timeless Investing Lessons." ValueWalk, March 30, 2017. https://www.valuewalk.com/2017/03/seth-klarman-30-timeless-investing-lessons.

Shah, Bhavin. "My Best Pick 2018." Outlook Business, January 8, 2018. https://outlookbusiness.com/specials/my-best-pick_2018/bhavin-shah-4052.

Siegel, Jeremy. "Valuing Growth Stocks: Revisiting the Nifty Fifty." *American Association of Individual Investors Journal*, October 1998. https://www.aaii.com/journal/article/valuing-growth-stocks-revisiting-the-nifty-fifty.

Silver, Nate. *The Signal and the Noise: Why So Many Predictions Fail—but Some Don't*. London: Penguin, 2015.

Simon, Herbert A. "Designing Organizations for an Information Rich World." In *Computers, Communications, and the Public Interest*: edited by M. Geenberger. Baltimore, MD: Johns Hopkins Press, 1971. https://digitalcollections.library.cmu.edu/awweb/awarchive?type=file&item=33748.

——. *Models of My Life*. Cambridge, MA: MIT Press, 1996.

Sinclair, Upton. *I, Candidate for Governor: And How I Got Licked*. 1934. Berkeley: University of California Press, 1994.

Smith, Terry. "Bond Proxies: Can You Afford Not to Own Them?" *Financial Times*, June 26, 2015. https://www.ft.com/content/1c359352-18f1-11e5-a130-2e7db721f996.

Soe, Aye M., Berlinda Liu, and Hamish Preston. *SPIVA U.S. Scorecard*, S&P Dow Jones Indices, Year-End 2018. https://www.spindices.com/documents/spiva/spiva-us-year-end-2018.pdf.

Solin, Dan. "Do You Have 'Prediction Addiction?'" *Huffington Post*, May 25, 2011. https://www.huffingtonpost.com/dan-solin/do-you-have-prediction-ad_b_66570.html.

Sonkin, Paul D., and Paul Johnson. *Pitch the Perfect Investment: The Essential Guide to Winning on Wall Street*. Hoboken, NJ: Wiley, 2017.

Sparks, Evan. "John Templeton." Philanthropy Roundtable. http://www.philanthropyroundtable .org/almanac/hall_of_fame/john_m._templeton.

"Special Situation Videos: Lecture 1 and 2." Greenblatt Columbia Lecture 2005. CS Investing, September 25, 2012. Video. http://csinvesting.org/2012/09/25/special-situation-video -lecture-1.

Spier, Guy. *The Education of a Value Investor: My Transformative Quest for Wealth, Wisdom, and Enlightenment.* New York: St. Martin's, 2014.

"Spin-Offs—The Urge to Demerge." SBICAP Securities, June 19, 2017. https://drive.google .com/file/d/0B5meW_TNaEhNcFY4ME9ZeTBUNWM/view.

Stewart, James B. "Amazon Says Long Term and Means It." *New York Times,* December 16, 2011. https://www.nytimes.com/2011/12/17/business/at-amazon-jeff-bezos-talks-long-term -and-means-it.html.

"Study History." Investment Masters Class. http://mastersinvest.com/historyquotes.

Sullivan, Tim. "Embracing Complexity." *Harvard Business Review,* September 2011. https:// hbr.org/2011/09/embracing-complexity.

Surowiecki, James. *The Wisdom of Crowds: Why the Many Are Smarter Than the Few.* London: Abacus, 2014.

Szramiak, John. "This Story About Warren Buffett and His Long-Time Pilot Is an Important Lesson About What Separates Extraordinarily Successful People from Everyone Else." *Business Insider,* December 4, 2017. http://businessinsider.com/warren-buffetts-not-to -do-list-2016-10.

Taleb, Nassim Nicholas. *Antifragile: Things That Gain from Disorder.* New York: Random House, 2014.

——. *The Black Swan: The Impact of the Highly Improbable,* 2nd ed. New York: Random House, 2010.

Taleb, Nassim Nicholas, and George A. Martin. "How to Prevent Other Financial Crises." *SAIS Review* 32, no. 1 (Winter–Spring 2012). http://www.fooledbyrandomness.com/sais .pdf.

Talley, Madelon Devoe. *The Passionate Investors.* New York: Crown, 1987.

Tanous, Peter J. *Investment Gurus: A Road Map to Wealth from the World's Best Money Managers.* Upper Saddle River, NJ: Prentice Hall, 1997.

Task, Aaron. "Money 101: Q&A with Warren Buffett." *Yahoo Finance,* April 8, 2013. https:// finance.yahoo.com/news/money-101--q-a-with-warren-buffett-140409456.html.

Tervooren, Tyler. "Advice from Warren Buffet [*sic*]: Games Are Won By Players Who Focus on the Field." Riskology. https://www.riskology.co/focus-on-the-field.

Tetlock, Philip, and Dan Gardner. *Superforecasting: The Art and Science of Prediction.* New York: Broadway, 2016.

Thaler, Richard H., and Cass R. Sunstein. *Nudge: Improving Decisions About Health, Wealth, and Happiness,* rev. ed. New York: Penguin, 2009.

"There Are 3 Stages in a Typical Bull Market." *Ivanhoff Capital* (blog), February 2, 2012. http:// ivanhoff.com/2012/02/02/there-are-3-stages-in-a-typical-bull-market.

Thorndike, William. *The Outsiders: Eight Unconventional CEOs and Their Radically Rational Blueprint for Success.* Boston, MA: Harvard University Press, 2012.

Thorp, Edward O. *A Man for All Markets: From Las Vegas to Wall Street, How I Beat the Dealer and the Market.* New York: Random House, 2018.

Tilson, Whitney. "Notes from the 2002 Wesco Annual Meeting." Whitney Tilson's Value Investing Website. https://www.tilsonfunds.com/motley_berkshire_brkmtg02notes.php.

——. "Notes from the 2003 Wesco Annual Meeting." Whitney Tilson's Value Investing Website. http://www.tilsonfunds.com/motley_berkshire_wscmtg03notes.php.

——. "Notes from the 2004 Wesco Annual Meeting." Whitney Tilson's Value Investing Website, May 5, 2004. https://www.tilsonfunds.com/wscmtg04notes.doc.

——. "Notes from the 2005 Wesco Annual Meeting." Whitney Tilson's Value Investing Website, May 4, 2005. https://www.tilsonfunds.com/wscmtg05notes.pdf.

——. "Whitney Tilson's 2007 Berkshire Hathaway Annual Meeting Notes." Whitney Tilson's Value Investing Website, May 5, 2007. https://www.tilsonfunds.com/Berkshire_Hathaway _07_annual%20meeting_notes.pdf.

——. "Whitney Tilson's 2007 Wesco Annual Meeting Notes." Whitney Tilson's Value Investing Website, May 9, 2007. https://www.tilsonfunds.com/Whitney%20Tilson's%20notes%20 from%20the%202007%20Wesco%20annual%20meeting-5-9-07.pdf.

——, ed. "Three Lectures by Warren Buffett to Notre Dame Faculty, MBA Students and Undergraduate Students." Whitney Tilson's Value Investing Website, Spring 1991. http:// www.tilsonfunds.com/BuffettNotreDame.pdf.

"Time Arb." Investment Masters Class. http://mastersinvest.com/time-arb.

Tkaczyk, Christopher, and Scott Olster. "Best Advice from CEOs: 40 Execs' Secrets to Success." *Fortune*, October 29, 2014. http://fortune.com/2014/10/29/ceo-best-advice.

Train, John. *The Money Masters*. New York: Harper Business, 1994.

Tupy, Marian L. "Corporations Are Not as Powerful as You Think." HumanProgress, November 1, 2017. https://humanprogress.org/article.php?p=785.

Twain, Mark. *Pudd'nhead Wilson*. 1894. Reprint, Mineola, NY: Dover, 1999.

Vartak, Samit S. *SageOne Investment Advisors Letter*. August 10, 2017. http://sageoneinvestments .com/wp-content/uploads/2017/08/SageOne-Investor-Memo-Aug-2017.pdf.

"Visita a Warren Buffett." Think Finance, 2005. http://www.thinkfn.com/wikibolsa/Visita_a _Warren_Buffett.

Waitzkin, Josh. *The Art of Learning: An Inner Journey to Optimal Performance*. New York: Free Press, 2008.

"Warren Buffett on the Stock Market." *Fortune*, December 10, 2001. http://www.berkshirehathaway .com/2001ar/FortuneMagazine%20DEC%2010%202001.pdf.

"Warren Buffett Remarks on European Debt Crisis, the 'Buffett Rule' and the American Worker: Interview by Business Wire CEO Cathy Baron Tamraz." *Business Wire*, November 15, 2011. https://www.businesswire.com/news/home/20111115006090/en/Warren-Buffett-Remarks -European-Debt-Crisis-.

"Warren Buffett's Career Advice." CNN Money, November 16, 2012. Video. http://money.cnn .com/video/magazines/fortune/2012/11/16/f-buffett-career-advice.fortune/index.html.

Wasik, John F. *Keynes's Way to Wealth: Timeless Investment Lessons from the Great Economist*. New York: McGraw-Hill Education, 2013.

Watts, William. "Birthday Boy Warren Buffett Reaffirms His Love for Apple, but Sinks Mondelez." MarketWatch, August 30, 2017. https://www.marketwatch.com/story/birthday -boy-warren-buffett-reaffirms-his-love-for-apple-but-sends-mondelez-tumbling -2017-08-30.

Wilhelm, Ian. "Warren Buffett Shares His Philanthropic Philosophy." *Chronicle of Philanthropy*, March 8, 2010. https://www.philanthropy.com/article/Warren-Buffett-Shares-His/225907.

"Words of Estimative Probability." Central Intelligence Agency, March 19, 2007. https://www .cia.gov/library/center-for-the-study-of-intelligence/csi-publications/books-and -monographs/sherman-kent-and-the-board-of-national-estimates-collected-essays /6words.html.

Zeckhauser, Richard. "Investing in the Unknown and Unknowable." *Capitalism and Society* 1, no. 2, article 5 (2006). https://sites.hks.harvard.edu/fs/rzeckhau/InvestinginUnknownand- Unknowable.pdf.

Zweig, Jason. *The Devil's Financial Dictionary*. New York: PublicAffairs, 2015.

——. "The Secrets of Berkshire's Success: An Interview with Charlie Munger." *Wall Street Journal*, September 12, 2014. https://www.wsj.com/articles/the-secrets-of-berkshires-success-an-interview-with-charlie-munger-1410543815.

——. *Your Money and Your Brain: How the New Science of Neuroeconomics Can Help Make You Rich*. New York: Simon and Schuster, 2008.

Zweig, Martin. *Martin Zweig's Winning on Wall Street*, rev. ed. New York: Warner, 1997.

INDEX

Page numbers in *italics* indicate figures or tables.

on restricted earnings, 165; on risk, 58, 262–263; on role models, 45; on savings accounts, 214; on sector tailwind, 315; on shareholders, 229; on simplicity, 72; on staying power, 266; on stocks, 121; on success, 209, 327; on time, 216; on turnarounds, 294; on wealth, 258–259, 363; on Wells Fargo, 317–318

Buffett indicator, 218

Buffett Partnership Ltd., 88–95

bull markets, 61, 173–174; end of, 237; Marks on, 233; Neill on, 250; stages of, 233; Templeton on, 233

Bullock, Sandra, 322

Burger, Edward B., 31

Business Adventures (Brooks), 264

business models: Buffett on, 219; earnings in, 211; evaluation of, 211; gruesome, 213; intrinsic value in, 216; longevity of growth in, 212; Munger on, 214–215; switching costs in, 211

business ownership: exiting in, 120–121; flexibility and, 120–121; managers in, 119; partial, 118; rare opportunities in, 120; terms of, 119–120

business-to-business (B2B), 213

business-to-consumer (B2C), 213

buybacks, share, 226

bystander effect, 230

Cadila Healthcare, 197–198

CAGR. *See* compound annual growth rate

Calcutta Electric Supply Corporation (CESC), 311

calmness, 353

candor, 125–127

CAP. *See* competitive advantage period

CAPE ratio, 236

capital allocation, 170, 302; ROIC and, 226–227

Capital Cities Communications, 117

capital cycle: illustrating, *194*; red flags, 182–184

capital discipline, 124

capital expenditure, 131, 164

capitalism, 278, 316; brutality of, 222; correcting forces of, 250; Greenblatt on, 202

Capital Returns (Chancellor), 182, 189, 369

capital stewardship, 124–125

Capital Trust, 340

capital work in progress, 132

cap-to-sales ratio, 191

Carlson, Ben, 73; on diversification, 243

Carnegie, Andrew, 64–65, 286

Caro, Robert, 12

Carr, Nicholas, 14

cash, 254; value of, 299

cash balances, 131

cash flow, 124, 177–178; analysis, 131; discounted, 290; free, 131

cash flow from operating activity (CFO), 131

Cassel, Ian, 371, 372

categorical imperative, 93–94

CBOE VIX, 264

Central Intelligence Agency, 293–294

CEOs, 123, 126

certainty: in bear markets, 212–213; stocks and, 212; uncertainty and, 54–55

CESC. *See* Calcutta Electric Supply Corporation

CFO. *See* cash flow from operating activity

challenger brands, 222

Chancellor, Edward, 182–183, 189, 369

change, 32; of mind, 297–300; Munger on, 297–300; starting small, 111–113

Charles Munger (Griffin), 26

chartists, 185

chauffeur knowledge, 335

checklists, 128; psychological, 133–138

chronic diseases, 357

Cialdini, Robert, 335, 341

Cicero, 17

cigar butts, 175–176, 217

circle of competence, 303; defining, 59, 61–62; enlarging, 59–60; humility and, 56–62; reading and, 60

circle of incompetence, 58

Clason, George, 79

Classics: An Investor's Anthology, 85

Clear, James, 20, 42, 357, 361

Close, Chuck, 42

Coca-Cola, 171

cocaine brain, 137

Code of Hammurabi, 149

cognitive dissonance, 342–343

Cohen, Aaron, 4–5

Collier, Charles, 64